NEW
BIBLICAL COMMENTARY

Old Testament Editors,
Robert L. Hubbard Jr.
Robert K. Johnston

DEUTERONOMY

Old Testament Series

NEW INTERNATIONAL BIBLICAL COMMENTARY

DEUTERONOMY

CHRISTOPHER J. H. WRIGHT

Based on the New International Version

Copyright © 1996 by Hendrickson Publishers, Inc.
P. O. Box 3473
Peabody, Massachusetts 01961–3473
All rights reserved.
Printed in the United States of America
ISBN 1–56563–171–4

Second printing — March 1998

Library of Congress Cataloging-in-Publication Data

Wright, Christopher J. H., 1947–
    Deuteronomy / Christopher J. H. Wright; Old Testament
editors, Robert L. Hubbard, Jr., Robert K. Johnston
    (New International biblical commentary; 4)
    Includes bibliographical references and indexes.
    ISBN 1–56563–171–4 (pbk.)
    1. Bible.   O.T.   Deuteronomy—Commentaries.   I. Hubbard, Robert L.,
1943–   .   II. Johnston, Robert K., 1945–   .   III. Title.   IV. Series.
BS1275.3W75   1996
222′.1507—dc20   96–28350
                                                                              CIP

British Library Cataloguing in Publication Data

Wright, Chris, 1947 Oct. 9–
    Deuteronomy.—(New international biblical commentary; 4)
    1. Bible.   O.T. Deuteronomy — Criticism, interpretation, etc.   I. Title.
    222.1′5′06

ISBN 0–85364–725–9

For
My dear wife
Liz

Table of Contents

Foreword
New International Biblical Commentary

As an ancient document, the Old Testament often seems something quite foreign to modern men and women. Opening its pages may feel, to the modern reader, like traversing a kind of literary time warp into a whole other world. In that world sisters and brothers marry, long hair mysteriously makes men superhuman, and temple altars daily smell of savory burning flesh and sweet incense. There, desert bushes burn but leave no ashes, water gushes from rocks, and cities fall because people march around them. A different world, indeed!

Even God, the Old Testament's main character, seems a stranger compared to his more familiar New Testament counterpart. Sometimes the divine is portrayed as a loving father and faithful friend, someone who rescues people from their greatest dangers or generously rewards them for heroic deeds. At other times, however, God resembles more a cruel despot, one furious at human failures, raving against enemies and bloodthirsty for revenge. Thus, skittish about the Old Testament's diverse portrayal of God, some readers carefully select which portions of the text to study, or they avoid the Old Testament altogether.

The purpose of this commentary series is to help readers navigate this strange and sometimes forbidding literary and spiritual terrain. Its goal is to break down the barriers between the ancient and modern worlds so that the power and meaning of these biblical texts become transparent to contemporary readers. How is this to be done? And what sets this series apart from others currently on the market?

This commentary series will bypass several popular approaches to biblical interpretation. It will not follow a *precritical* approach that interprets the text without reference to recent scholarly conversations. Such a commentary contents itself with offering little more than a paraphrase of the text with occasional supplements from archaeology, word studies, and classical theology. It mistakenly believes that there have been few insights into the Bible since Calvin or Luther. Nor will this series pursue an *anticritical* approach whose preoccupation is to defend the Bible against its detractors, especially scholarly ones. Such a commentary has little space left to move beyond showing why the Bible's critics are wrong to explaining what the biblical text means. The result is a paucity of vibrant biblical theology. Again, this series finds inadequate a *critical* approach that seeks to understand the text apart from belief in the meaning it conveys. Though modern readers have been taught to be discerning, they do not want to live in the "desert of criticism" either.

Instead, as its editors, we have sought to align this series with what has been labeled *believing criticism*. This approach marries probing, reflective interpretation of the text to loyal biblical devotion and warm Christian affection. Our contributors tackle the task of interpretation using the full range of critical methodologies and practices. Yet they do so as people of faith who hold the text in the highest regard. The commentators in this series use criticism to bring the message of the biblical texts vividly to life so the minds of modern readers may be illumined and their faith deepened.

The authors in this series combine a firm commitment to modern scholarship with a similar commitment to the Bible's full authority for Christians. They bring to the task the highest technical skills, warm theological commitment, and rich insight from their various communities. In so doing, they hope to enrich the life of the academy as well as the life of the church.

Part of the richness of this commentary series derives from its authors' breadth of experience and ecclesial background. As editors, we have consciously brought together a diverse group of scholars in terms of age, gender, denominational affiliation, and race. We make no claim that they represent the full expression of the people of God, but they do bring fresh, broad perspectives to the interpretive task. But though this series has sought out diversity among its contributors, they also reflect a commitment to a common center. These commentators write as "believing critics"—scholars who desire to speak for church and academy, for academy and church. As editors, we offer this series in devotion to God and for the enrichment of God's people.

ROBERT L. HUBBARD JR.
ROBERT K. JOHNSTON
Editors

Preface

Having taught Deuteronomy in India and England for some seven years with deepening appreciation of the challenge and relevance of the book, I responded enthusiastically to Carl Armerding's original request to contribute this volume to the NIBCOT series. The enthusiasm has occasionally struggled to survive the merciless tyranny of the written word in comparison with the more congenial medium of preaching and lecturing, but it is still intact. Since Deuteronomy itself is the deposit of the preached word, I have tried to let the living voice be heard and not be stifled in the conventions of academic style.

Commentaries, unlike the Bible itself, need to justify their existence. If there is anything fresh in the presentation offered here, it will mainly be due to my concern to engage with the *missiological* relevance of Deuteronomy. In a sense, the whole Bible is related to mission—the mission of God in God's world, the mission of God's people in the midst of the nations. But Deuteronomy is particularly pregnant with implications and reflections on what it means to be the people of God, to be entrusted with the knowledge of the one living God, and to be challenged to live out that knowledge in the sight of the nations. Deuteronomy has much to teach any who care about the uniqueness of the biblical faith in the context of the ambient cultural idolatries of our age.

The additional notes will show my enormous debt to the writings of many scholars. Books and articles are cited in an abbreviated form, with full details in the bibliography. For the sake of the assumed readership of the series, the bulk of citations are in English, or in English translation. An author's name followed by a Bible book signifies a commentary.

At the heart of Deuteronomy stands chapter 15, with its laws on the *release* of debts and slaves. The writing of this commentary was made possible only by a number of "releases" for which I wish to express my appreciation. I am grateful to my colleagues on the staff of All Nations Christian College for the release of a sabbatical term in the summer of 1993, and to the students of my 1992–93 tutorial group who released their tutor, but not without their continued love and support. I spent the term at Tyndale House, Cambridge, and warmly thank the Warden, Bruce Winter, the Bursar, Iain Hodgins, and the Librarian, Andrew Clarke, for making my stay so comfortable and profitable.

All would have been in vain, however, without the willingness of my dear wife, Liz, to release me from so much domestic responsibility during that time. She has borne with me as I have borne with Deuteronomy, and together we have proved yet again how precious it is that "underneath are the everlasting arms" (Deut. 33:27). The book is dedicated to her with renewed love and gratitude.

Easneye, Ware, England

Abbreviations

ABD	*Anchor Bible Dictionary*
AnBib	Analecta biblica
Bib	*Biblica*
CBQ	*Catholic Biblical Quarterly*
cf.	*confer,* compare
ch(s).	chapter(s)
e.g.	for example
EvQ	*Evangelical Quarterly*
etc.	and so forth
f(f).	and following
GNB	Good News Bible
Hb.	Hebrew
HTR	*Harvard Theological Review*
HUCA	*Hebrew Union College Annual*
i.e.	that is
Interp	*Interpretation*
ISBE	*International Standard Bible Encyclopedia*
JBL	*Journal of Biblical Literature*
JETS	*Journal of the Evangelical Theological Society*
JJS	*Journal of Jewish Studies*
JQR	*Jewish Quarterly Review*
JSOT	*Journal for the Study of the Old Testament*
JSOTSup	Journal for the Study of the Old Testament, Supplement Series
KJV	King James Version
lit.	literally
LXX	Septuagint
MT	Masoretic Text
NEB	New English Bible
NICOT	New International Commentary on the Old Testament
NIV	New International Version
NRSV	New Revised Standard Version

NT	New Testament
NTS	*New Testament Studies*
OT	Old Testament
REB	Revised English Bible
RSV	Revised Standard Version
SBLDS	Society of Biblical Literature Dissertation Series
TynBull	*Tyndale Bulletin*
v(v).	verse(s)
VT	*Vetus Testamentum*
VTSup	Vetus Testamentum Supplements

Introduction

Deuteronomy has been aptly described as the heartbeat of the OT. Feel the pulse of Deuteronomy and you are in touch with the life and rhythm of the whole Hebrew Bible. Indeed, if we add the influence of the book on Jesus, Paul, and the early NT church, it is a profoundly significant book in the whole Christian canon of scripture. If another measure of the relative importance of any biblical book is the amount of secondary literature it has generated, then on that scale, Deuteronomy weighs very heavy indeed. Deuteronomic bibliography, though presumably as finite as Stephen Hawking's universe, seems without boundaries and ever expanding.[1]

Title

The English name of the book comes from the Greek translation of 17:18, where the Hebrew speaks of "a copy of this law." The LXX used the term *deuteronomion,* meaning "second law." In a sense, this is misleading, since the book is certainly not a second law, but rather a renewal and reinforcement of the law given at Mt. Sinai. About half of the "Book of the Covenant" (Exod. 21–23) is reproduced in Deuteronomy, but usually with additional motivational and explanatory preaching. The title of the book in the Hebrew canon is its opening words, *ʾēlleh haddᵉbārîm,* "These are the words." This more aptly points to the prophetic character of the book as both words of Moses and word of God, to be heard, heeded, and obeyed in each generation. These opening words also point to the similarity between Deuteronomy and the ancient Near Eastern treaty documents that often began in the same way. The covenantal nature of Deuteronomy is thus already signaled in its title.

Structure

Deuteronomy is so rich in content and texture that, like a rich fruitcake, it can be sliced in various ways. No single view of the structure of the book can be said to be the only possible or "right" approach. At least four approaches are valid and helpful.

Speeches of Moses. The most natural reading of the text as it presents itself to us is as a record of speeches made by Moses to the Israelites just before his death. Using the similar phrases, "These are the words" (1:1), "This is the law" (4:44), and "These are the terms [lit. words]" (29:1), as markers, we can isolate three major sections of Moses' speeches:

1:1–4:43	A historical review followed by exhortation
4:44–28:68	Exhortation to covenant loyalty followed by the law, covenant renewal, blessings, and curses
29:1–30:20	Summary and concluding challenge

This is then followed by a kind of epilogue of the last acts of Moses: his commissioning of Joshua, his Song and Blessing, and finally his death.

Because these speeches are presented as immediately prior to Moses' death, they give the whole book a testamentary character that thus enhances the seriousness of its challenge to Israel.[2] Von Rad regarded this as linked to the alleged use of Deuteronomy in ceremonies of covenant renewal at Shechem. Polzin's more recent literary study of the speech form of the book exposes how the voice of the narrator, the voice of Moses, and the voice of God are intermingled, as are the two audiences of the book—Moses and his audience, and the narrator and his. The effect, according to Polzin, is to enhance the status of the voice of the narrator, in preparation for "his" authoritative interpretation of the following history of Israel from Joshua onward.[3]

Covenant form. Ever since the discovery of the texts of vassal treaties from the Hittite empire of the 2d millennium and the Assyrian empire of the 1st millennium, there has been a vast amount of work on the comparison between these treaties and the biblical covenant as a way of describing the relationship between Yahweh and Israel.[4] It is clear that Deuteronomy is not in itself simply the text of a treaty. Nevertheless, it does speak of ongoing acts of covenant renewal, and its structure bears the marks of the regular form of ancient Near Eastern treaty texts.

This provides another way of dividing up the book. The italicized terms that follow are the key elements in the treaty form, with the matching section of Deuteronomy alongside:

(a) *Preamble,* identifying the speaker and addressees (1:1–5)

(b) *Historical prologue,* relating significant events in the relationship between the parties (1:6–4:49)

(c) *General stipulations,* outlining the broad terms of the treaty (5–11)

(d) *Detailed stipulations,* the specific requirements of the imperial state on its vassal (12–26)

(e) *Blessings and curses,* as sanctions and motivation for observing the treaty (27–28)

(f) *Witnesses* (cf. 30:19; 31:19; 32)

In addition, the treaties usually contained some instructions for the storage and public reading of the treaty document, such as those found in Deuteronomy 31:9–13, 24–26.

Deuteronomy has done more than simply apply the secular model of the vassal treaty to Israel's conceptualization of its relationship to Yahweh. Deuteronomy has transformed the political form into a vehicle for a very powerful theological message, in which the first three sections become the foundation for all the rest. That is, the detailed requirements of God on Israel are all founded upon the grace of God manifested in their history. This is not only a structural matter but is also reflected in the way the very vocabulary of Israel's response to Yahweh in chapters 12–26 mirrors that of Yahweh's actions toward Israel in chapters 1–11.[5] This priority of grace and divine action within the covenant framework will become more and more apparent in the commentary below.

Concentric literary pattern. Whereas more traditional literary criticism has been absorbed with isolating sources and layers of the redactional history of Deuteronomy, newer literary interest in the book has explored its qualities as a work of amazing literary skill and artistry. D. L. Christensen has analyzed in great depth the poetic features of the composition of the text and has observed in particular the feature of concentricity. Sometimes called chiasmus, this is the technique of arranging material in a balancing order in which a number of points are made and then, after a central point is established, the original points are repeated or balanced in reverse order. There is thus a movement "in" to the center and then back "out" to the frame again. The aesthetic appeal of balance and symmetry is very broad; it is often found in the visual arts, in music, and in poetry. Christensen argues that, although Deuteronomy is not strictly poetry in the same form as, say, the Hebrew Psalms, its rhythmic prose and repetitive phraseology point to a poetic, and possibly a musical, composition whose form facilitated its memorization and preservation.[6]

Concentric structures can be observed at all levels in the book, and the more obvious ones will be pointed out in the commentary. Christensen presents the whole book in the following structure, which can be supported by numerous textual links and echoes in the related sections.[7]

A THE OUTER FRAME: A Look Backward (Deut. 1–3)
  B THE INNER FRAME: The Great Peroration (Deut. 4–11)
    C THE CENTRAL CORE: Covenant Stipulations (Deut. 12–26)
  B′ THE INNER FRAME: The Covenant Ceremony (Deut. 27–30)
A′ THE OUTER FRAME: A Look Forward (Deut. 31–34)

The outer frame could be read continuously, its connecting figure being Joshua, commissioned to lead Israel on from the past victories (chs. 1–3) into the land ahead (31–34). Likewise the inner frame could be read continuously, similarly joined by the references to blessings and curses, and the ceremony on Mt. Ebal. The intricate patterning of the material in this form, with the many internal signs of literary art as well, would seem to militate against the common critical view of Deuteronomy (e.g., Mayes) as a book that has grown from a basic law code by a lengthy process of additions and redactions.

An expanded Decalogue. The clearest feature of Deuteronomy is its call for total loyalty to Yahweh as sole God. This, of course, is also the fundamental demand of the first and second commandments of the Decalogue. The great didactic section in chapters 4–11 is designed to inculcate by every means possible the importance of these opening commandments. Several scholars, however, have gone beyond this observation to suggest that the arrangement of the laws in the central section, chapters 12–26, is also governed by the Decalogue.[8] Those who have taken this general view have not agreed on the precise identification of particular sections with specific commandments, but the broad outline seems generally convincing. The links are clearer with some commandments than with others. Fuller discussion follows in the commentary, but the following correlations are worth noting.

12–13	The first, second and third commandments are reflected here in the demand for purity of worship and exclusion of all foreign gods.
14:28–16:17	The fourth commandment (sabbath) underlies this section with its emphasis on the "holy rhythms" of Israel's life, and on care for the poor.
16:18–18:22	The fifth commandment (honoring parents) is the foundation for the respect for legitimate human authority that in this section is focused on judge, king, priest, and prophet.
19:1–21:9	The sixth commandment (prohibiting murder) underlies the opening and closing laws in this section. In between, the eighth and tenth (19:14) and ninth (19:15–21) are also alluded to.
22:13–30	The seventh commandment (prohibiting adultery) is the basis for regulating a number of related sexual offenses.
23–26	The laws become more miscellaneous in this final section, but the eighth and tenth commandments (against theft and covetousness) may be here translated into a community ethos of care and compassion, especially for the weak and poor.

Even if the analysis is not clear-cut, it seems broadly convincing that the Decalogue has influenced the ordering of the legal material in Deuteronomy. The effect is not merely to produce literary or structural balance, but to amplify the theological and ethical challenge of the commandments and thus draw out the spirit and "ethos" of the law.[9]

Date and Setting

The book presents itself to us as a record of some speeches
of Moses shortly before his death, in the context of a renewal of
the covenant on the plains of Moab before the people of Israel
crossed the Jordan and settled in the land. However, since the
work of de Wette in 1805, modern critical scholarship has tended
to regard the book as the product of a much later period. The
dominant view locates the book in the seventh century, in vary-
ing degrees of relationship to the great reforms of Josiah in the
last quarter of that century. The primary reason for this link is
that Josiah's reform centralized worship in Jerusalem, and centralization of worship is assumed to be the dominant thrust of
Deuteronomy (esp. Deut. 12). Since de Wette it has been virtually
universally accepted that the "Book of the Law" that was discovered in the temple in Josiah's reign (2 Kgs. 22) was all or part of
the book now known as Deuteronomy. A common view is that
what was found was a law book containing Deuteronomy 12–26
and the present book is the result of a long process of additions
to that core by later Deuteronomists.

While some would associate the original Deuteronomy
closely with the reform itself, and therefore envisage it as having
been written shortly before that event in the late seventh century,
others would see it as the product of a reforming tradition in
Israel that goes back to the early seventh and eighth centuries. If
the book is seen as the work of a group, or movement, or party,
the identity of this circle is still a matter of considerable disagreement. How one identifies the authors depends on one's view of
the content of the book and its purpose in relation to the historical
conflicts, trends, and achievements of the late monarchy period.
Some see Deuteronomy as the end product of the eighth-century
prophetic movement and would associate it particularly with the
prophetic circles of northern Israel.[10] Others have linked it with
Levites from the north, who came to Judah after the fall of Israel
and preserved their traditions there.[11] Some have noted the
similarities with the Wisdom tradition and associated Deuteronomy with the royal court circle in Jerusalem, as a book produced
by the scribes for the support and education of the king.[12] Others,
in contrast, have argued that the book, because of its allegedly
northern, covenantal, ethos was radically critical of the Judean
style monarchy, and aimed to reform its cultic tradition,[13] or
included the "centralization law" as a concession to buy accep-

tance in Jerusalem, [14] or that the "centralization law" was a later addition to the original core of the book. [15]

This sample of the great variety of views on the identity and motives of the Deuteronomists shows the difficulty of tying the book down to one particular group with one particular aim. Furthermore, the link between the book as we have it and the actual reforms of Josiah is not as clear as was once alleged.[16] Once the direct link with Josiah's reform is recognized as decidedly tenuous, the original prime reason for confidently dating Deuteronomy in the seventh century as a "fixed point" of historical criticism is correspondingly diminished and the date of origin becomes a much more open question.[17] Some of the supporting arguments for a seventh-century production are less convincing by themselves if the Josianic assumption is questioned. "The tendency to date Deuteronomy in the seventh century owes much to habit; the data themselves are capable of quite other constructions."[18] When some scholars see Deuteronomy as the product of a prophetic group, others as the work of priests, and yet others attribute it to scribal wisdom sources, such diversity causes one to wonder if the reverse direction of influence is not more probable, and certainly simpler as an explanation: namely, that Deuteronomy precedes the development of these movements and it is *it* which has influenced *them*. The strongest connections are, of course, with the prophets. In that regard, it is significant that one of the most marked features of prophetic rhetoric (the covenantal lawsuit) and one of the most dominant themes in their theology of history (God's judgment on Israel at the hands of the nations, but an eventual reversal in which it falls on the nations and Israel is vindicated), are both expressed very powerfully in the Song of Moses in Deuteronomy 32, which is regarded by many scholars as very early poetry, probably the oldest material in the book, and very likely premonarchic.

The position adopted in this commentary is that, first, historically, the arguments for a seventh-century *origin* of Deuteronomy are outweighed by those that see a much more ancient tradition enshrined in the book. Many scholars who regard the book itself as a product of the seventh century acknowledge that it contains much earlier material. The historical figure of Moses is clearly so central to the book and, without denying the very obvious likelihood of editorial updating of the material for subsequent generations, there seem to be no compelling reasons why a substantially Mosaic legacy should not underlie the book, i.e., material that owes its origin to his creative and spiritual genius and that was profoundly formative in emergent Israel. Second, hermeneutically, it seems best to interpret and comment upon the text from the standpoint assumed in the book itself. There is no doubt that the abiding relevance of Deuteronomy was powerfully at work in different generations of Israel's history in the land (e.g., in the reforms of Jehoshaphat, Hezekiah, Josiah), and indeed could speak a vital word to the generation of the exile and return.[19] The constantly future orientation of the book virtually guarantees that ongoing relevance and address to later generations and centuries. But the book presents itself to us as the exhortations of Moses to Israel on the verge of the original settlement in Canaan, and it seems best, when expounding the text, to respect the integrity of that explicit context rather than to find explanations and meanings that depend upon the assumption that particular texts were actually pursuing a subliminal agenda related to issues of much later eras.

Missiological Significance

Deuteronomy is a book for a people on the move, literally at first, spiritually and morally thereafter. It sets Israel on the boundary of the land and looks beyond that boundary to what lies in store for Israel as it moves into the future with God. Furthermore, it is a book addressed in the name of a God on the move—Yahweh, the God who has been dramatically involved in Israel's own past movements, and indeed also in the movements of other nations on the great chessboard of history. It presents, therefore, a God of sovereign worldwide purpose and a people with a sharp spiritual mandate and moral agenda. The combination forges a dynamic factor in the biblical concept of the mission of those who claim to be the people of the biblical God. To explore the thrust of the book from this angle rescues the exercise from the rather static "list of themes" approach. Deuteronomy bends every rhetorical, literary, emotional, and moral skill to the task of equipping and motivating God's people to live for the purposes of God in each generation. This missiological edge can be felt in the following areas. Fuller discussion of each point will be found in the commentary on relevant texts.

The challenge to loyalty in the midst of culture change. Mission is sometimes defined (from the human angle) as the crossing of boundaries (cultural, geographical, linguistic, religious, etc.). On this definition, since Israelites were not "sent" anywhere, the OT (with the exception of Jonah) is often regarded as decidedly nonmissionary, in comparison with the centrifugal missionary expansion of the NT church.[20] Yet the OT is actually full of boundaries that God's people were challenged to cross, whether in faith and obedience or in times of judgment and restoration: Abraham leaving Ur for the land of promise; Jacob and his family going down to Egypt; the exodus generation crossing the Sea of Reeds from slavery to freedom; the Deuteronomic generation, about to cross the Jordan into the land; the generation that went to Babylon; and the generation that faced the challenge of returning. Each "crossing" involved the facing of risks and dangers and questions from the new cultural context in which the people of God found themselves. For Abraham, the land of promise was also the land of Sodom, and his own nephew succumbed. Egypt became the place of bondage. The wilderness was an awesome time of testing in which a whole generation failed. The promised land was full, not only of giants in the eyes of the Israelites, but of idolatry and wickedness in the eyes of God. Babylonian imperialism threatened the very survival of the nation. The postexilic generations faced prolonged frustration of their hopes. In each case, the primary challenge was to faith and loyalty in the midst of change.

Deuteronomy is a book on the boundary.[21] The people of Israel faced the challenge of an idolatrous and polytheistic culture that, in spite of initial hostility, would prove enormously enticing and seductive. Would they remain loyal to the knowledge and love of the living God that had been entrusted to them through exodus and Sinai, or would they succumb to the pressures of syncretism by treating Yahweh as one among the gods of Canaan? Would they live as a distinctive ("holy") community by the standards of justice and compassion that characterized Yahweh, or would they sink to the inequalities, corruptions, and perversions that were sanctioned by Baalism? Inasmuch as the relationship between the gospel and human cultures is a central missiological issue, the story of Israel's engagement with Canaanite culture is a rich vein for cross-cultural missiological reflection, though not as yet greatly exploited for that purpose.[22] It is significant, though not surprising, that when Jesus crossed his personal Jordan from the obscurity of village craftsman to the temptations and hostilities of public ministry, he turned to Deuteronomy for the resources to confirm his own loyalty and obedience, as he wrestled with the implications of the mission he had embarked upon (Matt. 4:1–11).[23]

The challenge of monotheism. Deuteronomy is uncompromisingly, ruthlessly monotheistic. It affirms that Yahweh alone is God and there is no other.[24] As will be discussed in the commentary (especially on chs. 4 and 6), this is no mere philosophical principle. The purpose of Deuteronomy is not to posit the singularity of deity, but to define the character of deity. God is God as revealed in Yahweh. It is crucial to insist on the specificity of biblical monotheism. The first commandment was not, "You shall believe in only one God," but "I am Yahweh, the God of redemptive power and action demonstrated in the exodus liberation; you shall have no other gods to rival me." But alongside this exclusiveness of Yahweh in relation to Israel there was also a definite universality regarding Yahweh's dealings with the nations. Their movements are under his control (2:9–12, 19–23). By identifying Yahweh with El Elyon, the Most High God, the Israelites accept his disposition of the boundaries and destinies of the nation also (32:8f.).

From a missiological perspective, there is first of all a clear contrast between such historico-redemptively defined monotheism and all forms of polytheism and idolatry, whether fertility cults (7:5), astral deities (4:19), or gods of national pride (32:31). A primary feature of Israel's mission (i.e., a major reason for their election) was to be the stewards of the knowledge of this unique God. "*You* were shown these things *so that you might know* . . ." (4:35, cf. the importance of the theme of "witness," in Isa. 43:10–13, echoed in Luke 24:45–49 and Acts 1:8). The reason, therefore, for the totally uncompromising attitude to all forms of idolatry was not a racist hatred of foreign religions, but a total commitment to the saving truth. The tragedy of polytheism and idolatry is not the arithmetic (many gods instead of one), but that they exchange the only true source of salvation for lifeless and powerless substitutes, and in doing so, introduce injustice, bondage, and cruelty into human life (cf. Rom. 1:21–32). Baalism is an example, but it has many modern counterparts in western and other cultures. The category of the idolatrous in every culture (including especially one's own, where it is most invisible) is one that needs far more careful attention and exposure than most biblical and theological scholarship currently affords it. For it is surely still as much the responsibility of the people of God to confront human idolatries with the reality of the living and saving God as it was for those addressed by Deuteronomy. Methods may change radically, but the mission is the same in principle.

Secondly, there is the relevance of OT monotheism to the uniqueness of Christ—the key missiological issue today as it has always been. In the dialogue between Christians and those of other faiths, there is a temptation to regard Jesus as simply the founder of Christianity in a way that cuts him loose from his deep roots in the Hebrew scriptures. Both in his own understanding of his mission, and in the interpretation of his identity and significance by his immediate followers in the NT church, Jesus shared in the uniqueness of Israel and in the uniqueness of Yahweh, the God of Israel. The historical particularity and redemptive character of OT monotheism coincide in the person of Jesus. It is not enough to acclaim merely the unique power of Jesus' life, or insights, or teaching, or example. The NT witness is that in Jesus the mission of Israel was accomplished (as the gospel went to the nations in fulfillment of the promise to Abraham) and that in Jesus Yahweh himself had been encountered in human life. God is God as revealed in Jesus of Nazareth.[25] Reflection, therefore, on such heartbeat texts as Deuteronomy 4:32–40 and 6:4f. must go on to detect their monotheistic but now Christocentric pulse in texts like 1 Corinthians 8:5f.[26]

Israel as a model for the nations. God's call of Abraham was explicitly for the ultimate purpose of blessing the nations (Gen. 12:1–3). This fundamentally missionary intention of the election of Israel echoes through the OT at almost every level.[27] There was a universal goal to the very existence of Israel. What God did in, for, and through Israel was understood to be ultimately for the benefit of the nations.

More to the point as regards Deuteronomy, what God ethically required of Israel served the same universal, missionary purpose. Genesis 18:19 makes this connection very explicitly. Having repeated the divine agenda in verse 18, "all nations on earth will be blessed through him," God goes on,

> For I have chosen him, so that he will direct his children and his
> household after him to keep the way of the LORD by doing what
> is right and just [lit. "doing righteousness and justice"], so that the
> LORD will bring about for Abraham what he has promised him.

Syntactically and theologically, the verse binds together
election, ethics, and mission, with ethics as the middle term. It
will be the moral nature of the people of Abraham, who keep the
way of Yahweh in righteousness and justice and bless the nations, that will enable God to fulfill the point of choosing Abraham. The text has a programmatic nature, all the more powerful
by being in the form of direct divine speech. The very election of
Israel (which is of great importance in Deuteronomy), in all its
particularity, not only has a universal "missionary" goal but also
leads to a clear and distinctive ethical agenda for God's people in
the world as part of the condition of that goal being accomplished. Exodus 19:4–6 is a similarly definitive text that links
Israel's obedience to the covenant law to their identity and role
as God's priesthood in the midst of the nations. The idea of Israel
as "a light to the nations" is another way of expressing the idea
(cf. Isa. 42:6; 49:6b), and it is clear that the imagery of "light" is
strongly moral (not just religious) in content (cf. Isa. 58:6–8; 60:3).

Deuteronomy is sometimes accused of being narrowly focused on Israel alone with no regard for this wider vision of
Israel's role in God's purpose for the nations. Certainly its primary focus is on Israel as a society, but it would be unfair to take
this as either an unawareness or an exclusion of the tradition of
the blessing of the nations through Israel. The emphasis on the
Abrahamic covenant alone would make such an oversight unlikely. Furthermore, the broader issue of Yahweh and the nations
is to be found quite explicitly in the theology of the Deuteronomic History (cf. Josh. 4:23f.; 1 Sam. 17:46; 2 Sam. 7:22–26;
1 Kgs. 8:41–43, 60f.; 2 Kgs. 5:15; 19:15–19). In Deuteronomy itself,
the nations are treated in a broadly dual role: on the one hand, as
a problem and snare to be resisted, and on the other hand, as the
observers of Israel. In the latter role, the nations appear as witnesses to the quality of Israel's life or the blessing of God on them
(4:6–8; 28:10), as well as to the judgment that Yahweh would pour
out on Israel for their sin (28:37; 29:22–25).

The most significant of these texts for the case being made
here is Deuteronomy 4:6–8 (see commentary). Its point is that if
Israel would be shaped and characterized by the laws and insti-

tutions of the Sinai covenant, then they would be a highly visible exemplar to the nations both as to the nature of the God they worshipped and as to the quality of social justice embodied in their community.[28] This seems to be a deliberate linking of Israel's role among the nations to the socio-ethical structure of their corporate life: mission and ethics combined. The mission of Israel was to be a model to the nations. Mission was not a matter of going but of being; to be what they were, to live as the people of the God Yahweh in the sight of the nations.

Hermeneutically, this perspective also offers a potentially more fruitful way of handling the law as regards contemporary ethical relevance. The issue of the status and applicability of OT law in the Christian context has been a major point of debate and division in the church since the NT itself. Part of the problem seems to be that the law is discussed as an entity in itself, whereas it needs to be set explicitly in the context of the mission of Israel. The purpose of the law must be set in the light of the universal significance of Israel for the nations as a presupposition of any extended application. In order to answer the question, "Why the law?" we need to ask "Why Israel?"

> The law was designed to mold and shape Israel in certain clearly defined directions, within their own historico-cultural context. That overall shape . . . thus becomes the model or paradigm intended to have a relevance and application beyond the geographical, historical and cultural borders of Israel itself. . . . The point is that this paradigmatic nature of Israel is not just a hermeneutical tool devised by us retrospectively, but theologically speaking, was part of God's design in creating and shaping Israel as he did in the first place.[29]

Adopting such a paradigmatic assumption in interpreting OT law (which I have developed more fully elsewhere[30] and which is the stance adopted in this commentary) leads to several further steps as a hermeneutical strategy.

(a) One must ascertain in as much depth as possible *the function* of particular laws within the overall Israelite social system and use all appropriate critical tools in doing so. This requires historical and sociological understanding of Israel and its sense of community identity, worldview, and social objectives. There is an increasing body of research in this field.[31] This will help us to discern what kind of law any particular legislation represents and whether it is central or more peripheral in relation to Israel's major ideals.

(b) One should then articulate as precisely as possible *the objective*, within the ancient Israelite context, of any particular law or institution. What was it there for? This can best be done by asking further questions. What kind of situation was this law designed to promote, or to prevent? Whose interests did it pro-tect—i.e., who would have benefited from it? Whose power was restricted or controlled by it? What social ideals are expressed or implicit in it? What effect would the functioning of this law have had on the social shape and ethos of Israel?

(c) Finally, one steps out of the ancient Israelite world into one's own modern socio-cultural context and seeks to *preserve the objective while changing the context*. If the answers to the questions above express something of God's intentions and ideals for Israel, then, assuming Israel's paradigmatic nature and God's moral consistency, what should we be aiming at in our own society? What policies, laws, structures do we need in order to achieve comparable or equivalent objectives? What critique can we bring to bear on existing social realities in the light of the biblical paradigm? Clearly we will not all come up with the same answers or identical proposals. But we will have released the power and authority of the OT law to affect and shape our ethical responses. In all this it is assumed that, since Deuteronomy was ad-dressed initially to the covenant people of God, it must be allowed to challenge the church today at a primary level, as regards its faithfulness or failure in embodying in its own community life the paradigm of justice, compassion, and neighborly love. But if Israel were to be a "light to the nations," then the paradigm must be applied beyond the church in our witness and challenge to wider secular society. Thus the missiological significance of Israel and its law will be given practical and context-specific ethical expression in a way that seems faithful to the dynamic pattern of the OT law and prophets themselves. In Deuteronomy then, we shall look for a substantial part of that social shape of Israel as an ethical model that can dynamically inform our ethical and missional objectives as those who are committed to the same God in the same world.

Deuteronomy's theology of history. While Deuteronomy is firmly grounded in the past events of election and redemption, it is predominantly a future-orientated book. It looks not only to the immediate future—the crossing over to the promised land—but also to the long-term future of Israel in relation to God and of both Israel and God in relation to the nations. In this respect it is immediately relevant to a biblical understanding of mission, since nothing is more central to that than a vision of God's ultimate purpose, which draws each generation of God's people toward the future. And in its prophetic anticipation of the broad shape of Israel's history as it unfolds in the OT, Deuteronomy also gave shape to the historical-eschatological theology of mission that is central to the NT.

At its simplest, Deuteronomy's anticipation of history was that Israel, although called and given every possible incentive to live in loyalty to its covenant Lord, would in fact fail to do so. The Israelites' "stiff-necked" nature would lead to rebellion and disobedience. As a result, the curses of the covenant would fall, including the terrible threat of scattering among the nations. However, beyond that judgment there lay the expectation of restoration and new life, if the people would return and seek God once more. This is the scenario that flows through the great concluding section of the book, chapters 27–32 especially. While the dominant issue is undoubtedly the fate of Israel, the nations are woven into the picture in several ways. They witness Israel's failure and judgment and are shocked by it (28:37; 29:22–28). They are also the human agents through which that judgment is carried out (28:49–52; 32:21–26). And yet finally, in the amazing inversion and paradox of chapter 32, God vindicates his people in the midst of the nations (as enemies) in such a way that the nations are called upon to praise Yahweh and rejoice *with* his people (32:27–43). Thus, the history that will see the judgment and restoration of Israel will also see the judgment and blessing of the nations, each pair interwoven with the other.

It would exceed the scope of this introduction to trace the pervasive presence of these connected ideas through the OT itself. What is more important is to point out their influence on the NT. It is clear that Jesus linked his own mission to the hope of the restoration of Israel and that the Gospel writers had the same interpretation of the significance of his ministry. N. T. Wright, for example, suggests that Matthew has shaped his Gospel not merely in terms of the five books of the Torah (a common scholarly view), but specifically in terms of the sequence of thought in the great final section of Deuteronomy 27–34. In doing so, Matthew brings out the significance of the story of Jesus "as the continuation and climax of the story of Israel, with the implicit understanding that this story is the clue to the story of the whole world."[32] Although Jesus limited his own ministry to the primary objective of the restoration of Israel, he left in his actions and words many hints of an expected ingathering of the nations, and he made that ingathering the explicit mission of his disciples after his resurrection.[33]

It was, however, the Apostle Paul who made the most use of Deuteronomy in his theological and missiological reflection. Not only did he see in the continued suffering of Israel a kind of prolongation of the exile (a view shared by many first-century Jews) but he also saw in the death and resurrection of Jesus as the Messiah the climax of the judgment and the restoration of Israel respectively. Linking this with his central understanding of the significance of Israel for the nations (as the purpose of the Abrahamic covenant), Paul recognized that the fulfillment of God's purpose for Israel could never be complete without the ingathering of the nations as well. At the heart of Paul's whole theological system was his redefinition of the meaning of Israel's election in relation to the nations for whose sake Israel was elect and for whose sake the Messiah had come in fulfillment of Israel's election and mission.[34] Hence the apparent paradox of his personal calling as the "apostle to the nations," and his actual missionary strategy of "to the Jew first." The failure of many Jews to respond led to the extension of the Good News to the Gentiles (e.g., Acts 13:44–48; Rom. 11). But never, in Paul's thinking, did this mean a rejection or replacement of the Jews. Rather, Paul picks up a rhetorical pun in Deuteronomy 32:21, on God making Israel "jealous," and develops it into a theology of history and mission: the ingathering of the Gentiles will arouse jealousy among the Jews, so that ultimately "all Israel," extended and inclusive of believing Jews and Gentiles, will share in salvation (Rom. 10:19–11:26). Clearly Paul reflected deeply on Deuteronomy 32 especially (it has been called "Romans in a nutshell") and quotes its final doxology (32:43) in his exposition of the multinational nature of the gospel and its implications for the need for cross-cultural acceptance and sensitivity between Jewish and Gentile Christians (Rom. 15:7–10).[35]

It can be seen, therefore, that although it is true to say that Deuteronomy is primarily absorbed with God's dealings with, and requirements of, Israel, it contains perspectives on Israel and the nations that ultimately led "over the horizon" of its own context and that influenced and shaped the mission of Jesus and Paul in theory and in practice. Such perspectives, with their overall canonical significance, need to be the broader framework for our understanding and application of the relevance of the content of the book, both in its urgent rhetoric and in its earthy legislation.

Notes

1. See Christensen, *Deuteronomy,* pp. xxii–xxxix, for the most comprehensive recent bibliography.
2. Disseminating teaching by means of farewell speeches was apparently an Egyptian didactic technique; cf. Weinfeld, *Deuteronomy,* pp. 4f.
3. See Polzin, "Deuteronomy," and *Moses and the Deuteronomist.*
4. Cf. Mendenhall's seminal study, "Ancient Oriental" (1954), which generated a flood of treaty-covenant studies in the following two decades. For a comprehensive survey, see McCarthy, *Covenant.* Although exaggerated claims have been made, it remains the case that there is a clear relationship between Deut. and the tradition of ancient Near Eastern treaty texts which stretches back to the late second millennium.
5. This point is established in great detail by McConville, *Law and Theology.*
6. Christensen's theory that the text had an original musical dimension, designed to be sung or chanted as a form of memorization and dissemination, would help to explain some of the features of the text, especially its rhythmic and metrically balanced nature, recurring phraseology, and carefully interwoven patterns. For further detail on the stylistic distinctives of Deut., cf. Driver, *Deuteronomy,* pp. lxxviii–lxxxviii, and Thompson, *Deuteronomy,* pp. 21–26, 30–35.
7. See Christensen, *Deuteronomy,* p. xli.
8. The most detailed work on the Decalogue structure of Deut. 12–26 has been done by Braulik. See especially "The Sequence."
9. Cf. Walton, "Spirit of the Law."
10. E.g., Nicholson, *Deuteronomy and Tradition;* Phillips, "Prophecy and Law."
11. Cf. von Rad, *Studies.*
12. Cf. Weinfeld, *Deuteronomic School; Deuteronomy,* pp. 55ff., 62ff.
13. Cf. Clements, "Jerusalem Cult Tradition."
14. Cf. Nicholson, *Deuteronomy and Tradition,* pp. 94–101.
15. Cf. von Rad, *Studies,* p. 67.

16. See commentary and additional notes on ch. 12. Clements, as part of a very thorough survey of all the positions on Deuteronomy's background and purpose, calls for

> considerable caution in asserting a precise identification between the book found in the temple in Josiah's time and the present book of Deuteronomy. . . . In the minds of many recent scholars, the more the character and assumptions of Josiah's reform are examined, the more oblique would appear to be the link with the book of Deuteronomy. (*Deuteronomy*, p. 72)

17. Apart from those who maintain a substantially Mosaic heritage in Deut., the book has been attributed to the premonarchic era, perhaps associated with Samuel, to the time of the united monarchy, to the reforming reign of Hezekiah in the eight century, and to the exilic and postexilic periods. For a helpful survey of scholarship on the question of dating, see Thompson, *Deuteronomy*, pp. 47–68.

18. McConville, *Grace in the End*, p. 56. McConville also provides a thorough survey of the scholarly positions on the date, authorship, and purpose of Deut. (op. cit., pp. 15–64). See also Clements, *Deuteronomy*, pp. 69–83.

19. Cf. Hoppe, "The Meaning of Deuteronomy."

20. This understanding of the nonmissionary nature of the OT accounts for a mere four pages being devoted to it in the magisterial theology of mission by Bosch, *Transforming Mission*.

21. This aspect of the book is emphasized especially by Miller, *Deuteronomy*, and shapes the interpretative framework for his exposition.

22. Senior and Stuhlmueller see Israel's relationship with pagan culture as a recurring pattern of "violence—indigenization—challenge," which is reflected in the whole history of mission; *Foundations*, pp. 36–81. For other stimulating reflection on the theme, cf. Brueggemann, *Prophetic Imagination*, chs. 1–3; Goldingay, *Theological Diversity*, pp. 59–96; C. J. H. Wright, "People of God," and *Eye/Living*, pp. 174–96.

23. Cf. C. J. H. Wright, *Knowing Jesus*, pp. 181–91.

24. There is an unsatisfactorily a priori character about the tendency among commentators to diminish the force of such statements by saying that they "cannot" have implied full monotheism, but only mono-Yahwism for Israel. The latter is obviously intended, but if an Israelite had wanted to make an explicitly monotheistic declaration in absolute terms, what more could he (or she, cf. 1 Sam. 2:2) have said than Deut. 4:39 or 32:39?

25. This contrasts starkly with monistic pluralism, which asserts that "ultimate divine reality" is one, but refuses to allow that any of the world's religions embodies final truth or revelation about it, or has access to that ultimate as it is in itself. Jesus is thus relativized as one among many "points of contact." But for the religious pluralist, Jesus is no more a definitive revelation of the ultimate divine than Yahweh

himself ever was (Yahweh being merely another human construct for expressing something about the transcendent).

26. Cf. C. J. H. Wright, *Unique,* pp. 65–82. N. T. Wright argues strongly for the Deuteronomic basis (Deut. 6:4f., the *shema*) of Paul's Christological monotheism in 1 Cor. 8, in *Climax,* pp. 120–36. Cf. also B. Rosner, " 'No Other God.' "

27. Cf. C. J. H. Wright, *Knowing,* pp. 34–54; Scobie, "Israel and the Nations;" Senior and Stuhlmueller, *Foundations,* pp. 83–109.

28. McBride, "Polity," portrays Deut. as a kind of "constitution" for Israel, in line with what is being suggested here. The balance of idealism and harsh realities is characteristic of the attempt to provide a model or pattern. Cf. also the stimulating ethical study of Deut. by Goldingay, *Theological Diversity,* pp. 134–66. Even at an individual level, the figure of Moses in Deut. is a "model within a model," portraying many of the features that should be found in a godly people and certainly in godly leadership. Cf. Miller, "Moses, My Servant."

29. C. J. H. Wright, "Ethical Authority," pp. 227f.

30. See C. J. H. Wright, *Eye/Living, God's Land,* and "The Authority of Scripture."

31. The classic work of de Vaux, *Ancient Israel,* is still a helpful resource for such broad understanding of Israel as a society. More recent work is well surveyed in Clements, ed., *The World of Ancient Israel.*

32. N. T. Wright, *People of God,* pp. 387–90. Cf. also Grassi, "Matthew."

33. Cf. C. J. H. Wright, *Knowing Jesus,* pp. 136–80 and bibliography.

34. This crucial theme is very thoroughly expounded in N. T. Wright, *Climax.*

35. On the full extent of Deuteronomy's influence on Paul's missiology, cf. Scott, "Restoration of Israel."

§1 At the Boundary (Deut. 1:1–5)

1:1 / The opening words of the book give it a prophetic flavor from the start—**These are the words Moses spoke** (cf. Isa. 1:1; Amos 1:1; etc.). This is reinforced by the repeated emphasis on the role of Moses in verses 3 and 5. His task was to proclaim **all that the LORD commanded him,** a task in which he was also a model for all future prophets (cf. 18:17f.). The relationship between the words of Moses and the words of God in Deuteronomy is sometimes so close that they merge imperceptibly, making exegetical separation quite difficult. "To claim . . . that the Bible nowhere claims to be the 'Word of God' is to fail to hear a central claim of Deuteronomy" (D. Christensen, *Deuteronomy*, p. 9). He was also **to expound** the law (cf. Deut. 27:8 and Hab. 2:2). Deuteronomy is thus "preached law"—that is, law explained with prophetic urgency, divine authority, and a preacher's clarity. Whatever one's view of the authorship of the book, it was given this introduction in order to stress its abiding relevance **to all Israel.** This is a frequent phrase in Deuteronomy, occurring in the first verse of the book (referring to Moses' words), in the last verse of the book (referring to Moses' acts), and about fourteen times between. It stresses the covenant unity of Israel, both horizontally (all in each generation, cf. 29:10ff.) and vertically (throughout all generations, cf. 5:3; 29:14).

Having established the source and the authority of the words to follow, the introduction goes on to fix them in their specific geographical and historical context (another feature of the prophetic books). The word of God is not a message without context. It intersects with the reality of a particular time and place, and is thereby all the sharper in its ongoing relevance. These verses form a bridge with Numbers 36:13, just as the closing chapter links the book with Joshua. The continuity and wholeness of the canon of scriptural books is clearly visible in these short strips of editorial velcro.

The geographical context was **in the desert,** or wilderness, **east of the Jordan . . . in the territory of Moab** (vv. 1, 5). The precise location is uncertain from the list of the place names given. But the point is clear. Israel was still in the wilderness. This last book of the Torah begins and ends with them awaiting possession of the promise that had shaped both their destiny and the literary structure of the Pentateuch itself—namely, the land that God had promised to Abraham. Wilderness, certainly, was the place of God's grace, protection, and provision, but it was not the place where they were meant to remain. Indeed, the reason they were still there was that it was also a place of God's judgment and discipline. Both points will be underscored in the rest of this chapter and in the lessons applied in chapter 8.

1:2–3 / The historical context is fixed in two ways. First of all it is dated very precisely to **the fortieth year** after the exodus from Egypt. The generation that had experienced God's liberation in the exodus had failed to enter into God's promise of the land because of their fear and rebellion, and had perished in the wilderness. The present generation is here addressed as if they had shared in that collective failure (1:26ff.). It is this implication of verse 3a that may explain the otherwise enigmatic note in verse 2, about the length of time it normally takes to travel from Mt. Sinai to Kadesh Barnea (the oasis just to the south of the land, from which they could have launched their invasion a whole generation earlier). A journey that should have taken them **eleven days** had already lasted forty years. The implication, which is hammered home repeatedly in the following chapters, is that they should not squander the opportunity this time.

1:4 / Secondly, however, and more cheerfully, Moses' exposition of the law is dated **after he had defeated Sihon . . . and . . . Og.** These events (recorded in Num. 21:21–35 and recollected in Deut. 2:24–3:11) were powerful reminders of God's past victories, and therefore equally powerful encouragement to move forward to face the even greater challenge ahead. The introduction thus alludes to both negative and positive motivation that Moses fully exploits in the following chapters.

The opening verses thus set the scene for the rest of the book. Geographically, historically, and theologically, Deuteronomy is a book "on the boundary," speaking powerfully through the ages to every generation of God's people called to move across the ever shifting boundary from past experience of God into future unknown circumstances (cf. Miller, *Deuteronomy,* pp. 20f.).

Additional Notes §1

1:1–2 / For a full discussion of the journeyings of Israel in the wilderness, and the problems involved in identifying many of the sites, including Mt. Sinai itself in particular, see G. I. Davies, *The Way of the Wilderness,* and "Location of Mount Horeb."

1:4 / **Amorites:** See additional note on 7:1.

§2 Structures for Growth (Deut. 1:6–18)

The recollection of this particular event out of all the memories of the wilderness period is a key to one of the book's main purposes, which was to provide Israel with a social, political, moral, and spiritual charter (cf. McBride, "Polity"). Here, and in greater detail in 16:18–18:22, the people are provided with different levels and structures of leadership. Those leaders are then given their primary responsibilities. Deuteronomy thus outlines a theology and an ethos of leadership in the people of God that has both spiritual dimensions and social applications.

1:6 / **You have stayed long enough at this mountain** was God's way of saying that the purpose for which Israel had been brought to Mt. Sinai was then complete. It was time to move on. The phrase is repeated in 2:3 as a signal that the time of wilderness wandering was also over. For God's pilgrim people, moments come when God says "long enough." There is a boundary to cross, a new phase to enter. Deuteronomy is a book for such times of movement and change.

1:8–11 / This moving forward was grounded in God's promise. The covenant with **Abraham** had three main elements (cf. Gen. 12:1–3) and all of them are woven into vv. 8–11.

People (v. 10). God had promised to make Abraham into a great nation, as numerous as sand and stars. This theme of posterity dominates the Pentateuch (cf. Clines, *Theme*). In the book of Genesis it generates suspense, but in Exodus 1:1–7 it is seen as secured. By the time of the exodus, the multiplication was such that new structures were needed to cope with its extra demands (vv. 12–17).

Blessing (v. 11). God had promised a relationship of special blessing with the descendants of Abraham, a relationship later described in covenantal terms (Gen. 15, 17). Blessing within covenant relationship is the focus of God's dealings with Israel at Mt. Sinai, as recorded in Exodus and Leviticus. The second term of the Abraham covenant thus forms the second major element in the structure of the Pentateuch. Moses prays for that blessing to continue as promised, even as he struggles to cope with its consequences!

Land (v. 8). This becomes the dominant theme of the Pentateuch from the point in Numbers when God told Israel to leave Sinai and head toward the land (Num. 10:11). From then on the focus of the narrative and the perspective of the laws is the promised land, even though the Pentateuch ends just a day's march short of it (Deut. 34). The geographical extent of the land (v. 7) includes the whole of Palestine from the edges of the Sinai desert (the **Negev**), from Mediterranean coast to Jordan valley (the **Arabah**), and as far as Syria in the North (to the **Euphrates**)—a larger area, in fact, than Israel ever historically controlled, even under Solomon. Verse 8, however, expresses Israel's theology of land in a nutshell. It was **the land that the LORD swore he would give** . . . and did. Possession of the land would thus be in itself a monumental, tangible proof of the faithfulness of Yahweh to his promise. The land-gift tradition was a central factor in Israel's sense of dependence on Yahweh. They could never consider themselves an autochthonous people ("sons of the soil"), for they would have been no people and would have had no land apart from the divine gift. The land was thus also a proof of God's grace. But it was land that they had to **go in and take.** Crossing the boundary would mean war and work for this people. The sovereign act of God and human responsive action go together. God's gift of grace needed to be appropriated by faith, obedience, and action. Centuries later, prophets would threaten that the gift could be lost again through unbelief, disobedience, and complacency.

God's promise to Abraham had more in mind than Israel alone. Although it is not explicit in the text at this point, the universal dimension of the Abraham covenant is never far from the surface whenever it is mentioned. The "bottom line" of that covenant was that all nations would be blessed in or through Abraham and his descendants. In the ultimate purpose of God, therefore, a lot more was at stake in Israel's crossing the Jordan into the promised land than merely getting them out of the wilderness. Their next step of obedience was also the next step in the redemption of the world. They needed to be motivated to take that step not just for their own sake, but to move forward in God's historical strategy for bringing blessing to the nations. There was a missionary dimension to Deuteronomy's call for

committed obedience. There always is. The church as a whole
and individual Christians need to see every step of obedience
that is called for in response to God's grace as being invested with
the significance of being woven into God's great plan of blessing
the nations.

1:9–12 / **You are too heavy a burden for me to carry
alone.** (Cf. Exod. 18:13–26 and Num. 11:10–17.) The problem did
not lie in the population growth in itself. That was due to God's
blessing, and Moses forestalls any suggestion that he was complaining about it by his prayer that God would multiply them **a
thousand times** more (v. 11)! The growing people, however, had
turned this blessing into a heavy one with **problems and . . .
burdens and . . . disputes** (v. 12). The words are graphic and
remind us of the many occasions in the wilderness narrative
when the people murmured, complained, disputed, and argued—taxing even Moses' outstanding leadership ability.

1:13–15 / The qualifications for those who were to be
appointed to subordinate leadership include both ability (**wise** and
understanding), and social standing (**respected**, lit. "known").
They would thus have the gifts and the respect to carry the
judicial responsibilities laid on them. The more explicitly moral
requirements of spiritual and personal integrity that Jethro had
proposed ("men who fear God, trustworthy men who hate dishonest gain," Exod. 18:21) are implied here by the instructions
given in verses 16ff.

1:16–17 / The responsibilities given to the tribal judges
echo other passages where a heavy emphasis is laid on judicial
integrity (cf. Exod. 23:1–9; Deut. 16:18–20; 2 Chron. 19:5–7). God's
concern was not merely that God's people should have good
laws, but that there should be good administration of law. Three
aspects of their duty are highlighted here. (a) They were to **judge
fairly** (lit. "judge the right"). The primary duty of judges is to
discover where right lies and act accordingly. (b) They were
to **not show partiality,** i.e., to not favor the Israelite over the non-
Israelite or the rich over the poor. The equal status before the law
of the resident alien in Israel is a marked and distinctive feature
of Hebrew law (cf. Exod. 12:49; Lev. 24:22; Deut. 29:10ff.; 31:12f.).
(c) They were to **not be afraid of any man,** because in exercising
justice they were doing the work of God himself. Whether the
phrase **judgment belongs to God** means that justice in general is

God's domain or that it was God who gave the judgment (verdict) in particular cases, through human agents, is uncertain, but the second is more probable (cf. 2 Chron. 19:6; Prov. 16:33). Either way, it underlines the elevated status given to judicial activity in Israel. It also enshrines a major feature of constitutional law, namely, that the law has a transcendent value. Promulgated and administered by humans, it possesses an authority above even those who so promulgate and administer it. Behind the law stands the God who loves and requires and gives justice.

The early church modeled itself on the Deuteronomic pattern of devolved leadership portrayed here. When rapid growth under God's blessing (echoing 1:10f.) led to disputes and organizational needs, these were met by a response similar in nature to that of Moses in 1:13–15 (cf. Acts 6:1–7). And inasmuch as Israel was intended to be a model, "a light to the nations" with paradigmatic relevance, there are interesting points of relevance to political and judicial forms of power in any human society today. We shall explore these more in our discussion of chapter 17.

Additional Notes §2

1:8 / The theme of **this land** is clearly one of the most central themes in the whole book and indeed is a key factor in Israel's theological understanding in the whole Hb. Bible. It had two major dimensions, of which the first is expressed in this verse: (a) divine gift; (b) divine ownership—the land still belonged to Yahweh as ultimate divine landlord (cf. Lev. 25:23). Modern study of this theme owes much to the seminal study of von Rad, "The Promised Land." See also Brueggemann, *The Land*, and C. J. H. Wright, *God's Land*.

1:15–16 / Three terms are used here for leaders in Israel. **Commanders:** The *śārîm* are primarily military officers here, but the term is also used of civil officers entrusted with supervision of work forces. Later it describes princes and court officials. **Officials:** similarly, *šōṭᵉrîm* (the term used in 16:18) are civil officials, probably with secretarial skills, who assist judges and other higher ranks of officialdom. **Judges:** the *šōpᵉṭîm* are those responsible for the administration of justice throughout Israel; this is one of the most important roles in the whole society and comes under constant moral scrutiny by the later prophets. On parallels between these officials and the instructions given them and other ancient Near Eastern societies, especially Hittite and Egyptian documents, cf. Weinfeld, *Deuteronomy*, pp. 140f.

1:16 / **An alien:** The *gēr/gērîm* denotes a class of people who were landless but resided in Israel's land under the protection of Israelite families. They may have been remnants of the original population or people who immigrated for various reasons. Being without the natural double protection of land and family, they were vulnerable to exploitation and oppression. Israel's memory of its "resident alien" status in Egypt was a powerful moral spur to humane treatment of aliens in its own midst (cf. Exod. 23:9). The Israelites' status before Yahweh as the supreme landlord is elsewhere expressed by the description of them as *gērîm* with him on his land (Lev. 25:23). On the social and economic situation of this class, cf. C. J. H. Wright, *God's Land*, pp. 58–64, 99–103; van Houten, *The Alien*.

§3 A Reminder of Wasted Opportunity (Deut. 1:19–46)

The journey from Horeb (Mt. Sinai) to the oasis of Kadesh Barnea takes about eleven days (v. 2). But when the newly freed Israelites got there, they lacked the nerve to possess the promised land, and thus had to wait for thirty-eight years in the wilderness. The events (cf. Num. 13–14) are recalled here in order to challenge the new generation to not fail again. One wasted generation was enough. It is an interesting feature of Deuteronomy, however, that the succeeding generations of Israel are treated as if they were the actors in that earlier drama. **All of you came to me . . .** (vv. 22ff.). Conversely, the covenant relationship that had been established at Sinai is explicitly said to have been made also with this next generation (cf. 5:3; 11:2–7; 29:14f.). All people of God have a solidarity and continuity in their actions and relationships, and this is the essence of the covenantal structure and ethos of Deuteronomy.

1:22–23 / **Then all of you came to me and said . . . The idea seemed good to me.** This is an interestingly different way of describing the initiative in the sending out of the spies from how the matter is presented in Numbers, where it is at God's command (Num. 13:1–3). But there is no need to assume that everything Moses interpreted as a word or command from Yahweh had to come by direct revelation. God could speak to him through the ideas and suggestions of others. In a similar way, vv. 9–14 describe a proposal that originally came from Jethro as if it were Moses' own idea. It seems unnecessary to regard the differences as coming from different documents (cf. Mayes, *Deuteronomy*, p. 126). It is perfectly natural to envisage a suggestion of the people being interpreted by Moses as the will of God, and then the actual command being given by Moses himself.

1:24–46 / With the return of the spies and the good report of some of them (the bad report of the others is suspended until v. 28), the original command **Go up and take possession of** the land (v. 21) has been reinforced by the encouragement, **it is a good land that the LORD our God is giving us.** This makes the people's next response all the more surprising and shocking: **But you were unwilling to go up** (v. 26). The rest of the section is presented as an ever intensifying resistance to all Moses' encouragements, ending in the debacle of an attempted conquest and humiliating defeat. Structurally, the narrative has a dramatic dialogue form, with alternating responses among the people, Moses, and God. The people's initial refusal (vv. 26–28) is countered by Moses' encouragement (vv. 29–31). This meets the people's continued refusal (vv. 32–33), which in turn arouses God's anger against them (vv. 34–36) and even against Moses (vv. 37–40). The people then change their minds (v. 41) in spite of God's warning (v. 42), and their final rebellion ends in disaster (vv. 43–46).

Three reasons for the people's failure of nerve are highlighted in the text.

Grumbling rebellion (vv. 26–27). The theme of Israel's murmurings and discontents chimes dolefully all through the narrative of their movements ever since the immediate aftermath of the exodus itself. "Stiff-necked" had become Moses' favorite term for them, echoing God's own opinion (Exod. 32:9; 33:3; 34:9; Deut. 9:6). But this time there is something of a climax. Of all their rebellions this was surely the most serious and the most costly. The bitterness of their disobedience is expressed in their words, in which they accuse God of quite absurd motives in what he had done for them. **The LORD hates us . . .** (v. 27). The very events that had been the greatest proof of God's love for them and of God's faithfulness to the promise to their ancestors are inverted into proof of God's malevolence (cf. 7:6–8)! Such a reaction, though certainly shocking in its context here, is not surprising as a symptom of depression and despair. It is sadly typical that even the people of God turn on God in accusation and blame when things go wrong, when obstacles seem insuperable, or when prolonged frustration leads to exhaustion.

Fear (v. 28). The bad report of the majority of spies (Num. 13:26–33) weakened the Israelites' resolve; they felt inferior and panicked. There were giants ahead! The irony is that they were in the kind of state of mind that God had promised to inflict on their enemies (cf. 2:25)—and later did (Josh. 2:11; 5:1; cf. Exod. 14:10).

Unbelief, in spite of evidence (vv. 29–32). One antidote to such fear is a good memory. Moses urges them to be unafraid in view of what they had already seen in their own recent past—God's victory over the Egyptians (v. 30) and God's parental care for them in the wilderness (vv. 31, 33). They had experienced Yahweh both as fighter and as father, as savior and as provider—a powerful combination of metaphors that echoes through the whole Bible. But **in spite of this, you did not trust in the LORD your God.** In spite of such evidence, they would not move forward in faith. Faith was no leap in the dark, but a perfectly reasonable step forward with eyes opened wide to what God had already done in the past and had promised to repeat in the future. God would be **ahead of** them as he had been behind them (v. 33). Israel's refusal in this circumstance was not prudence or realism but sheer unbelief that exhausted God's patience and led to judgment.

The seriousness of God's reaction to such a litany of rebellion is seen in the fact that the same expression is used for God's declared intent in judgment (vv. 34–36) as for the original promise of blessing: **the LORD . . . solemnly swore.** This particular generation had finally excluded itself from the enjoyment of the covenanted blessing of the promise to Abraham. The covenant as such was not revoked, but this generation would not **see** its fulfillment. Their eyes were sealed in unbelief. With such eyes they would never see the promised land.

Rebellion turns to presumption. Mortified by God's response, the people decide to "have a go" and in the process turn their delayed obedience to God's earlier command into direct disobedience to the latest instruction (vv. 40–46). The most serious flaw in the whole enterprise was that God had said, **"I will not be with you."** The last time Israel had heard such dreadful words was after the terrible golden calf apostasy at Mt. Sinai (Exod. 33:1–3). On that occasion Moses had realized only too clearly the implications of such an absence of God in their midst and told God that he would prefer to stay put in the wilderness rather than move forward without the presence of God (Exod. 33:15f.). Here, however, the people show no such awareness of the reality of their situation. The result demonstrated beyond all doubt that the only criterion of their success or failure lay in whether or not Yahweh was with them. Presumably this expedition did not differ in physical strength, military resources, or the number of fighting men from the expedition

God had originally commanded. The only difference was the lack of God's presence; but then, that was the only difference that mattered.

It is possible for the same action in the same circumstances to be an act of obedience or an act of disobedience, depending on the word of God in relation to it. It is possible for it to succeed or fail, depending on the presence or absence of God in the enterprise. Israel later learned through equally humiliating events (the loss of the ark to the Philistines) that the presence of God could not be physically or magically dragooned into the service of a disobedient people either (1 Sam. 4). Later still they expressed this principle in a psalm that sees all basic human action— building, working, raising a family—as fruitless without God (Ps. 127).

The whole section, 1:26–46, is a litany of disaster, punctuated by the sad refrain of the people's attitudes and actions. The sequence of verbs is poignant, climactic, and sobering. It stands as a warning to every generation of God's people to avoid such a chain reaction: **you were unwilling . . . you rebelled . . . you grumbled** . . . you were afraid . . . **you saw** but . . . **you did not trust** . . . you thought **it easy . . . you would not listen . . . you rebelled . . . you came back** . . . you wept . . . **you stayed.**

Additional Notes §3

1:28 / The **Anakites** was a term used for the previous inhabitants of Canaan, some of whom were apparently of unusual stature. The LXX translates it as "giants" (cf. 2:10f., 21; 9:2).

1:31 / The metaphor of God **as a father** who, in this case, **carries** Israel as **his son,** is found again, with a disciplinary flavor, in 8:5. The fatherhood-sonship theme is also reflected in the call for distinctive living (14:1) and is appealed to negatively in the powerful "prophetic" accusation of Israel in 32:5f., 18–20. It also underlies the description of the land as Israel's "inheritance" from Yahweh. It was, in fact, another way of expressing the covenant relationship and added a more personal and relationally durable dimension to it. See C. J. H. Wright, *God's Land,* pp. 15–22.

1:37 / On the exclusion of Moses also from the land, see commentary below at 3:26ff., and cf. 4:21f. and 34:1–4.

1:38 / The appointment of Joshua as successor did not actually take place at Kadesh Barnea in the context of the events being recalled here, but Moses adds it as an aside since obviously if Moses himself was not going to lead the people into the land, it was natural to ask who would. The mention of Joshua as his successor here at the beginning of the book, linking up with the full description of it at the end, adds to the effect of the whole book standing as "the last will and testament" of Moses. It is also a significant factor binding together both parts of the "outer frame" of the whole book (cf. 31:1–8, 14, 23; 34:9).

§4 Reminder of Past Victories (Deut. 2:1–3:29)

The first three chapters of Deuteronomy not only warn the people from past failures but also encourage them from past victories. The words to Joshua near the end of the section (3:21f.) give the point of the whole: God can do again what they had seen God do before, even for other nations. Their God did not lack experience! The structure of the section can be presented as follows:

2:1–8	Encounter with Edom
2:9–18	Encounter with Moab
2:19–23	Encounter with Ammon
2:24–37	Encounter with Sihon
3:1–11	Encounter with Og
3:12–20	Settlement of the Transjordan tribes
3:21–22	Encouragement of Joshua
3:23–29	Exclusion of Moses

The narrative summarizes and systematizes the events of Numbers 20–21 around two concerns. First, it underscores the sovereignty of Yahweh in all the events described. His initiation and direction of Israel's movements are repeatedly mentioned, and even the parenthetical footnotes of the chapter (2:10–12, 20–23) attribute previous national migrations and conquests to Yahweh's sovereignty.

Secondly, it seems designed to explain why some nations along Israel's route remained unmolested while others were conquered and dispossessed. The claims of brotherhood (an important ethical motivation later in the book) protected Edom (2:4, 8; cf. 23:7a). Moab and Ammon have a similar claim, being distantly related to Israel in the Genesis family archives (Gen. 19:30–38), but in their case the reason they are protected is explicitly told: Yahweh had already given them their lands by driving out earlier inhabitants, and the present arrangements were not to be dis-

turbed (2:9–12, 19–21). However, when Sihon and Og resisted
and attacked Israel, in spite of peace overtures in the former case,
they met their doom.

2:1 / By echoing 1:40, the last explicit command of God,
the narrative signals Israel's return to a more obedient behavior
and thus prepares the way for the positive flavor of the following
two chapters, in contrast to the gloom of 1:19–46.

2:2–8 / There are some differences between the account of Israel's dealings with Edom contained in Deuteronomy
and that in Numbers 20:14–21. Deuteronomy uses **descendants
of Esau** rather than Edom, in order to highlight the claim of
kinship (cf. Gen. 36). Deuteronomy omits the request of Moses
to pass through Edomite territory and its outright rejection by
the king of Edom, thus passing over the hostility implied in the
Numbers narrative. These differences doubtlessly stem from Deuteronomy's overall theological aim to compare the fates of the five
nations. Conversely, the idea of Yahweh having given the land of
Edom to Esau is not found in Numbers, but is Deuteronomy's
way of adding to the theological interpretation of history.

The accounts do not necessarily conflict. Numbers tells us
that the king of Edom displayed his military strength to deter
Israel from marching through his land (Num. 20:20); he did not
actually attack Israel and so would not have merited the fate of
Sihon or Og. It is also possible (cf. Driver, *Deuteronomy*, p. 34) that
the Numbers account describes Israel's earlier request to Edom,
whereas Deuteronomy refers to their march around Edom just
before their actual entry into the land. The geographical details
of the stages of Israel's route are obscure, so that we do not know
exactly how Israel **went on past** Edom, though it seems likely that
they skirted it on its eastern border.

2:9–12 / Moab was not to be conquered either, not because of a particularly benevolent attitude toward Moab (cf. 23:3–6),
but simply because Yahweh had **given Ar to the descendants of
Lot as a possession.** When Deuteronomy's prominent land theology in relation to Israel's possession of Canaan is taken into
account, this direct statement that Yahweh had given other lands
to other peoples, supported by the parenthetical notes that follow, is quite remarkable. Three times this passage says that Yahweh had given land to other peoples—to Edom (v. 5), to Moab
(v. 9), and to Ammon (v. 9)—using the same vocabulary as is

characteristically used of his land-gift to Israel. On top of this, the antiquarian footnotes (vv. 10–12 and vv. 20–23) inform us that the processes of migration and conquest that lay behind the then current territorial map had also been under the control of Yahweh. Not only is the same language used as for Israel's settlement, but the comparison is explicitly drawn: other nations had conquered and settled **just as Israel did in the land the LORD gave them as their possession** (v. 12).

More theology is tucked into these obscure notes than the NIV's understandable use of parentheses might suggest—some of it explicit, some latent. First, these notes unambiguously assert Yahweh's multinational sovereignty. The same God who had declared to Pharaoh that the whole earth belonged to God (Exod. 9:14, 16, 29) had been moving other nations around on the chessboard of history long before Israel's historic exodus and settlement. This universal sovereignty over the nations mattered a great deal to Israel in subsequent centuries as they themselves joined the ranks of the attacked and the dispossessed. Later prophetic understanding of Yahweh's "use" of the Assyrians, Babylonians, and Persians as agents of Yahweh's purposes in history is in fact consistent with this deeper theme of God's ultimate, universal direction of the destiny of nations (cf. Deut. 32:8; Jer. 18:1–10; 27:1–7).

Secondly, these notes relativize Deuteronomy's land-gift tradition itself, though not in the sense of questioning or undermining it. The affirmation of Yahweh's gift of land to Israel in fulfillment of his promise to Abraham is one of the fundamental pillars of Deuteronomy's whole worldview. However, it was, in principle and at a purely historical level, no different from what God had done in other nations. In the immediate context, Israel's defeat and territorial takeover of the lands of Sihon and Og was no different from other nations' earlier migrations and forceful settlements; all are attributed to the sovereign disposition of Yahweh.

Because God had also given lands to other nations, Israel's uniqueness lay, not in having merely received land from Yahweh, but in its covenant relationship with Yahweh. And that covenant was based on God's faithfulness to the promise to Abraham and God's historical act of redemption from Egypt. If that covenant were to be threatened by Israel's neglect, then the mere historical facts of exodus and settlement would count for nothing more in the face of God's judgment than the migrations of other nations.

Elsewhere Deuteronomy warns Israel against reading any kind of privileged superiority or pride into their remarkable history, whether numerical (7:7–8), economic (8:17–18), or moral (9:4–6). Amos shocked the people by putting Israel's exodus on the same level as other migrations orchestrated by Yahweh (Amos 9:7), and Jeremiah risked a public lynching by suggesting that Yahweh could destroy his temple and revoke the gift of land by expelling the people (Jer. 7:1–7, 26). Such prophetic threats sounded radical and shocking to the complacent people they addressed, but did no more than amplify the principles already laid down in the Torah. The driving out of nations and the gift of land to Israel were a tremendous historical encouragement and also a tremendous historical warning. God could and would do the same to Israel if they gave cause by following the ways of the nations (cf. Lev. 18:24–28; 20:22–24).

2:13–15 / Almost as a hidden echo of the implicit warning just referred to, these verses remind the present generation that the very generation that had experienced the incredible blessing of the exodus itself had forfeited their enjoyment of its purpose and had perished outside the land. It is a flashback to the negative account of 1:26–46. It gains its rhetorical power by an inversion of the "holy war" motif. That is, it takes phrases normally used against the enemies of Israel (**perished . . . the LORD's hand . . . against them . . . completely eliminated**) and directs them at Israel itself. Paul used the same event as a continued warning to God's people, on the explicit hermeneutical principle that "these things happened to them as examples and were written down as warnings for us" (1 Cor. 10:1–13).

2:16–23 / Israel's nonharassment of the Ammonites (on this occasion!) is noted in the same way and is for the same reason as in the case of the Moabites. This time, however, the explanatory geographical note adds a reference to a region not involved at all in the current narrative, namely, the "Gaza strip," which had been populated by the Avvites and was taken over by the Caphtorites, usually thought to be the Philistines migrating from Crete and the Aegean region (v. 23). The very incidental nature of this piece of information, which has no other apparent reason for inclusion, seems to underline the affirmation of Yahweh's sovereignty in international history and geography.

2:24–30 / **The Arnon Gorge,** running into the Dead Sea, marked the northern boundary of Moab and the southern boundary of Ammon. The Ammonite territory, however, lay to the east, stretching as far north as the Jabbok, which flowed into the Jordan. The territory to the west of the Ammonites actually bordered the eastern bank of the Jordan and belonged to **Sihon the Amorite, king of Heshbon.** The Israelites needed to pass through this territory in order to cross the Jordan into the promised land. Sihon's refusal to let them do so led to his land being not merely traversed, but conquered and annexed to Israel's tribal allotments.

The narrative that follows is a small-scale example of the Old Testament's view of historical responsibility, of which the story of Pharaoh and the plagues of Egypt is the classic case study. Why did Israel capture the land of Sihon? At one level, it was because Sihon chose to reject a request for peaceful transit (vv. 26–30)—a decision for which he was fully responsible. But at another level it was because Yahweh had already **given** Sihon's land into the hand of the Israelites and for that purpose **had made his spirit stubborn and his heart obstinate** (v. 30). Neither pole of the explanation should be collapsed into the other. That is, we should not view the theological explanation as merely a post factum spiritualization of historical events, nor should we think of Sihon (or Pharaoh) as a mere puppet stripped of personal accountability by a manipulating God. It is characteristic of Deuteronomy and the Hebrew scriptures generally to affirm with equal strength the divine will and purpose and the human responsible choice. History is the mysterious combination of both, neither operating independently of the other. Other examples of the same dual responsibility for a course of events include the stories of Joseph (Gen. 50:20), the division of the kingdoms after Solomon (1 Kgs. 11:29–12:24), and the death of Ahab (1 Kgs. 22:1–38).

Just as 2:1 signaled Israel's return to obedience, so 2:25 signals Yahweh's return to the active fulfillment of his promise (Exod. 15:14, 16). The fact that Sihon defied the divinely induced panic of the nations (expressed with characteristic rhetorical hyperbole—**all the nations under heaven**) underlines his own culpability for the destruction that followed.

2:31–37 / Since Sihon was a king of an Amorite people, this battle really represents Israel's first victory over the peoples of the land God had promised. It is thus described in language characteristic of the later accounts of the conquest. There is the same unselfconscious linking together of divine will and human action: **I have begun to deliver . . . [you] begin to conquer** (v. 31); **the LORD our God delivered him over to us and we struck him down** (v. 33); **we took all his towns** (v. 34) . . . **The LORD our God gave us all of them** (v. 36). There is also the application of the rules of war fought in the name of Yahweh (often called "holy wars," a nonbiblical term that is generally worth avoiding because of its later connotations; see discussion in additional notes §23). This involved the "devotion" to Yahweh of the enemy through total destruction. Sometimes, but not always, this included the destruction of all booty as well—on this occasion Israel kept what they captured (v. 35). The laws of war and the problems associated with the ban on confiscating goods *(ḥērem)* will be discussed further in the commentary on chapters 7 and 20.

It might be slightly fanciful to detect a note of "I told you so!" in the bald statement, **not one town was too strong** (lit. "too high") **for us** (v. 36). But it does seem to be a rebuking answer to the fear of the people (1:28). The previous generation had squandered their opportunity to take the land because they were intimidated by tall people and tall cities. Now their offspring discovered that height was no hindrance to the hand of God and a people moving in obedience (v. 37).

3:1–11 / The account of the defeat of Og and the capture of his territory in Bashan follows the earlier narrative in Numbers 21:32–35 closely and is very similar to the encounter with Sihon. Bashan is the territory to the northeast of the Jordan river, famed for its fertility and rich pastureland (cf. Amos 4:1). Clearly it was also well-populated and urbanized (3:4–5). As with the cities of Sihon, the fortifications and defenses were no obstacle to Israel. As a result, therefore, of Sihon's (and presumably Og's) resistance to Israel's initially peaceful request, Israel gained possession of large tracts of land on the eastern side of the Jordan, **from the Arnon Gorge as far as Mount Hermon** (v. 8).

3:12–17 / This summary of the settlement of the transjordan tribes (Reuben, Gad, and half the tribe of Manasseh) simply gives the result of a heated discussion between their leaders and Moses about their right to settle there. The full record is in Numbers 32. It is again characteristic that the Deuteronomic summary narrative somewhat changes the "flavor" without introducing serious conflict. What matters here is the outcome, not the emotions, of the decision.

3:18–20 / These verses emphasize the unity and solidarity of God's people. It would have been easy for the Transjordan tribes to settle down in their land and let the other tribes get on with their conquests. So Moses reminds them first that **the LORD your God has given you this land to take possession of it** (v. 18); they have no "natural right" of conquest, and secondly that God is giving much land to their brothers **across the Jordan** (v. 20). So it was not a matter of who conquered what. All the tribes would owe their land to God's gift, and so all the tribes must fight together to possess what God had given to all. Only when God had given **rest** to all would any be free of obligation to help the others.

The principle expressed here remained an ideal in Israel. In fact, in the turbulent centuries that followed, about the only thing that united the scattered tribes of Israel was this sense of mutual obligation, arising from a common awareness of being "Israel" and a common sense of commitment to Yahweh as the God of Israel. This unity was an ideal that was usually recognized only when it was broken. Thus, at the time of the great conflict with the Canaanites under Deborah and Barak, Deborah celebrated those tribes that had come to help in the battle and roundly condemned those that had not, including, unfortunately, the Transjordanians (Judg. 5).

3:21–22 / To close his opening historical survey, Moses looks forward to the future as entrusted into the hands of his successor, Joshua. The lessons of the past were especially for him, and the most important lesson of all was that God's victories were infinitely repeatable. If God could defeat two kings, God could defeat many more. Yahweh was a God who was not coincidentally lucky, but consistently victorious. These words, placed here, are picked up again in 31:1–8, when Moses actually commissions Joshua. They thus reinforce the nature of Deuteronomy as the "last testament" of Moses and give the whole book a forward look toward life in the land. This is confirmed again when the book of Joshua opens with a repetition of Moses' encouragement to Joshua, placed this time in the mouth of God (Josh. 1:1–9).

3:23–25 / There is a touching pathos in the way Moses turns from his encouraging words to Joshua, who has a bright future ahead of him, to his own sad longing to be allowed to share that future. **I pleaded** is a strong expression meaning to beg for grace and mercy out of desperation (cf. Ps. 30:8–10). Moses' plea is an impassioned one. He addresses himself personally to the God he knows by name: **Sovereign LORD**—a title for God that in Deuteronomy is used only in the prayers of Moses, for himself here and for the people in 9:26. He calls himself **your servant**—the privileged title that Moses shared with only a few people in the OT. He has a long-term understanding of God's will and purpose, such that he can look back over the incredible acts of God in two generations and realize that they were only "the beginning" of God's greatness (rather like the way Luke can describe his gospel as merely what Jesus "began to do and to teach," Acts 1:1)! Surely God will allow him to witness the next stage of that purpose. Moses acknowledges the uniqueness of Yahweh in terms he will later impress on Israel (4:35, 39). And finally, he knows that the whole point of his life's work, ever since the fiery encounter at the burning bush propelled him so reluctantly back to Egypt, has been to get this people into **the good land beyond the Jordan.** How could God keep him from seeing the fruition of all his labors?

3:26–29 / How indeed? Yet God said "no." The depth of the pain and disappointment that the divine refusal caused Moses can be seen in the number of times he refers to it. (1:37; 3:26; 4:21; cf. 31:2; 32:48–52; 34:4). So even if he stopped talking to God about it (v. 26 suggests he had been making a persistent request), he didn't stop reminding the Israelites of it: **because of you the LORD was angry with me**! The exclusion of Moses from entering the promised land figures so largely here, and was probably as much a surprise to the original readers as it is to us, that it invites some theological reflection.

When one puts together all the passages that bear on Moses' exclusion, they offer us at least two perspectives. On the one hand, our text here and the two closest to it in Deuteronomy, 1:37 and 4:21, give the impression that it was the people's fault. Moses suffered "because of" them. On the other hand, Deuteronomy 32:48–52 reflects the narrative in Numbers 20, in which Moses himself, under provocation from the people's complaining about lack of water at Meribah, apparently failed in some unspecified way to uphold God's holiness among them (Num. 20:12).

So was it Moses' own fault or was he the victim of the people's rebellion? Probably we should not try to separate the two perspectives so rigidly. Least helpful of all, in my view, is to try to solve the problem on source critical grounds by suggesting that in the original Deuteronomic account Moses was entirely innocent but suffered with and for the people, and that it is only the priestly writer, under the alleged influence of Ezekiel 18, who introduced the idea that Moses himself must have sinned. This might account for Numbers 20:9–12, but it also requires the questionable assumption that Deuteronomy 32:51f. is a Priestly addition to Deuteronomy.

Since Moses' purpose was to exhort the new generation *not* to go on failing as their parents had done, one can understand why his reference to his own exclusion dwells on the people's part in it and omits his own. In a sense, then, the phrase **because of you** is justified. Though not without fault himself, Moses was bearing the punishment of his own generation (that of the exodus) along with them, and bearing the punishment that even the following generation should have had. *Nobody* deserved to go into the land! Moses' death outside the land would witness to the reality of judgment, just as Joshua's victorious entry would witness to the reality of forgiving, covenant grace. This perspective seems close to the surface in 4:21–22. Moses will die, but the people will live. Judgment and grace are interwoven.

So, while it is right not to use the expression "vicarious suffering" for Moses' exclusion (after all, the original rebels also died in the wilderness, so Moses did not die "for them"), nevertheless, in some sense Moses was bearing more of the suffering of his people than was his personal due. He was not himself an innocent victim. But he suffered "because of" the people's sin—a sin that he had not directly shared, yet that had somehow induced his own failure. He entered into the suffering of his people and of the God of his people in a way that, like so much else in his life, foreshadowed that future servant of Yahweh who would indeed offer a blameless life for the sins of us all (Isa. 53:4–6). Would it have eased Moses' pain and disappointment, we might wonder, if he could have known that one day he would stand in the land on another mountaintop and have a conversation with that very servant about the sacrifice (indeed, the "exodus," Luke 9:31) *he* was about to accomplish?

And so this remarkable introduction to the book comes to a close, in a way that anticipates the sequence with which the whole book will end: the commissioning of Joshua, Moses' ascent and death at Mt. Pisgah, and the positioning of the people at Beth Peor—a day's journey from the promised land itself. The boundary has been very clearly drawn—geographically, historically, theologically, and morally. Moses has kindled his people's memories: memories of blessings so great that new organizational structures were required to cope with them (1:9–18); memories of rebellion so horrific that a whole generation had forfeited further blessing and perished in the wilderness (1:19–46); memories of divine guidance that negotiated a path through lands God had given to others (2:1–23); memories of past victories that inspired future courage (2:24–3:11, 21f.); memories of commitments to unity and solidarity in the struggles of God's people (3:12–20). It is time now to move forward and cross that boundary, because **you have stayed long enough** on this side of it (1:6; cf. 2:2).

Additional Notes §4

2:10–12, 20 / The identities of the groups mentioned in these verses are shrouded in uncertainty. On **Emim** and **Zamzummim,** cf. Gen. 14:5. **Rephaim** are a legendary race of giants (Deut. 3:13; Gen. 14:5; Gen. 15:20; Num. 13:32; Josh. 13:12) who later seem to have survived among the Philistines and around Hebron (2 Sam. 21:15–22; Josh. 11:22).

3:11 / Apart from his defeat by Israel, the only thing Og has bequeathed to the annals of history is the size of his bed! Commentators have puzzled over the purpose of this detail. The size was probably honorific—a truly "king-size" bed, though Og, as one of the last of the notoriously large **Rephaites,** was likely a very tall individual. Millard has argued from archaeological evidence, first that Og's "iron bed" was indeed a bed and not (as many commentators and an NIV footnote suggest) a basalt sarcophagus, and secondly, that it was probably a wooden frame plated or decorated with iron, not solid iron (like "ivory palace," Ps. 45:8). At this point in history, the transition from the Late Bronze to Early Iron Age, iron is still a precious and costly metal and therefore fit for the decor of the royal bedroom. Millard also suggests that since iron became the common metal of following centuries, this small incidental note about a remarkable "iron bed" is consistent with an early date for Deut. Cf. Millard, "King Og's Bed." Unlike Og, the matter has not been laid to rest: cf. Drews, " 'Chariots of Iron,' " and Millard, "Iron Bed."

3:26 / A stark contrast between the Deuteronomic explanation for God's denial of Moses' desire to enter the promised land and the one given in Num. 20 is argued by Mann, "Denial of Moses," linking it questionably with reflection on the death of Josiah.

The severity and apparent injustice of God's refusal to allow Moses to enter the promised land, and the circumstances of his death outside it, has greatly exercised the minds of Jewish commentators from the earliest times. For a fascinating survey of some of the relevant midrashic and haggadic interpretations, see Goldin, "The Death of Moses."

§5 Obedience and Loyalty to Israel's Unique God (Deut. 4:1–43)

The historical recollections now give place to urgent exhortation. This chapter is the natural conclusion to the lessons of this first speech of Moses and comes to a powerful climax in 4:32–40. At 4:44 and 5:1 we are introduced to the second major discourse, which includes the rest of the law itself. With this chapter we also move into the "inner frame" of the book's structure, comprising chapters 4–11 and 27–30, with their many common themes. Chapters 4–11 show a careful structure with its own concentric patterning of material (see additional note).

Deuteronomy 4 is in itself a remarkably well-constructed sermon with a quite clear concentric structure. The opening section (vv. 1–8) and the closing section (vv. 32–40) reflect each other, impressing on Israel the necessity of obedience. This necessity is reinforced with rhetorical questions that express the incomparability of Yahweh, the uniqueness of Israel's historical experience, and the excellence of their law itself. The affirmation of Yahweh's uniqueness in these "sandwich" verses ties in with the prologue and first commandment of the Decalogue (cf. Deut. 5:6–7). The central section of the chapter (vv. 9–31) is an extended reflection on the second commandment, which prohibited images and warned Israel of Yahweh's jealousy (cf. Deut. 5:7–10). The whole chapter, therefore, as an extended sermonic amplification of the opening chords of the Decalogue, powerfully presents the very pillars of Israel's nationhood in covenant with their God.

Internal and External Benefits of Obedience (4:1–8)

4:1 / The primary purpose for keeping God's law is **so that you may live.** This phrase is repeated frequently in Deuteronomy, climaxing in the veritable evangelistic appeal of 30:15–20. Indeed, the link between law and life is an authentic OT vision (cf.

Lev. 18:5; Pss. 1; 19; 119; Ezek. 18) that Jesus himself endorsed in conversation with the rich young man (Matt. 19:16ff.). It is a perspective that needs to be kept in view when wrestling with Paul's perception (from a different standpoint and in a different debate) of the law as an agent of death.

Life for Israel, in the setting of Deuteronomy, meant life in the land across the Jordan. Hence, Moses adds as further motivation to obedience the expectation of entry into, and possession of, the land. This introduces one of the features of the book that some scholars have regarded as a tension. On the one hand, it seems that the taking of the land is here made conditional on obedience to the law. On the other hand, the gift of the land was an unconditional act of Yahweh, motivated by his faithfulness to his promise to Israel's ancestors. The first part of the verse expresses the first point: **so that ... you may go in,** while the second expresses the other point: **the land that the LORD, the God of your fathers, is giving you.** Rather than seeing the two as in conflict, we can understand them within the balance of indicative and imperative that underlies the relationship between God and God's people throughout the whole Bible. Behind everything stands the unconditioned grace and faithfulness of God to the divine promise. The land would be given. But secure possession of it, long life, and enjoyment of it were dependent in each generation on the people's response of committed loyalty and obedience.

4:2 / The warning against tampering with the law by adding or removing anything (repeated in 12:32) expresses a concern for the integrity of God's revelation. It was not to be treated like a menu from which one could select what suited one's taste, nor as a mere foundation for personal inventiveness. God's word must be taken whole in its overall meaning and thrust. It is not to be trifled or tampered with. Such a concern certainly underlies the canonical principle, which some scholars see in its origins in this text and in its finality in Revelation 22:18f.

4:3–4 / In 1:26–46 Moses described the most signal failure of the exodus generation, namely, their rebellion at the very edge of the promised land. Here he refers to the most recent memory of the present generation—their idolatry and immorality in connection with **the Baal of Peor,** which resulted in large numbers of their contemporaries being struck down by plague (Num. 25; cf. Ps. 106:28–31; Hos. 9:10). The point of the reminder in this context was to underline by a negative example how precious a gift was the life God offered in the land, how easily it could be forfeited, and how it was only by their loyalty to Yahweh that Moses' hearers were **still alive today.**

4:5–8 / Obedience to the law was not for Israel's benefit alone. It is a marked feature of the OT that Israel lived on a very public stage. All that happened in its history was open to the comment and reaction of the nations at large. Apart from being inevitable, given the international scene of the ancient Near East, this "visibility" of Israel was a deliberate part of its theological identity and role as the "priesthood" of Yahweh among the nations (cf. Exod. 19:4–6). It could be either positive, as here, when the nations are impressed with the wisdom of Israel's law (cf. 28:10); or negative, as when the nations are shocked by the severity of Israel's judgment when they abandon the ways of their God (28:37; 29:22–28). Either way, faithful or unfaithful, the people of God are an open book to the world, and the world asks questions and draws conclusions (see the introduction, on the missiological dimension of Deut.).

So the point of verse 6 is not merely that obedience to God's law is a sensible result of **your wisdom and understanding.** This Wisdom perspective that keeping God's law is beneficial for the one who does so is certainly a thread running through Deuteronomy. But by suddenly introducing **the nations** as observers and commentators, the text opens up the whole significance of Israel's law to a much wider horizon. The nations **will hear about all these decrees,** that is, they will notice and inquire and take an interest in the phenomenon of Israel as a society, with all the social, economic, legal, political, and religious dimensions of the Torah. And that social system will lead them to the conclusion that Israel as a people qualify as a **great nation,** regarded as **wise and understanding.**

That is as far as the nations may be expected to go in their external observation. And even thus far it is a remarkable expectation, given the situation of those addressed in the text—an as yet landless people, descendants of refugee slaves who had precisely *opted out* of one of the "great nations" of the world, Egypt. But Moses goes on, with two rhetorical questions, to sharpen the point by emphasizing the foundation of the national greatness so defined. First (v. 7), it is based on the nearness of Yahweh to his people. Second (v. 8), it is based on the righteousness of the Torah. In both respects, the effect of the rhetorical questions is to claim that *Israel is incomparable*—in the same way that the rhetorical questions of verses 32–34 are designed to claim that *Yahweh is incomparable*. Israel would have an intimacy with God and a quality of social justice that no other nation could match. These would be the factors that would lie behind the external reputation. As far as the nations could see, it was simply a matter of wisdom and understanding. The inner reality was the presence of God and the justice of God's Torah.

These verses invite hermeneutical and missiological reflection. First, hermeneutically, the force of the rhetorical questions is to *invite comparison*, but in the confident expectation that nothing will invalidate the claims being made. The claim for Israel's social uniqueness was being made on a crowded stage, with plenty of other claimants for admirable systems of law. Israel knew of the ancient and acclaimed legal traditions of Mesopotamia; as a matter of fact, its own legal traditions intersect with them at many points. Yet this claim for the primacy of OT law is lodged quite possibly with deliberate polemical intent, since the law code of Hammurabi also claimed a divine quality of social righteousness (see M. Weinfeld, *Deuteronomic School*, pp. 150f.). Old Testament law explicitly invites, even welcomes, public inspection and comparison. But the expected result of such comparison is that Israel's law will be found superior in wisdom and justice. This is a monumental claim, similar in its formal and theological shape to the sermon's closing claim of the uniqueness of Yahweh in the midst of the gods of the nations. It grants to the nations and to the readers of this text, including ourselves, the liberty to analyze OT law in comparison with other social systems, ancient and modern, and to evaluate its claim. It thus sanctions the hermeneutical principles and methods outlined in the introduction by which OT law is granted a paradigmatic function in relation to our social ethics. For indeed, the humaneness and justice of Israel's overall social and legal system have been favorably commented on by many scholars who have done the most meticulous studies of comparative ancient law. Also, the social relevance of ancient Israel's system has increasingly been recognized in our very different modern world.

Secondly, missiologically, these verses articulate a motivation for obedience to the law that is easily overlooked. The point is that if Israel would live as God intended, then *the nations* would notice. Israel existed for the ultimate purpose of being the vehicle of God's blessing the nations. That was in their "genetic code" from the very loins of Abraham. Here we find that at least one aspect of the blessing of the nations would be that when exposed to such a model of social justice, the nations would observe and ask questions. The missiological challenge, therefore, is that the ethical quality of life of the people of God (their obedience to the law, in this context) is a vital factor in the attraction of the nations to the living God. The motivation for God's people to live by God's law is ultimately to bless the nations. As so often in the OT, mission and ethics are inseparable. There is a vital link between the religious claims of the people of God (that God is near them) and their practical social ethic. The world will be interested in the former only when it sees the latter.

The Danger and Consequences of Idolatry (4:9–31)

The high vision of Israel functioning as a model for the nations expressed in verses 6–8 could be jeopardized in at least two ways. First, it could be lost by sheer neglect. The possibility that the Israelites might forget (a) what God had done for them and (b) what God required of them, led Moses to reemphasize the importance of teaching both these things (vv. 9–14). Second, it could be lost by Israel being enticed into the idolatries of the nations (vv. 15–24). If this happened, then the Israelites would lose their primary distinctiveness and be scattered among the very nations they were supposed to be separate from (vv. 25–28). Only wholehearted return to the Yahweh of the ancestral promise could restore them from such calamity (vv. 29–31). The negative warnings of this central section of the chapter, then, should be seen in the light of, and for the sake of, the positive "missionary" potential of verses 6–8. That is what is at stake.

4:9 / The opening words are emphatic, and the command to **watch** (be careful; lit. keep, guard) **yourselves** is repeated in verses 15 and 23. The educational thrust of the book of Deuteronomy as a whole is reinforced by frequent instructions for parents to take seriously their own teaching role within the family network of the nation (see 6:7, 20ff.; 11:19; 31:13; 32:46; and cf. Exod. 12:26f.; 13:8, 14; Josh. 4:21f.).

4:10–14 / To warn the people against idolatry (vv. 15–20), Moses first draws their minds back to two features of their Mt. Sinai (Horeb) experience. First, there was the terrifying nature of the event and what it said about the God at the center of it. The

Sinai theophany ("appearance or manifestation of God") was an event of such a scale that it burned itself very deeply into the national collective memory of Israel. In times of crisis it was to the God of Sinai they appealed, in memory of the awesome demonstration of power that had happened there (cf. Deut. 33:2; Judg. 5:5; Ps. 68:8). The description in verse 11 summarizes the lengthier narrative of Exodus 19, with the paradoxical combination of blazing **fire** and **deep darkness**. Fire, however, is the dominant symbol, recurring in verses 12, 15, 33, and 36 (cf. 5:4, 22–26) and climaxing in the description of Yahweh himself as **a consuming fire** in verse 24. With such a memory and concept of God, any enticement to idolatry would be "playing with fire"—suicidal folly.

Second, there was the remarkable fact that at Sinai God had been heard but not seen. **You heard the sound** (lit. "voice") **of words but saw no form; there was only a voice** (v. 12). And the substance of that voice was not mere noise either, but the specific, clear, terms of the covenant, **the Ten Commandments** (v. 13; lit. "the ten words," see ch. 5). What really mattered at Sinai, then, was not that there had been a *theophanic manifestation* of God, but that there had been a *verbal revelation* of God's mind and will. Sinai was a cosmic audio-visual experience, but it was the audio that mattered. It has been observed that Hebrew society never developed a visual religious culture, unlike Greek society. Part of the reason lies in the aniconic (imageless) nature of Israel's worship, linked to the point made in verse 15 about seeing no "form" of God. But a more significant and more positive reason lies in the emphasis Israel placed on its "auditory" culture. God was to be heard, and through hearing, obeyed. The ear, as the organ of understanding and obedience in relation to the spoken word of God, was more religiously and ethically significant than the eye.

4:15–20 / This specific warning against idolatry is prefaced with a reminder of the point just made, **you saw no form** (v. 15). Any attempt, therefore, to make an image as an object of or aid to worship, was bound to be inadequate. But the reason for the prohibition should be carefully expressed. Sometimes it is claimed that Israel here affirmed an invisible deity, as against visible idols. Or that the contrast is between God as spiritual and idols as material. But neither of these two contrasts is what the text stresses. In the context of verses 12ff., the contrast is not between visible and invisible, or between spiritual and material, but *between the visible and the audible*. Idols have "form" but do not speak. Yahweh has no "form," but he decisively speaks. Idols are visible but dumb. Yahweh is invisible but eloquent, addressing his people in words of promise and demand, gift and claim. This introduces a fundamentally moral distinction into the contrast between the faith of Israel and surrounding visual polytheism. What sets Yahweh apart is not that *he* looks different, but that he calls for a people who will look different, with a different way of life, a different social order, and a different dynamic of worship. It is these powerfully redemptive and ethical qualities that burst the limits of language in verses 32ff. At this point, all that matters is that Israel should beware of cheap but attractive alternatives.

The words, **an idol, an image of any shape** (v. 16), are identical to those used in the second commandment (5:8). The list of possible "shapes" that idols might take (vv. 16–19) is given in an order that precisely reverses the order of the creation narrative: human beings, land animals, birds, fish, the heavenly bodies. The point, probably being made deliberately through this literary feature, is that idolatry not only corrupts God's redemptive achievement for God's people (v. 20), but perverts and turns upside-down the whole created order.

The heavenly bodies were among the most powerful of the deities of the ancient Near East and were associated with its most powerful civilizations. Hence the temptation to **be enticed** (v. 19) by them. Idolatry always has its fascination; this ancient warning still has force in the midst of the seductions of modern idolatries.

The second half of this verse has proved puzzling for many and takes its place among many controverted texts in the modern debate over the plurality of religions. It appears to say that the worship of sun, moon, and stars taking place in other nations was actually ordained by Yahweh himself. If that is what it means, how can it be squared with the almost universal condemnation of the idolatry of the nations elsewhere in the OT?

One way of handling this text is to take it in the context of the Israelites' habit of attributing to the sovereign providence of Yahweh all that they observed in the world. If nations were seen to be worshipping the sun, moon, and stars, then in some sense it must have been with Yahweh's permission. The point would then be that Israel had been privileged with a higher revelation and delivered from such subordinate objects of worship by God's redemptive power (v. 20). God's "assignment" of such lesser objects of worship to the nations would then be seen as *provisional* and intended to be replaced by the true worship of the living God presently entrusted to Israel. This would then be another dimension of Israel's role as the agent of God's blessing the nations. Such an assumption of provisionality would fit with Paul's affirmation of God's leniency toward those who imagine God is to be worshipped through created things, until they are confronted with the revelation of his truth and the challenge of the gospel, at which time they are called to repent and turn to the living God (Acts 14:15–17; 17:29–31).

One may question, however, whether the text actually affirms that *worship* of the heavenly bodies was positively intended by God. The Hebrew of the last clause of verse 19 can be translated simply, "and you worship what Yahweh your God assigned to all the peoples under all the heavens." The sentence might mean " . . . for them to worship," but no such words are in the text. In the context of the preceding inverted creation narrative, the thought may be merely of the gift of the heavenly lights to the whole of humanity for the purposes described in Genesis 1:14–18. The worship of these objects by nations was not God's original intention and must be rejected by Israel. Thus Mayes is probably right to say that the intention of verse 19 is "not to express either tolerance or ridicule of the nations and their practices, but rather to prepare the way for the contrasting picture of Israel's favored status in the next verse" (*Deuteronomy*, p. 154).

Verse 20 gives the double reason for the prohibition on Israel bowing down to any created thing: their experience of redemption **out of Egypt,** and the exclusive covenant relationship to Yahweh as **the people of his inheritance.** This last phrase, less common than the frequent designation of the land as Israel's inheritance, points to the strong filial nature of the relationship between God and Israel in Deuteronomy. Only a few times is the actual phraseology of sonship used (1:31; 8:5; 14:1; 32:6), but inheritance language presupposes sonship, for the heir was the firstborn son—a description already used of Israel in the exodus tradition (Exod. 4:22). The verse is also one of several echoes in Deuteronomy of the special identity of Israel as Yahweh's "treasured possession" in Exodus 19:5 (cf. Deut. 7:6; 9:26, 29; 14:2).

4:21–23 / See comments on 3:23ff. The reference to his own dismal fate outside the land may be Moses' way of reinforcing his warning. If this was the judgment on *him*, then what could a seriously rebellious people expect?

4:24 / In the course of this central section of the sermon, Moses affirms two climactic points, two apparently contradictory definitive statements about Yahweh. This is the first. The second is in verse 31. Sinai itself had demonstrated the nature of Yahweh as **a consuming fire** (cf. Exod. 24:17), but the point was not merely a matter of physical fear in the presence of spectacular cosmic pyrotechnics. The fire of Yahweh as **a jealous God** is the fire of an exclusive commitment to this people that demands an exclusive commitment in return. It is, in short, the fire of redeeming love that had brought them out of the fires of bondage (v. 20) and would therefore tolerate no rival. The apparent contradiction between verse 24 and verse 31 is in reality a vital consistency. For mercy functions precisely in the context of judgment. It was the fire of God's jealousy that protected the strength of God's mercy and covenant faithfulness to this people. In rebellion and idolatry they would find the God of verse 24. In return and obedience they would find the God of verse 31. This is the same unchanged God, responding to a tragically changeable people.

4:25–28 / Having pointedly looked to the past in the opening chapters, Moses equally pointedly looks to the future and is just as unromantic in his assessment of the people's likely behavior. This is the first of several such passages in the book (cf. 28:15–68; 29:22–28; 31:16–29). The threat of the Israelites being scattered among the nations need not be taken as evidence that such texts must have been written in the light of the exile of Judah in the sixth century. The experience of conquest, deportation, and scattering—and specifically as a punishment for treaty violation—was well enough known in the ancient world to explain the presence of this threat many centuries before it became a historical reality for Israel.

Just as the people's idolatry would reverse the very order of creation (vv. 16–19), so also it would entail a judgment that would reverse the covenant with Abraham: **only a few of you will survive** (v. 27) clearly contrasts with the promise of growth and multiplication (cf. 1:11).

The thought in verse 28, that **you will worship man-made gods,** seems to be ironic: under judgment they will have to do what they had freely chosen to do—serve other gods. But they will then discover precisely the impotence of those gods, an impotence proven at the point of need (cf. Jer. 2:27f.). If these gods cannot perform the equivalent of even basic bodily functions, what hope is there of any saving power from them? In Isaiah 46:1–2 the prophet takes the sarcasm to its zenith. The mightiest gods of Babylon, far from being any assistance to their worshippers in their hour of need, could not even rescue their own fallen idols, which consequently become a needless burden to living people! If Israel, knowing a God who had carried them (Exod. 19:4; Deut. 1:31; Isa. 46:3f.), wanted to go after gods they would have to carry for themselves, then they had a hard lesson ahead.

4:29–31 / Moses turns the dynamic of the covenant into a theology of history. No place would be too far and no time too distant for Israel to come back to God. Beyond sin and judgment there was always hope—as their recent past history had already proved. Ever since the apostasy of the golden calf in Exodus 32–34, Israel had known that its very survival depended not on its ability to keep the covenant but on God's willingness to sustain it by God's own forgiving grace and unswerving commitment to the ancestral promise and oath. God would not forget God's word. And since that same event, Israel had known that remarkable statement of divine self-identity: "The LORD, the LORD, the compassionate and gracious God, slow to anger, abounding in love and faithfulness . . ." (Exod. 34:6). The basis of their future hope, then, was the definitive character of God; **the LORD your God is a merciful God** (v. 31). But the condition of their finding that God was wholehearted, repentant recommitment (vv. 29f.). As in 1:19–46, the sequence of verbs is rich, giving a ripple effect in describing Israel's restoration: **You seek . . . you will find . . . you look . . . you will return . . . and obey.** Similarly, in response, God's commitment is affirmed in three staccato negatives: **he will not abandon . . . not destroy . . . not forget.** On the basis of such reciprocal truth, Jeremiah could write echoing words of hope to a generation for whom verse 27 had crashed into reality (Jer. 29:11–14).

Unique Events Reveal the Unique God (4:32–40)

These verses are the climax, not just of chapter 4, but of the whole first discourse of Moses in the book. They are fittingly exalted, in content and style. As mentioned earlier, this whole section mirrors the opening eight verses but elevates the theme tremendously. The stylistic device of rhetorical questions that expressed the incomparability of Israel in verses 6–8 is employed again to affirm the incomparability of Yahweh, and for a similarly combined ethical and missiological purpose. The supreme point is a monotheistic acclamation wreathed in cosmic language, demonstrated in historical experience, and demanding ethical response.

4:32–34 / A research project is proposed of truly cosmic scale, encompassing the whole of human history hitherto (**from the day God created man on the earth**) and the whole of space (**from one end of the heavens to the other**). Such is Moses' confidence that the questions he is about to pose will find no answer.

Stylistically, there are three questions: 32b, 33, and 34. But the second and third are really just subdivisions of the first. Moses refers to both the Sinai theophany and the exodus deliverance, but in his opening question they are seen together as a single "great thing." The whole of Israel's recent history is one mighty act of God. As in verse 7, the NIV slightly distorts the simplicity of the Hebrew with its **. . . anything so great as this.** The sentence literally reads, "Has there happened [anything] like this great deed/thing/event *(dābār)* or has there been heard [anything] like it?" The point is not quite that nothing *greater* had happened but that nothing *like it* had happened. What God did in the events of the exodus and Sinai was unprecedented and unparalleled. God had not done such things anywhere else, at any other time or for any other people. There was a uniqueness about Israel's experience that is powerfully affirmed here. Yahweh spoke to them in a way no other people had experienced (cf. Ps. 147:19f.), and Yahweh redeemed them in a way that no other people had known (cf. Amos 3:1f.).

4:35 / It is important to take the preceding verses as seriously as the comments above, and not to dismiss them as mere hyperbole simply because of their rhetorical form, especially in view of what hangs on them in this verse, namely, the unequivocal affirmation of the uniqueness of Yahweh as God. This is the theological freight that the rhetorical rolling stock is carrying. The people of Israel can be confident in their knowledge of God because of the unique experience of God's revealing and redeeming power that was entrusted to them. *You* (the pronoun is emphatic) **were shown these things so that *you* might know . . .** Monotheism in Israel was not the conclusion of an evolution of religious speculation, but an assertion generated out of historical experience and grounded there. In very similar fashion, Isaiah 40–55 builds its theology of Yahweh's sole and universal deity out of the interpretation of history, and likewise also links it to the concrete experience of Israel as Yahweh's "witnesses" (cf. Isa. 41:1–4, 21–29; 42:8f.; 43:8–13; 44:6–8; 45:20–25). There is no need, however, to argue that this Deuteronomic text must be late and dependent on the Isaiah tradition (cf. Mayes, *Deuteronomy*, p. 158). There is no reason to exclude an affirmation such as this from the earliest period of Israel's formative history, even if the history of Israel's religious pilgrimage through the subsequent centuries blurred and sometimes buried it. Virtually the same affirmations are made in the two "songs of Moses" recorded in the Pentateuch, both of which are commonly regarded as among the earliest examples of poetry in the Hebrew Bible (Exod. 15:1–18, esp. vv. 11 and 18; Deut. 32:1–43, esp. vv. 12, 15–21, 39).

4:36 / The purpose of God's self-revelation to Israel was not merely monotheistic enlightenment (**so that you might know . . .** , v. 35), but ethical **discipline.** The two are inseparable. The one who will not live as Yahweh requires (v. 40), does not "know God" as Yahweh (v. 39; **acknowledge** in Hb. is simply "and you will know . . ."). This fundamental connection inspired Jeremiah's profound reflection on "knowing God" as a matter of being committed to the same "kindness, justice and righteousness on earth" as God delights in (Jer. 9:23f.; cf. 22:13–16). If this was his understanding of what it means to know God, then his vision of a new covenant, in which all God's people would truly know God (31:34), must imply more than the devotional or mystical spiritualization of the phrase common in Christian circles. Covenantal (old or new) knowledge of God entails covenantal commitment to justice, just as covenantal love for God entails covenantal love for the neighbor.

4:37–38 / If God's purpose for Israel was to discipline and shape them through ethical obedience, his "subjective" motivation was his love for their **forefathers.** This forestalls any illusions of superiority Israel may have cherished (cf. 7:8ff.; 9:4–6). The theme of God's love for Israel and their ancestors is unique to Deuteronomy in the Pentateuch (cf. 10:15; 23:5). It is a love that is "axiomatic." That is, while it is used as an explanation and motivation for other things, no attempt is made to find any explanation standing behind it. It is a reality in the heart of God. To the question, "Why did God love Israel's ancestors?" the only answer would have been, "Because God chose to." But if we are

tempted to regard this as mere exclusive chauvinism, we must
recall that the ultimate goal of God's loving choice of Abraham
and his descendants was the blessing of all the nations, even
though it entailed the proximate judgment on specific nations
(v. 38). Ultimately, as Psalm 47 so confidently celebrates, the nations would applaud the saving work of God, which paradoxically included the defeat of some of their number by Israel,
because in the end it would enable them to become part of that
very people of the God of Abraham (Ps. 47:9). The particularity of
God's historical actions must always be set within the universality of God's redemptive purpose. To paraphrase a familiar NT text,
God so loved the world, that he chose Israel.

The grand climax of the whole sermon invites similar missiological and ethical reflection as its opening challenge. The
emphasis on the uniqueness of Israel and of Yahweh speaks to
the contemporary question of the uniqueness of Christ in the
context of religious pluralism. Far too often, in this latter debate,
the uniqueness of Christ is argued over without reference to
Jesus' own self-conscious deep roots in the Hebrew scriptures.
He is presented as if he were the founder of a new religion, which
assuredly was not his purpose. He came, by his own claims and
in the united NT witness to him, to complete the saving work of
Yahweh, God of Israel, for the sake of Israel and the world.
Theologically as well as historically, a line runs from exodus and
Sinai in our text to the incarnation and Easter events. What
Yahweh (and no other god) had redemptively initiated in the
history of Israel (and no other people), he brought to completion
for the whole world in Jesus of Nazareth (and no other person).
The uniqueness of Jesus as the Messiah of Israel, and thereby as
savior of the world, is grounded in the uniqueness of Israel itself
and of Yahweh as God, for according to the NT Jesus embodied
the one and incarnated the other. And the central struggle of
early Christianity, to which the NT bears witness, was to recognize and express this final truth within the parameters of an
undiluted commitment to the dynamic monotheism of Israel's
own faith as affirmed here. The missiological urgency of the
interfaith debate must be grounded in a fully biblical understanding of the uniqueness of God's saving work in history,
which means starting with the affirmation of this and similar OT
texts and not with a Jesus severed from his scriptural and historical roots. For this same reason, Christians are not at liberty
to abandon the Hebrew scriptures of the OT, or to regard the

scriptures of other religions or cultures as equivalent and adequate preparations for Christ. For the thrust of this text is clear: it is *these* events (and no others) that witness to *this* God. (Cf. Wright, *Unique,* chs. 3–4, and *Knowing,* chs. 3–4.)

We must conclude, however, by noting that the final thrust of the rhetoric of our text is ethical. For unless Israel would live in accordance with God's law, what value would their incredible historical and religious experience retain? And furthermore, how would the nations come to know of the uniqueness of Yahweh as the living God and of his saving action in history unless they are drawn by the ethical distinctiveness of God's people (cf. vv. 6–8; Peter urged this point upon his readers as the messianic people of God, 1 Pet. 2:9–12)? If God's people abandon their ethical distinctiveness by forgetfulness, idolatry, or disobedience, then not only do they jeopardize their own well-being (v. 40), they also frustrate the broader purposes of the God who brought them into existence by electing love and "out of darkness" by redeeming power.

4:39–43 / See commentary on 4:36.

Additional Notes §5

Christensen, *Deuteronomy,* p. 69, portrays the concentric structure of Deut. 4–11 as follows:

A "And now, O Israel, obey Yahweh's commandments" (4:1–40)
  B "Then Moses set apart three cities" (4:41–43)
    C "This is the Torah"—the Ten Words (4:44–6:3)
      D "Hear, O Israel, Yahweh is our God, Yahweh alone" (6:4–7:11)
        E When you obey, you will be blessed (7:12–26)
        E' When you disobey, you will perish (8:1–20)
      D' "Hear, O Israel, you are about to cross the Jordan" (9:1–29)
    C' At that time, Yahweh spoke the Ten Words (10:1–7)
  B' "At that time, Yahweh set apart the tribe of Levi" (10:8–11)
A' "And now, O Israel, what does Yahweh ask of you?" (10:12–11:25)

The careful structure of ch. 4, and especially the balance of its opening and closing sections, has led some scholars (particularly Lohfink and Braulik) to argue for its authorial unity, as against the view that it exhibits many layers of Deuteronomistic redaction. Cf. Christensen, *Deuteronomy,* pp. 71–73. The unity of this chapter has also been strongly argued for by Mayes, "Deuteronomy 4," though his view that Deut. 4, along with other sections, is the work of an exilic editor who expanded an earlier shorter law code and introduced the treaty pattern and terminology, is questionable.

4:1 / The implicit tension in the text between the imperative-conditional pole ("obey, so that you may possess") and the indicative-unconditional pole ("the land Yahweh promised your fathers to give you"), can best be understood in the light of the "father-son" relationship between Yahweh and Israel. Sonship is an unconditional "given" of life—a status that cannot be earned. Yet it also intrinsically involves obligations and commitments, especially to obedience. For further discussion of this, see C. J. H. Wright, *God's Land,* pp. 15–22.

4:6 / **Wisdom,** *ḥokmâ,* and **understanding,** *bînâ,* are frequently combined (cf. Gen. 41:39; 1 Kgs. 3:12). The fame of Solomon's wisdom and understanding among the nations in his early reign may be an intentional echo of this Deuteronomic text (1 Kgs. 4:29–34). The same pair are included among the purposes of the book of Proverbs (Prov. 1:2) and would be among the effects of Yahweh's Spirit that would rest on the messianic Davidic king (Isa. 11:2). In this text they are proffered as within the reach of all Israelites collectively as the fruit of obedience.

4:7–8 / The NIV shifts the emphasis of the text somewhat with, **what other nation is so great as to . . .** The Hb. is lit. "What great nation [is there] whose . . ." Moses was not claiming that Israel was the *greatest* nation on earth, but that it was *different* from other great nations. He was claiming that Israel stood among the "great nations," but on very different grounds from the usual criteria of national greatness. In Israel's case, its greatness rested on the intimacy of its relationship with the living God and the justice of its social system. The parallel rhetorical questions show that the two are inseparable functions of each other. A government such as Ahab's, which exchanged Yahweh for Baal, soon found it possible to sacrifice Yahweh's just laws and Naboth's honor and patrimony all on the same altar of covetous greed (1 Kgs. 21). The prophet Hosea saw that the demise of a just and caring society was the result of the loss of the knowledge of Yahweh (Hos. 4).

4:11 / On the symbolism of **fire** here and elsewhere in the OT, see Miller, "Fire."

4:19 / On the apparent toleration of the worship of the heavenly bodies by the nations, cf. Goldingay and Wright, " 'Yahweh Our God.' "

4:24 / The impact of this verse is all the greater because the imagery of Yahweh as **a consuming fire, a jealous God** (*ʾēl qannāʾ*)

frequently refers to his judgment on his enemies (cf. Deut. 9:3; Isa. 29:6; 30:27–30; Nah. 1:2), whereas here it is targeted on Israel.

4:26 / Witnesses were an essential part of ancient treaty texts, and usually lists of gods were invoked for this purpose. In their place, the OT called **heaven and earth as witnesses.** The effect was to bind together the creative and redemptive power of God in sanctioning the demands of the covenant relationship. Cf. Deut. 30:19; 31:28–30; 32:1; Isa. 1:2; 44:23; Mic. 1:2; 6:1f.; Pss. 50:1–6; 96:11ff.

4:28 / A common theme in the OT polemic against idols is the impotence and lifelessness of all other claimed gods. Cf. Lev. 26:30; Pss. 115:4–8; 135:15–18; Isa. 2:8, 20; 17:8; 30:22; 40:18–20; 44:9–20; 46:1f., 5–7; Jer. 2:5, 11, 27f.; 10:1–16; 51:17f.; Hos. 8:6; 13:2; Hab. 2:18f.

4:33–34 / **The voice of God ... Has any god ever tried ...:** The NIV here mixes up two possible exegetical ways of reading these verses, when it would probably be better to opt for either one or the other in both verses. In Hb., *ʾelōhîm,* without a definite article, can mean God (i.e., assumed to be Yahweh), or a god, or gods. Contexts usually leave no doubt as to which is intended in each case. If we take the second of the NIV's options (v. 34) first, then Moses' questions are primarily contrasting Yahweh with other gods: "Has any people heard the voice of a god [i.e., their own god] speaking out of fire [i.e., in the same way that Yahweh spoke to you]? Has any other god ever tried to take a people ... ?" Taken thus, the emphasis is clearly on the uniqueness of Yahweh himself. No other alleged god has done either of these things. But this would leave open the possible question whether or not Yahweh himself had done such things for other peoples. No other god had, but Yahweh could have.

My view, however, (in commentary above) assumes the stronger meaning of *ʾelōhîm* in *both* questions. Not only, with NIV, **Has any other people heard the voice of God [Yahweh] ... ?** (expected answer, No, because God has spoken to no other people in such a way), but also "Has God (i.e., Yahweh) ever tried to take for himself one nation out of another ... ?" (expected answer, No, because no exodus has been like Israel's as described here). Taken thus, the emphasis is more clearly on the uniqueness of Israel's experience of the work of God, but the first affirmation is still preserved. Only Yahweh had made himself known in such ways and only Israel had experienced it. This seems to fit better with the thrust of vv. 35–40. It was precisely because Israel had experienced what no other nation had, that *they* were entrusted with the true knowledge of the one living God and were called to live in the light of such dynamic monotheism.

4:41–43 / These verses seem strange at this point, but their effect is to preserve the narrative context within which the speeches that make up Deut. are set. See further the commentary on ch. 19.

§6 Introduction to Israel's Covenantal Constitution: The Decalogue (Deut. 4:44–5:6)

Here opens Moses' second discourse (chs. 5–26), the central section of the whole book. It is subdivided into two main parts. Chapters 5–11 are a broad exhortation to covenant loyalty and obedience, following up and amplifying the theocratic and covenantal challenge set forth in chapter 4. Chapters 12–26, with their subheading in 12:1, are more detailed legislation, much of which renews, expands, and sometimes modifies laws already given in more basic form in the Book of the Covenant (Exod. 21–23).

Chapters 5–11 are concerned with orientation, ethos, commitment, and loyalty and not initially with the specific legal details. Deuteronomy recognizes that law in itself is not enough for a wholesome society. There is a need for a fundamental, collective choice to do the will of God out of gratitude and covenant loyalty. In a somewhat similar way, Jesus' Beatitudes describe a whole life-stance and orientation toward God and others, before the detailed teaching of the rest of the Sermon on the Mount. For Jesus himself, it seems that Deuteronomy 5–11 were especially significant chapters in relation to his own commitment to do the will of his Father. The narrative of his testing in the wilderness records that all of his scriptural answers to Satan come from Deuteronomy 6 and 8, probably as the fruit of deep personal meditation on their implications for his own sonship and mission (cf. C. J. H. Wright, *Knowing Jesus*, pp. 181–91).

4:44–49 / These verses introduce the whole following section of the book with a summary of the story already given in more detail in chapters 1–3. Such summary repetition is not uncommon in OT and other ancient Near Eastern narrative texts, and so need not be seen by itself as evidence of different editorial stages.

5:1 / **Hear, O Israel** (cf. 6:3, 4, etc.) . . . **in your hearing,** (lit. in your ears); note the constant emphasis on the ear as the organ of response and obedience, corresponding to the reality of Yahweh as the God who could not be seen but was unmistakably heard (cf. commentary on 4:15–19). Before reciting the Ten Commandments, Moses makes three prefatory points, of which the third is actually the opening declaration of the Decalogue itself.

5:2–3 / First, *the continuity of the covenant* is declared. **Not with our fathers . . . but with us,** should probably be taken as a case of Hebrew "relative negation"; i.e., the meaning is "not only . . . but also" (cf. Hos. 6:6). The **fathers** in question were probably the immediately preceding generation, rather than the patriarchs to whom the term usually refers. Moses' point is that this present generation (which he emphasizes with some repetitive Hb. phrasing)—and therefore by implication all future generations—was just as much a partner in the covenant concluded at Sinai as those who actually stood at the foot of the mountain itself (cf. 1:26ff.; 11:2–7; and 29:14f.). The covenant was never a thing of the past, because Yahweh, as the living God, was the contemporary of every succeeding generation—a fact that could have positive or negative results depending on their response (cf. 5:9b–10).

5:4–5 / Secondly, *the personal nature of the covenant* is stressed. **The LORD spoke to you face to face** should be understood metaphorically. It does not contradict 4:12 and 15. Even with the role of Moses as mediator (v. 5 with further explanation in vv. 23–31), Israel had experienced a powerfully direct and personal encounter with God. Here, as everywhere in the Hebrew Bible, ethics is not some abstract duty in relation to impersonal universal principles. Still less is it a moral philosophy. It is a matter of personal address by, and personal response to, a personal God with a "face," though no "form." This is the nature of covenant relationship and this is what is at stake in every ethical decision and action. It is also the reason why those Israelite psalmists who revel most in the delights of the law, do so as an overflow of their joy in personal relationship with Yahweh the lawgiver.

5:6 / Thirdly, *God's redemptive initiative of grace* is presented as the foundation of the law. This majestic opening chord of the Decalogue, identical with Exodus 20:2, launches it in the indicative, not the imperative mood. The demands of the law are based on who God is (**the LORD your God:** i.e., Yahweh in relation to his people) and on what God has done (**who brought you out:** i.e., his historical act of saving grace). This is a crucial perspective that is commonly overlooked or perverted in Christian attitudes to the Hebrew Bible—at least at a popular level. The simplistic view is taken that in the OT salvation was achieved by keeping the law, whereas in the NT salvation is by grace through faith. The very first sentence of the Decalogue prevents such a view. The commandments were given to Israel, not so they could perhaps gain salvation by keeping them, but because God had **already** redeemed them and this was how they were to live in the light of that fact. This prefatory sentence to the Decalogue thus mirrors the very shape of Exodus, which has nineteen chapters of salvation before any chapters of law. The pivotal text, Exodus 19:3–6, makes the same important point. "You have seen what I have done . . . ," said God, thus directing Israel's attention to God's own redemptive initiative before calling for their responsive obedience and covenant loyalty. Similarly, in Deuteronomy 6:20–25 the very meaning of the law that fathers are to give to inquiring children is nothing less than a narrative of redemption. The priority of saving grace to human responsive obedience is as much a principle of OT ethics as of NT theology.

Before we embark on commenting on each commandment, several points may be made on the Decalogue as a whole:

(a) The unique status of the Ten Commandments among all OT law can be seen in several ways. They were given a special name, "the ten words" (Exod. 34:28; Deut. 4:13) or just "the words" (Deut. 5:22; 9:10) and linked in each of these texts to the covenant. They alone were inscribed on two tablets of stone, with the expression "by the finger of God" probably a metaphor for the direct revelation by which they were given (Exod. 31:18; 34:1, 28). They alone were deposited in the ark of the covenant (Exod. 40:20f.; Deut. 10:1–5). They were thus the essential, constitutional core of the covenant. And the narrative context in both Exodus and Deuteronomy emphasizes the unique and special character of these "ten words." Although Moses acts as a mediator, he simply receives and passes on the divine speech, rather than teaching and interpreting the law as he does the subsequent legislation. And Deuteronomy also conveys the categorical uniqueness of the Decalogue by the "signature" of 5:22, **These are the commandments the LORD proclaimed . . . and he added nothing more.** It can be seen, therefore, that the exalted place given to the Ten

Commandments in both Jewish and Christian tradition is not an arbitrary selection, but is in accord with the clear signals of the OT text itself. The Decalogue is a key text: hermeneutically, in facilitating systematic understanding of the rest of the laws that in countless ways reflect and apply the fundamental principles it sets forth; and ethically, in its almost limitless capacity to address the whole range of moral issues—personal and societal—that ever-changing human cultures wrestle with.

(b) Verse 6 anchors the Ten Commandments specifically in the immediately preceding history of Israel, namely, their liberation from slavery in Egypt. Now this is not, of course, to suggest that the moral principles set forth in the Decalogue were totally unknown to humanity before the revelation on Mt. Sinai. The book of Genesis illustrates awareness of the basic morality of the commandments as early as the story of Cain and Abel and even on the part of "pagans" such as Pharaoh (Gen. 12:10–20) and Abimelech (Gen. 20). The point is, however, that by giving them explicitly, collectively, and directly to Israel immediately after the exodus, God injected them with the flavor of that event and with the memory of what preceded it. The Ten Commandments were given to a people who three months previously (Exod. 19:1f.) had been groaning in political, economic, social, and spiritual bondage. Liberated from that, how were they to organize their own community life? How could a liberated people preserve the benefits of their liberty? In the light of the exodus, the Ten Commandments become a kind of "Bill of Rights" for a free people under a covenant that was expressed in characteristic biblical language of responsibility (cf. C. J. H. Wright, *Eye/Living*, pp. 142ff.)

In Egypt, Israel had labored under a Pharaoh who not only claimed divinity but refused to recognize Yahweh as God—at least in his land (Exod. 5:2). A major theme of the subsequent narrative is to prove to Pharaoh, as well as to the Israelites, that Yahweh is God, not only in Egypt but in the whole earth (Exod. 6:7; 7:5; 8:22; 9:14, 29; 10:2). The first commandment follows naturally on such manifest proof, and the second prevents any temptation to indulge in the divine statuary for which Egypt was noted. The exodus story also involved a fresh revelation of the divine name (Exod. 3:13ff.; 6:2–8) and demonstrated its power. No Israelite must attempt to use the power of that name, which had operated for the national benefit, for any personal, malevolent, or frivolous purpose (third commandment). In Egypt, the harshest aspect of reality for Israel was the unrelenting labor imposed on them (Exod. 1 and 5). With no freedom they had no rest. The sabbath commandment was a distinctive gift, explicitly geared to the needs of the most vulnerable of the working population (cf. Exod. 23:12; Deut. 5:14b). In Egypt, Israel had been subjected to intolerable intrusion and destruction of their family life (Exod. 1:15f.). Their free society was to be structured around the network of viable extended family households, whose internal authority and sexual integrity were protected by the fifth and seventh commandments. In Egypt, Israel had been the victims of a state-sponsored program of selective genocide (Exod. 1:22). Freed from such murderous tyranny they were to protect human life from all unlawful killing (sixth commandment). In Egypt, Israel had been economically exploited, robbed of the benefit of their own productive labor. God's intention for them was a land of their own and a distinctive economic system, within which theft and greed would seriously violate the community dimension of the covenant (eighth and tenth commandments). In Egypt, Israelites were the victims of massive structural injustice. In their society, therefore, the integrity of justice and the legal system must at all costs be protected from the threat of malicious falsehood (ninth commandment).

Thus, although mostly framed negatively, the commandments have a strikingly positive function in protecting and preserving the blessings of the freedom achieved by God's liberation from Egypt. Liberation is no advantage in itself unless consolidated into social structures that maintain its objectives for the whole community. The Decalogue is the foundation block of such consolidation.

(c) It has long been common to observe the vertical and horizontal dimensions of the Decalogue, with its dual orientation toward God and toward other human beings. Jesus reflected this when, in line with various Jewish precedents, he summarized it in the two "great commandments," love for God and love for neighbor (Matt. 22:34–40; cf. also Rom. 13:8–10). On the rabbinical summarizing of the law, see Flusser, "The Decalogue."

However, the sequence of commandments also presents a scale of values that reflects God's design for human life. Unquestionably, *God* comes first. God is to be worshipped exclusively, without images and without abuse of God's name. The fourth commandment exhibits a concern for the health and benefit of society as a whole, with its specific benefit for workers. The sabbath day is sanctified "*to* the Lord your God" but observed *for* the benefit of human beings. The fifth commandment shows the central importance of the family, which the seventh also protects in its sexual integrity. As we shall see in the commentary on individual commandments, the interests of the family can take priority in law even over the life of an individual who threatens it (cf. 21:18–21), just as the protection of the wider society from the wrath of God takes priority over obligation to one's family (13:6–11). After the family, however, individual human life takes priority over all else. The sixth commandment thus precedes the eighth and tenth, which were concerned primarily (though not exclusively in the case of the tenth) with material property. People matter more than things. It would be going too far to assert a strict sequential order of values in the Ten Commandments, but the overall impression seems valid. God's priorities for human moral attention are: God, society, family, life, sex, property. It hardly needs to be pointed out that in Western society at least, modern culture has almost precisely inverted this order of priorities. Having built a whole ideological worldview on breaking the tenth commandment, it is hardly surprising that we have trampled over the preceding ones until the first is virtually meaningless. Why call on people to worship no *other* God when most would claim to worship no God at all?

Taken together, these three points reinforce the hermeneutical principles outlined in the introduction. Among all OT law, which was intended to function paradigmatically as part of Israel's identity as a "light for the nations," the Decalogue has a pride of place that makes it the most "universalizable." Its purpose was not restrictive but protective. That is, its restrictions are for the positive benefit of preserving freedoms within human society and, as Walter Harrelson shows, still have much to offer to any society *(Human Rights).* And it displays a scale of moral values, based on response to God and the saving action of God, which can help us in the complex task of wrestling with competing moral priorities in our own day.

Additional Notes §6

4:44–49 / It is widely held that we have here an introduction to an earlier form of Deut., and that chs. 1–3 were added as an introduction to the longer historical work known as the Deuteronomistic History, which is 5–34. See Noth, *The Deuteronomistic History,* pp. 12–17, and Clements, *Deuteronomy,* chs. 2 and 4, for further discussion and bibliography. To the contrary, arguing the unity of the book on the basis of parallels with the Hittite treaty form, is Kline, *Great King,* pp. 27–44 (esp. p. 31).

5:4–5 / On the relationship between these verses and the Exodus Sinai narrative with its version of the Decalogue, cf. Nicholson, "The Decalogue."

§7 The Ten Commandments (Deut. 5:7–21)

The First Commandment

5:7 / **You shall have no other gods before me.** Lit. "There shall not be for you other gods before (or over against) my face." Herein lies the source of the stream of biblical monotheistic faith. But it is not a philosophical monotheism that is at stake in these seven Hebrew words. The commandment does not explicitly deny the existence of other gods (nor is that surprising: it is a command, not a proposition). Rather it prohibits Israel from having any other gods instead of, or more likely, in addition to, Yahweh. If it does not deny the validity of polytheism in theory (though it equally emphatically does not affirm it either), it certainly denies the legitimacy of polytheism for Israel. The primary purpose of the primary commandment is to assert and protect the exclusive covenantal sovereignty of Yahweh as God over the Israelites and their exclusive covenantal allegiance to him. In other words, the fundamental thrust of the verse is not Yahweh's sole deity but Yahweh's sole sovereignty over Israel, on the basis of the historical fact just stated in verse 6.

This first commandment follows up chapter four's affirmation of the incomparability of Yahweh. No other god had done or said what Yahweh had done; nor had Yahweh done anything similar elsewhere. It is this unique incomparability that is now crystallized into the only logical response—there are no other gods. Other gods are not gods in reality, for chapter four twice denies any comparable divine beings alongside Yahweh God (vv. 35 and 39).

The NIV adds "besides me" as an alternative rendering to **... before me.** Different interpretations of the phrase are offered, including "in my presence," "before my face," i.e., in my sight, "over against, in opposition to me." The phrase may have a flavor of "to provoke me," with the thought that any god placed as an object of worship where Yahweh could "see" it would arouse his jealousy and wrath, just as we use the expression "to my very face" to describe gross effrontery. This fits with the strong connection between the first and second commandment (which some traditions actually combine as one single commandment).

A possible translation would be, "You shall have no other gods *as rivals to me*." For what is at stake is not a matter of philosophical orthodoxy ("You shall believe that only one God exists"), but a matter of practical loyalty. Otherwise, mere monotheism can become a virtual cloak for a denial of the first commandment. It is sometimes alleged that, if there is only one God in reality, then whatever people worship must be (or must represent) that God. This is the kind of twisted logic that underlies the ideology of pluralism in the debate over world religions. Such a view requires a concept of "God" that is so abstract that, even though it is grammatically singular, it can accommodate any number of "faces." Thus phrases like Ultimate Divine Reality, or The Real, or Transcendent Being, are used, and we are asked to accept that all religions, all concepts of God (or denials of personal deity as well) are equally valid in their partial portrayal of this mysterious, ineffable reality at the center. Against this one must, first of all, point out that the first commandment is inseparably linked to the prologue. That is, it does not say, "You must acknowledge that there is only one ultimate divine reality, however you choose to define or worship 'it' "; but rather, it says quite explicitly, "I am Yahweh . . . no other gods before *my* face." God is as God is defined by Yahweh and has no other "face." And secondly, one has to point to the NT development of this issue precisely in a highly pluralistic religious context. The difference then is that God is portrayed as defined in Jesus Christ. Thus, Paul, in applying his Hebrew monotheism to the issue of meat sacrificed to idols, does not allow his monotheistic denial of the ultimate reality of any idol to imply that worship of idols is therefore either neutral or acceptable as de facto worship of the one true God. There is only one God, but there are many *so-called* gods and lords, which can include demons. The facade of idolatry can therefore mask the demonic, and Christians need to be aware of both in their choices and actions (1 Cor. 8:5f.; 10:19f.).

The Second Commandment

5:8–10 / You shall not make for yourself an idol . . . The word *pesel* means an object, such as a statue, carved out of wood, stone, or metal, a physical image. From this commandment flows another great distinctive of Israelite worship alongside its monotheism (or perhaps more precisely, its mono-Yahwism), namely, its aniconic nature. The history of Israel's religion shows a varied degree of loyalty to this commandment, but it remains a remarkable fact that Israel has left virtually nothing significant archaeologically in the way of images of Yahweh. And it is probable that it is images of *Yahweh* that this commandment prohibits, rather than images of other gods, which are prohibited by implication in the first commandment. In fact, Jewish tradition (followed by Augustine, and Lutheran and Roman Catholic tradition) regards verses 8–10 as part of the first commandment. This can be supported from the fact that the natural antecedent of **them** in verse 9 is **other gods** in verse 7. The combined thrust of both commandments (or the dual thrust of the one, depending on your numeration!) is thus that Israelites were neither to have nor to serve other gods than Yahweh and that they were not to make any image of Yahweh **in the form of anything** in creation.

For what reason was the faith of Yahweh to be imageless? One view (e.g., Mayes, *Deuteronomy*, p. 166) is that the use of an image of deity makes the deity subject to human manipulation, and so is an attack on divine freedom and sovereignty. This may well be so, but it is perhaps more an explanation of the prohibition on misuse of the divine name in the third commandment, which is concerned with such human attempts to tap the resources of divine power for wrong ends. Also, the second commandment specifies bowing down to, or "serving" idols, which seems somewhat the reverse of manipulation.

Another view is that the living God is invisible and spiritual, and a carved idol is visible and material and therefore cannot rightly represent God. Again, this has an element of truth, but runs up against the fact that although the Israelites repudiated actual physical images of Yahweh, they were not lacking in creativity when it came to rhetorical imagery for Yahweh, drawn vigorously from the created and human order. Israel's language imagery for Yahweh made him very "visible" to the mental eye through a rich and often daring anthropomorphic and metaphorical style. The affirmation that Yahweh is *personal* seemed more urgent than fear about his invisible spirituality. This point gives us perhaps a more significant clue to the rationale of the second commandment. Yahweh is the *living* God, and any carved statue is necessarily lifeless. Something that can *do nothing* is no image of the God who can *do all things.* The only legitimate image of God, therefore, is the image God created in his own likeness—the living, thinking, working, speaking, breathing, relating human being (not even a human statue will do, but only the living person).

Chapter four also influences how we interpret the commandment in this context. First, Yahweh is the God who cannot be seen in any "form," but whose voice was clearly heard (4:12, 15ff.). As the *speaking* God, Yahweh reveals, addresses, promises, challenges, confronts, demands. Any attempt to turn Yahweh into a voiceless statue effectively gags God. Idolatry therefore is fundamentally an escape from the living voice and commands of the living God. As Moses will point out later, Canaanite idolatry had done nothing to establish a just and caring society in Canaan. On the contrary, idolatry allows injustice and cruelty to flourish, because it does not challenge the human proclivity to oppression and violence (e.g., 12:31). Yahweh is the liberating God who brings up out of Egypt, the God who works justice and demands justice. Let no statue stifle the voice of the God who speaks. It is hardly surprising that the twin dominant themes of the prophets, as the voice of Yahweh, are idolatry and social injustice.

Second, Yahweh is the *incomparable* God (4:32–39). Since there is nothing in all creation to compare with who Yahweh is or with what he has done, then it is futile to imagine that anything **in heaven above or on the earth beneath or in the waters below** could be an adequate representation. No created thing can function satisfactorily as an alternative to the living God—a lesson that human beings have not yet learned in spite of countless generations of trying. Modern investment of ultimate value in our own ideological, economic, political, and techno-scientific creations has proved equally barren, devoid of divinity, and prey to the demonic.

The text gives its own motivation for obedience, in the character of God: **for I, the LORD your God, am a jealous God.** The jealousy of Yahweh is a function of his covenant commitment to his people. Having committed himself exclusively to them, he requires exclusive loyalty in return. In a context of committed love, the exclusion of rivals (i.e., jealousy) is a perfectly proper concern, as that celebration of human love declares:

> Love is as strong as death,
>   its jealousy as unyielding as the grave. (Song Sol. 8:6)

So essential is this dimension of divine love to God's very character that one of the five texts using the expression "a jealous God" actually gives it as God's name (Exod. 34:14; cf. Exod. 20:5; Deut. 4:24; 5:9; 6:15; cf. also Josh. 24:19 and Nah. 1:2). It is a feature of the OT's portrayal of Yahweh that easily grates on the modern person because of the infectious pluralism that disapproves such exclusivity. But it is also, of course, fundamentally reassuring. The covenant relationship between God and God's people really means something only if God is totally committed to it. A God who was not jealous for the reciprocal commitment of God's people would be as contemptible as a husband who didn't care whether or not his wife was faithful to him. Part of our problem with this profound covenantal reality is that we have come to regard religion, like everything else, as a matter of "consumer choice," which we have virtually deified for its own sake. We resent monopolies. But the unique and incomparable, only living God makes necessarily exclusive claims and has the right to a monopoly on our love.

If jealousy is God's love protecting itself, then the desire and direction of that love is seen in the clauses in verses 9b, 10. Sin, and especially the sin of idolatry, reaps its reward in the living generations of those who practice it. Israelite extended families included three and often four generations, and the effects of one generation's failure in covenant loyalty **(those who hate me)** would detrimentally affect the succeeding ones, who would grow up without teaching and with an idolatrous example and environment. But verse 10 shows the dominant longing of God's heart. While three or four generations may suffer for their sins, God's agenda for blessing extends for thousands ("generations" is probably understood, cf. 7:9), where there is loyalty and love. "A thousand generations" is a very, very long time, longer than recorded human history—as good as "for ever." Such is the nature of God that God speaks of punishment in terms of living memory and of covenant love in terms of an unimaginable long-distance future. It is a sad distortion that popular caricatures of the OT God get stuck on verse 9b and miss the breathtaking vistas of promise in verse 10.

Together, the first and second commandment are truly the most fundamental of all, for everything that follows hangs on them. Their importance is reflected in the fact that Deuteronomy chapters 4 and 6, like an envelope around the Decalogue in chapter 5, are really extended meditations on the challenge of the

prologue and first two commandments (which offers some justification for the disproportionate space devoted to them in this
commentary). Their prominence also reflects the fact that bib-
lically, idolatry is the fundamental human sin. The essence of
our fallenness is that we choose to reject the authority of our
creator God and to substitute in God's place an allegiance to
other authorities, other presumed ultimates, other systems and
values of our own creation. Apostasy and idolatry are the classic
root sins of Israel in the OT, because they are the essential marks
of the human condition. Jeremiah captured their poignancy and
absurdity in his memorable imagery,

> My people have committed two sins:
> They have forsaken me,
>   the spring of living water,
> and have dug their own cisterns,
>   broken cisterns that cannot hold water. (Jer. 2:13)

The Third Commandment

**5:11 / You shall not misuse the name of the LORD your
God** (lit. "You shall not lift up the name of Yahweh your God to
worthlessness"). The knowledge of the personal name of God,
Yahweh, was arguably the greatest gift God entrusted to Israel.
This commandment protects the name of God from being used
"in vain." The Hebrew *šāw'* signifies something empty or worthless and is often used in association with evil or trouble-making
intention (cf. Ps. 12:2; Prov. 30:8; Isa. 59:4). The commandment
therefore has more in mind than thoughtless bad language.

The precise meaning of "lifting up" Yahweh's name is debated, but some light may be shed by other significant phrases
involving the name. "To call on the name of Yahweh" was a
synonym for worship. But worship could be corrupt, empty, or
rendered abominable by association with private or public wickedness. The name of Yahweh would thus be lifted up in vain (Isa.
1:10–17; 29:13). Judicial proceedings included swearing in the
name of Yahweh to tell the truth (cf. Deut. 6:13). To take Yahweh's
name in oath and then tell lies was also to "lift up the name to
vanity," for perverse ends. The corruption of the courts was one
of the major complaints of the prophets, and part of their recipe
for full repentance was a return to effective honoring of the third
commandment and the ninth (cf. Isa. 48:1b; Jer. 4:1f.).

In the modern world, the commonest misuse of God's name is in its trivialized use in blasphemy, in common speech, and in the media. A secularized society feels free to use the personal names of God and Christ with no concern for who they belong to. Then there is the equally trivialized use of God's name in the commercialization of religion, whether by the overt forces of mammon or by the more subtly damaging forces of organized religious empires, the "televangelists" and other latter-day Tetzels with their prosperity gospel and unscrupulous marketing of hopes and promises. (Tetzel was the man whose blatant selling of indulgences sparked Luther's protest, which in turn launched the Reformation.) By "giving God a bad name"—i.e., by blatantly using God's name in the interests of their own selfishness, power, or pride—they are in principle breaking the third commandment.

The Fourth Commandment

5:12–15 / Observe the Sabbath day by keeping it holy. Probably the sabbath day and the rhythm of a seven-day week with six days of work and one of rest was a unique Israelite institution (and gift to humanity). See additional note.

This commandment follows and reinforces the previous three. We have seen that the primary human failing is toward idolatry—giving ultimate value and worship to that which is not God. Human beings were created to live and work in the earth. Alienated from God as the source of our fulfillment and rest, we endow work and the whole economic enterprise with a significance beyond its God-given role. Work itself and the material produce it generates can then become an idol to be served without the limitation of God's own higher claim on our lives. In fact, it can come to dominate the whole of life and to define our very being ("you are what you do"), thereby usurping the God in whose image we are made. This idolatrous potential is particularly evident in our "workaholic" and "economaniac" society. The command to rest from work on the sabbath day forces a pause in this compulsive process and reminds us that time, like the earth itself, belongs to God, as does everything by which we are able to create wealth (cf. Deut. 8:17f.). The sabbath is thus a further bulwark against idolatry, building the claims of the primary commandments into the ceaseless regularity of daily life itself.

Further, observe the motivational clauses that support the sabbath commandment. In Exodus 20:11, the sabbath day is based upon God's own resting on the seventh day after the completion of God's work of creation (Gen. 2:2f.). It is thus a day that celebrates creation and enables us to enjoy symbolically the rest that describes the "end" of creation (in both senses). But it is enjoyed in the recognition that it is indeed God's earth, not primarily ours, that the cessation of work points to. Deuteronomy 5:15 calls on Israel to **remember** the historical events of their redemption from Egypt. The sabbath is thus linked to salvation history and all that was achieved through it and anticipated by it (cf. its eschatological significance for Christians in Heb. 4:1–11). Hence the sabbath could be regarded as a "sign of the covenant" (Exod. 31:16f.). The sabbath thus has the nature both of a creation ordinance and of a redemptive sign, and in both respects it directs human minds to the living God. As a creation gift it has relevance to all human beings; as a sign of redemption it has particular relevance to God's people, who exist for the sake of the rest of the nations. Thus, in Isaiah 56:2, 4, 6, it features in the description of those foreigners who would choose to identify themselves with Israel and Israel's God. Knight, calling the sabbath "an Instrument of Mission," comments that "even the sabbath becomes . . . an instrument of God's redemptive love . . . , as it works out when a member of the New Israel 'redeems' an outcast or a foreigner into the covenant fellowship" (*Isaiah 56–66*, pp. 4f.).

The more immediate practical motivation and effect of the sabbath commandment, however, was socio-ethical. It is the pivot of the Decalogue that, along with the fifth commandment, directs attention both to God and to human society. The liberation from slavery in Egypt and the gift of a land of their own set Israel's world of economic work in a totally new context. They would now work as free people, no longer in the indignity and insecurity of economic bondage. On that basis, they were to avoid oppressing and exploiting the weak and vulnerable in their own society. Hence the sabbath commandment is specifically for the benefit of the whole working population, animal as well as human (v. 14). That indeed is its express purpose: **so that your manservant and maidservant may rest, as you do** (cf. Exod. 23:12). The benefit of sabbath was not to be enjoyed only by Israelite landowners, while dependent laborers continued to work. The rest was specifically for the benefit of those laborers. Significantly, even the alien, non-Israelite residents were included in this "surprisingly egalitarian law," (van Houten, *The Alien,*

p. 92). Lohfink has also pointed out that while many human societies divided work and leisure along class lines (slaves, women, and the lower classes did the work; leisure was for the more privileged), the biblical sabbath principle by contrast divides work and leisure horizontally in time, not vertically in society. All should work and all should have rest (*Great Themes*, pp. 203–21). The sabbath was thus one part (arguably the most important part) of OT law's concern for workers, and especially for those most at risk in the world of work (cf. C. J. H. Wright, *Eye/Living*, pp. 77–81). Harold Macmillan, the British Prime Minister from 1957 to 1963, is reported to have described the sabbath as the first and greatest worker-protection act in history.

The moral seriousness of the sabbath commandment now comes more clearly into focus, especially for modern people who find it peculiar and inexplicable that the mere observance of such a day should even figure in the Ten Commandments, let alone be sanctioned by the death penalty. As a brake on the accelerating processes of idolatry it *protected the uniqueness of Yahweh* as creator and redeemer, and as a brake on the parallel tendency of human economic exploitation and oppression it preserved the social liberation that *reflected the character of Yahweh*. Sabbath was a sign of the covenant precisely because it embodied the essential vertical and horizontal dimensions of covenant commitment. It was "unto the LORD," but also for the good of society. Not surprisingly, prophetic passages that attack sabbath breaking also condemn the guilty ones for their greed, their exploitation, and their maximizing of gain at the expense of others (Amos 8:4–6; Isa. 58:13f., in the context of the whole ch.; cf. Neh. 13:15–22).

The Fifth Commandment

5:16 / Honor your father and your mother. The sequence of thought from the fourth commandment to the fifth is clearly from society as a whole to the family that forms the basic unit of society. The close link between the two commandments is seen also by their pairing in Leviticus 19:3 (and also by their link with the second commandment, Lev. 19:4).

This commandment was not addressed primarily to *children*, though they would obviously be included in its scope. The Decalogue is covenantal law for the whole Israelite community, and we should beware of reducing the impact of this commandment by reading it solely in the light of Paul's use of it in the "household codes" (Eph. 6:1–3; Col. 3:20). It addresses adults and reminds us of the broad, extended nature of the Israelite family, in which several generations lived "together" under the authority and protection of the "head of the household"—probably the senior living male. Honoring parents was thus a broader reality than childhood obedience, though it would, of course, have included that (cf. Prov. 4; 10:1; 13:1; 15:5; 19:18). Just as the fourth commandment does not merely describe a cultic taboo day, but governed Israel's social and economic life as a whole society under God, so here the fifth commandment forms part of the structure and fabric of Israel's covenantal relation with God and is not merely a recipe for happy families.

The family, or "father's house," was the basic unit of Israel's society in three ways. *Socially,* it was the source of judicial authority at the "grassroots" level, through the functioning of the elders; it had a role in the military structure of the nation's defense; and it was the primary place of education and transmission of tradition. *Economically,* it was the basic unit of land tenure. The land was divided up, not merely to tribes, but to clans and father's houses, so that every household was to have its inheritance or share in the land. And since possession of the land, as the gift of Yahweh, was tangible proof of the relationship of Israel to Yahweh, each household thus had a "material" share in that relationship. *Spiritually,* or theologically, the family in both the above respects—i.e., as a kinship unit and as a land-holder—was fundamental in the social realization and preservation of the covenant relationship between Israel and Yahweh. Whatever threatened the family ultimately threatened the wider social basis of the whole covenant relationship. Such threats were therefore treated seriously (cf. Deut. 21:18–21).

By placing the fifth commandment, with its capital sanction, in this light, we resist the temptation to see it as a relic of a harshly vindictive patriarchal society (which is made unlikely by the inclusion of the mother along with the father as the recipient of honor; cf. Lev. 19:3 where she is named first). Rather, we can understand it as a witness to the seriousness with which Israel was to take the covenant and protect it for the sake of the nation.

This perspective also illuminates the motive clause for this commandment: **so that you may live long and that it may go well with you in the land the LORD your God is giving you.** The promise and hope for long life in the land is common in Deuteronomy, but it is specifically attached to the fifth commandment, because the health, integrity, and economic viability of Israel's households held the key to the nation's survival in the land.

The fourth and fifth commandments offer us a paradigm for societal health that has implications for the objectives of social and legislative policy today. For example, a legal limit on Sunday commerce may be just one factor in the struggle against being utterly consumed by the idolatry of consumerism, but it is a significant one because it is related to questions of justice for the most vulnerable sections of the national workforce (as it was in Israel), to the values of family time together, and to the health of relationships in general. Similarly, our application of the fifth commandment's concern for the health of families must go beyond moralistic condemnation of parents for the lawless state of today's youth and critically examine those social policies (e.g., on employment, taxation, welfare, etc.) that increasingly undermine the economic viability, social dignity, and physical cohesion of extended families. By articulating the objectives of these laws in Israel's society, we can seek creative and relevant ways of achieving comparable objectives in contemporary social policy.

The Sixth Commandment

5:17 / **You shall not murder.** The translation **murder** is appropriate, rather than the simple "kill." The verb, *rāṣaḥ*, is more specific than the more common verb for killing, *hārag*. It describes any form of unlawful or unauthorized killing.

The commandment itself is not specific as to the circumstances or conditions under which it applies. On the one hand, that is part of its strength, since it puts the onus of moral proof on anyone who seeks to justify a particular act or policy of killing. The presumption is always that killing is wrong, unless compelling reasons indicate otherwise (such as, for example, in the OT itself, where legitimized taking of life in warfare or in judicial execution was sanctioned in the context of proper divine or human authority and not considered murder). This bears on all ethical matters in which human life is at stake, from its beginnings in the womb to its waning in old age or terminal illness. The application of the sixth commandment as a *first* principle to the difficult ethical issues involved, for example, in genetic engineering, abortion, and the many varieties of euthanasia, is certainly hermeneutically and theologically correct.

The OT's protection of human life has explicit theological roots in the declaration that God created human beings in the image of God. This identification is the climax of the creation narrative (Gen. 1:27) and is the basis of God's reaction to homicide in Genesis 9:5f. God requires an accounting for human lifeblood, even from the animals, precisely because "in the image of God has God made man." However, it is probably not strictly accurate to speak of "the sanctity of human life" in OT terms (though one is fully aware of the importance of that concept in Christian ethics). If the phrase implies that all life is absolute and inviolable in and of itself, then we will have difficulty with Yahweh's commands to kill in war or in judicial punishment—as indeed many do. Absolute sanctity would mean it could never be right to take a human life in any circumstances. (It becomes even more problematical, of course, if the sixth commandment is extended to other organic life-forms that are alleged to have the same right to life as human beings. Such an extension ends up destroying the categorical *theological* difference between human and other forms of life.) The Bible does not make life "holy" in and of itself. Human beings are made in God's image, an image that no human has the right to destroy without the maker's authority. But God does have that authority. Human life is a gift from God and belongs to God, and no human has the right to destroy the gift or steal what belongs to God. But God has the right of disposal over what belongs to God. On these grounds, it is clear that we can distinguish between unlawful taking of life by evil *human* intention and authorized taking of life in circumstances carefully defined by *God*, "the Lord and giver of life." The prohibition on murder, therefore, is a matter not merely of horizontal human rights, but of our accountability to God for the lives of our fellow human beings. It presupposes the vertical and horizontal axes of human moral responsibility.

The high value placed on individual human life that this commandment shows permeated very deeply into the whole ethos of OT Israel. The shedding of "innocent blood" was one of the most severely condemned crimes in the prophets, the Psalms and the Wisdom literature. But not only the overt action was condemned. The dangers of all that leads up to acts of violence and murder were also recognized in the stories of Cain's jealousy (Gen. 4), David's lust (2 Sam. 11), or his vengeful rage (1 Sam. 25), in Wisdom's portrait of murderous greed (Prov. 1:10–19), and in the penetrating law of Leviticus 19:17f., "Do not hate your brother in your heart . . . Do not seek revenge or bear a grudge against one of your people, but love your neighbor as yourself." It was an authentic extension of this OT perception that led Jesus to condemn anger as the moral root of murder (Matt. 5:21f.).

The Seventh Commandment

5:18 / You shall not commit adultery. The fifth commandment protected parental authority and inculcated transgenerational respect. The seventh commandment protected the sexual integrity of the marriage bond at the heart of the family. Again, we should remember that for the Israelite, family was not just one couple and their own children but the cluster of such families in three generations that constituted the extended household. Within that kinship "molecule," the marital integrity of each "nuclear" couple was carefully defined, both by this primary prohibition on adultery and by the range of limitations on sexual intercourse in Leviticus 18:6–18, which has been shown to be primarily designed to protect the inner sexual relationships of the extended family (see Porter, *The Extended Family*).

Adultery was clearly a very serious offense in ancient Israel. The legislation that supports the seventh commandment makes it a capital offense for both parties involved (Deut. 22:22; Lev. 18:20; 20:10). The prophets attack it as a social evil (e.g., Hos. 4:2; Jer. 7:9; 23:10; Ezek. 18:6ff.; 22:11; 33:26; Mal. 3:5; etc.) and use it as a metaphor for Israel's spiritual apostasy.

Now all human societies, including Israel's ancient Near Eastern neighbors, have sanctions to protect whatever marital arrangements are customary there. But why is adultery treated so prominently and given such severe punishment in the OT? The answer to this lies in the nature of the Decalogue, in which fundamental covenant law is combined with the central importance of the family in Israel's social realization of the covenant—in other words, this commandment has the same social and religious context as the fifth commandment. As moderns, we have difficulty conceiving of this context, because we have largely consigned adultery to the realm of private morality or civil proceedings. In Israel, however, adultery was anything but a private concern.

> Adultery was a crime against God inasmuch as it was a crime against the relationship between God and his people, Israel; and it was a crime against that relationship inasmuch as it was an

attack upon the social basis on which it rested. . . . . Any attack on the stability of the household unit was a potential threat to the nation's relationship with God. This applied internally if there was disruption of the *domestic authority* within the family—hence the importance of the Fifth Commandment and related injunctions. It applied externally as well, if the *economic viability* of the household was threatened by theft, debt, eviction, and so forth, hence the significance of the Eighth and Tenth Commandments and related prophetic protests. It can now be seen that the Seventh Commandment also comes into this category and is based on the same principle, since adultery strikes at the very heart and stability of the household by shattering the *sexual integrity* of the marriage. . . . This explains why it is so frequently singled out by the prophets for condemnation and why it is included in the Decalogue—because both were concerned above all to preserve the relationship between Israel and Yahweh, which they saw to be threatened at its familial roots by the crime of adultery. (C. J. H. Wright, *God's Land,* pp. 206f.)

The legal and prophetic view of adultery is fully borne out by the Wisdom tradition, which characteristically looks to the consequences of such affairs, and, in line with the above comments, observes the disastrous social effects on a man's whole family and substance and standing in the covenant community (Prov. 2:16–19; 5:1–23; 6:23–35; 7:1–27). Wisdom also offers the first step toward Jesus' radical view of the roots of the sin of adultery in lustful looks (cf. Prov. 6:25; Job 31:1, 9ff.).

The Eighth Commandment

5:19 / **You shall not steal.** This commandment is distinctive in a way that is not immediately obvious from the Decalogue itself. The Decalogue does not prescribe legal penalties, but in the rest of Israel's legislation, all the offenses that carry a death penalty can be related, directly or indirectly, to commandments in the Decalogue. However, the eighth commandment is exceptional; in normal Israelite judicial practice (i.e., excluding exceptional cases like Achan, where laws of war were also involved), no kind of theft of property carried the death penalty. Only theft of persons (i.e., kidnapping, usually for slave sale) was a capital offense (Exod. 21:16; Deut. 24:7).

This feature of Israelite law stands in sharp contrast to the laws of theft in other ancient Near Eastern law codes, where there was a wide range of penalties, including mutilations and death, for different kinds of theft, as well as a gradation of penalties according to the social rank of the victim. In the OT, theft was penalized and remedied by restitution, sanctioned by the threat of slavery if necessary to cover what needed to be repaid, but never punished by death. The other side of this principle, as we have seen in the sixth commandment, was that the murderer's penalty could not be commuted for financial compensation (which was allowed for certain classes of people in other ancient Near Eastern codes). Material property and human life were not to be measured in terms of each other, or substituted for each other. The priority of the sixth commandment over the eighth, then, was more than just numerical. It reflects a scale of values in which human life is of immeasurably higher value than property.

However, just because theft was not punished with the severity found in other ancient Near Eastern codes does not imply that theft was regarded lightly in Israel. Its very inclusion in the Ten Commandments shows that it was viewed as a serious offense against the covenant relationship. This is seen in the range of texts *outside* the strictly legal texts, and the great depth of feeling in them, that condemn theft and thieves in no uncertain terms. Theft was condemned by the prophets as an indication of social breakdown and lack of knowledge of God (Hos. 4:2; 7:1), as the mark of a city that has degenerated to the level of Sodom and Gomorrah (Isa. 1:10, 23), and as utterly incompatible with claims to acceptable worship in the temple (Jer. 7:9f.). Psalm 50:16–18 ranks it with adultery as irreconcilable with covenant loyalty. Proverbs 30:9 fears the temptation to steal because it would be a profanation of the very name of Yahweh, while Proverbs 29:24 curses even those who witness a theft and do not give evidence. Zechariah 5:3–4 pronounces a very mobile and active curse on both the thief and the perjurer, indicating divine reaction even when human justice is foiled.

It is clear, then, that the prohibition was treated seriously and applied to a wide range of antisocial behavior, alongside other forms of economic exploitation and injustice. Calvin's instinct was valid, then, in seeing the eighth commandment as concerned not only with the precise crime of burglary or robbery but with all forms of unjust gain at the expense of others.

> It follows, therefore, that not only are those thieves who secretly steal the property of others, but those also who seek gain from the

loss of others, accumulate wealth by unlawful practices, and are more devoted to their private advantage than to equity. . . . there is no difference between a man's robbing his neighbour by fraud or force. . . . Craft and low cunning is called prudence; and he is spoken of as provident and circumspect who cleverly over-reaches others, who takes in the simple, and insidiously oppresses the poor. Since, therefore, the world boasts of vices as if they were virtues, and thus all freely excuse themselves in sin, God wipes away all this gloss, when He pronounces all unjust means of gain to be so many thefts. (J. Calvin, *Harmony*, Vol. III, p. 111)

Calvin goes on to include in his discussion of the eighth commandment a whole variety of socioeconomic pentateuchal legislation including exploitation of hired workers, just treatment of aliens, accurate weights and measures, security of landmarks, laws relating to debt, interest and pledges, bribery, trespass, injury, and damage to property. He also argues that the prohibition implied a corresponding affirmative—to seek the good of the neighbor by generosity and kindness. Accordingly he also includes in his "supplements" laws concerning rights of gleaning, sabbatical release of slaves and debt pledges, jubilee and redemption laws, and levirate marriage! In this he has the support of Ezekiel, who defined his typical righteous person as one who not only refrained from theft but exercised positive generosity (Ezek. 18:7), a combination claimed by Job (Job 31:16–22, 31f., 38–40), commended in the Psalms (Ps. 112:4–9), and applied practically in the NT (Eph. 4:28).

Like the sixth commandment, then, with its wide range of ethical applicability in matters involving human life, the eighth commandment has a comparably broad relevance to matters of material property and economic institutions, policies, and practice.

The Ninth Commandment

5:20 / You shall not give false testimony against your neighbor. Literally this reads, "You shall not respond (i.e., when giving witness in court) against your neighbor with worthless testimony." The commandment is not simply about telling the truth in general, but about telling the truth in the place where it counts most, because that is where lying can cost most—the court of law. The protection of the process of justice was a major concern in Israel, and in the Decalogue the full weight of the identity, character, and action of Yahweh is thrown behind it. Breaking the ninth commandment would frequently involve breaking the third, which increased its seriousness. A nation founded by an act of Yahweh's righteousness must guard the righteousness of its own legal system, and every citizen was accountable for that.

Elsewhere OT law recognized the temptations to false witness that come from fraud and greed (Lev. 19:11–13), slander and hatred (Lev. 19:16–18), crowd pressure or conspiracy (Exod. 23:1f.), misplaced favoritism (Exod. 23:3, Lev. 19:15), and even family loyalties (Deut. 13:6–11). It therefore established a remarkably retributive law on perjury: anyone discovered to have given false testimony was to be punished with the same punishment that the victim of his accusation would have received if the verdict had gone against him (Deut. 19:16–21). One wonders what a salutary effect such a law might have in the modern world, which is plagued with miscarriages of justice notoriously caused by false testimony and conspiracy.

Along with religious idolatry and socioeconomic oppression, the perversion of justice was one of the primary targets of prophetic anger. Indeed, all three were linked. The story of Naboth shows a king and queen simultaneously seeking to expunge the worship of Yahweh, flouting the basic economic institutions in family land-tenure that Yahwism sanctioned for the sake of equity among the whole population and unscrupulously using Israel's own legal rules (regarding witnesses and capital crimes) to pervert Yahweh's justice for their own ends (1 Kgs. 21). If that event was exceptional in the ninth century, it had become endemic in the eighth, so much so that Amos complains that justice is turned to wormwood in "the gate" (the public place where courts convened) and truthful witnesses were hated and intimidated (Amos 5:7, 10, 12f., 15; cf. Isa. 5:20–23; 10:1f.; Hos. 4:1f.; Jer. 5:1f., 26–28; 7:9).

However, though the primary reference of the commandment is to false testimony in court, it also embodies a concern about truthfulness in the wider spheres of human relating. The OT, especially in the Psalms and Wisdom literature, has a passionate interest in truth, partly as a reflection of an essential characteristic of Yahweh himself, and partly out of a thoroughly practical and consequential awareness of the cost to individuals and society as a whole when lying becomes endemic.

The Tenth Commandment

5:21 / You shall not covet . . . anything that belongs to your neighbor. The climax of the Decalogue takes us to the heart of the matter, to the source of so much of what the previous commandments have prohibited, namely, human covetous desire. We should remember that the Decalogue is not a code of laws in the legislative sense. It is never called "laws," but "words." It sets out the boundaries of required and prohibited behaviors for the covenant people as matters of fundamental principle. The inclusion of coveting shows that covenant loyalty in Israel went far deeper than external conformity to statute law. The God who claimed the people's love also claimed the rest of their affections and desires. "If anyone says, 'I love God,' yet hates his brother, he is a liar. For anyone who does not love his brother, whom he has seen, cannot love God, whom he has not seen" (1 John 4:20). These words were not written by the author of Deuteronomy, but they might well have been. For in terms of the dynamic of the covenant, covetous desires toward the wife, household, or possessions of a brother-neighbor constitute hatred. Deuteronomy is concerned to inculcate a social ethos in which motives and desires, intentions and attitudes, matter greatly. All the rhetoric, the didactic, hortatory style, the urgent appeals, glowing promises, and dire warnings are directed precisely to the heart and mind, the inner world of will and purpose. There is nothing at all surprising, therefore, in the tenth commandment being posted to the same address.

The radical nature of the tenth commandment (i.e., the realization that it goes to the roots of human wickedness in so many other fields) is fully endorsed in the NT. Jesus warned his hearers about the dangers of covetous greed and reinforced his teaching with several parables (Luke 12:13–21). His challenge to the rich ruler who claimed to have kept the commandments probably intended to show that the man's claim foundered on his failure to live up to the tenth commandment through his attachment to his wealth (Matt. 19:16ff.). Paul fastened on the tenth commandment as the one that awakened his awareness of sin and lawbreaking (Rom. 7:7). James recognized the insidious and far-reaching effects of covetousness in producing behavior that breaks the other commandments (Jas. 4:1ff.). So serious, indeed, is covetousness in its stranglehold on human minds and intentions that Paul twice equated it with idolatry (Col. 3:5; Eph. 5:5).

Thus the commandments come full circle. To break the tenth is to break the first. For covetousness means setting our hearts and affections on things that then take the place of God. It is not surprising, then, conversely, that a whole culture that systematically denies the transcendent by excluding the reality of the living God from the public domain, as Western societies have been doing for generations, also ends up turning covetous self-interest into a socioeconomic ideology, rationalized, euphemized, and idolized. Knowing full well that you cannot serve God and mammon, we have deliberately chosen mammon and declared that a person's life *does* consist in the abundance of things possessed. And when a society has so profoundly and deliberately abandoned the first and tenth commandments, the moral vacuum that results from the loss of all those commandments in between soon follows.

Additional Notes §7

The literature on the Decalogue is enormous. Selected works are cited in the for further reading section at the back of the book, and a more complete bibliography is available in Christensen, *Deuteronomy*, pp. 101–3.

There has always been some variation in the precise ordering of the commandments forbidding murder, adultery, and theft. They appear in different orders in Hos. 4:2 and Jer. 7:9, in the LXX version of Exod. and Deut., as well as in later Jewish and Christian listings (e.g., Matt. 19:17–20; Mark 10:18–20; Luke 18:19–20). Cf. Freund, "Murder, Adultery and Theft?"

The numbering of the Ten Commandments is not consistent in various Jewish and Christian traditions. For a useful tabulation of the different systems, see W. Harrelson, *Human Rights*, pp. 45–48. The order followed in this commentary is the traditional Reformed Protestant numbering.

5:7–10 / The questions of the origins of Israelite monotheism, and the extent to which Israelites were monotheistic in religious practice at different stages of their OT history, are very complex and have generated much scholarly research and very divergent views. In my view, though we may never be able successfully to distinguish the "official" canonical OT faith from the empirical religion of average Israelites in any given historical period, there is no compelling reason to doubt that the roots of biblical monotheism go back to Moses himself, though his legacy had a troubled history in the preexilic centuries. Among the more recent writings, which take into account the relevance of archaeological and epigraphical evidence, the following are prominent and contain full bibliographical information on other and older works: de Moor, *Rise of Yahwism;* Smith, *Early History;* Tigay, *No Other Gods;* Hess, "Yahweh and His Asherah?"

5:12–15 / The observance of special days, taboo days of ill-omen, festivals for gods, market days, astrologically significant days, etc. is, of course, common in many, if not all, human societies. But the cycle of seven days as a week and the nature of the seventh as a sabbath appear to have been unique to Israel. For a survey of research and theories as to its origins, see Hasel, "Sabbath," who writes:

> In spite of the extensive efforts of more than a century of study into extra-Israelite sabbath origins, it is still shrouded in mystery. . . . The quest for the origin of the sabbath outside of the OT cannot be pronounced to have been successful (p. 851).

See also, McCann, "Sabbath," and the bibliographical information in both articles.

For a thorough survey of all the OT sabbath texts and traditions, see Andreason, *Sabbath.* For helpful discussions of the significance and contemporary relevance of the sabbath, see Miller, *Deuteronomy,* pp. 79–84; Brueggemann, *The Land,* pp. 63–65; Harrelson, *Human Rights,* pp. 85–92. On the relation between OT sabbath and NT "Lord's Day," see Carson, *Lord's Day,* and Beckwith and Stott, *Day.*

5:16 / **Honor** is the strong word *kabbēd,* lit. "to give weight to, regard as of high value and worth, to glorify." Its opposite is *qillēl,* which means "to curse," but is lit. "to make light of, regard as of no value, despise." This latter verb is used in the capital offense that sanctioned the fifth commandment, "Anyone who curses his father or mother must be put to death" (Exod. 21:17; cf. Deut. 27:15). Both verbs can be used about God, 1 Sam. 2:30 being a good example of the contrast: "Those who honor me I will honor, but those who despise me will be disdained." Likewise, in Lev. 19:3, the verb *yārē'* ("to fear, respect"), which even more commonly is used of God, is used of parents. The vocabulary of the commandment thus contributes to the long-standing interpretation that sees the honoring of parents as a reflection of, and early training in, the duty of honoring God. This is reinforced by the combined command to "rise in the presence of the aged, show respect for the elderly and revere your God" (Lev. 19:32).

For the view that the commandment also included deceased ancestors in its scope, see Brichto, "Kin, Cult, Land and Afterlife." For a critique that rejects this hypothesis but finds value in other aspects of Brichto's study, see C. J. H. Wright, *God's Land,* pp. 151–59. Also, on the centrality of the household-plus-land units in the entire covenant structure of Israel and its implications in many spheres, including its relevance in NT and Christian ethics, see idem, pp. 44–114.

5:17 / Whereas in the Exod. version each of the following commandments stands as a separate sentence, Deut. joins them together as one whole sentence by putting the conjunction "and" at the beginning of vv. 18, 19, 20, and 21. Flusser, "The Decalogue," relates this to Jas. 2:10–11 and the Jewish-Christian tradition of summarizing the second five commandments in terms of Lev. 19:18, "Love your neighbor as yourself." The article helpfully illuminates the continuities between Jewish and NT traditions on the matter of summarizing the law.

5:18 / Adultery in the OT law is still sometimes mistakenly described as a property offense, on the alleged grounds that wives were regarded as the property of their husbands in ancient Israel. Against this, it can first be said that no other property offense in Israelite law carried a death penalty, which would make the capital nature of adultery anomalous (see note on the eighth commandment). Also, the view that wives were property in the OT has been shown for nearly half a century to be simplistic and false, but it keeps surfacing in both popular and scholarly writings. For a full survey of the legal and social status of wives in Israel and the wide range of scholarship on the issue, see C. J. H. Wright, *God's Land,* ch. 6, pp. 183–221.

It is also often pointed out that in terms of legal technicality, adultery was an offense that a woman could commit only against her own marriage, and a man could commit only against another man's marriage. That is, it was not technically adulterous (in respect to his own marriage) if a man had sexual intercourse with an unmarried girl, a concubine (slave woman), or indeed a prostitute; it was adulterous only if he had intercourse with another man's wife, in which case he was "adulterating" the other marriage. However, it is going too far to take from this that the primary or only motive for the sanction against adultery was that a man could be sure his children were his own and that there was no concern for sexual morality as such (cf. Phillips, *Criminal Law,* p. 117). Even non-adulterous sexual assault, though it did not carry a death-penalty, required a guilt-offering to atone for the sin, as well as compensation (Lev. 19:20–22). And Hosea very emphatically exposes and condemns the "double-standard morality" of Israelite males in Hos. 4:14. See further, McKeating, "Sanctions," and Phillips, "Adultery."

5:19 / The theory (which goes back to rabbinic interpreters but was revived by Alt) that the original form of the eighth commandment was a prohibition on "stealing a man," i.e., on kidnapping, and that it would therefore have been a capital offense is now generally regarded as unnecessary and probably mistaken. For a full discussion of this question and a survey of the whole range of Israel's laws on theft, see Jackson, *Theft;* Gnuse, *You Shall Not Steal;* Dearman, *Property Rights;* C. J. H. Wright, *God's Land,* pp. 131–38.

5:21 / It was early Jewish interpreters who first suggested that the meaning of *ḥāmad* (**covet**) here was not so much coveting as an emotional craving, but the taking of steps toward actually stealing the thing coveted (i.e., the tenth commandment prohibited actual theft).

The probable reason was to interpret the commandment in conformity with the others as enforceable legislation. In modern times this idea was revived initially by German scholars, though apparently without awareness of its premedieval Jewish roots, most prominently by Alt, "Das Verbot." For details of the early Jewish interpretation and its development, see Rofé, "The Tenth Commandment." The most thorough study of the issue, however, concludes that there are no adequate grounds, exegetically, historically, or theologically, for rejecting the traditional sense of the tenth commandment in favor of a concrete meaning referring to overt action: Jackson, "Mere Intention." This also renders unnecessary the view that the eighth commandment originally prohibited man-stealing (kidnapping) on the grounds that the tenth commandment covered ordinary theft.

The fact that the tenth commandment includes the neighbor's wife in its list of what was not to be coveted has often been used as a somewhat facile argument for the view that wives were considered the property of their husbands in OT Israel. But it is obvious that possessive suffixes or pronouns have different objects and cannot be treated as signifying equivalent value. "My wife" expresses a relationship and an evaluation somewhat different from "my shoes," and if it does not imply that my wife is merely an item on my list of goods and possessions in English, why should it have had such a meaning in Hb.? See C. J. H. Wright, *God's Land*, pp. 196f. Likewise, the fact that Deut. places the wife before the rest of the list (changing the order from Exod.) may indicate a desire to elevate women's position, though this change by itself hardly signifies a major shift in her legal or covenantal status as Phillips argues, *Criminal Law*, p. 152. Cf. Moran, "Conclusion."

§8 Moses the Mediator (Deut. 5:22–6:3)

We now return to the narrative framework that envelops the Decalogue. The main thrust of this section is to amplify and explain the mediatorial role of Moses, described parenthetically in 5:5, and thus to reinforce the authority with which Moses teaches the following sections, beginning especially with the exposition of the first commandment in 6:4ff.

5:22 / **These are the commandments;** in Hebrew, "these words," the standard name for the Ten Commandments (cf. 4:13; 9:10; 10:2, 4), are emphatically placed first and the rest of the verse reinforces this emphasis, with terse phrases that express the divine source of the Commandments (**the LORD proclaimed in a loud voice**), their authority over all Israel (**to your whole assembly**), their majesty (**out of the fire, the cloud and the deep darkness**), their completeness and finality (**he added nothing more,** which obviously does not mean that God gave no more laws, but that God gave nothing else comparable to the Ten Commandments), and their fixed and permanent nature (**he wrote them on two stone tablets**). The distinct status of the Ten Commandments is thus assured. They function as a kind of constitution, or charter, the norm and policy that inform all the rest of the detailed legislation to follow.

5:23–27 / These verses recall and expand on the simple account given in Exodus 20:18–21. On the one hand, the people are amazed at witnessing such a theophany of God's **glory** and **majesty** and especially at hearing **the voice** of God (24, 26; cf. 4:33). On the other hand, they are afraid and prefer to avoid any more of the same while they are still, miraculously, alive! Such a mixed reaction is not at all surprising, indeed it is psychologically very plausible. There is no need to postulate contradiction between verses 24 and 25 and see them as coming from "different hands" (Mayes, *Deuteronomy*, p. 173). The common understanding was that nobody could *see* God and survive (though cf.

the mysterious experience of the elders in Exod. 24:11), but, as we have emphasized before, the point of Sinai was that God could not be seen but *could be heard.* He was invisible but not inaudible. Nevertheless, even that was terrifying enough, and the leaders of the people, while acknowledging that it was possible to survive an encounter with God (v. 24b), opted for safety (v. 25). (There is some irony in the fact that these people fear they will perish merely by being in the presence of God, when in later years they blatantly flout God's covenant with no such fear.) And so, the people ask Moses to be their mediator, the one who will risk the intimate presence of this awesome God (v. 29). And, in case it might sound like they are trying to avoid obedience also, they make it clear that they will accept whatever Moses brings as the word of God and obey it (v. 27b).

Speaking, then, on behalf of the whole people, the representatives of Israel do three things: (a) they recognize that the terrifying physical phenomena they are witnessing are nothing less than a theophany—a manifestation of the presence of Yahweh their God, in which they are being unmistakably addressed; (b) they unanimously commission Moses to be their mediator (**Go near and listen**), their means of further revelation, and their teacher (**Then tell us whatever the LORD our God tells you**); and (c) they commit the people of Israel to obedience (**We will listen and obey**).

5:28–29 / God's response is warm and positive: God accepts what they say as **good**. But awareness of their past and their likely future generates a divine wistfulness, **Oh that . . .** , which surfaces quite often in the OT (cf. Isa. 48:18f.; Jer. 2:1–3; 3:19–20; Hos. 11—the climax of such divine longing is reached when Jesus himself weeps over Jerusalem, Luke 19:41–44).

5:30–31 / The people's commissioning of Moses to be their mediator is now complemented by God's personal invitation to him, thus authorizing his role and status from both parties. There is an intimacy and almost a hint of conversational politeness in the way God speaks to Moses in verse 31. There is a suggestion that when the people go home, God can stop thundering and talk rather more *sotto voce* with Moses alone. (So, e.g., Craigie: "But as for you, stand here with me and let me speak to you . . . " [*Deuteronomy*, p.165].)

The topic of their conversation would be **all the commands**. In Hebrew, the word is actually singular here ("the whole command," *kol-hammiṣwâ*, as also in 6:1; 11:22; and 19:9, where the NIV inexplicably prefers plurals), and probably refers to the whole substance of the law considered as a single entity, i.e., the fundamental principle of covenant loyalty, perhaps especially as summed up in 6:4f. In each of the above contexts, keeping "the whole command" is also closely linked with "walking in the way of Yahweh," (cf. v. 33). Moses would thus be entrusted not only with the details of specific legislation (**decrees and laws**) but also with the grasp and insight into the whole law that would make him a faithful interpreter of the mind of God.

The result of the three-sided dialogue, then, is that Moses' confirmation as the authorized mediator between God and the people comes both by the people's request and by divine invitation. There is no doubt that this was an important point to have established, in view of the several challenges to Moses' authority that had been mounted in the wilderness. But there is an even greater significance to this interchange. In 18:14–20, Moses looks forward to the means by which God will continue to speak to the people after Moses' own death: God will raise up "a prophet like Moses." This promise is then specifically linked to the people's request and God's answer at Horeb, precisely as recorded here (18:16f.). Thus God's intention to continue a line of prophets who will carry on Moses' role as spokespersons for God is grounded in the people's own desire to have it so. Their commitment to hear and obey God's word through Moses is likewise carried forward as an ongoing commitment to hear and obey it as delivered by those whom God will raise up to be "like Moses," (18:19). The two passages, therefore, not only highlight the effrontery and fickleness of the people in their complaints and rejections of *Moses'* authority as divine spokesman (in view of the fact that they had requested it) but also serve as a critique of subsequent centuries of rejecting the word of God through *the prophets* (whom, by implication, they had also requested). This was a part of Amos' accusation against the people (Amos 2:11f.). It also illuminates Jeremiah's challenge to the false prophets who plagued his life and confused the people. His complaint was precisely that they had not "stood" in the presence of God, as Moses had done, and yet they dared to speak in God's name (Jer. 23:18, 21f.).

5:32–6:3 / This section links the earlier recollection of the past events at Horeb and the actual exhortation and teaching of the law to the present generation that is launched at 6:4. Since it has now been established that Moses is God's authorized spokesman, then the people's obedience to what he tells them is effectively obedience to God, and any deviation **to the right or to the left** will be a rejection of **the way** of the Lord. In Hebrew, chapter 6 begins with "*And* this is the command . . . ," which suggests that it is a continuation of the previous verses. The sequence of meaning is: "God gave me all this command (5:31) . . . So you be careful to do it (5:32f.) . . . And this is it (6:1ff.) . . . !"

The emphasis on motivational factors is almost overwhelming in this short passage. Five times we read "so that" or "that." The stakes were high. The rewards were great. The blessing and promise were in place. But obedience was the heart of the matter, **so that you may live and prosper and prolong your days . . . so that you . . . may fear the LORD your God . . . so that you may enjoy long life . . . so that it may go well with you and that you may increase greatly.** Not that obedience would *earn* such blessing. The final line of 6:3 recalls that the lush future in the land will be theirs because of God's faithfulness to the promise made to their forefathers. It was a gift of grace, but to be appropriated and enjoyed through obedience—a constant biblical pattern in both Testaments.

Additional Notes §8

5:22 / **Your whole assembly:** Deut. likes to use the word *qāhāl* to signify the wholeness and unity of the people of Israel, just as it frequently uses "all Israel." It uses it most frequently to refer to the "day" of the great original assembly at Horeb (Sinai), 4:10; 9:10; 10:4; 18:16; and 33:4. Cf. also 23:2–4; 31:12, 30. On the wider OT significance, see Anderson, "Israel: Amphictyony."

Two stone tablets: Cf. Exod. 24:12; 31:18; 32:15f.; 34:1–4, 27f. When the first tablets are smashed in reaction to the people's apostasy, two fresh ones are prepared. It is said that Moses himself wrote the words on the latter (Exod. 34:28). Whether this is deliberately to distinguish them from the original ones carved by God himself or whether it implies that the expression **he wrote them** was understood anthropomorphically in the first case as well (i.e., that Moses did the chiseling while God did the speaking) is not certain. The expression "the finger of God" (Exod. 31:18; Deut. 9:10) could certainly be used metaphorically elsewhere (Exod. 8:19; cf. Luke 11:20). The important truth conveyed by the repeated phraseology is that the Ten Commandments were a direct revelation from God, however they came to be carved in stone.

On the relationship between spoken and written word, between scriptural and prophetic authority, with particular reference to Deut. 4 and 5, cf. Moore, "Canon and Charisma."

§9 One Lord, One Love, One Loyalty (Deut. 6:4–25)

6:4–5 / Just as the Decalogue is both statement (Deut. 5:6) and command (5:7ff.), so this most fundamental of Israel's "credal" traditions, the "Shema" (Deut. 6:4–5), is both an affirmation *about* God and a call for commitment *to* God. Its Jewish name, "Shema," is the first Hebrew word of the summons, **Hear, O Israel,** a favorite form of address in Deuteronomy (cf. 5:1; 6:3; 9:1; 20:3; 27:9) that is similar to the Wisdom tradition's portrayal of parents calling a child's attention to their teaching for the child's own good (cf. Prov. 1:8). It is also a constant reminder that Israel was a people summoned by God to hear God's word. They were not merely spectators at a divine "show," but the recipients of divine revelation in words. They were to *hear* the truth and to respond to it. Even at a formal level, therefore, these two verses expose the falseness of the view that religious truth and revelation are "personal, not propositional"—i.e., the view that God does not reveal timeless truths propositionally, but simply acts in love and leaves to each individual his or her own interpretative conclusions as we respond in personal relationship to him and one another. Such reductionist views of revelation ignore the reality that truth in human experience is *both propositional and personal* and deny the biblical emphasis on both. Deuteronomy 6:4–5 is one whole sentence; nothing could be more "propositional" than 6:4 and nothing more "personal" than 6:5.

The LORD our God, the LORD is one. The NIV is most probably correct in its translation of verse 4 (see the NIV's footnotes and the additional notes for other possible renderings stemming from the absence of an explicit "is" in the Hb.). In the first half of the declaration, the Hebrew word "our God" is a qualifier, functioning like a relative clause: "Yahweh, who is our God, this Yahweh is one." But what does this mean?

An exegetical understanding would be that the second two Hebrew words mean "Yahweh is one," rather than "Yahweh alone." The uniqueness and incomparability of Yahweh are a major affirmation of the context, as we have already seen (Deut. 3:24; 4:35, 39; cf. 32:39; Exod. 15:11; Ps. 18:31), and there is doubtless a lingering flavor of that uniqueness in this text (note how Mark 12:32 adds the uniqueness formula to the great commandment). A problem with this contextual approach is that the verbal forms that usually express the uniqueness and incomparability of Yahweh are quite different from the expression in verse 4, which seems to suggest the oneness or singularity of Yahweh. There are various suggestions as to how this is to be understood.

One possibility is that there is a polemical intent to define God as wholly different from the multitude of gods that surround Israel, perhaps especially from the multiple manifestations and forms of Baal in the Canaanite cults. Yahweh is not the brand name of a cosmic corporation. He is one God, our God, and Yahweh is his personal name. On this understanding, the emphasis lies on Yahweh's *singularity.*

Another possible understanding is that the oneness of Yahweh implies a unity of will and purpose. Yahweh is not inwardly divided, despite the fact that in the OT text Yahweh sometimes appears to act in contradiction to the declared purposes and character of God (e.g., Moses' intercession in Exod. 32–34; Num. 14; cf. Deut. 9:7–29; Ps. 73; Job; Hos. 11). But, whatever the appearances, at the deepest level Yahweh is one, consistent, faithful, and true within. The idea here would be the same as when we say of a particular individual, "There is only one John." We imply he is not two-faced or inconsistent; you can rely on John to be the same whatever happens. Likewise, to say "Yahweh is one" is to affirm unchangeableness and consistency. There is no divine schizophrenia. The harmony of God's purpose for the world and its people is grounded in the ultimate unity of God's own being. On this understanding, the emphasis lies on Yahweh's *integrity.*

Whether, then, we read the verse in terms of Yahweh's incomparability (from the context, but not the text itself), his singularity (explicit, and probably the most likely meaning), or his integrity (implied, but not directly stated), it is clearly a most important text in relation to Israel's monotheism. It is beside the point to insist that the verse is not explicitly monotheistic in the philosophical sense of categorically denying the existence of other deities than Yahweh. The incontrovertible emphasis was that Yahweh (alone) was God in covenant relationship with Israel; that Yahweh had done what no other god had done or could do; that Yahweh was one, not many.

Whether the full implications of all this were understood from the start may be impossible to verify, but such convictions certainly generated a hope that was missiological, universal, and unquestionably monotheistic. The Deuteronomistic historian records prayers of both David and Solomon that express the wider vision and hope of other peoples coming to recognize what Israel already knew regarding Yahweh (2 Sam. 7:22–26; 1 Kgs. 8:60; cf. 1 Kgs. 8:41–43, and the reflection of Deut. 6:5 in 1 Kgs. 8:61). And the only clear quotation of Deuteronomy 6:4 in the rest of the OT is both eschatological and clearly monotheistic: "The LORD will be king over the whole earth. On that day there will be one LORD, and his name the only name" (lit. "Yahweh will be one and his name will be one," Zech. 14:9).

Finally, it is worth repeating the point made in relation to Deuteronomy 4:35, 39. The declaration at the heart of the Shema, and especially in its eschatological form in the text just cited (Zech. 14:9), is made about *Yahweh in particular*, not just about *deity in general*. That is why a preoccupation with abstract monotheism can lead us to overlook the primary challenge of the text. It is not being said simply that there is ultimately only one divine reality. Such a claim would certainly not be unique among the religions and philosophies of humankind. Nor is the eschatological hope of Zechariah merely that some day all human beings will profess monotheism of some sort per se. A philosophical monotheism that leaves the divine reality unnamed and characterless is alien (both unknown and hostile) to the OT faith. It is vital to see that, in OT terms, *it is Yahweh who defines what monotheism means*, not a concept of monotheism that defines how Yahweh should be understood.

This has very serious implications for the so-called "theocentric" theory of religious pluralism, according to which the ultimate divine reality at the center of the religious universe cannot be definitively or absolutely named in terms of any of the great divine names of human religions, including Yahweh or Jesus Christ or Allah or Brahman, etc. These are described as penultimate "personae" or "impersonae"—masks of human creation that attempt to express the inexpressible "noumenon" of the divine reality. The "theos" at the center thus becomes abstract, impersonal, and finally ineffable (nothing at all can be said about him/her/it). But the sharp precision of the Shema cannot be evaporated into a philosophical abstraction or relegated to a penultimate level of truth. Its majestic declaration of a monotheism defined by the history-laden, character-rich, covenant-related, dynamic personhood of "Yahweh our God," shows that the abstract and definitionally undefinable "being" of religious pluralism is really a monism without meaning or message.

"And you shall **love the LORD your God.**" Statement and response is the typical form of Deuteronomic exhortation, characteristic indeed of the biblical faith. "We love, because he first loved us," is a NT text that could as easily have been at home in Deuteronomy. So here in verse 5, the affirmation about Yahweh is followed by the claim upon Israel's total allegiance. The two halves of the Shema thus mirror the opening of the Decalogue, with the declaratory preface followed by the exclusive claims of the first two commandments (5:6–10).

The command to love God is one of Deuteronomy's favorite ways of expressing the response God expects from the people (10:12; 11:1, 13, 22; 13:3; 19:9; 30:6, 16, 20). It features also in the covenant renewal texts, Josh. 22:5; 23:11, which draw so much on the Deuteronomic model. In the context of a broken covenant, it is found in the prayers of Daniel (Dan. 9:4) and Nehemiah (1:5), drawing, perhaps on the worship of the Psalms as well as Deuteronomy (Pss. 31:23; 97:10; 145:20). A very early poetic use in the context of the early wars of Israel in Canaan is in Judges 5:31.

For Deuteronomy, the command to love is so often linked with the command to obey, in a sort of prose parallelism, that the two terms are virtually synonymous (though they should not be simply identified; "love" clearly has a distinctive range of affective meaning not entirely equivalent to the practical sense of "obey"). The simple fact that Deuteronomy's love is one that can be commanded shows that it is not merely an emotion. It is also a commitment to Yahweh, which generates corresponding action in line with his word. "If you love me, keep my commandments."

This committed, covenantal response to Yahweh was to be total: **with all your heart and with all your soul and with all your strength.** The wholeness, or oneness, of Yahweh (v. 4) is to be met with a response involving the wholeness of the human person (v. 5). The expression "heart and soul" is another characteristic Deuteronomic phrase (seen in 4:29; 10:12; 11:13; 13:3; 26:16; 30:2, 6, 10). The **heart** *(lēbāb)* in Hebrew was not so much the seat of emotions and feelings—as it is in English metaphors—as the seat of the intellect, will, and intention. You think in your heart, and your heart shapes your character, choices, and decisions. It is also the center of the human being as a moral agent (cf. also its prominence in Proverbs). It is understandable, therefore, that the gospel version of the great commandment adds the word "mind" (*dianoia*) to the list. *Dianoia* (understanding, intelligence) is the word the LXX uses to translate *lēbāb*, in this text and most others.

Soul is more often than not a misleading translation of Hebrew *nepeš*, since it has connotations in English that are simply not present in Hebrew. *Nepeš* means the life of each individual, and applies to animals as much as humans (cf. Gen. 1:20, 24; 2:7; Lev. 17:11, 14). In the legal texts it is frequently used in the sense of "a person, an individual, anyone," or in the sense of "a life" that can be taken or lost. But most often it is used to express the whole inner self, with all the emotions, desires, and personal characteristics that make each human being unique. "Bless the LORD, O my *nepeš*," sings the Psalmist, who then amplifies his meaning, "and *all that is within me* bless his holy name" (Ps. 103:1 RSV).

To love God, then, **with all your heart and with all your soul,** means with your whole self, including your rationality, mental capacity, moral choices and will, inner feelings and desires, and the deepest roots of your life. To this profound pair, the Shema adds a third, remarkable item: (lit.) "and with all your very-muchness" (*mᵉʾōd*). This word is everywhere else used adverbially, meaning "greatly," "exceedingly." Here it is almost uniquely used as a noun in its own right and is open to various translations, of which **strength** is the most common. However, the earliest Jewish versions (including the Targum) translated it as "your substance" or "your possessions"—an acceptable possibility that has some support in Proverbs 3:9 and may lie behind some of Jesus' parables and conversations (such as Matt. 6:19–24; Luke 12:13–21). It may even be that this third word is simply intensifying the other two as a climax. "Love the Lord your God with total commitment (heart), with your total self (soul), to total excess!" Loving God should be "over the top!" Such commitment characterized Josiah in his reforming zeal after the discovery of the Book of the Law of the LORD. Josiah alone in the Deuteronomistic History is credited with explicitly measuring up to the second verse of the Shema (2 Kgs. 23:25).

6:6–9 / The law, however, was not just for kings like Josiah. It was for everyone. It was to be in the heart as well as the head, in the home as well as the courts. These verses powerfully dispel two misconceptions. The first misconception is that OT law was a matter of legalistic conformity to an external code. On the contrary, Deuteronomy 6:6 is part of a strong stream of OT teaching that calls for the internalizing of the law in the heart, i.e., at the center of a person's mind, will, and character (cf. 4:9; 10:16; 11:18; Jer. 4:4; 31:33; Ezek. 18:31; 36:26f.). The second misconception is that religious traditions and observances are the preserve of a professional elite with esoteric knowledge, whether clerical or academic. The priests of Israel were, indeed, to teach the law, but not as something only they within the confines of the professional guild could understand. On the contrary, the law was to be the topic of ordinary conversation in ordinary homes in ordinary life, from breakfast to bedtime (v. 7; cf. the comments on the law being accessible and "near" in 30:11–14). Such would be its popular scope and relevance.

Once again, the rapid sequence of verbs helps us feel the force of the advice: **impress them** [the commandments] . . . **talk about them** . . . **tie them** . . . **bind them** . . . **write them.** The law of God is thus to be applied to the *individual* (**your hands** and **your foreheads**), the *family* (**your houses**), and public, civic *society* (**your gates,** the place of public business, courts, markets, etc.). The believer must work out the meaning of loving God in appropriate ways for all three levels. The love-commitment of the whole person in verse 5 is thus expanded to the whole community in verses 7–9.

Christian readers of 6:8–9 may be tempted to dismiss the Jewish use of *tefillin* (phylacteries) and *mezuzot* (scrolls inscribed with these verses, placed in cases, and fixed on doorposts) as unnecessary literalism (see additional note). However, the question is whether we are any more serious or successful in flavoring the whole of life with conscious attention to the law of God (v. 7, which is not at all "symbolic") as a personal, familial, and social strategy for living out our commitment to loving God totally.

6:10–16 / Nothing, said the Apostle Paul, can separate us from the love of God (Rom. 8:35–39). Unfortunately there is plenty that can separate God from the love of God's people. Verses 10–19 follow the positive commands of 6:4–9 with a sharply contrasting warning against three ways Israel may be distracted from the wholehearted love of Yahweh. These verses are often regarded as an insertion, in view of this sudden change of tone, and in some ways verses 20–25 do follow very naturally from verses 7–9. The effect of the whole passage, however, is to sandwich the negative thrust of the warnings (vv. 10–19) in between two very positive sections on Israel's response to Yahweh (vv. 4–9, 20–25). The overall flavor of the chapter is thus characteristic of the balance of Deuteronomy as a whole: obedience, though sanctioned by the reality of God's wrath, should be primarily motivated by gratitude and love in responding to God's grace.

The three warnings are indicated by the triple **do not** in verses 12, 14, and 16, each of which flashes danger lights marking temptations Israel would be exposed to. Each of the three warnings, given in brief form here, is considerably expanded in the following two chapters, so our comments at this point will be similarly brief and preliminary.

The danger of forgetting God because of affluence (6:10–13). There is no embarrassment in Deuteronomy in anticipating the abundance and richness of life in the land that lay ahead. God's desire for the people of God was (and still ultimately remains) a full life, enjoying the gifts of creation. But equally there is no illusion regarding the likely behavior of the people; in the enjoyment of the gift they might **forget** the giver. So these verses build up to that danger with rhetorical skill. First, there comes the reminder that the land itself is a promise-gift of God's grace (10a). Next, there is a description of the land, full of material bonuses that had a traditional prestige (10b–11; cf. Josh. 24:13; Neh. 9:25), climaxing with "and you will eat and (lit.) be full." The dreamlike sequence is shattered with the opening words of verse 12: "Watch out!" Fullness can lead to forgetfulness, especially forgetfulness of where they came from and what Yahweh had rescued them from—**the land of slavery.**

In order not to forget, they must determine to **fear** Yahweh and **serve him only** (v. 13). The English obscures the sharpness of the Hebrew, in which "slavery" and "serve" are the same root word (and the NIV spoils the contrast further with its paragraph break after v. 12). Those whom God had emancipated out of slavery to Egypt must live as God's own loyal slaves. The structure of verse 13 in Hebrew emphasizes that God should be first in allegiance; God comes first in the word order of the sentence; (lit.) "The LORD your God shall you fear and him shall you serve and in his name shall you swear." To swear in the name of Yahweh was to acknowledge Yahweh as the highest authority (hence the seriousness of doing so frivolously or with evil intent, 5:11). This entire chapter seems to have been foremost in Jesus' mind when he went into the wilderness following his baptism. Jesus cited this verse when he refused to bow down and worship Satan or acknowledge Satan as in any way comparable to his Father God (Matt. 4:8–10).

The danger of abandoning God because of surrounding idolatry (6:14–15). In 4:16–19 the warning was given to avoid being enticed into worshipping the heavenly bodies. Here Canaanite idolatry is in view. The temptation would be very strong to adopt the religion of the people of the land in order to reap any potential benefits. But that would be fundamentally incompatible with covenant loyalty and would therefore arouse the jealousy and anger of Yahweh (see commentary on 5:9).

The danger of doubting God because of hardship (6:16). Deuteronomy 8:1–5 draws further lessons from Israel's experience of need and hardship in the wilderness years. This verse singles out one event, the murmuring at **Massah,** when there was a shortage of drinkable water (Exod. 17:1–7). Both here and in the Exodus narrative the people's reaction is described as "testing" the LORD. The Hebrew word (*nissāh,* from which the place was named) does not mean to tempt someone by trying to entice them to do what is wrong, but rather to test or prove whether someone will really do what they say. This is precisely the nuance of the people's challenge at Massah (Exod. 17:7), "This God Yahweh, can he do what he promised, is he really competent, is he really with us?" Such "testing" of Yahweh flows from a lack of belief in Yahweh's word and comes despite the fact that this people has witnessed Yahweh's previous faithfulness (cf. 1:31–33). This kind of testing is commonly induced by need and hardship and this warning comes because life will not always be as idyllic and effortless as pictured in verse 11.

Jesus indicates the depth of his meditation on this chapter when he quotes this verse in response to Satan (Matt. 4:5–7). The suggestion that he should "prove" God's protective commitment to him by jumping off the temple in Jerusalem when he still had ringing in his ears the voice of his Father God, with its combination of recognition, approval, and commissioning, was rightly resisted as utterly out of line with the command of Deuteronomy

6:16. Where Israel, God's first-born son (Exod. 4:22), had so often distrusted and disobeyed, in spite of spectacular demonstrations of God's benevolence, the Son of God would trust and obey.

6:17–19 / The positive antidote to such forgetfulness, desertion, or doubting of God is the determined positive effort to keep God's commands. Thus the negative **do not**s of the previous verses are replaced by the positive **Do . . .** of verse 18. There is no thought here of Israel *earning* possession of the land by doing **what is right and good;** rather, the land-gift was entirely grounded in the ancestral promise (v. 18b), and given **so that it may go well with you.** Possession without blessing would be worthless, and the driving out of their enemies would be a mere prologue to their own evacuation (8:19f.). These verses echo and balance the earlier challenge of the chapter in verses 2–3.

6:20–25 / Bringing both balance and climax, this final section of the chapter returns to the teaching theme of verses 6–7. It continues the message of verse 9, with the intervening warnings serving to reinforce the importance of their message. Like a number of other texts (see additional note), this passage envisages internal family teaching, in which parents answer children's questions regarding specific events, memorials, rituals, or observances. The child's question then becomes the springboard for explanation and teaching, rather like a catechism (which some scholars suggest is what we have fragments of here). The first thing to notice is that such questions and teaching opportunities would arise only if the parents themselves were conspicuously observing the laws. What was true for Israel as a whole (cf. Deut. 4:6–8) was true for each family—no observance, no questions.

The son's question in verse 20 is (lit.) **"What [are] the stipulations, decrees and laws . . . ?"** He is presumably not asking what they are in content, since he would already know that through the family's observation of them. So we have to assume the question means something like "What is the meaning of . . . ?" or "What is the real significance of . . . ?" or "What is the point of . . . ?" or even, "*Why* do we keep these laws?" In fact, as it turns out, the father's answer combines the historical basis of the law, its divine origin, and the beneficial value of keeping it.

It would have been quite easy to imagine the text going straight from verse 20 to verse 24, "Why do we keep these laws?

Because **the LORD commanded us.**" Period. (Most parents will have felt the temptation to answer children's "why's" in similar fashion.) The moral obligation of an imperative from God should be enough to elicit obedience. But will it be? If this is all that is given by explanation, the son might very well give Pharaoh's response, "Who is Yahweh that I should obey him?" (Exod. 5:2) The full answer, therefore, takes the same classic form as the Decalogue itself by stating the facts of redemption on which Yahweh's identity and Yahweh's claim on Israel were simultaneously founded. The LORD who commanded us (v. 24) is the LORD who delivered us (vv. 21–23). These are the additional reasons for these stipulations, decrees, and laws.

Verses 21–24 provide such a concise but comprehensive summary of the central elements of Israel's faith that some scholars regard them as an example of Israel's earliest "creeds" (see additional notes), incorporating the traditions of exodus, land-gift, and patriarchal promise. It is virtually the OT "gospel" in a nutshell. The crucial point here, however, is that this definitive statement of Israel's salvation history is given as the answer to a fundamental question about *the law*. The son asks about the law and is answered with a story—the old, old story of Yahweh and his love. *The meaning of the law is to be found in the gospel.* The basis of the law lies in the history of redemption (vv. 21–23); the reason for keeping the law is to enjoy the blessings of redemption (v. 24); the fruit of obeying the law is the righteousness that is the goal of redemption (v. 25).

In the light of the emphatic thrust of the previous verses, it is impossible to read into verse 25 any kind of alleged "works righteousness." The context makes it impossible to think that righteousness (in a salvific sense, which is in any case almost certainly not its meaning here) is somehow *achieved* by obedience to the law. Rather the point of the father's whole answer is that obedience to the law is the only *right response* to the saving acts of such a God as Yahweh. Indeed, "the righteousnesses of Yahweh" is one way the OT sums up his saving actions for Israel, done out of the redemptive initiative of his grace. **Our righteousness** is the obedient response that flows from the gratitude of those enjoying liberty, life, and well-being as God's gift. It probably also includes that enduring blessing on family and social life that is the equally God-given fruit of such obedience. It is, in short, a righteousness that presumes the experience of redemption, not a righteousness that presumes to achieve redemption (see additional note).

Additional Notes §9

6:4 / The Hb. words have no verb, because Hb. normally omits the verb "to be" in simple predicative sentences. The verse reads, *Yahweh ʾelōhênû Yahweh ʾeḥād*. Its sense is then governed by where we assume "is" should be understood and whether it should be understood once or twice. Thus, as the NIV footnote points out, four readings are possible:

(a) Yahweh is our God; Yahweh is one.

(b) Yahweh is our God, Yahweh alone.

(c) Yahweh our God, Yahweh is one.

(d) Yahweh our God is one Yahweh.

The best recent discussion of the exegesis is by Moberly, "Yahweh is One." Moberly excludes (a) and (b) on the grounds that "our God" is never used predicatively (i.e., with "is" understood) anywhere else in Deut. but is used exclusively (in its 300 instances) in a descriptive or adjectival sense. Also, it is questionable whether *ʾeḥād*, which is simply the numeral "one," is ever used anywhere else in the OT to mean "alone" (for which *lebādād* was used). He therefore argues that we must choose between senses (c) and (d), and he prefers (c) because of its easier sense and in view of its similarity to Zech. 14:9.

On the idea of the integrity of Yahweh as the implication of the text, cf. Janzen, "Shema."

6:5 / On the covenantal significance of the command to love Yahweh, its background in the treaty texts, and its filial significance, cf. Moran, "Love of God"; McCarthy, "Love of God"; McKay, "Man's Love for God." On the probable influence of these ideas on Jesus' own conception of his divine sonship, cf. C. J. H. Wright, *Knowing Jesus*, pp. 117–35.

In Jewish tradition, the full form of the Shema, which was for daily recitation, was a composite text including Deut. 6:4–9; 11:13–21; and Num. 15:37–41, with appropriate benedictions attached. A very helpful exposition of the meaning of the Shema, including its Jewish interpretation, its NT forms, and its contemporary force, is McBride, "Yoke of the Kingdom."

6:8–9 / While there is no reason why these instructions could not have been intended literally (esp. those regarding doors and gates), it seems more likely that at least v. 8 was intended metaphorically, since the same imagery is used regarding specific ritual activities in

Exod. 13:9 (the passover) and Exod. 13:16 (the sacrifice of first-born animals and the redemption and dedication of first-born sons). Cf. also Prov. 3:3; 6:21; 7:3. Jewish tradition has taken both verses literally. For details, see Hirsch, "Phylacteries."

6:16 / On the incident at Massah and other references to Israel "testing" Yahweh, cf. Exod. 17:1–7; Num. 14:22; Deut. 9:22; 33:8; Pss. 78:18; 95:8f.; 106:14. Ahaz misused Deut. 6:16 by refusing to ask for a sign when God actually offered him one in order to confirm the prophetic word (Isa. 7:10ff.). Ahaz piously quotes this verse in an attempt to conceal the very refusal to believe God's word that the verse itself is directed against! No wonder Isaiah's patience snapped (Isa. 7:13).

6:20–25 / This pattern, in which a child asks a question and is given a clearly didactic answer, is found in four places, all of which relate to important aspects of Israel's early history: Exod. 12:26f. (the passover); 13:14f. (the rite of the first-born); Deut. 6:20–25 (the meaning of the law); Josh. 4:6f., 20–24 (the stones from the crossing of the Jordan). It has been suggested that these texts may be evidence of a liturgical form of catechesis. See Soggin, "Catechesis." Whether or not this was so, it is certainly evidence of the importance of the family in the preservation and inculcation of Israel's historical faith and its implications (cf. the comments on the fifth commandment). Cf. C. J. H. Wright, *God's Land,* pp. 81–89.

Verses 21–24 were isolated by von Rad as an example of what he described as an early Israelite "credo." Other examples include Deut. 26:5–9 and a more expanded form in Josh. 24:2–13. On the basis of the fact that these summaries of Israel's history do not explicitly refer to the tradition of the giving of the law at Mt. Sinai, von Rad ("Problem") argued that the Sinai tradition was originally totally separate from the historical exodus-conquest tradition. For a survey and critical discussion of the large literature this proposal generated, see Hyatt, "Credo," and Nicholson, *Exodus and Sinai.* Both of these scholars reject von Rad's separation of the traditions on this basis. See also C. J. H. Wright, *God's Land,* pp. 13–15, 24–43.

6:25 / It is unlikely that the word "righteousness" is being used here in a forensic sense, i.e., of being "in the right" legally. This seems to be the basis (misleadingly in my view) of the REB "For us to be in the right we should . . . ," and the NRSV, "If . . . we will be in the right." That is hardly the issue in the context and if it had been intended would probably have been expressed differently in Hb. ("we shall be righteous [ones], *ṣaddîqîm*"). The Hb. text is (lit.) "and righteousness *(ṣ^edāqâ)* there will be for us." The construction normally expresses a possessive relationship, as in the grammatically identical "There will be for you no other gods" (5:7), i.e., "You shall have no other gods." The most natural meaning, then, is "*ṣ^edāqâ* will be ours," i.e., "We shall have *ṣ^edāqâ.*" It is then more probable that the word *ṣ^edāqâ* (a notoriously flexible word) has a passive rather than an active meaning here. That is, it is not, "we shall be doing what is right," (doubtless true, but somewhat redundant), but rather, "we shall have, experience, enjoy the blessing of, everything being right—in our family, in our society, and in our relationship with God." Elsewhere, the fruit of Israel's obedience is God's blessing, and there are other contexts where righteousness and blessing *(bᵉrākâ)* are virtually synonymous, including the very appropriate Ps. 24:4–5. This view is indebted to Moberly's stimulating study of the meaning of the righteousness reckoned to Abraham (Gen. 15:6), to Phinehas (Ps. 106:31), and in the text: "Abraham's Righteousness."

An interesting point of style in the whole chapter is that **this law** in the final verse is singular and is the same word as **the commands** in v. 1 *(hammiṣwâ)*. If this singular expression, "this whole command," has a particular reference to the Shema, as some think, then the beginning and end of the chapter "enclose" it rather attractively.

§10 Israel's Election and Its Implications (Deut. 7:1–26)

Like several of these opening chapters of Deuteronomy, chapter seven displays a careful stylistic structure, a concentric arrangement of several layers. It begins and ends with the destruction of the Canaanites and their idols (vv. 1–6, 20–26). The reason for that destruction lies in Israel's distinctive identity and relationship to God, succinctly expressed in verse 6 and spelled out in more colorful detail in verses 13–15 and 17–24, with verse 16 summarizing the "outside" themes again. But at the center of the chapter, as the basis for Israel's elect status and blessings, stands the description of the action and character of Yahweh (vv. 7–10), which is the bedrock on which all the rest stands. The concentric arrangement can be portrayed as follows:

A Destruction of Canaanites and their gods: Israel to be holy (7:1–6)
   B God's love for the forefathers (7:7–8a) as reason for the exodus (7:8b)
      C Yahweh as the faithful God of covenant love (7:9–10)
   B′ God will fulfill the promise to the forefathers (7:11–16), so remember the exodus (7:17–19)
A′ Destruction of Canaanites and their gods, lest Israel become detestable (7:20–26)

To observe this formal structure of the chapter, however, is to be faced immediately with its ethical, theological, and missiological challenge. The "outer skin" of the chapter, as we have said, is the command to exterminate the Canaanites and destroy all physical evidence of their religion. That skin is stretched over a structural "skeleton" of a nation that must be distinct and exclusive. Yet when we finally arrive at the "heart" of the chapter, we find it beating with the passionate love of God, expressed with poetic repetition and variety. Divine love and grace stand at the core of a chapter commanding total destruction! The moral issues raised by the conquest of Canaan are significant (and we shall take them up more fully in ch. 9), but the theological issues are equally weighty. Nor can we forget the missiological dilemma. This people who are here being instructed to have no mercy on the nations in Canaan are the very people through whom, we were told, God intends to bless the nations! The paradox is quickly apparent. Whenever one teaches or preaches about the universality of the Abrahamic covenant, or the calling of Israel to be a blessing to the nations, and no matter how eloquently one does so, one will very soon face the response, "What about the Canaanites, then?" Has that universal blessing inherent in the ancestral promise been suspended or overlooked here? These are some of the questions we must bear in mind as we turn to the text.

7:1-2 / The emphasis in these verses, right up until the final instructions that come at the end, is on God's own action in bringing Israel victoriously into the land ahead of them. It would be God who would cause Israel to "enter and possess" the land and "drive out" the nations. God would "deliver" the nations into Israel's hand. To emphasize the need for divine initiative and action, the **many** nations are listed and described as **larger and stronger** than the Israelites. This is a perspective that Deuteronomy is keen to stress in order to deflate any incipient Israelite arrogance (v. 7) and to exalt the power and initiative of Yahweh (cf. 4:38; 9:3; 11:23). When Yahweh had done his part, however, the Israelites were to do theirs—**destroy them totally.** As the NIV footnote informs us, the Hebrew word translated here "totally" (*heḥerîm*) had a technical sense. The common explanation that it meant "devoting" things or people to Yahweh is probably not the best. A better explanation seems to be that it is an absolute and irrevocable *renouncing* of things or persons, a refusal to take any gain or profit from them. Thus, in obedience to this command, things or persons could be renounced without necessarily being destroyed. This explanation provides a context in which the instruction prohibiting treaties or intermarriage with the inhabitants of the land would make sense. If the local people needed to be destroyed, then verse 3 would be rather unnecessary, since everyone should have been exterminated (see additional note).

7:3-5 / The major challenge of these verses is that the Israelites were to be utterly distinct from the nations whose land they would enter. Three aspects of this crucial distinctiveness are listed here. (For a discussion of the concept of "holy war" see additional notes §23.)

Political (v. 2b). **Make no treaty with them.** The word for treaty, *bᵉrît*, is normally translated "covenant." But it was, of course, a secular word as well, and it is used in that sense here. The covenant between Yahweh as "great king" and Israel as his "vassal" required, as did all such vassal-type treaties, the total exclusion of any other alliance or treaty made unilaterally by the vassal. For Israel to enter into treaties with Canaanite nations would therefore prima facie be an act of disloyalty to their own covenant commitment to Yahweh. This suspicion of disloyalty to Yahweh remained a potent theme in the later interaction between prophets and those kings of Judah and Israel who joined in the alliance-hunting politics of the ancient Near Eastern international power games. Treaties with other nations would also require some recognition of the gods of those nations, which would likewise be intolerable for Yahweh.

Social (vv. 3–4). **Do not intermarry with them.** This prohibition was not on ethnic grounds alone; mixed marriages were not in themselves out of bounds for Israelites. Moses himself had a Cushite wife (Num. 12:1), and a later law in Deuteronomy allowed an Israelite to take a wife from among captives of war (21:10–14). What was ruled out here was the kind of intermarrying that involved the social bonding of families and joint religious rituals (something that the circumstances of 21:12f. clearly did not include). Since the prohibition in verse 3 follows so closely after verse 2b it might also be forbidding intermarriage as an adjunct to the making of treaties, a practice for which Solomon was later condemned (1 Kgs. 11; cf. Neh. 13:26). Any type of marriage that would involve compromise with idolatry was banned in the critical days of the settlement in the land (v. 4; cf. the similar motivation in the postexilic resettlement period, when Israel's distinctiveness among the nations was again threatened, Ezra 9–10; Neh. 13:23–27).

Religious (v. 5). **Break down their altars,** etc. Here lies the crux of the matter. The moral justification for the destruction of the Canaanites will be expressed later, in terms of the wickedness of their society. But in the context of the last three chapters, in which the demands of the first and second commandments have been laid bare so thoroughly, the primary object of Israel in Canaan must be the eradication of Canaan's idolatry. The polytheism of many **altars** and **idols** cannot coexist with the God of the Shema. The **sacred stones** *(maṣṣēbôt)* were standing stone pillars (a number of which have been discovered on various archaeological sites) that probably had phallic symbolism (as they still do in fertility cults in other parts of the world). The **Asherah poles** *(ᵃšērîm)* were probably made of wood, since they could be chopped down and burnt, and may have been carved images of the Canaanite goddess Asherah, female consort of Baal (1 Kgs. 18:19). Together the stone pillar and wooden image would have represented the male and female element in the fertility cult (note how Jeremiah sarcastically inverted them, Jer. 2:27!). The moral factor in the condemnation is beneath the surface but not completely absent; it is in a different but unmistakable form in 12:31.

7:6 / The actions commanded in verses 1–5 were intended to protect Israel's distinctiveness. The basis of that distinctiveness is that **the LORD your God has chosen you.** This is one of the clearest statements in Deuteronomy of Israel's election (see also 4:37; 10:15; 14:2). But it is carefully surrounded by phrases that immediately recall the key declaration of Exodus 19:4–6: **a people holy . . . out of all the peoples . . . his treasured possession.** The stress is again on Israel's distinctiveness in the midst of many other nations. They were to be "holy to Yahweh," i.e., set apart, different, belonging exclusively to him, but with the warm coloring of the last word, *sᵉgullâ.* This word was used for the private treasure of a king, who owned everything else as well, but valued his personal possessions particularly (cf. 1 Chron. 29:3; Eccl. 2:8).

The echoes of Exodus 19:4–6 are very clear in Deuteronomy, usually in places that are explicitly sanctioning or motivating Israel's distinctiveness. In 14:2, 21, Israel's holy distinctiveness is the reason for observance of the clean *food laws,* just as it is in much greater detail in Leviticus. (Lev. also echoes Exod. 19:4–6 in several contexts, including its most fundamental *social legislation* [Lev. 19:2; 20:7f., 23–26; 22:31]). In Deuteronomy 26:17–19, it is seen as the goal of the *covenant relationship,* succinctly described. In Deuteronomy 28:9f. Israel's distinctiveness is linked to *blessing for obedience,* which significantly is described in language similar to what follows here in 7:13–15 and even more significantly is linked to the observation and recognition of "all the peoples on earth" (cf. 4:6–8).

The intertextual links between all these passages in Deuteronomy and Leviticus and their foundational text in Exodus 19:4–6 are both suggestive and challenging. On the one hand, it grounds a diversity of practice in the same theological reality. The call to renounce utterly the Canaanites and to destroy their religion comes from the same source and has the same explicit theological motive and basis as the call to preserve distinctions in clean and unclean foods and to exercise social neighborliness. This makes it impossible for us simply to excise the commands relating to the Canaanites and relegate them to some allegedly inferior stage of Israel's development or to dismiss them as somehow out of symmetry with the more palatable parts of OT faith and ethics. They are too interwoven with precisely these fundamental threads of Israel's self-identity and theological affirmation to be dismissed as merely peripheral lapses into the barbaric.

On the other hand, it is impossible to observe these connections with Exodus 19:4–6 without calling to mind the additional phrase in the text that Israel was to be God's "priesthood" in the midst of the nations, a term implying a representative, mediatorial role. Israel would bring the knowledge of Yahweh to the nations (just as the priests taught the law of Yahweh to his people) and would ultimately bring the nations into covenant fellowship with Yahweh (just as the priests enabled sinners to find atonement and restored fellowship through the sacrifices). Israel's very existence in the earth was for the sake of the nations, and had been since God's promise to Abraham. But how can this be reconciled with the command to destroy the Canaanite nations? It seems extremely unlikely that the universal dimension of the Abrahamic covenant or the idea of Israel's priestly role among the nations was either unknown or simply ignored (still less rejected) by Deuteronomy. Deuteronomistic literature elsewhere is very aware of the universal intentions of God's actions in Israel (cf. Josh. 4:24; 2 Sam. 7:25f.; 1 Kgs. 8:41–43, 60; 2 Kgs. 19:19; and see introduction).

Three reflections may ease the dilemma. First, even the Abrahamic covenant had its sharp edge, its negative side. It included not only the promise of blessing but also the declaration of curse upon those who would despise Israel. From that point of view, as the book of Deuteronomy has already shown in the cases of Sihon and Og and as Exodus showed in the case of Pharaoh, resistance to God's people is self-destructive and brings God's judgment.

Secondly, the eschatological promise that all the nations of the earth would ultimately be blessed did not mean that particular nations in history would not be judged. For example, in the lifetime of Abraham, Sodom and Gomorrah suffered God's judgment. The fact that God would ultimately use the Israelites as the *vehicle of God's blessing* for the nations did not disqualify them from also being the *agent of God's judgment* on wicked and idolatrous nations. As a matter of fact, God even used the Assyrians and Babylonians in later centuries as the agents of judgment upon Israel itself. The fact that Israel's possessing the promised land involved the proximate destructions of its former inhabitants does not neutralize or contradict the fact that Israel would be the vehicle by which God would ultimately bless the nations. Israel found it possible to envisage the nations one day even applauding in worship the history of God's mighty acts for Israel, even though they included their own defeat (Ps. 47:1–3)!

Thirdly, from a missiological perspective, what was at stake was not merely the survival of the Israelites, but the preservation of the truth of the revelation of God entrusted to them and so majestically articulated in chapters 4–6. For Israel to have syncretized that revelation with Canaanite idolatry and fertility polytheism would have been no favor to the Canaanites or any other nation, but a fundamental betrayal of Israel's vocation. The progress of salvation-history included judgment, but its goal was still salvation, based on the revelation of the true God.

> The purpose of God's particular action in the history of Israel is ultimately that God, as the saving and covenant God Yahweh, should be known fully and worshipped exclusively by those who as yet imperfectly know him as El. The end result of what God began to do through Abram was of significance for the Canaanites precisely because it critiqued and rejected Canaanite religion. (Goldingay and Wright, " 'Yahweh Our God,' " p. 49)

From a canonical perspective, setting these harsh commands in the context of Israel's distinctiveness from the nations and its theological basis in verse 6 enables more fruitful reflection on the theme in a NT context. We have seen that the holiness of Israel, in the sense of their separateness from the nations, is the theological basis in Leviticus and Deuteronomy for (a) the distinctions between clean and unclean animals, which symbolized the distinction between Israel and the nations respectively; (b) the command to eradicate the Canaanites and their religion; and

(c) the social and neighborly code of conduct so profoundly set forth in Leviticus 19. Now, in the NT it is clear that the Messiah Jesus abolishes the distinction between Jews and Gentiles and that believers from both communities together constitute Israel, redefined and extended in Christ. This is the reason why, for Christians, the distinction between clean and unclean food is no longer relevant. Its basis in the national separation of Jews from the nations is gone (cf. Mark 7:1–23, followed by the story of the Syro-Phoenician woman; and Acts 10–11).

Presumably, in the same way and for the same reason, the idea of the people of God engaging in warfare against other allegedly "pagan" nations is no longer an option because the original basis of national distinctiveness (as expressed in Deut. 7:6) does not apply to the multinational community of the followers of Jesus. This, be it understood, is a theological argument based on the transformation of the nature of Israel in Jesus Christ, not merely on presumed higher Christian ethical standards or sentiments. Nevertheless, it has further basis in the oft-quoted saying from Jesus' Sermon on the Mount, "Love your enemies" (Matt. 5:43ff.). Just before this Jesus says, "You have heard that it was said, 'Love your neighbor and hate your enemy.' " "Love your neighbor" is a quotation of Leviticus 19:18—we have seen that chapter 19 is headed by the fundamental call to national holiness based on Yahweh's holiness and categorically contrasted with the nations (Lev. 18:3, 30). But it is well-known that the second half of Jesus' quote, ". . . and hate your enemy," is not from any OT text. Jesus' command, "Love your enemy," has its roots in the command that balances Leviticus 19:18, "Love [the alien] as yourself" (Lev. 19:34). The alien in Leviticus 19:34, however, was the nonthreatening, *vulnerable foreigner* who lived in Israelite communities and was easily oppressed. The radical challenge of Jesus' command was that he spoke of *the alien who was the enemy*—the powerful, oppressing enemy—Rome! The detail he added to his command makes it clear he meant the Romans (cf. Matt. 5:40f.). In the society that surrounded Jesus, Romans were viewed with the same antipathy that the Canaanites are spoken of in Deuteronomy, and for at least some sections of the population, commitment to the holiness of Israel required a fresh purging of the land of those latter-day idolatrous enemies of God and God's people. Jesus set a radically new agenda that won him few friends, but he did so without shedding an ounce of commitment to the distinctiveness of God's people. On the contrary, he emphasized it even more in calling for his followers to be utterly different from the world around them and its standards, expectations, and behaviors. That, he said, was what it meant to be "perfect" as God is perfect, or "merciful," as God is merciful—these are his distinctive interpretations of the OT demands (Matt. 5:48; Luke 6:32–36).

And so, the concept and implications of the distinctiveness of the people of God and their separation from the unholiness of the world around are not lost in the NT, even though it seeks a very different practical outworking from that envisaged in Deuteronomy 7. Even at the personal level, there are habits to be put to death (Col. 3:5–11). Even in the context of the Christian's freedom, there are idolatries to be shunned in fear of arousing God's jealousy (1 Cor. 10:14–22; 1 John 5:21). Certain kinds of alliance with unbelievers are also prohibited; this may include marriage, though the text probably does not mean that specifically (2 Cor. 6:14–18, a text that follows the prohibition on "unequal yokes" with OT warnings about idolatry and the importance of separation). But the most critical area of distinctiveness is in the ethical lives of those who have known God's "exodus" deliverance and are therefore called to be a holy, chosen people, living for God's glory. First Peter 2:9f. chains together a number of texts (including Exod. 19:5f. and Deut. 7:6) to make this point, and then immediately follows it with a recipe for Christian living "among the nations" that looks very different from what the Canaanites experienced.

7:7–8 / Thus far, the chapter has moved from the instructions as to what the Israelites were to do (vv. 1–5), to the basis of those instructions, i.e., Israel's identity as the holy, chosen, and treasured people of Yahweh (v. 6). Israel's status is grounded in the action of God in such a way as to remove any possible claims on Israel's part that their chosen status reflected their own superiority. Three times, in fact, Moses sets out to prick any self-inflated bubbles of Israelite pride. Numerical superiority is rejected as even a remotely possible reason why God should have loved them; they were a minnow among the nations. Economic arrogance is targeted in 8:17; they owed everything to the gift of God. Finally, moral self-righteousness is trounced most heavily of all in 9:4–6; the Israelites were a congenitally stiff-necked people.

The bottom line remains, as it always does in the OT, the inexplicable, self-motivated love of God. Having decided to love Israel's **forefathers,** and having made them specific promises under **oath,** God proved faithful to that promise in the exodus (v. 8). Earlier, we described the love of God as "axiomatic"—that is, having an undefined, inexplicable nature. These verses come closest to expressing that. Two different words describe God's love. God **set his affection** *(ḥāšaq).* This word denotes passionate, committed love; in human relationships, this love is often tinged with strong desire (cf. Gen. 34:8; Deut. 21:11; cf. 10:15). The other word is the commonest, *ʾāhab,* which we encountered in 6:5. The running sentence from the beginning of verse 7 to the beginning of verse 8 thus reads, (lit.) "Not because of your being numerous . . . did Yahweh desire you . . . but because of Yahweh's loving you . . . " *God loved you because God loved you!* And God proved it through action.

7:9–10 / And so we come to the core of the chapter, affirming Yahweh as God and affirming God's character as Yahweh. In the final analysis, it is because Yahweh *is* God, as well as being **your God,** and because Yahweh is **the faithful God, keeping** a **covenant of love,** that God acted as God did toward Israel. Because of that action, Israel was constituted a unique people committed to preserving a distinctiveness among the nations. On that basis, they were to make no compromise with the idolatrous and perverted polytheism of the Canaanites. It is again characteristic of the OT that Yahweh's claim to ultimate deity is founded on his action, and specifically his saving action (v. 8). "Claim to divinity is found here in the power to break the chains of slavery and oppression (cf. Ps. 82)" (P. D. Miller, *Deuteronomy,* p. 113). In the context of conflicting religious claims for rival deities (in the ancient world as much as in the modern), such a statement has considerable power and missiological cutting edge. Who is truly God? The one who proves the claim in faithfulness, integrity, committed love, and liberating, ransoming power. The same dynamic throbs through the polemical rhetoric of Isaiah 40–48.

The reactions of God to those who are God's (lit.) "lovers" and God's "haters" is developed from the second commandment (5:9b, 10), only here the order is reversed because of the emphasis on God's love in verses 7–9. Those who **love** God **keep** God's **commands** (cf. John 14:15, etc.), an interesting reverse parallelism to the fact that God also specializes in **keeping** a **covenant of love.**

Those who **hate** God are therefore those who disobey and reject God's word and hinder the fulfillment of God's covenant purposes. The verse allows no middle ground, no apathetic shrug. You either love God or hate God. But the consequences of each choice are wildly disproportionate (a thousand generations to one), showing where the overwhelming balance of God's own desires lies: Yahweh is the God who simply loves to love. The combination in these verses of the definitive nature of Yahweh in his covenant love, with the affirmation of Yahweh as God, is perhaps the nearest the OT comes to drawing the final conclusion of the logic: "God is love" (1 John 4:16; cf. Rom. 5:8).

7:11 / This verse is like a pause for breath! Its conventional exhortation is also a stylistic clue that the preceding verses do in fact represent a climax and that we have thus come to the central point of the chapter's argument. It has gone as follows: Israel needs to adopt a policy of complete renunciation of the Canaanites and their religion (vv. 1–5), because their identity and status as the people of Yahweh demands their distinctiveness from the nations (v. 6). Their distinctiveness is based on God's electing love, promise to the ancestors, and historical redemption of God's people from Egypt (7–8). This, finally, was based on the very nature and character of Yahweh himself as God (vv. 9–10).

In some ways, the rest of the chapter repeats these points in reverse, with additions and implications (see p. 108). Having "come in" and arrived at its climax, the chapter now takes us "out," returning us to the point of entry—the destruction of the Canaanites.

7:12 / And so, we take the first step back from the center and touch on the promise to the **forefathers.** This promise was not dependant on Israel's qualities, but the future enjoyment of its benefits was dependant on obedient response to the God who made it. Again we see that obedience to the law was not the means of gaining the covenant, but the means of maintaining and enjoying it.

7:13–16 / Abraham's blessing promised posterity and land. Verses 13–15 add local color to the bare words, describing what it would mean to have a growing population in a fertile land. The description is rich and rhetorical, but it is also polemical in a concealed way. The things so graphically described here, especially the fertility of wives, of land, and of domestic animals, were precisely the things that the gods of Canaan were supposed to deliver. Destroying those gods (v. 16, again), the Israelites need not fear the loss of these things. For Yahweh is Lord of all these living realities. Fruitfulness and fertility flow from Yahweh's blessing, not from the phallic and fertility cults of Baal. This lesson was sadly forgotten by Hosea's day (cf. Hos. 2:5–23).

How literally are we to take texts like Deuteronomy 7:12–15? At face value it promises Israel an idyllic, poverty-free, sickness-free life. It is easy to see how such texts can be taken up by proponents of the so-called prosperity gospel as the biblical warrant for contending that health and wealth are guaranteed to believing Christians. It certainly has to be said that the words have literal reference in their context. That is, they are talking about real crops, animals, and children and should not be spiritualized into some metaphor for any other kind of blessing. There is a healthy earthiness and physical affirmation in OT faith that should serve as a corrective to false forms of Christian world-denying asceticism or hyperspirituality.

However, there are several factors that put these verses into a wider biblical perspective that rules out a simplistic "prosperity" interpretation. First, in the OT itself health and wealth are not in themselves a reliable sign of faith and obedience (i.e., the mere enjoyment of circumstances described in vv. 13f. does not prove that the condition described in v. 12 has been met). Some people gain prosperity through oppression of others, as the prophets pointedly depict. And the lack of or loss of the good things of life may have nothing to do with personal sin or disloyalty to God, as the book of Job explores so profoundly. On the contrary, simple observation shows that often the wicked prosper and the righteous suffer, and God's covenant seems strangely inactive (Ps. 73; etc.). Secondly, a straightforwardly "mechanical" view of God's response does not fit verse 10 either. There we are told that God **will not be slow to repay to their face those who hate him.** Yet in human experience, not only are evildoers sometimes repaid very slowly, even generations later, but the very fact of the delay is elsewhere theologically interpreted in terms of God's grace leaving time for repentance (e.g., 2 Pet. 3:9 and context). Verse 10, therefore, has to be understood in terms of the unquestionably true general principle that God's judgment awaits the wicked. But it is not instant. And it is not automatic, inasmuch as God leaves room for repentance—"space for grace," as it has been called. In a similar way, verses 12–15 have to be taken as true in principle: God rejoices to bless those who are obedient and loyal to God's covenant, and their lives are enriched in many ways, not excluding the material blessings of God's world. But the connection between faith, obedience, and material blessing is neither instant and automatic, nor universally experienced. Sickness and barrenness are not the exclusive lot of the wicked even in OT times.

7:17–24 / Corresponding, now, to verse 8, the exodus is used, as it so often is in the OT, as the great encouragement for future challenges. The antidote to fear is a good memory. **Do not be afraid . . . remember well.** The same spiritual-historical psychology was directed at Joshua in 3:21–22. The emphasis throughout these verses is once again on the initiative and power of God. God would do all the driving out and delivering. All Israel would do was **wipe out their names.** The historical reality ended up somewhat differently, but the clear message is that the conquest of Canaan was the act of God, not merely an arbitrary territorial aggression.

7:25–26 / Finally the chapter returns to its opening concern, the vital importance that Israel remain unimpressed, untempted, unsnared, and uncontaminated by the idolatry of Canaan. The seriousness with which Deuteronomy treats idolatry and the insidious nature of idolatry's enticement for God's people call for a more reflective and realistic treatment for the modern missiological context than is usually offered in many discussions of the question of world religions. There is a strength of language here (**detestable . . . utterly abhor**), matched by a strength of action in chapter 13, that portrays a divine attitude toward idolatry that cannot be easily relativized or patronized with an allegedly more enlightened perspective. Yet, if we are not called to violently literal iconoclasm, and still less to the destruction of idolaters (however defined), what then is the practical relevance of such texts? We shall return to this theme in chapter 13.

Additional Notes §10

7:1 / The listing of **seven nations** is for rhetorical effect. The list is fairly standardized, but elsewhere the list can be shorter or longer (cf. Gen. 15:19–21; Exod. 3:8; 23:23; 34:11; Josh. 3:10; 24:11; 1 Kgs. 9:20; etc.). The **Hittites** were a sizable empire to the north, with their core in

Anatolia (modern Turkey) but obviously with some colonization of Palestine. **Amorites** and **Canaanites** are more general terms for the majority population. The **Jebusites** were the original inhabitants of Jerusalem, who certainly survived in the land up to the time of David (2 Sam. 5:6–8). Virtually nothing is known about the other named nations. See Ishida, " Pre-Israelite Nations."

7:2 / **You must destroy them totally:** The Hb. word found here as a verb, *hhrm* in Hiphil, and the related noun, *ḥērem,* have a complex history of interpretation. They have sometimes been said to be characteristic of Israel's concept of "holy war." But the alleged features of such a holy war are neither unique to Israel nor inherently very different from ordinary wars, and more recent scholarship advocates the disuse of the term as a way of describing OT wars. It seems that *ḥērem* denoted a specific kind of war in which all "proceeds" (booty, animals, captives) were to be renounced by Israel through being devoted to Yahweh alone. But the rules for this were not uniform. (Cf. Jones, "Holy/Yahweh War?"; Craigie, *The Problem of War.*) It appears that the number of wars that were explicitly characterized by *ḥērem* were in fact few. The law of war in Deut. 20 does not equate all war with *ḥērem,* and makes some significant distinctions. See further Lohfink, *"haram; herem,"* Lilley, *"Ḥerem,"* and additional notes §23.

7:5 / The listing of **altars, sacred stones, Asherah poles and idols** is found frequently in texts describing and condemning both Canaanite polytheism and the later Israelite syncretism that, in defiance of this law, made use of such items in corrupt Israelite worship (cf. Exod. 23:24; 34:13; Lev. 26:1; Deut. 12:2f.; 16:21f.; Judg. 3:7; 6:25–30; 2 Kgs. 18:4).

7:12–16 / An attempt to take the Deuteronomic philosophy of blessing for obedience seriously, but without a facile mechanistic connection, and to apply it to modern issues of war and peace, world hunger, and conservation, is provided by Baker, "Deuteronomy and World Problems."

7:22 / **Little by little ... not ... all at once:** Cf. Exod. 23:29. Joshua and Judges show that after the initial foothold in the land and destruction of key power centers, the actual process of conquest and settlement was a lengthy, confused, and incomplete affair (e.g., Josh. 13:1). The accounts in Joshua also reflect the "idiom and vocabulary" of conquest, which deal in generalizations that are later qualified. On the one hand, Josh. 10:29–11:23 describes conquest in terms very similar to Deut. 7—total destruction of all that breathed. On the other hand, there is clearly an element of either rhetorical or stereotypical language here; we later discover that various lands were not conquered and certain groups of Canaanites were definitely still breathing, even if somewhat heavily from being put to forced labor (Josh. 13:13; 15:63; 16:10; 17:12f.; Judg. 1).

7:25–26 / In Josh. 7, Achan disregards God's command, "do not covet . . . do not take [silver and gold] for yourselves." The subsequent destruction of his whole family was not the normal judicial consequence of theft (theft was not punishable by death in normal law), but a ruling under the special laws of the *ḥērem,* which he had violated.

§11 Not by Bread Alone (Deut. 8:1–20)

Like chapter 7, this chapter is also very skillfully organized in a loose chiastic fashion, with the same "in and out" pattern as in chapter 7.

A The land sworn to the forefathers; command given today (v. 1)
  B Wilderness as place of humbling, testing, and provision (vv. 2–6)
    C A good land (vv. 7–9)
      D You will eat and be satisfied (v. 10)
        E Bless the LORD; **Do not forget** (v. 11)
      D' You will eat and be satisfied (v. 12a)
    C' A good land (vv. 12b–14)
  B' Wilderness as place of humbling, testing, and provision (vv. 15–16)
A' Wealth, covenant with forefathers; as at this day (vv. 17–18)

Verses 19–20 stand outside this pattern and are a final emphasis of the central point of the chapter, **do not forget**, with a solemn warning.

8:1 / Another way of looking at the chapter is to see that the wilderness, which was a place of testing, produced blessing in the end (16b), whereas the land, which would be a place of blessing, would also be a place of testing of the people's loyalty and humility. There is, therefore, a twofold message to the chapter: *(a) Remember God in the hard times of the past,* and *(b) Do not forget God in the good times in the future.*

8:2 / There is always more than one way of looking at history. The most obvious evaluation of the wilderness period (1:19–46) could be that it was a monumental waste of a golden opportunity because the generation that came out of Egypt failed to go up and take the land at that time. However, in retrospect, one can see that the ensuing years were not all wasted. As Moses looks back on that time, he discerns a purpose in having a generation wander about in the wilderness. God turned it into a learning experience that must never be forgotten.

This verse has a strong sense of that purpose. God had led the people **all the way in the desert,** *in order* **to humble . . . to test . . . to know.** It was not just a matter of salvaging something positive from the wreckage of a failure. Like other events in biblical history (e.g., the story of Joseph, the rise of the monarchy, and ultimately, of course, the cross itself), the wilderness wandering is presented to us *both* as arising out of human sin and rebellion *and* as having a divine purpose.

To humble (vv. 2, 3, 16) is a verb, *ʿānāh* (in Piel), that is often used in the sense of "to afflict" by abuse or humiliation (e.g., Gen. 16:6; Exod. 22:21). When God is the subject, it can mean to punish in discipline (1 Kgs. 11:39; Isa. 64:12) or for educational purposes, as here (cf. Ps. 119:71, 75). As a response to their rebellion at Kadesh Barnea, the wilderness was indeed punishment. But as a place of learning, it was an ideal classroom. The irony is that in that very classroom the Israelites thought they were testing God (cf. 6:16 and commentary), whereas in fact it was the other way around; it was God who was testing them. The meaning of **test** is the same in both cases. It does not mean to tempt someone into doing something they would not otherwise do, but rather, it means to *prove* a person's word and intentions. Israel wanted to know if Yahweh really could do what he promised (after the exodus?!); Yahweh wanted to know if the people really would do what they had promised (cf. Exod. 24:3, 7). The wilderness was thus a learning experience for God as well as the people. God wanted **to know** what was in Israel's heart—i.e., what would be their settled disposition, attitudes, and thinking. The issue was, and still is, obedience. God's learning goes on, for the challenge of these words addresses every generation of God's people. When God puts people in the crucible of humbling affliction, what experimental results does God get from such testing of hearts and wills?

8:3 / The sharpest learning curve and the most significant lesson to be learned came through the most basic and universal form of human need—hunger. Once again we notice the paradoxical bond between natural fact and divine intention. The people's hunger in the wilderness was not just an accidental by-product of their inhospitable location. The three opening verbs all have God as the active initiator: "he humbled you and he made you hungry and he fed you . . . " The narrative of the

manna in Exodus 16 puts more emphasis on the people's grumbling, but still portrays the same sort of reciprocal learning. Thus, God was testing the people regarding their obedience (Exod. 16:4), but equally the people, as a result of the daily miracle to follow, would "know Yahweh" (Exod. 16:6, 12, 15). This gives a clue to the significance of the second half of our verse, which reads (lit.) "in order to cause you to know that not on the bread only does (or shall) humanity(*ʾādām*) live, but on everything that goes forth from the mouth of Yahweh does (or shall) humanity live."

This familiar saying is not *negating* bread and its importance (elsewhere the OT rejoices in bread as a fundamental gift of God, cf. v. 9). Moses knew as well as we do that human beings *do* live on bread. It does not quite get to the heart of the verse, either, to say that it contrasts human self-sufficiency with total dependence on God (this is closer to vv. 17f.), for the bread in question was not what Israel produced themselves but precisely a gift of God and as such a humbling daily reminder of their dependence. Nor is it merely contrasting bread as a physical thing with the spiritual word of God. In fact the form of the sentence is not so much a contrast as a climax: "not bread only, but the mouth of God." The point was that God had given the Israelites food in order to teach them something far more important than the mere fact that God was able to provide food for them. That was a significant lesson in itself (though they were no better at remembering it than most of us are in times of need). But this verse points higher. "Everything going forth from the mouth of God" includes the declaration of God's promises, the claims of God's covenant, the guidance of God's Torah, the articulation of God's purpose for creation and humanity. Words that promised bread came from the same mouth that promised much, much more. A similar contrast is given tremendous poetic and prophetic power in Isaiah 55, with its exposure of bogus breads (vv. 1f.) and its confidence in the word that goes forth from God's mouth (v. 11). So could Israel, enjoying bread, believe and act on the rest of God's utterances, trust God's guidance, obey God's commands?

All life on earth needs bread (or its equivalent); *human* life needs the mouth of God that first breathed into our nostrils. For while bread will keep us physically alive, it is the word of God that uniquely gives human life its meaning, shape, purpose, and value. It is perhaps significant that the text speaks of humanity (*ʾādām*) and not just of Israel. For when any individual or group of human beings turn a deaf ear to what has gone forth from the mouth of God, they sink to the subsistence level of consuming only bread, forfeiting the very ground and goal of their humanity. Western culture has been doing this systematically for two centuries, simultaneously trying to live by bread alone and turning the self-sufficient boast of verse 17 into a regnant economic and social policy. The resultant loss of "life"—both literally and in the loss of any undergirding consensus on the meaning, purpose, and dignity of human existence—signals, in the view of many observers, the death-throes of a culture.

8:4 / Whether this verse signifies a miraculous experience of tailoring and podiatry to match the daily manna or (as seems more likely) is a rhetorical and figurative flourish describing the remarkable survival of a whole nation in such tough conditions (cf. 8:15; 29:5; Neh. 9:21), is open to the reader to decide. Whatever was in the manna was nutritious enough, at any rate, to prevent the symptoms of famine edema. It may well have been the combination of food and clothing in these verses that inspired the teaching of Jesus about faith in God's provision in Matthew 6:25–34. It is clear that he meditated deeply on these words in the context of his "temptations" (see below), and his teaching follows the thrust of Deuteronomy 8:3 by pointing his disciples' minds beyond the mere fact of God's ability to provide, to the priority of seeking the reign of God and God's justice— matters that undoubtedly flow from the mouth of God and not just from the experience of daily bread.

8:5 / With perhaps a touch of irony, Moses presents God as doing to Israel what Deuteronomy repeatedly urges human parents to do—to exercise educative discipline over their children. The metaphor of Israel as child was used in 1:31, but with a different point. There the picture was of God's parental protection and support for a young child who needs carrying. Here the emphasis is on God's parental discipline of the growing child who needs to learn life's lessons. This was the purpose of the Sinai theophany (Deut. 4:36). The wilderness, then, was the time of Israel's adolescence, in which God taught them and disciplined them through hardship and suffering.

It is, of course, impossible to read verses 8:1–5 without thinking of Jesus and his use of Deuteronomy 8:3 when tempted by Satan in the wilderness. In fact, it is worth reading the whole paragraph through the eyes and mind of Jesus. The Synoptic

Gospels all portray the temptations of Jesus as following directly from his baptism. At his baptism, Jesus received affirmation of his identity and mission as the Son of God, in words that quoted at least two scriptures, Psalm 2:7 and Isaiah 42:1. The burden of messianic sonship and the mission of obedient, suffering servanthood that flowed from the combined texts led him into a period of intense wrestling with the future laid before him. It is hardly surprising that he turned to the opening chapters of Deuteronomy for the resources that would undergird the orientation of his life to doing the will of his Father God, for that, as we have seen, is the whole thrust of these great sermons.

There is no doubt that the evangelists intend us to notice the significance of Jesus, the Son of God, spending forty days in the wilderness suffering hunger and thirst, just as Israel, the child of Yahweh, spent forty years in the wilderness facing similar privation. No doubt Satan's repeated insinuation, "*If* you are the Son of God . . . ," was intended to induce in Jesus the same spirit of "testing God" that had so characterized Israel. Had God really meant what God had said, even in the scriptures? It was the same trick Satan had played on Adam and Eve with such tragic success. If God could feed the Israelites, why be hungry now when a miracle would solve the problem? But Jesus sees through Satan's temptations to the reality of God's testing, in its Deuteronomy 8:2 sense: what was in Jesus' heart? Would he live by the word and will of God? Would he be covenantally faithful and obedient where Israel had failed? The ancient word of Deuteronomy pierced the fog of Satan's confusing question and confirmed Jesus on the pathway of filial obedience that led ultimately through Gethsemane to the cross. Perhaps the combination of the Deuteronomic text with the tradition of Jesus' temptation and the final battle in Gethsemane is what lies behind the profound meditation on sonship, suffering, and obedience in Hebrews 5:7–8 and its implications for us in Hebrews 12:7–11.

8:7–9 / In terms of syntax, the sentence beginning at verse 7 (**For** would be better translated "When," as in 6:10) runs on continuously until the main command is finally reached in verse 11—**Be careful that you do not forget** . . . The train of thought is thus: "When God brings you into the good land . . . and you have eaten and you are satisfied and you bless the LORD . . . *then be careful* . . . " It thus follows an identical pattern to its shorter form in 6:10–12. The description of the land is rhetorical and poetic but the main point, in view of the previous context, must be the expectation that **bread will not be scarce** (v. 9). Whatever lessons God may have taught through hunger in the wilderness, God's desire for people is not scarcity but sufficiency. And **you will lack nothing;** the verb is the same as expresses the psalmist's familiar confidence that, with Yahweh as his shepherd, he would lack nothing (Ps. 23:1).

8:10 / The experience of God's blessing should produce the response of blessing God. **Praise** is more correctly "Bless" **the LORD your God.** **When you have eaten and are satisfied** refers more fully to the enjoyment of all the material gifts of the good land, but it is appropriate to take it literally as well and see in the verse a biblical justification for "saying grace" by blessing the LORD *after* meals as well as before (as in Jewish custom). The substantive point is that, however it be expressed, gratitude to God the giver is the only fitting response to realities such as the good land promised in verses 7–9 and its equivalent in any context of human life.

8:11 / Unfortunately, a more common response than gratitude is the forgetfulness this verse warns against in the climax of the chapter. Forgetfulness is not merely a matter of amnesia. To **forget the LORD** involves at least two things, both of which are characteristic of what it means to "forget a person" (as distinct from merely forgetting a fact). First, it means forgetting all the history of what God had done for them, both the lessons of the hard times (vv. 2–5) and the blessings of the good times (vv. 7–9). To forget a person is to lose touch with the story of the relationship and all it meant in the past and should still mean now. That is why it is such a hurtful and diminishing thing to "feel forgotten" by other human beings (or by one in particular) with whom one has shared a story in relationship. This is no less true for the God of Israel. Such "forgetting" is felt as deliberate rejection, not just as a mental lapse. So much of the pain of God expressed through the prophets (who frequently shared it in their own lives) is the result of this kind of forgetting.

Secondly, forgetting God is defined in verse 11b as moral disobedience, as **failing to observe** God's **commands.** In the OT memory is closely linked to obedience. It is possible, according to this verse and those following it, to be enjoying the material blessings of God and yet be living in fundamental and forgetful disobedience to God. While this situation will not ultimately last

(vv. 19f.), it has lasted long enough to cast serious doubt on the kind of automatic and immediate connections that purveyors of prosperity gospels would like to make between material wealth and personal faith and obedience.

8:12–16 / The phrase **eat and are satisfied** is repeated, alerting us to the literary structure. We have heard the central point in verse 11; the "preacher" will now lead us back "out" through his points in reverse. This is not an exact repetition, however. A number of small additions give a fresh coloring to this second half of the chapter. The source of forgetfulness will be pride, and the exodus is mentioned as another "foil" to the sheer unnaturalness of forgetting such a God (v. 14). How could they forget all God had done? The hardness and danger of life in the wilderness is spelled out more graphically, and the gift of water as well as manna is recalled (v. 15). The beneficial effect of God's discipline in the wilderness is highlighted: **so that in the end it might go well with you** (v. 16b), just as parents may say, as they punish a child, "You'll thank me for this some day!"

Another subtle difference between the verses leading up to the central v. 11 and those coming away from it may lie in the two descriptions of Israel's life in the land. In verses 7–9 the emphasis is on the land and its natural resources that will provide the people with enough to live without scarcity. The response should be to praise God (v. 10). In verses 12–13 the emphasis is on Israel's own productive use of the resources so given, resulting in abundance of everything, luxury, settling down, and great wealth. The tragic pitfall would be to become proud and forget God (v. 14) and to have an attitude of self-asserting achievement (v. 17). (Actually, vv. 12–18, like 7–11, are one whole sentence. The verbs in vv. 15–16 are all participles describing God's actions. The main verb is **remember** in v. 18). Thus there seems to be a balancing truth—which is fairly characteristic of OT thinking on economic matters and is well illustrated in Israelite history—that *sufficiency generates praise* (vv. 7–10), *but surplus generates pride* (vv. 12–14).

8:17–18 / The source of forgetfulness was the kind of pride that could ignore the incredible history of Israel with its God. Again, it helps to run the verbs by in rapid sequence, as indeed their participial form invites, as a kind of verbal "action replay." **The LORD your God** is the one who "saved you" (**brought you out,** v. 14), **led you** (v. 15), "watered you" (v. 15b), "fed you"

(v. 16), and "gifted you" (v. 18). What was there to be proud about? Nevertheless, Moses anticipates the boast of the self-made man worshipping his creator (v. 17). How well he knew human nature! The portrayal of the "yuppie's" boast is so perceptive and so accurate—psychologically as well as empirically. This verse could also be read as a capitalist charter, because it implies that whatever **my power and the strength of my hand** produce in the way of **wealth** is **for me**. That is, it is mine to enjoy, to exploit as I wish. My abilities, my strength, my hard work, my cleverness, and my professional skills, produced it, *ergo,* it is mine. Self-exaltation and self-interest underlie the claim.

Now the OT certainly praises hard work and the achievements that flow from it (Prov., passim). But the rest of the law (as we shall see in later sections) undercuts any idea that "what's mine is mine because I produced it," by subjecting it to the demands of compassion and the common welfare. "I made it so I own it" is never the bottom line of biblical economics. Verse 18 sticks a very simple but fundamental pin in verse 17's balloon of complacency and pride. "You say your own power and strength produced this wealth? And where do you think *they* came from?" The fact is that all human strength, gifts, abilities, and life itself, along with the material resources out of which the wealth has been created, are the gift of God. We are as little the makers of our own strength as we are the makers of the earth. So, to **remember the LORD** is to recognize that all is from God, as David later expressed with great eloquence. This is the first principle of biblical economics. The earth is the Lord's and everything in it (Ps. 24:1), but he has given it to the human race for our use (Ps. 115:16). Humility in the accountable stewardship of what has been given to us is thus as much a principle of human use of the resources of the earth as it was for Israel's use of the land God gave them in fulfillment of God's promise.

8:19–20 / These verses reinforce the central warning of the whole chapter and then follow it with a serious threat. If the people persist in forgetful idolatry, they will face destruction **like the nations the LORD destroyed before you.** Following chapter 7 with commands to ruthlessly exterminate the nations, this threat is particularly chilling. In the earlier chapter the destruction of the Canaanites was not arbitrary, but was morally required by reasons that are about to be spelled out more explicitly in chapter 9. God's giving the land to Israel was not the whimsey of divine favoritism, but was part of a two-way obligation, requiring the obedience of Israel if it was to be permanently enjoyed. If Israel behaved like the nations it had dispossessed, it in turn would be dispossessed like them. This chapter is a solemn affirmation of the consistency of Yahweh as God as well as a solemn warning against presumption (cf. Heb. 4:1–11; 10:26–31).

Additional Notes §11

The concentric structure of ch. 8 was observed and laid out by Lohfink, *Hauptgebot,* p. 195. Lohfink's outline has been refined and modified in much greater verbal detail by O'Connell, "Deuteronomy viii 1–20."

8:1 / **Every command:** Better, "all the command." The focus is on the law as a whole, in principle, and in its fundamental purpose, rather than on every detailed command (cf. the following verses, where the Hb. is similarly singular: 6:1, 25; 7:11; 11:8, 22; 15:5; 19:9; 27:1).

8:3 / Part of the literary artistry of this chapter is that the expression "what goes forth from the mouth of Yahweh" uses the same word as is used for God's bringing Israel forth from Egypt (v. 14) and bringing water forth from the rock (v. 15). On the wordplay, see van Leeuwen, "God's Mouth."

8:5 / The association of the wilderness with Israel's adolescence is a powerful metaphor used by Hosea and Jeremiah. For Hosea, it was the time when God, in parental love, brought God's child Israel out of Egypt, but then experienced the pain of Israel's rejection and rebellion (Hos. 11:1–2). Nevertheless, Hosea also used the wilderness as an eschatological motif looking forward to when God would again betroth Israel as a bride (Hos. 2:14ff.). Jeremiah portrayed Israel as that bride in the historical wilderness period, seeing it as a honeymoon period of youthful married love and devotion (Jer. 2:2).

8:12–15 / A very close parallel to these verses is found in Hos. 13:4–6, which also includes a clear allusion to the opening of the Decalogue.

§12 Not because of Israel's Righteousness (Deut. 9:1–10:11)

The warnings against false assumptions continue. Moses has already demolished any idea of national chauvinism arising from Israel's election (7:6–10) and also any economic arrogance arising from their future prosperity (8:17f.). In this chapter he targets what is perhaps the most pernicious and perennial distortion of all—moral self-righteousness in the interpretation of military conflict. Together, these three challenges penetrate deeply to the evergreen sources of human pride: the idolatries of racism, materialism, and militarism. The thrust of this chapter, though directed at Israel, goes to the heart of a universal phenomenon in the behavior of human beings, governments, and nations. In its prophetic power to challenge a complacent people, it matches the uncompromising rhetoric of Amos. In its unwelcomeness to national leaders and myth-makers, it stands alongside the parables of Jesus and the speech of Stephen in Acts 7. In its relevance to modern claims and counterclaims to "right" in international conflicts, it still speaks today.

9:1–3 / The opening verses of Deuteronomy 9:1–10:11 summarize many of the themes of the book from the beginning to this point. The task ahead was formidable. The **cities** and **nations** that had induced such fear in the exodus generation were still there and the next generation knew all about them (v. 2). Moses even chants the litany of inferiority that the spies had brought back (cf. 1:28). But his strategy to counter that fear was not to try to shrink the enemy by false propaganda but rather to strengthen faith in Israel's one great ally—Yahweh their God. God would be in the vanguard, going **ahead of** them. The **devouring fire** that they had feared so much at Sinai (4:24; 5:25) would be turned against their enemies. God is the one who will **destroy** and **subdue** (v. 3a).

9:4–6 / The euphoria of victory is as likely to produce moral self-congratulation as the rewards of economic labor is likely to produce imagined self-sufficiency (8:17). There is a regular concern in these chapters for what people **say** to themselves (cf. 7:17; 8:17; 15:9). So Moses, with characteristically sharp instincts, envisages what will be said when the campaign dust settles. At a primary theological level, these verses reinforce the point made already in many ways that Israel owed all they were and all they possessed to the grace and gift of God, and not in any way to their own merit. They could stake no claim on divine favors in advance, nor could they retrospectively explain any success and prosperity that came their way as the due reward for their righteousness.

It is probably right to take the whole of verse 4 as what the people would say to themselves (see additional note), rather than breaking it by inserting **No** in the middle (NIV). They wanted to make a straightforward equation: *"Our victory = our righteousness + the enemy's wickedness."* But Moses disallows the validity of this equation. Verse 5 denies part of it (**not because of your righteousness or your integrity**), but affirms part (**but,** yes, as you say, **on account of the wickedness of these nations**). The Israelites would be right in their estimation of the Canaanites, but utterly wrong in their estimation of themselves. The wickedness of the Canaanites did not prove the righteousness of Israel.

To this correction of their false inference, Moses adds two other reasons why Israel could never attribute the conquest to their own righteousness. The conquest would simply be God keeping God's own promise, **to accomplish what he swore to your fathers** (v. 5b). Israel could not claim credit for the promise itself, or for its fulfillment. Additionally, far from the conquest being *because of* their righteousness, it was actually *in spite of* their stubborn provocations of divine wrath (v. 6b). It was only by God's grace (and the intercession of Moses, vv. 18–29) that Israel was not destroyed along with the rest of the nations. Thus, the corrected equation would be: *"Our victory = God's promise to Abraham, Isaac, and Jacob + the enemy's wickedness."*

Theologically, then, these verses stand along with the rest of Deuteronomy in affirming divine grace and denying human claims on God arising out of self-attributed righteousness. They present an OT theological equivalent of the arguments of the Apostle Paul in Romans 1–3. Israel had many advantages and blessings that were undeniable and based on God's election, but when it comes to moral standing before God, to matters of relative guilt or innocence, then there is fundamentally no difference between Israel and the nations, Jews and Gentiles. All alike stand under God's judgment (cf. Miller, *Deuteronomy*, pp. 121ff.).

Ethically, these verses offer an important perspective on the moral problem of the conquest. Was it not fundamentally immoral, it is often asked, that Israel should have invaded Canaan, defeated and destroyed the peoples there, and taken over their land? It does not ease the moral issue to point out that the process was certainly much more complex than the biblical narrative alone records, or that other factors, such as internal revolt, may have been involved, or that not so many people were actually exterminated as these texts envisage. The point is that these texts set up a picture of at least what *should have* happened and consistently present it as the command of Yahweh.

What does, however, transform the ethical landscape is the declaration of the wickedness of the Canaanites. For this sets the conquest within the moral framework of divine justice operative within history in and among nations. An act that would be immoral if committed arbitrarily and without justification (beating another human being, for example), can take on a very different moral significance when set in the context of punishment by legitimate authority for specific wrongdoing. We can recognize the wrongness of pain inflicted in the first case and the rightness (or appropriateness) of pain imposed in the second case, in principle, even if we might argue over cases, degrees, and methods.

The OT consistently declares that the reason for the destruction of the Canaanites was their wickedness. This is first expressed in advance in Genesis 15:16, where the "iniquity of the Amorites" is spoken of in the same breath as the forecast sin of the Egyptians, which would likewise be "punished." This text is significant not only because it links the punishment of the Canaanites with the fulfillment of the promise to Abraham, just as our text here does, but also because it explains the postponement of such judgment in relation to the *degree* of their wickedness: "the sin of the Amorites has not yet reached its full measure." In other words, in the days of Abraham, God, "the judge of all the earth," did not regard the wickedness of Canaanite civilization as having yet reached such a stage of depravity as to deserve the full weight of God's destructive judgment. That stage had now come.

The same perspective, namely, that the depravity of the Canaanites was the reason for their expulsion by God, is affirmed in Leviticus 18:3, 24–30; 20:22–24, and Deuteronomy 12:31; 18:12; 20:18. It is also the consistent interpretation found in the Deuteronomistic historical texts (1 Kgs. 14:24; 21:26; 2 Kgs. 16:3; 17:8; 21:2). However, in these texts we find the converse and equally challenging point that *God both threatened to do, and finally did do, to the Israelites exactly what he had done to the Canaanites for the same catalogue of wickedness.* Deuteronomy 8:19–20 has made this point in the immediate context of our text. God's action against the Canaanites, then, was not an arbitrary act of inter-ethnic violence, nor was it an act of divine favoritism toward Israel. God demonstrated divine moral consistency in ultimately dealing with both groups in the same way.

But there are other levels of significance in this text. The topic of the inner dialogue in verse 4 is the question of international right and wrong. Warfare was commonly considered in the ancient world as the arbiter of international justice. Those whom the gods adjudged to be in the right were the victors; the losers were clearly the opposite. The terms **righteousness** and **wickedness** in Israel's evaluation in verse 4 are probably forensic in the way they are used here. They are concerned with who was in the right and who was in the wrong; who was innocent and who was guilty. And the Israelites' conclusion from the historical events decides the matter with binary logic: if the nations were judged to be wicked, then Israel therefore must be deemed to be righteous. But this logic overlooks God's evaluation of *both* parties. The Canaanites' wickedness did *not* establish Israel's righteousness. Nor did God's *use* of Israel as the agent of God's judgment assume or confer righteousness on Israel's part. In later history, the same problem in reverse puzzled Habakkuk, who could not understand God's use of nations as wicked as the Mesopotamian empires to punish Israel themselves. And in the same way, the fact that God *did* use Assyria and Babylon as agents of judgment on Israel's wickedness did not make those nations righteous or treat them as such. Quite the opposite. The paradox of providence, unpopularly taught by the prophets, was that God could use the most deeply unjust nations as the agents of achieving God's own sovereign dispensing of historical justice in the international arena. The "rod of God's anger" (Isa. 10:5) did not have to be straight.

This brings us to the question of whether there can be a modern-day "just war." It may well be the case that God can use one nation (or several) as the agent of divine judgment on

another nation through war, for the restraining of evil ("defend-
ing the bad against the worse," as it has been called) or the
relative (and usually highly ambiguous) righting of wrongs. But
even where such a view is taken of a particular conflict, our text
warns against the facile assumption that righteousness adorns
the victorious nation or nations. Since the Bible so clearly shows
that God can use the wicked to punish the wicked, it follows that
a technically "just war" can be fought and won by a deeply unjust
nation that itself stands under the judgment of God. Unfortunately, however, modern nations are as prone as the Israel of our
text to opt for a monochrome morality that demonizes the enemy
and deifies one's own nation and its cause. The temptation to
equate military superiority with moral superiority, with all its
political and propaganda potential, is hard to resist. And so is the
idolatrous tendency to claim for one's own cause the name and
support of the God otherwise excluded from all consideration.
Recent history has given us, in the Falklands and Gulf Wars, for
example, some disturbing examples of military victories being
decked out with all the aura of self-righteous self-congratulation
that deserves to be publicly challenged with the prophetic "NO"
of these verses: **NOT because of your righteousness or your
integrity . . . !**

9:7–8 / If part of the intention of verses 4–6 was to justify
the conquest in terms of the wickedness of the Canaanites, one
might have expected the rhetoric to continue with a few choice
examples of that pagan wickedness (such as we find, for example,
in 12:31). Instead, we are given a lengthy and pointed recollection of an outstanding example of *Israel's* wickedness, plus a brief
catalogue of some lesser examples (v. 22f.). Clearly, Deuteronomy
is more concerned with the failures of God's people than with the
wickedness of the other nations, just as the OT in general pours
more condemnation on Israel's idolatry than on that of the nations. As a matter of missiological interest, it is arguable that
dwelling overmuch on the wickednesses and idolatries of "the
pagans" (so-called) can induce precisely the kind of national,
ecclesiastical, or cultural superiority complex that Israel's self-
righteousness illustrates here. The strategy of Deuteronomy
9:1–10:11 undermines such delusions by declaring that the
people of God are as deserving of God's destruction as the
worst of the nations (v. 8) and that only by God's grace are they
spared it.

The parting shot of the previous section's warning against self-congratulation was Moses' description of Israel as "a stiff-necked people" (9:6). This graphic metaphor pictures the hard, unbending neck of a stubborn animal that refuses to cooperate with its owner's wishes. As a term for Israel's stubborn rebellions against God it comes primarily from the story about to be recollected from Exodus 32–34 (cf. Exod. 32:9; 33:3, 5; 34:9). These words of introduction to the rest of the chapter show that Moses' intention was to douse completely Israel's self-righteousness by reminding them of past rebellion. Although Moses singles out a particular example, verses 7 and 24 show that this was no exceptional lapse, but simply the most horrendous illustration of their congenital and ingrained stubbornness.

The choice of the rebellion **at Horeb** (Sinai) is doubly significant. First, because that was where the covenant had been initiated. No sooner had it been made than the people broke its most fundamental requirements. The covenant had not been based on, and certainly could not be sustained by, Israel's own righteousness, so any grounds for future boasting were cut from under them. And secondly, on that occasion God **was angry enough to destroy** them—but didn't. The emphatic use of the same word, (hašmîd, "destroy") as was used in verse 3 for God's destruction of the Canaanite nations is very pointed. And it is reinforced in verse 14, where God actually threatened to do to the Israelites exactly what they were commanded to do to the Canaanites: to **destroy them and blot out their name from under heaven** (cf. 7:23f.). So, far from Israel's estimation of the reason for their successes, the fact was that if anyone deserved to be destroyed it was the Israelites themselves, and long ago. Their very existence on the edge of the promised land, let alone their future possession of it, was proof of the mercy and grace of God.

9:9–14 / What we have here, and continuing until 10:11, is a fairly free recollection of the great apostasy of the golden calf at the foot of Mt. Sinai (Exod. 32–34). There is a lot of common phraseology and the end result is the same. There are some difficulties in correlating the precise chronological order of events, particularly regarding exactly when Moses went up and down the mountain, when he fasted and interceded, and when God made various responses. But these are almost certainly due to the nature of this account as a recollection aimed at highlighting the significant theological point of the story, rather than to a confusion of sources and a complex redactional history. It greatly assists understanding of the Deuteronomy text to read Exodus 32–34 in full first. The main focus of 9:9–14, and continuing to verse 21, lies in the words of God to Moses in verses 12–14. The first of three striking features is the way God, speaking to Moses, refers to Israel as **your people whom you brought out of Egypt.** The double "you and yours" amounts to virtual repudiation of the people. It is not quite as explicit as "Not *my* people" (Hos. 1:9), but it implies as much. The Sinai covenant had been broken by the people; the smashing of the covenant tablets would demonstrate that. So the covenant words "my people" are pointedly avoided and the exodus is reduced to an act of human enterprise. The horrific import of the words was not missed by Moses, as we shall see from his intercession. It seems that Moses immediately began protesting such words, leading God to exclaim, **Let me alone . . . !** (v. 14; cf. Targum, "Stop your prayer from before me"; see also below, after v. 29). Worse was to follow.

The second striking feature of this section is when God threatens, not only to repudiate the Sinai covenant by disowning the people, but even to abandon the Abrahamic covenant by destroying the people and *starting all over again with Moses!* This incredible implication of the words, **and I will make** *you* **into a nation stronger and more numerous than they,** is even clearer in the explicit, verbal echo of the Abrahamic covenant in Exodus 32:10, "Then I will make you into a great nation." Such was the wrath of God with this people that God could contemplate a virtual repetition of the flood scenario: total destruction of this nation, and then a renewal of the promise and redemptive agenda with one faithful person, Moses (for a fascinating comparison of Exod. 32–34 with the flood narrative, see Moberly, *Mountain of God*, pp. 91–93).

9:15–21 / The shock of God's words is allowed to sink in by postponing the details of Moses' intercession, which in Exodus 32:11–14 followed immediately, until after describing the actions taken regarding the golden calf. Two of these are echoed from the Exodus narrative. The smashing of the two stone tablets of the covenant (vv. 15–17) was like a prophetic sign (cf. Jer. 19) that signified the broken covenant. Moses did not drop them accidentally in shock. This was a deliberate public action, **before your eyes,** with an unmistakable message. The burning and destruction of the golden image was an object lesson in what

Israel was to do to the idols of other nations (7:25). The people of God should not need to be treated like the other nations. What had once been earrings and ornaments of the Egyptians was now ground to dust as God despoiled God's own people in judgment (cf. Exod. 32:2f.; 33:5f.).

The third striking feature, however, is unique to the Deuteronomic account, namely, the reference to Moses' intercession on behalf of Aaron (v. 20). If even Israel's original high priest, with all the holiness the tradition attached to him and his family, far from being righteous in himself had stood under the anger of God and in danger of destruction but for Moses' intercession, what possible grounds could there be for the rest of the people to claim their own righteousness? Notice the double dose of near-destruction, **angry enough . . . to destroy you; angry enough . . . to destroy him** (vv. 19f.).

9:22–24 / Still the life-saving words of intercession are held in suspense as Moses throws into his argument a few more examples of rebellion from his wilderness diaries. The three place names in verse 22 all have sinister sounding meanings, related to the events that took place there: "burning" (**Taberah,** Num. 11:1–3); "testing" (**Massah,** Exod. 17:1–7); and "graves of craving" (**Kibroth Hattaavah,** Num. 11:31–34). The rebellion at **Kadesh Barnea** had already been fully exploited for its didactic value in 1:19–46.

9:25–29 / At last we reach the words that stood between God's anger and God's mercy: the prayer of Moses. God, we recall, had threatened to renounce both the Sinai covenant (by disowning the people) and the Abrahamic covenant (by destroying them and starting again with Moses). Moses, with incredible boldness, raises his hand to God on both counts and comes as close as one can imagine to rebuking God for suggesting such things. Whether he ever allowed the idea of himself taking over from Abraham as the father of a great nation to tempt him (was God also "testing" Moses in this encounter to see what was in *his* heart?), we cannot tell. Faced with the endless burden of a people who had been rebels as long as he had known them (v. 24), Moses could be forgiven for entertaining the thought of their instant extinction. But Moses is not only the model intercessor but also the model leader of God's flock (cf. Heb. 3:2–5). He was totally committed to them. Rebels they might indeed be, but they were

still the people of Yahweh, and Yahweh was a God with promises
to keep and a reputation to think of.

And so Moses' intercession focuses on three points, on
which he knew he was speaking to the heart of his God. (a) God
had entered into a covenant relationship with this people that
God simply could not now repudiate. The repeated second-person
in **do not destroy** *your* **people,** *your own* **inheritance that** *you*
redeemed . . . (v. 26), is meant to challenge the words of God in
verse 12. And the point is doubly emphasized by the concluding
repetition of the phrases in verse 29. Human beings in general
may prove false to their word. Israel in particular had spectacu-
larly done so. But Yahweh, the God who was "one," and whose
very being is defined by "faithfulness" (6:4; 7:9) surely could not
abandon his commitment. This people were Yahweh's people,
because Yahweh had made them so. (b) The people's status was
founded even further back in God's oath to the ancestors. So let
God **remember** them, as a judge "remembers" factors in favor of
a defendant (v. 27). God could not abandon the promise to Abraham without breaking God's own oath, sworn on God's own
very being (Gen. 15). It would be self-destructive. (c) And finally,
in a bold stroke, Moses appeals to God's jealousy for the honor of
God's own name. So much of what had happened thus far had
been explicitly so that the nations would know the truth about
who Yahweh was. What kind of God would they take Yahweh
to be, then, if he destroyed the very people he had so miraculously delivered (v. 28f.; this line of argument is developed
even more fully in Moses' other major intercession at Kadesh
Barnea, see Num. 14:13–16). People would not know what to
believe about God if God carried out the threatened destruction of Israel. Let God then protect God's own name.

The LORD listened to me (9:19; 10:10). The intercession of
Moses was effective because it went to the heart of God's own
priorities as Moses already knew them from his long intimacy
with God: God's people, God's promises, God's name. As a
model of intercession, his prayer stands at the head of a list of OT
prayers that follow a similar pattern and focus on the same
priorities (cf. Dan. 9:1–19; Neh. 9; Joel 2:17b); it is a powerful
model for God's people at all times.

There is, of course, a mystery about prayer in general and
intercession in particular, and this classic case study in intercessory prayer never fails to raise questions about the ways of God
and the implications of how the conversation unfolds between

God and Moses. Was God really serious in this declared threat? If Moses had not interceded, would God have carried out the destruction of Israel? Had God really forgotten the things Moses challenged God to "remember?" If God was not really planning to destroy the people (10:10b), did God only "pretend" to listen to Moses' prayer? Did Moses actually change God's mind?

In answering such questions it seems important first of all to say that there is not much point in wrestling with alternative hypothetical scenarios posed by such questions. The text purports to lay before us a genuine encounter between Moses and the God of Israel in which history meshed with prayer in a meaningful way. Asking "what if" serves little theological purpose. Secondly, however, it seems equally important to preserve the integrity of the encounter. Both God and Moses appear to be behaving straightforwardly. There is nothing in the text to suggest that God's anger was overdone for mere effect; no suggestion that God's threat was a bluff intended to secure a hasty repentance. Psalm 106:23 indicates the critical nature of the event: the threat of destruction was real. Likewise, Moses took God's words with utmost sobriety. His reaction to the divine wrath was not a patronizing dismissal of authority, "You can't be serious!" Rather, he recognized that this was a sincere threat that could be countered only with appeal to prior words and actions of the same God. The paradox is that in appealing to God to change, he was actually appealing to God to be consistent—which may be a significant clue to the dynamic of all genuine intercessory prayer. So, on both sides, it is vital to maintain the full seriousness of the words spoken and the intentions expressed through them, otherwise the whole encounter, and more significantly, the whole personal relationship between God and Moses, loses both credibility and personal integrity.

Yet perhaps there is a hint of the divine intention in the enigmatic words, **Let me alone . . .** (v. 14). As Childs points out (*Exodus*, p. 567), classic Jewish commentators have sensed deep meaning here. After all, God need not have spoken such words, or indeed any words at all, to Moses. In wrath God could have acted "immediately" without informing or consulting Moses in any way. Yet, just as God involved Abraham in the "consultation" prior to the judgment on Sodom and Gomorrah (which also led to intercession, though with a different outcome, Gen. 18:16–33), so here God pauses and makes the divine will "vulnerable" to human challenge.

The fact is that, far from human intercession being an irritating but occasionally successful intrusion upon divinely pre-fabricated blueprints for history, it is actually an integral part of the way God's sovereignty in history is exercised. That does not totally solve the mystery, but it puts it in its proper biblical perspective. God not only allows human intercession, God *invites* it (in later biblical texts God also commands it), and builds it into the decision-making processes of the heavenly council in ways we can never fathom. "God takes Moses' contribution with utmost seriousness; God's acquiescence to the arguments indicates that God treats the conversation with Moses with integrity and honors the human insight as an important ingredient for the shaping of the future" (Fretheim, *Suffering of God*, pp. 50f.).

Intercessory prayer, then, flows primarily not from human anxiety about God but from God's commitment to relationship with human beings. It reflects not just a dissonance between how things are and how we would like them to be but an even deeper dissonance in the heart of God over God's boundless love for an unlovely world and God's covenantal faithfulness to a covenantally unfaithful people. Moses was not so much arguing *against* God (though it doubtless felt like it), as participating in an argument *within* God (a tension expressed in Num. 14:17–19). Such prayer, therefore, not only participates in the pain of God in history, but is actually invited to do so for God's sake as well as ours. This is a measure of the infinite value *to God* of commitment to persons in covenant relationship. God chooses in sovereign freedom to link that divine sovereign freedom to human prayer. Intercessory prayer, then, as a divine-human engagement, is not merely a human duty to be fulfilled as part of the mission of the people of God, but ultimately flows from and into God's own mission in the created world (cf. Rom. 8:18–27).

10:1–5 / The outcome of Moses' intercession is made clear by the report of the renewed covenant in 10:1–5 and of the resumed journey in 10:6–11. The main focus of verses 1–5 is on the rewriting of the Ten Commandments and the storage of the two tablets in the ark as the tangible sign of a renewed covenant. Verse 5 is like calm after the storm of God's anger is averted by Moses' intercession. Having the commandments in the ark in the midst of the people was symbolic of the "nearness" of God again. Things can now move forward, away from the brink of God's threatened destruction.

With the narrative of Exodus 34 again in the background, the recollection of events is summary and general rather than sequentially precise. For instance, there is no mention of the making of the ark in Exodus 34 itself (the plans for it are given in Exodus 25:10–21). Although in verse 3 Moses claims **I made the ark,** the actual making of the ark was the work of Bezalel (Exod. 37:1–9). Moses is speaking here as the initiator behind the making of the ark by a craftsman.

10:6–9 / At first reading these verses seem to have little relation to the preceding narrative. Verses 6–7 seem to be extracted from the records of Israel's itinerary. Doubtless this accounts for the NIV putting them in parenthesis, since it is also clear that verses 10f. connect very naturally and conclusively from verse 5. Yet since the verses are in our text, we must examine their hermeneutical importance. It seems that at least three purposes are served by them. First, the historical note about the itinerary of Israel seems to be the narrator's way of saying that Moses' intercession for Israel was manifestly successful. The Israelites not only survived but they resumed their journey toward the promised land. Second, by choosing to mention the death of Aaron and Eleazar's succeeding him to the high priesthood, the narrative makes clear that Moses' intercession on Aaron's behalf (9:20) was also successful; not only did Aaron not die at the time of the great apostasy but his family remained the heirs of his priesthood. Third, by briefly summarizing the duties of the Levites, these verses establish that all the gifts of God mediated through the Levites are still intact: the ark itself, the proper service of God, and the blessing of the people in Yahweh's name.

10:10–11 / The whole section ends, as it began in 9:1, with the onward movement of the people into the land of promise. In the light of all that has come between the beginning and the end of the section, this should be a chastened people about to move into the land; a people with every confidence in their God, but with no illusions about themselves.

Additional Notes §12

9:2 / **Anakites:** Cf. 1:28.

9:3 / **Quickly:** In this context, "quickly" is used to give the people assurance of success, but is qualified in reality (cf. 7:22f.).

9:4 / The best sense is gained if the direct speech of the people is continued to the end of verse 4. This also avoids the apparently redundant repetition of verse 4b in verse 5. The word **No** is not strictly in the Hb.; it is an interpretative rendering of the simple conjunction "and," on the translators' assumption that the people's speech stops at **because of my righteousness** and Moses' answer begins with the following words. However, it seems probable that the people were making a "legal" double assumption of innocence and guilt (see commentary), which Moses corrects. Thus, the better translation would be, "Do not say to yourself, 'The LORD has brought me here to take possession of this land because of my righteousness, and because of the wickedness of the nations the LORD is going to drive them out.' It is not because of your righteousness . . .'"

9:6 / **Stiff-necked:** Cf. Deut. 10:16; 31:27; Jer. 7:26; 17:23; 19:15. For a profound interpretation of its significant role in the narrative of Exod. 32–34, see Moberly, *Mountain of God*, pp. 89–93.

9:7–10:11 / The critical questions involved in accounting for the similarities and the differences between this Deuteronomic version and Exod. 32–34 are complex, but the varied attempts at explaining them on source-critical grounds appear to pay little attention to the literary structure and coherence of both texts and seem to add very little to the theological understanding of either. For helpful collation of the texts and documentary approaches to the divergences, see Driver, *Deuteronomy*, pp. 112ff., and Mayes, *Deuteronomy*, pp. 198ff.

9:9 / **Forty days and forty nights; I ate no bread and drank no water:** This is probably a stylized idiomatic description of a prolonged and serious fast. It is probably not meant to be a precise statement of the length of the fast or to be taken literally as regards water. No human body, not even one with the octogenarian vigor of Moses, can survive forty days without liquid (eighty days if the fast of v. 18 is meant to signify a second period) and certainly not in the hot, dry climate of the Sinai peninsula. The intensity of Moses' fasting signifies the momentous, historic significance of the giving of the law and the horrendous threat faced by the people because of their sin.

The phrase "forty days and forty nights" may function as a literary "divider" in 9:9–10:11, breaking up the narrative into five sections by its five occurrences and thereby also showing the progression and unity of the passage: (a) 9:9f., the making of the covenant; (b) 9:11–17, the breaking of the covenant; (c) 9:18–21, dealing with the sin of the people; (d) 9:25–10:5, Moses' intercession and the renewal of the covenant; (e) 10:10f., the resumption of the journey toward the fulfillment of the promises (see Lohfink, *Hauptgebot*, pp. 214–16).

9:10 / On **stone tablets,** and **the assembly,** see the additional note on 5:22. **The finger of God,** as an expression for God's direct power, is also found in Exod. 8:19; 31:18; and Ps. 8:3. For a discussion of Jesus' use of it in Luke 11:20, in a controversy with some echoes of Deut. 9, see Wall, " 'The Finger of God.' "

9:21 / Deuteronomy records that the gold dust of the idol was scattered in the stream, which may symbolize that its curse was carried away. Exod. 32:20 says that Moses made the people drink it, which may have similar symbolism to the drinking of the water of the curse (Num. 5:17–28). Either way, the gold of the idol was destroyed beyond any possibility of recovery and reuse.

9:25–29 / On Moses as intercessor, see Miller, "Moses, My Servant"; cf. also Balentine, *Prayer,* pp. 135–39.

10:1–5 / Some scholars contrast the description of the ark here as a mere box to store the tablets of the Ten Commandments with the more elaborate descriptions of it as a putative throne symbol for Yahweh (Exod. 37:6–9) and with its use as a symbol of Yahweh's presence in Israel's travels (e.g., Num. 10:33–36) or in war (e.g., 1 Sam. 4). Some see the Deuteronomic account as negating the ark as symbol of divine presence by treating it a simple receptacle (cf. Nielsen, "Reflections." Others have taken the minimalization of the ark in Deut. as typical of a Deuteronomic theology of God's "distance," otherwise manifested in the so-called "Name-theology" (cf. von Rad, *Studies,* pp. 37–44). However, as Miller has pointed out, the nearness of God has already been linked with the law given to Israel (in 4:6–8), and so, as the law's container, "the ark continues to function in some fashion as the vehicle for God's presence in the midst of the people" (*Deuteronomy,* p. 56). The grounds for making a strong dichotomy between divine absence and presence in Deut., and thus also the grounds for von Rad's assertions, have been recently challenged by Wilson, *Fire.*

The point of Deut. 10:1–5 is not to give a detailed physical description of the ark or to explain every aspect of its religious significance, but rather, in the context of ch. 9, to see its construction for the purpose of storing the *new* tablets of the law as tangible proof of the forgiveness of the people and the renewal of the covenant by God's grace.

10:6–7 / The itinerary here contains some names in common with Num. 33:30–33, but in reverse order. There may have been several variant traditions of all the sites visited by the Israelites in their wilderness wandering, and it is more than likely that they visited the same sites in more than one direction of movement. Many of them cannot be identified with any certainty today. See additional note on 1:2.

10:8–9 / On the Levites, see commentary on 18:1–8.

These verses begin the buildup toward the climax of the opening exhortation of the book in chapter 11. Deuteronomy 10:12–22 is unquestionably one of the richest texts in the Hebrew Bible, exalted and poetic in its language, comprehensive and challenging in its message. It purposely tries to "boil down" the whole theological and ethical content of the book into memorable phraseology, packed and pregnant, rich and resonant of all the surrounding preaching. Indeed, there are not many dimensions of "OT theology," that are not directly expressed or indirectly echoed in this mini-symphony of faith and life.

10:12–13 / And now, O Israel. Rather like a Pauline "therefore," the words indicate a transition from the points that have just been forcefully made in 9:7–10:11 to the practical implications that follow from them, in the same way that the identical opening words in 4:1 link that chapter to the preceding historical recollections of chapters 1–3.

What does the LORD your God ask of you but. The intention is to get down to basics and show that the claim of God upon the covenant people is not complicated and esoteric but fundamentally simple. Not simple as in "easy"—if obedience were *easy* there would be little need for these chapters full of encouragement, warning, and promise. The motivation for obedience is total and exclusive commitment. The substance of obedience is relatively straightforward (a) because there is only one God to whom obedience is owed, so the moral confusion of polytheism is avoided, and (b) because Yahweh has made his moral will known with unmistakable clarity (cf. 30:11–13).

Already, Deuteronomy has indicated the essential unity of the demand of God, through the repeated use of the singular *miṣwâ*, "commandment," in important passages (5:31; 6:1, 25; 7:11; 8:1) and, of course, through the Shema (6:4f.). This sentence (vv. 12f.) is like a five-note musical chord. Each note has its own distinct tone, but taken all together they sound forth in a harmony that expresses the whole content of Deuteronomy and the Torah—**to fear . . . to walk . . . to love . . . to serve . . . to observe.** With a similar purpose, but different words, Micah 6:8 asks the question "What does the LORD require of you?" and answers it with a triplet of phrases that summarize the prophetic preaching, in the same way that these phrases summarize the Torah: "to act justly and to love mercy and to walk humbly with your God." **To fear the LORD your God** is to have a basic respect and reverence for the covenant Lord that permeates all other attitudes (cf. 5:29; 6:13; 10:20). **To walk in all his ways,** as the imitation of God, is perhaps the phrase in the Hebrew Bible that most nearly summarizes what we mean by "Old Testament ethics" (cf. 5:33; 8:6; 11:22). **To love him** is to have and express covenant loyalty and obedience flowing out of gratitude (cf. 6:5; 11:1, 13, 22). **To serve the LORD your God with all your heart and all your soul** is virtually identical to "loving" God, but with the added metaphor of bonded service to the one who has bought and therefore owns the people (cf. 6:13; 10:20; 11:13). **To observe the LORD's commands** is to give careful, conscientious, and constant attention to the terms and stipulations of the covenant relationship (cf. 7:11; 11:1, 8, 13, 22). As can be seen, the five phrases function as a kind of text for the remainder of the preaching in chapters 10 and 11, which are essentially a twisting kaleidoscope of all the colors and patterns that flow from the central commandment—to love God (which naturally stands central in the list of five).

For your own good. Only two words in Hebrew (*le ṭôb lāk*, "for good for you"), this phrase condenses all the blessings that Moses elsewhere expansively describes. Through obedience, Israel could enter into secure possession of the land, long life, enjoyment of all God's gifts, etc. (cf. 5:29, 33; 6:24; 30:15–20). It also condenses the important ethical point that the law itself was a gift of God's grace for the benefit of human beings, not an imposition for arbitrary divine satisfaction. As Moses has already pointed out (4:6–8), observing the law is wisdom—it not only pleases the giver of the law, but it benefits the keeper of the law. "Obedience is good for you," may not sparkle as an advertising slogan, but it captures the human perspective of OT ethics.

10:14 / The six verses of 10:14–19 are carefully structured as a pair of matching triplets: verses 14, 15, 16, and verses 17, 18,

19. In each of the two passages there is an opening, hymn-like exaltation of Yahweh with resounding superlatives (vv. 14, 17). The following verse describes something unexpected about God's action or character (vv. 15, 18). The concluding verse is a command for Israel to respond appropriately (vv. 16, 19). This stereophonic effect enriches the impact of the whole symphony. **Even the highest heavens** (lit. "heavens of heavens"—a superlative expression): This verse, with wonderful rhythmic cadence, affirms the universal exaltation and cosmic ownership of Yahweh (cf. 1 Kgs. 8:27; Pss. 24:1; 47:7–9; 68:34; 95:4f.; 115:16; 148:4f.; Jer. 10:10–13). There is absolutely nothing in creation "up there or down here" that does not belong to him. Some commentators insist on relativizing verses like this, based on their own certainty that such claims cannot be expressing monotheism, but reflect only a relatively special status for Yahweh. But if absolutely everything belongs to Yahweh (and the text could hardly have found more emphatic words to say so), what was left to be franchised out to other deities? The text attributes cosmic universality to Yahweh, and it is exegetically unsound to reduce its scope on the basis of a priori assumptions about Israelite religion.

10:15 / **Yet . . .** : the Hebrew word *(raq)* emphatically introduces a contrasting or surprising point. The wonder is that a God of such cosmic, universal ownership should have focused **affection** on the insignificant ancestors of insignificant Israel. This verse echoes 7:6–8 in expressing the wonder of Israel's election. There, the surprise was that God should have chosen Israel though they were so small. Here the surprise is because God is so great. In both cases, the message is that Israel's election was based on nothing in themselves that had evoked God's favoritism, but solely in the character and action of this amazing God.

It is important to read each verse (14–15) in the light of the other for they mutually qualify and "flavor" each other. On the one hand, the God of universal ownership exercised his sovereignty in the particular choice of Israel. On the other hand, the God who loved and chose Israel is the God who owns the whole world. Thus, the universality of God must not be separated from the particularity of God's electing love. However, neither must the particularity of God's action in Israel be severed from the universality of God's cosmic ownership of the world (cf. the same dual truth in Exod. 19:4–6).

Missiologically, it is vital to keep these two great biblical truths integrally related to each other. Otherwise the universality of verse 14 can evaporate into an unbiblical, ahistorical universalism or the particularity of verse 15 can be twisted into a chauvinistic, unbiblical exclusivism. The first danger is to conclude that if everything and everybody belongs to God, then all distinctions are dissolved between those who are the people of God and those who are not yet. The second danger is the temptation to infer from God's love for God's people that God hates, or at least has no interest in or plans for, the rest of the nations. The balance of these verses protects us from the unbiblical extremes of a monistic universalism that destroys all distinctions, on the one hand, and a narrow exclusivism that denies or restricts the universality of God's love, on the other.

10:16 / Instead of words of encouragement following vv. 14f., Israel finds a double-barreled call to repentance aimed at their metaphorical hearts and necks. Election, for Israel, was not so much a privilege as an awesome responsibility that could prove highly dangerous. The way this summary call for repentance follows an exalted statement of election is rhetorically and theologically very similar to Amos 3:2, where the uniqueness of Israel's relationship with Yahweh is stunningly followed by the words, "therefore I will punish you." The specific words, **do not be stiff-necked any longer,** 9:6 and the whole narrative of 9:7–29, go back to the original story of Exodus 32–34, where, as Moberly has shown, they are a key to the literary and theological structuring of the whole text (*Mountain of God,* pp. 89–93). Moses had appealed to God to forgive the people, not because they had stopped being stiff-necked, but because they still were! (In Exod. 34:9, *kî* should be translated "because," not "although," as NIV). God's forgiveness of Israel's apostasy on that occasion (as ever) was the fruit of God's own grace and faithfulness coupled with the effective intercession of Moses. The call to repentance and a more obedient, co-operative spirit was thus based on the amazing grace of God.

10:17 / The second triplet begins with another burst of hymnody, similar in form to verse 14, but with its emphasis not so much on God in relation to the created order (heavens and earth) as on God in relation to all other spiritual realities. **God of gods and Lord of lords;** like "heavens of heavens" in v. 14, these should be understood as superlative expressions. Yahweh is "the

highest God and supreme Lord." Whatever other spiritual realities exist, they are subject to Yahweh. Again the question of
monotheism arises, and again it seems inadequate to say, as some
commentators do, that only a relative mono-Yahwism is in view.
For the text does not say merely that Yahweh is the only God for
Israel (while allowing for the legitimate jurisdiction of other national deities), but affirms that Yahweh is the supreme God over
all. Yahweh's sovereignty is not just covenantal but cosmic. The
conviction expressed poetically here seems very similar to the
conviction expressed politically (and with scant regard for diplo-
matic niceties) at the international conference of Middle Eastern
states in Jerusalem in ca. 594 BCE by Jeremiah (Jer. 27:5ff.). The
same truth was acknowledged with surprise by the object of that
word, Nebuchadnezzar himself (Dan. 2:47; 4:25, 34f.). Yahweh,
the God who owns the world (v. 14), is also the God who runs the
world (v. 17).

The affirmation of Yahweh's universal ownership and universal lordship in vv. 14 and (especially) 17 clearly stakes out the
dynamic and polemical claims of Israel's faith. Israel lived in an
ancient Near Eastern macro-culture as religiously plural as any
era in which God's people have had to live. Unless verses such as
Deuteronomy 10:14 and 17 are dismissively relativized as cultic
hyperbole or as confessionally true only for Israel (not ontologi-
cally or definitionally true of ultimate deity), then they clearly
stand out against the dominant cultural polytheism and need to
be taken seriously. Similarly, and with greater missiological relevance for Christian claims within the modern controversy over
religious pluralism, the fact that early Christian worship could
apply such language to Jesus (Rev. 17:14; 19:16; cf. 1:18, etc.),
shows both the determination of NT Christians to affirm the
universal lordship of Christ in ways that clashed with all the
religious plurality of their context and also their determination to
do so within a consistent framework of scriptural monotheism.
They saw no incompatibility, in other words, in including Jesus
in the affirmation of Deuteronomy 10:14, 17 (cf. 1 Cor. 8:4–6).

Unlike human lords and so many of the members of ancient Near Eastern pantheons, Yahweh had no favorites and no
price (v. 17b). The expression **shows no partiality** is (lit.) "he does
not lift up faces," i.e., he does not base decisions on selective
favoritism. Now this might seem to be in considerable tension
with verse 15 until we remember that Deuteronomy has already
explicitly excluded the idea that God's election of Israel was some

kind of favoritism (7:7; 9:4f.). Unfortunately, the very notion of divine election is still frequently caricatured and dismissed by Christians as self-selection dressed up as divine will, or, worse, divine favoritism. The statement of God's love for Israel in verse 15 is bounded by (and so to be understood in relation to) affirmations of God's ownership of the whole earth (v. 14) on the one side, and of God's impartiality (v. 17) on the other. It should not be pulled out of that context and defined in a way that denies either of those enveloping truths.

10:18 / The moral character of Yahweh continues in verse 18 with the same kind of surprise as verse 15 introduced. In some ancient Near Eastern royal texts the exaltation of national gods is commonly followed by the derivative exaltation of the royal household. It was human kings who basked in the reflected glory of the ruling gods. But who, in this wonderful doxological definition, are the beneficiaries of Yahweh's supreme lordship? **The fatherless and the widow and . . . the alien!** Nothing could be more characteristic of Israel's "counter-cultural" faith. The majestic monotheistic superlatives of verses 14 and 17 are harnessed, not to the glory and power of the wealthy and strong, but to the needs of the poor, the weak, and the vulnerable (cf. the same pattern in Isa. 40:28–31). The rest of the law will demonstrate that this social concern was no facade. Rather, the fundamental character of Yahweh expressed so succinctly here, and enjoined on Israel in verse 19, pervades the legal sections of Deuteronomy and explicitly shapes much of the practical social legislation.

And loves the alien, giving him food and clothing. Apart from its relevance to the immediately following ethical command to Israel, this singling out of Yahweh's love for the alien must have a bearing on the meaning of his impartiality in the previous verse. God's electing love for Israel has been affirmed to be free of sheer favoritism and so not in conflict with the affirmation that God **shows no partiality.** That point is now expressed in a converse way. The impartiality of Yahweh is seen in that he not only **loved** Israel's forebears but he also **loves** the alien. The same word is used, and the additional phrase, that Yahweh feeds and clothes the alien, undoubtedly echoes that particular token of his loving grace experienced by Israel in the wilderness (8:3–4). Granted all the redemptive, covenantal uniqueness of Yahweh's action on Israel's behalf, it remains true that what Yahweh did for them was, quite simply, typical of him. Yahweh is the God who loves the aliens and feeds and clothes them. When the Israelites were the aliens in Egypt (v. 19b), God provided for them. Once again we find this remarkable balance-in-tension between the particularism of Yahweh's action for Israel in redemption and covenant and the universality of his character on which that behavior is based. His action for Israel was paradigmatic *for them*, but it was also paradigmatic *of God*. Jesus drew the same lessons about the generosity and breadth of God's love from nature and applied it with a similarly radical ethical thrust to the love of "aliens" (Matt. 5:43–48; 6:25–34).

10:19 / Here we have the Deuteronomic equivalent of the "second greatest commandment," like Leviticus 19:18 and 34. It is remarkable first of all because it is totally rooted in the character and action of God. What does it mean to "walk in all God's ways" (v. 12)? This verse is the answer. The ways of Yahweh in verses 14–19 begin with condescending love for the ancestors of Israel and climax in practical love for the strangers in Israel, the aliens. In between these two all-embracing dimensions of Yahweh's love are sandwiched impartiality, integrity, and commitment to justice. God is love; so to walk in God's ways will entail the exercise of practical love, for ethics in the Old Testament as much as in the New involves the imitation of God (cf. 1 John 3:17; 4:20f.).

But the second remarkable point is precisely the object of this love. Moses skips over, as it were, love commands that might have naturally followed—to love God, to love fellow Israelites as neighbors—to the most radical and demanding of the list—to love the alien—and makes that the content of this second great imperative in response to the greatness of God. Was it perhaps an assumption that if Israel could demonstrate practical love to aliens, they would be likely to sustain other aspects of the social charter God was giving them? Or was it perhaps the insight that love for aliens will always be the first feature of any society to evaporate in times of social pressure and conflict? Xenophobia, exploitation, and precisely the kind of scapegoat politics that Israel suffered in Egypt are much more typical. Whatever the reason, it is an astonishing singling out of that particular love commandment in such a lofty context. The Hebrew verb form *weʾāhabtā* ("and you [sg.] shall love") occurs only four times in the OT: Deuteronomy 6:5 and 11:1 (the LORD your God); Leviticus 19:18 (your neighbor); 19:34 (the alien). This verse (Deut. 10:19) is the only occurrence of the plural form *waᵓᵃhabtem* ("and you [pl.] shall love"), and it reinforces Leviticus 19:34 exactly.

Finally, we may note that in these six rich verses Israel is required to respond to God's universal reign and gracious action in only two ways: "Repent!" and "Love the alien!" (vv. 16, 19). It is challenging to sense the way Jesus drank deeply from the wells of Deuteronomy's spirituality and ethic when teaching about the kingdom of heaven, "Repent, for the kingdom of God is at hand," and when radically commanding, "Love your enemies."

10:20–22 / The passage reaches its climax with rhetorical repetition of its main points, perhaps actually running on to 11:1. **He is your praise** probably means Yahweh is the object of Israel's praise in worship, rather than that he is the reason why Israel will receive praise from the nations. If so, then it is a significant example of the worship of Israel being set within the context of the requirement of obedience. Yahweh would be acceptably praised only by those who do what Yahweh does in practical socio-ethical terms. And such ethical justice will be worked at only by those committed to **fear, serve,** and **hold fast** to Yahweh as their God. Other gods have other ways, but Israel must "keep the way of the LORD, by doing what is right and just, so that the LORD will bring about for Abraham what he has promised him" (Gen. 18:19). The reference to the growth of the people in fulfillment of God's great missionary promise to Abraham (v. 22; cf. Gen. 46:27; Exod. 1:5; Deut. 1:10) shows that the response required of Israel in this whole section would not be merely for its own good (v. 13b), but would be an integral part of God's ongoing redemptive purpose in the world through the people of Abraham. It is thus another indication of the fundamental link in the OT between ethics and mission.

Additional Notes §13

10:16 / **Circumcise your hearts:** Circumcision was the sign of covenant membership, but it could also be used metaphorically with the ears (Jer. 6:10 marginal note) or the heart to speak of willingness to hear and obey the word of God (cf. Deut. 30:6; Lev. 26:41; Jer. 4:4; 9:26; Ezek. 44:7–9). The phrase thus indicates an inner commitment to obedience that lives out the meaning of the physical sign in the flesh. Paul's observation in Rom. 2:28f. is not some new spiritual insight but an authentic articulation of the ethos of the Torah itself.

10:17 / On the vocabulary of this verse, cf. Pss. 24:8; 95:3; 136:2f.; Neh. 9:32; Isa. 42:13.

10:18 / On the identity of the **alien** (gēr), see additional notes on 1:16.

§14 The Crucial Choice: Blessing or Curse (Deut. 11:1–32)

This is the last chapter of the great introduction to the law that began in chapter 4. It continues to expound the summarizing text of 10:12f., but interweaves examples and illustrations around the repeated exhortations to obedience. The constant thrust is on the importance of choice—the benefits of the right choice and the disasters that will result from the wrong choice. Ultimately, obedience or disobedience is the only choice, blessing or curse is the only prospect. Chapter 11 thus ends by setting out the blessing and curse option, which is then expounded more fully in chapters 27–28. Since so much of the chapter echoes and reinforces themes that have occurred already or anticipates themes to come later, our comments at this stage can be brief.

11:1–7 / After an opening repetition of the fundamental commandment (v. 1), which may in fact be the conclusion to the previous section, this passage reinforces the call to obedience with two historical examples, one positive (3f., the exodus and crossing of the sea, Exod. 7–14), one negative (v. 6, the rebellion and destruction of Dathan and Abiram, Num. 16). The purpose is to impress on this generation of Israelites that it is their responsibility to obey Yahweh here and now (vv. 2, 7), neither relying on the obedience of previous generations nor passing off the responsibility to the next generation. Each generation has a continuity and a solidarity with previous generations in covenantal obligation (cf. 5:2f.), but at the same time each generation must make its own response and take the consequences.

11:8–9 / The entire section of 11:8–17 is devoted to Israel's future life in the land. It draws out some of the features first described in 8:7ff., reemphasizing the overall thrust of the critical importance of obedience and adding detail.

The opening exhortation in verses 8–9 uses the singular form "all this commandment" (cf. 5:31; 6:1, 25; 7:11; 8:1), indicating the wholeness of the law and the comprehensiveness of the response being called for. The two verses again put side by side the apparent necessity of obedience as a condition of entering and enjoying the land and the unconditional nature of the land gift as the fulfillment of the promise to Israel's ancestors. It seems unnecessarily divisive to regard these as distinct traditions stemming from different historical periods. They were two sides of the same truth, combining, as Deuteronomy characteristically does in so many other ways, the priority of divine grace and the necessity of human obedient response.

11:10–12 / Yahweh being God of all the earth, it is hardly surprising that Deuteronomy can happily draw theology out of meteorology! The geographical and climatic differences between Egypt and Canaan are described here as a prelude to the lessons of verses 13–17. Egypt, a land of scarce rainfall, is dependent on the humanly devised and humanly operated schemes of irrigation from the waters of the Nile (v. 10). Such irrigation projects, from ancient to modern times, are indeed a testimony to human achievement, but the Israelites know all about the hard work involved in them. In marked contrast, the land of Canaan has a precipitation climate and, apart from some streams and limited storage of rain water in cisterns, is almost totally dependent for its agricultural fertility on the regularity of the rains (v. 11). Not that God was any less responsible for the annual flooding of the Nile, but there is something about the mere direction and source of rain that justifies the picturesque description of Canaan as a land **that drinks rain from heaven** and the virtually Edenic portrayal of God's perpetual presence and attention there (v. 12).

11:13–15 / The climatic point having been made, the moral lesson is obvious. If you need rain to survive, and if Yahweh sends the rain, then you would be well advised to **faithfully obey the commands** of Yahweh and to maintain covenant love, loyalty, and service. The result would be agricultural abundance and sufficiency (cf. 8:6–10). In verses 11–12, the land is portrayed as enjoying the blessing of Yahweh by itself, as it were, simply as the object of his lavish care. But for Israel to enter into the enjoyment of that blessing in the land they must remain committed to obedience to Yahweh (vv. 13–15). Thus, their obedience would not *earn* the blessing of fertility, nor would it somehow magically induce fertility. That blessing was already "there" in the very nature of the land and its relationship to Yahweh, but it could be appropriated and enjoyed only by an Israel prepared to live a life of faith and obedience.

11:16–17 / The danger of disloyalty (cf. 4:15–19 and 6:14) is now similarly related to the weather and its dependent agriculture (cf. 28:23f. and Lev. 26:18–20.). The statements that *Yahweh* was responsible for the fertility of Canaan (v. 12), that it was he who gave the rain (v. 14), and that he could as easily withhold it (v. 17), are deceptively simple. They actually conceal a strongly polemical claim. For among the inhabitants of Canaan it was Baal who was lord of rain, fertility, and agricultural fecundity. The warning of verse 16 is thus very pointed. Israel would indeed face, and repeatedly succumb to, the temptation to pay homage to the gods that seemed to control agricultural success, yet no amount of prayer to these gods of rain and fertility would help. Hosea and Amos preached this message (Hos. 2:5–9; Amos 4:6–13). Elijah proved it (1 Kgs. 17–18).

The question arises as to how far one can generalize or dogmatize from the relationship in these verses between moral obedience and material blessing (cf. commentary on 7:12–16). Deuteronomy repeatedly correlates these two, and in the rest of the OT this equation remains as an underlying principle witnessing to a truth about God in relation both to the earth and to God's people. It is not, however, universalized in a mechanical way in the rest of the OT. Indeed, such a conviction is challenged head-on in books like Job and Ecclesiastes and fuels the baffled lament of Psalms like Psalm 73. The connections between obedience and prosperity are neither guaranteed nor "reversible." That is, we cannot deduce that prosperity proves prior obedience or that suffering necessarily proves personal guilt. But the abiding principle is that God does respond justly to our response to God, and that God remains in final control of everything that affects human life, including contingent factors like climate and fertility. God's historical justice and God's sovereign providence are the non-negotiable factors.

11:18–21 / The importance of regular inculcation of the law (cf. 6:6–9) takes on a new urgency in view of the preceding warnings.

11:22-25 / Before the Israelites could begin to enjoy agricultural success in the land, they had to have military success so as to actually settle there. These verses hang Israel's possession of the land upon the condition of faithful obedience (v. 22), repeating the message of 7:12-24.

11:26-32 / These verses have a present and a future aspect. They point to the immediacy of present choice: **I am setting before you today a blessing and a curse.** All the teaching and preaching of the previous chapters focuses on these alternatives. No apathy is allowed in making an immediate decision between the two options set out in verses 27 and 28. These verses also point toward the future and the need for a permanent reminder of the ongoing consequences of that present-day choice. So Moses arranges for a physical monument to the covenant alternatives that would be more visible and more durable than any memorial sculpted by human hands—two mountains! Gerizim and Ebal are mountains on either side of Shechem, a place later associated with a significant covenant ceremony (Josh. 24). Although the map coordinates of verse 30 are no longer very clear to us, it is clear that Gerizim, the mountain symbolizing blessing, was to the South and thus on the right as one faced East (the priority direction for orientation), while Ebal, symbolizing curse, was to the North and thus on the left. It is also suggested that Gerizim was covered with fertile vegetation whereas Ebal was barren (Mayes, *Deuteronomy*, p. 218). Further details of the ceremonies on these mountains are given in chapter 27. This physical representation of the fundamental choice between blessing and curse immediately precedes the central section of law that begins in chapter 12 and is the first thing recorded after that section closes in chapter 26. It thus functions as a kind of thematic "verbal velcro" for the two sections of the "inner frame" of Deuteronomy (see p. 4). This structure highlights the theological importance of blessing, curse, and law and is another indication of the careful and artistic structuring of the book. The same literary care is also seen in the final verses of this chapter (vv. 31-32), which bring the whole exhortation to a close on the same note as it began in 4:1f.

Additional Notes §14

11:10 / **By foot** may refer to foot pumps used to lift water from the river and canals to the fields, or to the foot-control of the small mud walls and dikes that control the irrigation flows. Since "foot" in Hb. is sometimes used as a euphemism for genitals, it may even have been a derogatory reference to urination. For further illumination, see Eslinger, "Watering Egypt," and Nicol, "Watering Egypt . . . Again."

11:14 / **Autumn and spring rains:** These are in Hb. the "early rains," which fall in October/November, bringing to an end the long dry summer and enabling plowing to take place, and the "later rains," which come in March/April, marking the end of the rainy season and enabling the final period of growth before the harvests. Both were essential features of the agricultural year.

I will send rain: There is an oscillation in these verses between God referred to in the third person with Moses as speaker (which is how v. 13 naturally reads) and God speaking in the first person, as here. This does not indicate disruption in the text, but is characteristic of the interlocking of the word of Moses and the word of Yahweh in Deut. as a whole—another feature of the book that illustrates Moses' prophetic role and stature.

11:24 / **Every place where you set your foot will be yours** (cf. 2:5; Josh. 1:3; 14:9): The act of walking over or around a plot of territory could be a symbolic declaration of legal ownership. The extent of the land within the stated limits was somewhat idealistic. Not until the time of the Solomonic empire (and for only a short time afterwards) did the Israelites have control over territory bounded by the desert (South), Lebanon (North), the Euphrates (East), and the Mediterranean (West).

§15 The Name above All Names (Deut. 12:1–32)

A new section is clearly indicated by the fresh heading in 12:1, even though we are still listening to the second speech of Moses, which began at 5:1. The next such heading is at 29:1, after the blessings and curses in chapters 27–28. Chapters 12–26 form the central section of the book, characterized by the preaching of specific laws and sometimes given the title, "the Deuteronomic Code." However, it is important not to be unduly influenced by this identification of separate sections. There is a temptation in reading Deuteronomy to regard chapters 1–11 as the grand sermonic introduction and then to treat chapters 12–26 as nothing more than a law code, to be investigated in comparison with the legal sections of Exodus and Leviticus and in the light of whatever historical reconstruction one posits for the origin of the Deuteronomic law. This has two unfortunate effects. First, it can mean that one interprets Deuteronomy as if it really were a "second law," a *new* code of laws that must then be given a historical setting somewhere in Israel's religious development, whereas the book presents itself as the preaching of *existing* law in the context of a renewal of the covenant. Some modifications and fresh motivation of older laws are undoubtedly present, but the overall intention is to induce loyalty to existing covenant law, not to initiate fresh legislation.

Secondly, such isolation of chapters 12–26 from chapters 1–11 obscures the depth and purpose of the interpenetration of vocabulary, themes, and theology in each. All the sections of laws in chapters 12–26 are presented in the light of, or more precisely, in response to, the great truths and principles that have been so eloquently expounded in chapters 1–11 (esp. 4–11). There is a mirror-like effect in the way the earlier chapters present what God had done for Israel, while the later chapters present what Israel must do in response, often employing the same vocabulary to show this reciprocal relationship. This theological schema may often be the reason that some laws in Deuteronomy have a different form than their equivalents in Exodus or Leviticus (rather than such difference being intentional changing of the law in response to historical development, cf. McConville, *Law and Theology*).

Chapter 12 is concerned with Israel's exclusive loyalty to Yahweh in its worship and thus reflects the first two Decalogue commandments. The chapter also echoes Exodus 20:22–26 in its concern for the legitimacy of the worship of Yahweh and Leviticus 18:3 in its concern for the distinctiveness of Israel from the nations (notice the key word in common with Deut. 12:4 and 31: "you shall not *do* as they *do*"; NIV **you must not worship**). There are also close links with Deuteronomy 7 with its emphasis on the reciprocal distinctiveness of Israel as elect and holy. McConville shows the correspondences between chapters 7 and 12 (*Law,* pp. 59–64), showing not only the structural similarities (see additional note) but also that the central thrust of both chapters is the concern for Israel's distinctiveness from the nations and its practical implications. In the light of these points, it seems that we are more likely to get to the heart of the chapter's message, not by regarding it as a program of cult centralization, written or adapted specifically for a particular historical reform, but by listening to its call for the purity and unity of Israel's worship in response to the blessing of Yahweh.

12:1–4 / The virtual repetition in verses 29–32 of the points made in verses 1–4 illuminates the careful literary structure of the chapter. This parallels the "sandwich" feature of chapter 7 (cf. 7:1–5 and 7:17–26) and enables us to see that the whole chapter must be interpreted in the light of this framework (several commentators lose the force of this inclusion by regarding 12:29–32 as the introduction to ch. 13). The primary point at issue is the contrast with Canaanite ways.

Verse 3 is virtually identical in purpose and vocabulary to Exodus 23:24; 34:13, and Deuteronomy 7:5. The instruction, however, to **wipe out their names from those places,** is additional and significant in the light of the emphasis on the name of Yahweh in the following verses. To remove the names of Canaan's gods was to remove *their* presence and *their* power, just as the putting of Yahweh's name in a place was to fill it with *his* availability and *his* nearness. But they could not coexist. The names of other gods must be deleted, destroyed, along with all their paraphernalia. The change must be radical.

> Negating one group of names and establishing another name in
> effect calls for a new order, a transformation: a shift from an order
> where there are multiple claims for human allegiance . . . and
> where human design determines the place and nature of wor-
> ship. This order is to give way to another, wherein divine control
> is placed over human worship and one name replaces all other
> names. (Miller, *Deuteronomy*, p. 131)

The religious transformation would entail enormous social, economic, and political change as well (cf. Gottwald, *Tribes of Yahweh*).

Now when we reflect missiologically on these instructions
in relation to Israel's attitude to the nations and their gods, some
interesting points arise. We know Israel did *not* "wipe out" all the
names of gods known in Canaanite religion; they actually accepted a few as legitimate titles for the God they knew as Yahweh. The acceptability of "El" and the total non-acceptability of
"Baal" as names for Yahweh are linked to the relationship
between the Mosaic Yahwism of the Exodus-Sinai era and the
broader El-worship of the ancestral (i.e., patriarchal) era (cf.
Moberly, *The Old Testament*). Undoubtedly, the exclusion of Baal
is related to his association with fertility cults and the oppressive
and licentious ethos of Canaanite society (cf. v. 31).

In the current debate over the Christian response to other
religions, the greater openness of the ancestral era to the gods of
the surrounding culture is sometimes cited as biblical justification for a more accepting and syncretistic approach to the divini-
ties of other faith traditions in our own day. However, a more
discriminating evaluation of the biblical evidence shows this not
to be the case. The historical progress of divine activity and
revelation sharpened the Israelites' understanding of the distinctiveness of their God and culminated in the demand for their
exclusive loyalty and the rejection of other gods. The Pentateuch
as a whole, therefore, presents us with a balance between the
universality of the God acknowledged as El in various ancient
Near Eastern cultures, including Israel's, and the particularity of
the same God acknowledged uniquely by Israel as Yahweh to the
exclusion of Baal. Both sides of the picture are missiologically
important and ought not to be collapsed in either direction (cf.
Goldingay and Wright, "Yahweh Our God"). The direction of our
particular text here, however, is clearly toward the latter pole of
an exclusive loyalty to the **Name** (v. 5) that eliminates all other
names (v. 3). And this in turn has both a negative and a positive
implication.

Negatively, it militates against the central affirmation of contemporary religious pluralism: the theory of the relativity of all religions as witnesses to an ultimate divine reality that is not identical with the divine as conceived in any of them. This text denies that any and all "names" and "faces" of deity in the religious traditions of the world can be valid and salvific. For pluralism, the possibility of one true revelation by one true God known by one saving name through one particular people is a priori ruled out. Ignoring the OT's own understanding of the universality of God's saving purpose behind the particularity of Israel's election, pluralists reject the very possibility of such a view of truth and salvation as being (a) chauvinistic and/or imperialistic and (b) incompatible with their epistemology of cultural and historical relativism. (That is, pluralists insist that truth cannot be known absolutely within any single cultural or historical context; all is relative and partial. They do not tell us, however, on what privileged epistemological grounds they themselves are able to make this intrinsically absolutist claim.)

For the pluralist, then, all of the names of deity in the religions of humanity have some validity, but, equally, *none* of them is uniquely or absolutely the *real* name or *final* revelation of the ultimate divine reality. No one name can arrogate to itself the right to deny, let alone destroy, the other names. Pluralism, therefore, is the reverse of our text. Multiple names and places are to be affirmed in the great project of religio-cultural pluralism. The only name to be rejected would be any name that refused to accept its own relativity and to coexist happily with the others. There is, then, an unavoidable clash between the pluralist agenda and the agenda of this biblical text. According to Deuteronomy, there are some divine names that cannot be tolerated alongside the name of Yahweh. And at least part of the reason lies in the depravity associated with those names—the phallic and fertility allusions to the Baal cult (v. 3) and the callous horror of child sacrifice (probably of children born to cult prostitutes, v. 31).

Positively, the substitution of the name of Yahweh for other names points us toward that exaltation of the "name above all names" that is conferred by God on Jesus. A line runs from this text, via Isaiah 45:22–24, to Philippians 2:9–11 and Ephesians 1:20–21. All these texts, OT and NT, were written against the background of religious plurality and the competing claims of rival divine names. The polemical intent of the NT texts is thus comparable to the instructions in Deuteronomy. The uniqueness of the name of Yahweh (most probably the meaning of the "name above all names" in Phil. 2:9) is now claimed for Jesus alone and will ultimately be acknowledged by all, just as Isaiah 45:24 envisages every tongue confessing that salvation/righteousness is in Yahweh alone. Thus, Deuteronomy's concern for the purity of Israel's faith through the utter renunciation of the very names of other gods cannot be relegated to an outgrown era of OT religious bigotry and replaced by a congenial "wider ecumenism" of faiths. If "the name belonging to Jesus" (a possible translation of Phil. 2:10) indeed implied the name of Yahweh (which seems very clear from the quotation of Isaiah 45:23 and the use of "Lord" in v. 11), then Christian concern to protect the name of Jesus Christ from being equated with any other names (for example in certain kinds of public multifaith worship) should be as keen as Deuteronomy's passion for the uniqueness of the name of Yahweh over against all other religious manifestations.

12:5 / Deuteronomy 12:5–12, dealing with the worship of Israel at the place God would choose, is the first of the two major central sections of the chapter. The other section is verses 13–28, dealing with the matter of "profane slaughter"—i.e., the nonsacrificial killing of animals for food. Both sections have a double-barreled form, with a kind of didactic parallelism between 5–7 and 8–12, and between 13–19 and 20–28. The reason for the repetitious nature of the material is more likely to be its teaching purpose rather than a literary history of successive redactions of separate laws. McConville's careful analysis of the intricate stylistic features, vocabulary distribution, and balancing chiasms also points strongly toward the essential unity of the chapter (McConville, *Law and Theology*, pp. 59–67).

In contrast to the pagan sanctuaries of Canaanite gods and their names, the Israelites were to **seek the place the LORD your God will choose.** Their worship was to take place neither at the religious sites of the former inhabitants nor at any place they happened to fancy (v. 13, cf. Ezek. 20:28f.), but only at the place of *Yahweh's* choice. The primary emphasis is on the distinguishing feature of the site as being *chosen by Yahweh*, not just on it being *one place rather than many.* The unity of Israel's worship consisted in its being offered to only one *God*, Yahweh, rather than in its being offered at only one *place.* Yahweh would choose the place **to put his Name there for his dwelling.** This expression denotes the presence of the tabernacle and ark, the visible symbols of

Yahweh's presence in the midst of the people (cf. Exod. 29:43–46). It probably also has connotations of Yahweh's ownership of the place, and judging from ancient Near Eastern parallels to the phrase, it may have overtones of possession by right of conquest. In other words, Yahweh's placing of his name there was symbolic of his ownership of the whole land (cf. Wenham, "Central Sanctuary," esp. pp. 112–14). The combined expression (the place of Yahweh's choice; the place where he put his name), or either part of it, become the standard designation throughout the rest of Deuteronomy for the legitimate sanctuary at which various cultic functions were to be carried out (e.g., 14:23ff.; 15:20; 16 [passim]; 17:8ff.; 18:6; 26:2).

The place itself is not named. It would have been perfectly possible to identify a specific place-name in advance, since knowledge of the topography of the land was not lacking, as the references to Mts. Gerizim and Ebal show. The lack of a place-name thus serves only to underline the importance of the name installed there—Yahweh's name. Scholars' preoccupation with "the place" in geographical terms through linking it to a specific historical program of centralization in *Jerusalem* has inverted the priority of the text, which is concerned not so much with the *location* of the place as with its *election* by Yahweh. What matters is not "where?" but "who?" Likewise, the Canaanite sanctuaries were to be destroyed, not because of *where* they were or because they were many but because of **their names,** i.e., *whose* they were. Whatever human name the place may come to have will be less important than the name that God will have put there. And if the name of Yahweh was not being honored there in the way God required, then the place itself had neither sanctity nor ultimate security, whether it was Bethel being attacked in the tenth century by an unnamed prophet from Judah (1 Kgs. 13:1–3) and by Amos from Judah in the eighth (Amos 5:4–6; 7:10ff.), or Shiloh (Jer. 7:12–15), or even Jerusalem itself (Mic. 3:9–12; Jer. 7:1–15). On internal OT critical perspectives on the Jerusalem tradition, cf. McConville, "Jerusalem."

In the wider canonical context, this valuing of a place because of Yahweh's choice and presence, rather than because of its location, sows the seeds for the NT's transference of the significance of the place of worship. The temple gives way to the person of Jesus Christ as the focus of worship in the messianic age (cf. John 4:19–26; Acts 7:44–50; and Davies, *Land*).

From the time of David onward, with the transfer of the ark
and the building of the temple by Solomon, the place could be
thought of only as Jerusalem. This identification is quite explicit
in the later Deuteronomistic History (e.g., 1 Kgs. 8:44, 48; 11:13,
32, 36; 14:21; 2 Kgs. 21:7; 23:27) and is reflected in the Psalms (Pss.
87; 122; 132). But in the premonarchic period it is undeniable that
other places served as "central sanctuaries" for shorter or longer
periods. Shiloh is the most obvious such place (cf. 1 Sam. 1–4; Jer.
7:12), because of the known presence of the tabernacle and ark
there. Shechem and Bethel are canvassed by some scholars as
earlier such sites, but the evidence is more dubious. Nonetheless,
the existence of a central sanctuary preceded the initial centralizing of the cult in Jerusalem by David or any of the subsequent
reform movements of Davidic kings such as Asa in the ninth
century BCE (1 Kgs. 15:11–14; 2 Chron. 15), Hezekiah in the
eighth (2 Kgs. 18:3–4; 2 Chron. 29–30) and Josiah in the seventh
(2 Kgs. 23:4–25; 2 Chron. 34–35). As many scholars recognize,
therefore, the "centralizing" law of Deuteronomy 12 cannot be
reliably linked solely to the Josianic reform in the seventh century or indeed necessarily and originally to Jerusalem. That identification, according to von Rad, "was probably too hasty . . . The
fact cannot indeed be disputed that later, during the course of
Josiah's reform, the law was applied to the sanctuary at Jerusalem, but this proves nothing at all about the origin of the requirement" (*Deuteronomy*, p. 94; cf. additional note).

12:6–12 / The repeating sections (vv. 6–7 and 11–12)
call for two things: (a) that the people should **bring** their **offerings** of all kinds to the sanctuary of Yahweh, and (b) that they
should **eat** and **rejoice** there in a community-inclusive way (v. 12).
The list of seven different items in verse 6 seems designed to be
as broad as possible, but is not concerned with precise or exhaustive listing. (On **burnt offerings** and **sacrifices**, cf. Lev. 1–7; on
tithes, cf. Deut. 14:22–29; on vows, cf. Deut. 23:21–23 and Lev. 27;
on **the firstborn**, cf. Deut. 15:19–23 and Exod. 13:1–16.) The point
is, *whatever* your worship requires you to bring, it must be brought
to the place Yahweh chooses. None of it must be squandered by
being falsely attributed to the gods of Canaan, no matter what the
temptation to credit them with the fertility powers associated
with them. Only Yahweh had "brought" the people to the land.
Only Yahweh would give its fruitfulness and fertility. Therefore only Yahweh should be the "destination" of their recipro-

cal "bringing" of his bounty in gratitude and worship. It bears
repeating that the primary point of the chapter is that the people's
worship and offerings should be brought to Yahweh's sanctuary
and not to Canaanite ones; the point is not that they should be
brought to one sanctuary as opposed to many.

The theme of "rejoicing before the LORD" is characteristic
of Deuteronomy (cf. 14:26; 16:11, 14; 26:11; 27:7; and Lev. 23:40).
Chapter 8 envisages a people enjoying the bounty of the land to
such an extent that they would be in danger of forgetting the
Lord in their satiety and pride. Here, a way to prevent that
danger is to regularly do some of their eating and rejoicing
specifically in the presence of Yahweh, so that there could be no
mistaking where the bounty came from (**because the LORD your
God,** and no fertility god or goddess, **has blessed you,** v. 7).

The emphasis on feasting and joy in the worship of Israel
is striking. The idea of a God who somehow disapproves of
human enjoyment of material things is far removed from these
texts. Eating and rejoicing are not just permitted; they are commanded! Furthermore, they are to permeate the whole of life **(in
everything you have put your hand to,** v. 7). They also filter
through the whole Bible, including the astonishing freedom of
Jesus' eating habits, by which he demonstrates the inclusiveness
of the kingdom of God in direct conformity with the ethos of this
Deuteronomic text and in equally direct conflict with the exclusiveness of table-fellowship rules among the Pharisees. It was an
infectiously attractive part of the life of the first Christian
community (Acts 2:44–47). And of course it characterizes the
eucharistic meal at the heart of Christian worship, which both
celebrates what God has done redemptively (echoing the historical dimension of blessing in our text) and anticipates the messianic banquet (for which the future orientation of verse 10 sows
an eschatological seed).

Two other points are worth noting about Israel's festal
worship. First, it was to be *morally pure.* The command to eat and
rejoice in the presence of Yahweh follows hard on the heels of the
command to destroy the phallic and fertility symbols of Canaanite religion in which cultic sex played such a role. All of that was
excluded from Israel's worship, which had to be **not . . . in *their*
way** (v. 4). However, not having orgies does not mean not having
fun. Canaanite depravity was to be replaced by Israelite purity,
but Israelites could still enjoy their worship, physically, and emo-
tionally: **eat and rejoice!**

Secondly, Israelite worship was to be *socially inclusive and responsible.* Verse 12 specifies that the whole household must share in the enjoyment of the worship and feasting at the sanctuary, including male and female slaves (**menservants and maidservants**). **The Levites** also must be included, since, having no land, they were dependent on the offerings of the people and a share in the meat of those sacrifices that were not wholly consumed on the altar. Hence the warning **not to neglect the Levites** in verse 19. This social inclusiveness and compassionate sensitivity of Israel's worship is expanded to include other categories of needy people: the widows, orphans, and aliens, in 14:27–29; 16:11, 14. It was not enough to insist that the poor and aliens be treated with judicial equality in court or to provide charitable storage depots for welfare handouts to them (14:28f.). They must be included in the very heart of Israel's life—the joyful worship and feasting in the presence of God. In this way Israel would add yet another dimension to the multiple ways in which their national life was intended to imitate and mirror what Yahweh was like and had done. For did not Yahweh himself defend the cause of the widow and orphan? Did not Yahweh also love the aliens, feeding and clothing them (Deut. 10:18)? No worship, then, that claims to love God but excludes those whom God loves can be acceptable to God—a point that the prophets expressed negatively with such damning ferocity and that the early church expressed positively in the social care associated with their worship (Acts 2:44–46; 4:32–37).

12:13–28 / The remaining section of the chapter, which again comes to us in two fairly parallel parts, 13–19 and 20–28, deals with the matter of "profane slaughter." It is related to Leviticus 17, which in its context had dealt with how the Israelites were to kill animals for food while they were a pilgrim people in the wilderness. The instruction there was that those classes of animal that were sacrificial (oxen, lambs, and goats) should be killed and eaten as meat only after proper sacrificial rituals at the tabernacle. The intention was to prevent their use in idolatrous rituals away from the tabernacle (Lev. 17:7). However, wild animals caught by hunting could be freely eaten (though with the blood properly drained, Lev. 17:13) since they were nonsacrificial anyway (Lev. 1:2). Deuteronomy looks ahead to the Israelites living throughout the land in scattered settlements (**in any of your towns**, v. 15; cf. v. 20). Then, unlike the Israel of the wilderness camped around the tabernacle, many would live at a distance from Yahweh's sanctuary. In such circumstances, to insist that no meat be eaten except that which had been sacrificed at the sanctuary would consign the majority of the population to a vegetarian diet supplemented by game birds or animals caught by hunting. Thus, the rules laid down here allow **animals from the herds and flocks** (v. 21—i.e., animals eligible for sacrifice) to be slaughtered and eaten with no sacrificial requirements (vv. 15, 20). For kitchen purposes, such animals could be regarded as no different from game animals (**gazelle or deer,** vv. 15, 22). And since it was simple butchery without sacrifice, the ritual distinctions between **the ceremonially unclean and the clean** did not apply to those who shared the meal. The ritually unclean could not partake of a sacrifice, but they could enjoy the family roast. Any food, however, vegetable or animal, that was specifically offered to God, in **tithe, firstborn,** or for any other reason, must be properly brought to the sanctuary (vv. 17f., 26f.). And whether profane or sacrificial, all killing of animals must be done with proper regard for the sacredness of the **blood** as vehicle of life (cf. Lev. 17:10–14). In ordinary butchery for food, they were to **pour it out on the ground,** with no atoning significance (vv. 16, 23f.), **but the blood of your sacrifices must be poured beside the altar of the LORD your God,** where it made atonement (v. 27).

12:29–32 / The final paragraph returns to the theme of the opening verses, with renewed warning against the temptation to imitate Canaanite religious practices. Here the warning is intensified by reference to **all kinds of detestable things** that characterize their idolatry. The moral aspect of God's judgment on the Canaanites is illustrated by the horrific practice of child-sacrifice. In Hebrew, the word **even** and the word order of the sentence emphasize the sense of revulsion at such a practice.

In conclusion, then, although the historical issues addressed by the chapter may be remote from us now, a number of timeless principles are enunciated regarding the worship of God's people. There is the call for *total renunciation* of all other names than the saving, covenant name of Yahweh. The careful identification and rejection of idolatry is as pressing a need in the modern church as in ancient Israel, just as the temptation to yield to the seduction of the gods of our day is as real now as then. There is the rich and liberating call for *wholehearted rejoicing* before God, which, by consecrating all of life to God, liberates the ordinary and the "secular" to be enjoyed under God's blessing. A line can be drawn from the freedom of the second half of this chapter to the freedom of 1 Timothy 4:3–5. And there is the challenging call for worship to be *socially responsible,* inclusive, compassionate, which finds some echoes not only in the practice of the NT church but also in the sharp words of Paul (1 Cor. 11:17–22) and of James (Jas. 2).

Additional Notes §15

The comparison McConville draws between Deut. 12 and Deut. 7 is as follows.

12:1–4	Command to destroy the peoples and religion of Canaan	7:1–5	Command to destroy the peoples and religion of Canaan
12:5–12	Israel's holiness reflected in command to worship at chosen place	7:6–11	God's choice of Israel as a holy people
12:13–28	Enjoyment of abundance of the land as corollary of holiness, and applied to cultic realm in terms of "free" slaughter	7:12–16	Enjoyment of abundance of the land as corollary of holiness
12:29–32	Warning against ensnarement by foreign religion	7:17–26	Warning against ensnarement by foreign religion (*Law and Theology,* p. 60)

12:2 / Mountains . . . hills . . . every spreading tree: These favorite places of Canaanite worship were imitated in later Israelite history as idolatrous shrines, in spite of this warning against them (e.g., Hos. 4:13; Jer. 2:20; 3:6; 17:2; 1 Kgs. 14:23; 2 Kgs. 16:4; 17:10). Cf. Holladay, " 'On Every High Hill' "; Vaughan, " '*Bāmā*' "; and Whitney, " 'Bamoth.' " It is noticeable, however, that the technical term *bāmôt* (usually translated "high places," but probably meaning "local shrines"), which is the repeated target of condemnation in the later prophetic and historical texts, is *not* used here or anywhere at all in Deut. This seems to indicate that Deut. 12 is not the alleged program of cult centralization from the time of Josiah (see introduction, pp. 6–8, and additional note on 12:5), since Josiah's program was the most sustained attempt hitherto in Israel to remove the *bāmôt* (cf. Manley, *Book of the Law,* p. 133), and Deut. never uses the word *bāmôt* at all.

12:5 / This is a key verse in the theory that this chapter calls for the centralization of Israel's worship at the sole sanctuary (i.e., Jerusalem) and in the consequent linking of Deut. to Josiah's seventh-century reform, of which cult centralization is said to be a major feature. The arguments around this question have been well rehearsed elsewhere, so only a few points need be raised here.

(a) The text is primarily concerned with the purity and exclusiveness of Israel's worship and its distinctiveness from *Canaanite* religion rather than with the centralization of *Israelite* worship as such. That is, the text does not demand a single place instead of many places of *Israelite* worship, but an exclusive place for the worship of Yahweh as opposed to the places of *Canaanite* worship.

(b) **The place** is not named (though it could have been, just as Gerizim and Ebal were named in advance), and as many scholars recognize, this text could thus have been appropriate at any time in Israel's history after the settlement in relation to several central but temporary sanctuaries (e.g., Shiloh) before Jerusalem permanently filled that role. The only name that mattered was the name of Yahweh that was to replace the names of any other gods. The text does not so much say that Yahweh would put his name in only one place as that Israel should seek only the place where Yahweh would put his name, wherever that might in future be. Such a place would be "central," even if temporary, as long as the ark stayed there.

(c) While the natural reading of the text certainly points to a specific central sanctuary, it is not necessarily implying a *sole* sanctuary for all Israel. There is an emphasis on the *unity* of Israel's faith and worship, but that unity is to be founded on the legitimacy of being chosen by Yahweh and bearing Yahweh's name, not necessarily on the numerical singularity of the place of worship. If Deut. had indeed intended the centralization of all worship on a single site, and that site is assumed to be Jerusalem, then the instructions for building an altar on Mt. Ebal (27:1–8) contradict that whole agenda and are thus inexplicable in terms of the theory.

(d) The syntax of v. 14 can be understood in a *distributive* sense—i.e., "at whatever place Yahweh will choose in any of your tribes." This would then imply that the single central sanctuary of v. 5 was not envisaged as necessarily one sole place for all Israel's history. The view that v. 5 was a later editorial or legislative corrective to the potentially ambiguous v. 14 seems to assume somewhat incompetent redactors who could have simply edited v. 14 (cf. Mayes, *Deuteronomy*, p. 227; Halpern, "Centralization").

(e) The singular **the place** can also be understood in a *generic* sense, that is, applied to a class or category. Even if the author had in mind a particular central place of worship, that would not necessarily exclude other legitimate sanctuaries. The use of generic or collective singular nouns to denote a whole class of people is a marked feature of Deut., e.g., the common use of "the alien," "the widow," "the orphan." The law of the king in Deut. 17:14–20 consistently uses the singular, even in the significantly similar phrase, "the king the LORD your God chooses" (17:15). Yet it obviously does not imply that Israel would always have only one king (vs. divided kingdom). Likewise, God promises to raise up "a prophet like Moses" (18:15–22). It is very clear that the text is speaking generically and not in a numerically singular sense. It provides a test for distinguishing the false prophet ("that prophet") from the true one; again, presumably not implying that there would be only one of each. What mattered was not how many prophets might come along, but their authenticity and legitimacy in relation to the name of Yahweh. This parallel suggests that a generic sense of "the place" in 12:5 (and subsequent references) can coexist alongside the vision of a particular chosen, central sanctuary.

(f) Finally, it is often overlooked that a generic sense of *hammāqôm*, "the place," *is actually present* in the immediate context. Frequently commentaries contrast **the place** (sg.) of v. 5 with **the places** (pl.) of v. 2 and argue from that to a policy of total centralization on a single sanctuary. However, they ignore the fact that the last two words of v. 3 are *hammāqôm hahû᾿*, "that place" (sg.; the NIV again shows its preference for plurals with **those places**). The word is just as *singular* as in v. 5, and yet it clearly refers generically to the plurality of *Canaanite* shrines that the Israelites were to destroy. Now if the plurality of Canaanite shrines can be collectively called "that place" in v. 3, then **the place** of v. 5 could admit a generic or a distributive sense and need not be limited exclusively to a *sole* sanctuary.

In conclusion, then, I am arguing that to regard Deut. 12 as a programmatic text for a seventh-century campaign to centralize all worship of Yahweh on a sole sanctuary is to read into it far more than is there. Its concern is with the unity, purity, and legitimacy of the worship of Yahweh, in vigorous polemical conflict with the polytheism, depravity, and idolatry of the gods of Canaan. And that was a concern that, according to the Deuteronomic History, characterized the attempts at reform of more than one king of Judah.

12:7 / **In the presence of the LORD:** This expression, *lipnê yhwh*, lit. "before the face of Yahweh" occurs 25 times in Deut., of which 13 are linked to "the place the LORD will choose," indicating God's presence there. Wilson, *Fire*, argues that it implies a true, localized presence of Yahweh for his worshippers when, for example, they **eat** and **rejoice** before him. Wilson strongly counters the view, advanced by von Rad (*Studies*, pp. 38f.) and widely followed, that Deut. "demythologized" the Jerusalem temple cult in which Yahweh actually dwelt in the temple and instead regarded God as transcendent, available on earth only indirectly through the placing of the *name* of God (so-called Name-theology). See also McConville, "God's 'Name.' "

12:15–25 / According to the Documentary Hypothesis, which regards the Priestly material (referred to as P) as the latest (exilic) source of the completed Pentateuch, Lev. 17 (part of P) has to be regarded as coming later than Deut. and as intended to repeal the permissiveness of the regulations in Deut. 12. It seems much more probable, however, that the reverse is the case, namely that the Deuteronomic text constitutes a relaxing of the earlier Levitical restriction of all slaughter for food to sacrifices at the sanctuary. On this issue, and on the relationship of both texts to the event in 1 Sam. 14:31–35, see McConville, *Law and Theology*, pp. 42–48.

12:31 / On the Israelite abhorrence of the Canaanite practice of child-sacrifice, cf. 2 Kgs. 16:3; 17:17; 21:6; Jer. 19:4; Ezek. 23:37; Ps. 106:37f.; and C. J. H. Wright, *God's Land*, pp. 231–35.

§16 Sources of the Temptation to Go after Other Gods (Deut. 13:1–18)

Continuing the concern for the purity of Israel's worship, in line with the first commandment, Deuteronomy warns the people of the kinds of situation in which they might be tempted or pressured into deserting Yahweh for other gods. First, the danger of false religious leaders (vv. 1–5); second, the possible conflict of loyalties when close family members are involved (vv. 6–11); third, the pressure of an influential group of leaders in a community (vv. 12–18).

Temptation from Apparently Authentic Prophets (13:1–5)

The canonical, normative force of the word that God had already given to Israel (12:32 [Hb. 13:1]; cf. 4:2) was to be given priority over any future prophetic words. This principle is further developed in the law relating to prophets in 18:15–22 by stating that "the prophet" envisaged must be "like Moses." No sign that appears to authenticate is to be given precedence over the content of the words spoken by a prophet. He may come with the signs of a true prophet, but if his words contradict the normative covenantal demand, then he is false and must be purged from the body of Israel like a lethal poison.

13:1–2 / **If a prophet, or one who foretells by dreams** . . . (lit. "dreamer of dreams"): there is nothing *prima facie* false about this description. Dreams were a recognized and authentic way by which God could give messages (cf. Num. 12:6; Joel 2:28, though contrast Jer. 23:25–32; 29:8). The prophet may try to establish himself as a genuine prophet by announcing **a miraculous sign or wonder,** which then **takes place**—perhaps a successful prediction or miraculous event. Both signs and wonders are associated with the mighty power of Yahweh, especially in the exodus-Sinai-conquest narrative (cf. Deut. 4:34). So far so good, then.

This hypothetical prophet has the standard means (dreams) and he apparently taps into divine power. However, if this seemingly authentic prophet suggests that the people should **follow other gods,** all the fire alarms in Israel should begin ringing, for no prophet sent by Yahweh would lead the people into head-on denial of the first and fundamental demand of Yahweh—*"no other gods besides me."* His words cancel out all his amazing deeds. No display of miraculous powers, no amount of signs and wonders can lend a moment's credibility to anybody with a message so clearly at odds with covenant truth and demand.

13:3 / The first response the Israelites must make to any such message, however dazzling its supporting act, is that they **must not listen.** The very words must fall on deaf ears. Rather, they must exercise the discernment to see through the false message to the **testing** of God. We must be careful to see that this does not mean God would be trying to entice Israel to sin, but rather testing them to discover whether their actions would tally with their profession (cf. 6:16; 8:2). And what was being tested was the most fundamental commitment that God's people are called upon to make, as verse 3's explicit echo of the Shema (6:5) makes clear. **To find out whether you love him,** does not quite capture the stress of the unusual Hebrew phrase, which means "to know if loving him really is the case with you," or, "to know if you *do* indeed love him." The challenge of idolatry provided a test of covenant commitment.

13:4 / Echoing 10:12f., this verse emphatically reverses the word order all the way through, as the NIV indicates at the start. "After the Lord your God you must walk, him you must fear, his commands you must keep, his voice you must hear, him you must serve, him you must cling to." A people consciously living with this orientation and commitment would have the spiritual health and vitality to recognize and reject idolatrous enticement as decisively as a healthy body deals with invading germs.

13:5 / The death penalty for incitement to idolatry is consistent with the foundational nature of the first commandment (cf. Exod. 22:20; 23:13). It needs to be seen, not as a vestige of religious fanaticism or primitive barbarism, but as a measure of the seriousness with which the covenant was taken as the foundation of Israel's whole national existence and peoplehood. To go after other gods, as well as to be in **rebellion against the**

LORD, was effectively a form of treason against the whole community—i.e., a serious criminal offense with potentially disastrous results for everybody. The prophet who led people in that direction would bring God's curse on the nation (11:28). So who should die, him or the whole nation? Hence the purpose of the execution as designed to **purge the evil from among you.** It was a self-preserving act of removing a threat to the nation's health and survival, like a body ejecting a poison.

Two further aspects of the offense are specified here. First, the phony prophet **preached rebellion against the LORD your God, who brought you out of Egypt and redeemed you from the land of slavery.** This, of course, was the basis on which Israel was commanded to love Yahweh and to have no other gods (5:6f.; 6:20–25). So deliberately going after other gods (and worse, leading others to do so) was, to say the least, gross ingratitude. In the light of all Israel owed to Yahweh, "no other god is owed anything" (Clifford, *Deuteronomy*, p. 82). But a more serious effect of such desertion was that it would cut Israel off from the very source of their salvation. Yahweh was not merely "their God," but their *saving* God. Where would they turn to for salvation if they abandoned God (cf. Jer. 2:27–28)? To go after other gods was to exchange the God whose saving power had been proved for gods who couldn't even save their own breath, let alone save their own worshippers. No wonder Jeremiah felt the heavens shudder with amazement at such folly (Jer. 2:10–12).

Transferring the matter to a Christian context, the clearest criterion of what constitutes false or potentially idolatrous teaching from religious leaders (whether claiming prophetic gifts or not, whether producing signs and wonders or not) is how their teaching relates to the central truth of the saving gospel. For Israel, that was the story of the exodus. For Christians it is the story of the cross. For both it is a matter of the essential priority of God's grace and the good news of God's historical redemption. To distort these essentials or to lead people away from them into figments of human speculation is culpably idolatrous, as this ancient text declares.

Secondly, the false prophet **has tried to turn you from the way the LORD your God commanded you to follow.** The expression, "the way of the Lord" usually has a strongly ethical meaning (cf. 10:12ff.). It implies a whole orientation of personal and social life toward the values, priorities, and will of God, including commitment to justice and compassion, to integrity and purity.

The way of Yahweh meant all these things for Israel, so to go after other gods was to go a different way, to adopt different social, economic, political, and personal values. To turn from the true God is to turn from the truly human also. Godlessness and inhumanity are correlative.

In a Christian context also, there is an ethical criterion of falsehood (one of the major factors, for example, in the way 1 John handles the matter). An alleged "gospel" cannot be true if, instead of standing with God alongside the poor and oppressed, it adds to their misery by dubbing their poverty lack of faith or it joins hands with their oppressors. Signs and wonders do not necessarily authenticate the truth of the message, the purity of the motives, or the integrity of the mission of those who perform them. The most awful perversions of biblical truth can sometimes be accompanied by the most awesome displays of "miraculous signs and wonders." We need to judge with our ears, not just with our eyes.

Temptation from the Domestic Circle (13:6–11)

13:6–11 / In the private realm of the home and family the temptation would be all the more subtle, more difficult to detect, being done **secretly** (v. 6), and much more difficult to resist because of the close relationships and family authority involved. The harshness of verse 8 has to be understood in this light. All human instincts would militate against exposing a renegade within the family or a close friend, so the law had to address those instincts with powerful negatives.

Now, in ancient Israelite society, ties of kinship were the strongest of all horizontal human loyalties. Theologically also, as we saw when discussing the fifth commandment, the family stood at the center of the triangular pattern of relationships between God, Israel, and the land. Moral and legal responsibility to the family therefore came higher than individual freedoms and rights (as the case of the rebellious son shows sharply, 21:18–21). But, although the family had priority over the individual, covenant loyalty to God had priority over both. Ties of family and friendship must not override covenant justice and the protection of the whole community.

Where family life and covenant loyalty intertwine, then the strongest possible bond, with tremendous potential for long-term blessing, is forged. But when they are thrown into conflict, then the most horrendous tensions arise; these are often the most painful and costly conflicts that believers have to face. The family seeking to be loyal to the living God agonizes over one rebellious member living in idolatry or profligacy. The individual seeking to be loyal to God, whether by mere profession of faith or by obedience to God's call, can be torn apart if that loyalty is not shared, or is actively attacked, by family and friends (as was Jeremiah's lonely lot, Jer. 11:18–23; 12:6). Jesus endured this tension and temptation. He faced pressure from his own close family (Matt. 12:46–50), and from a **closest friend** (Matt. 16:22f.) to deflect him from his path of covenant obedience to God. He warned his disciples that they too would face such opposition (Matt. 10:34–36). He even presented the potentially rival claims of God and family in the characteristic Deuteronomic terms of "love" and "hate" (Luke 14:26; Matt. 10:37). Neither Jesus nor Deuteronomy were, by any stretch of imagination, *antifamily*. They were both passionately *anti-idolatry* and recognized in the family one of the toughest and subtlest sources of hidden idolatry, on which many a profession of loyalty to the kingdom of God has foundered.

Temptation from Public Apostasy (13:12–18)

13:12–18 / Apostasy could grip a whole town under the influence of **wicked men.** These men could be a small but influential group who seek to reintroduce the Canaanite ways of the original place; or a new element, such as the prophets of Baal imported by Jezebel; or the kind of men who supported Jezebel in the civil community (cf. 1 Kgs. 21:8–14, where "scoundrels" is the same term as **wicked men** in v. 13 here). Any report that such things had happened in a town of Israel were to be treated most seriously. But not precipitately. The law has two features that operated to protect towns from wanton destruction by jealous or greedy neighbors on a trumped up charge of harboring apostasy. Clearly towns could be as much at risk from such injustice as individuals. First, a heavy stress is laid on the need to **inquire, probe and investigate it thoroughly** (v. 14). Obviously, any "inquisition" can turn nasty, but the law desires truth and justice, not mob witch-hunts. And secondly, if the charge proved true, then the whole town was to be put under the severest level of *ḥērem*. Because of this ban on acquiring goods during a war, all property and **livestock** was to be destroyed (v. 15). In other words, there would be no economic benefit for those who carried out the "execution." The law could not be exploited as a "raiders' charter," giving one town the ability to accuse another of apostasy, attack it, and carry off its wealth (see Vasholz, "A Legal 'Brief'").

The fact that the town, though Israelite, was to be dealt with through the *ḥērem* also shows that its idolatry effectively abolished its covenant membership and rendered the town virtually Canaanite (cf. Craigie, *Deuteronomy*, p. 226, and Weinfeld, *Deuteronomic School*, pp. 91–100). Being an Israelite settlement on the land of promise did not guarantee immunity from God's wrath. The law illustrates the precise opposite of the divine favoritism that Deuteronomy is sometimes accused of. If Israelites chose to go the way of Canaanite gods and cults, then God would do to Israelites, individuals and communities, exactly what had been done to the Canaanites. Eventually, the year 587 BCE would see, in the greatest national catastrophe of Israel's OT history, Deuteronomy 13:12–16 being executed on the very place where God's name would dwell, and that not by Israelites carrying out covenant justice, but by a pagan nation acting on God's behalf. The only difference would be that a "remnant" would return, and it would not **remain a ruin for ever, never to be rebuilt.**

Contemplating the severity of a chapter like this, one's first reaction may be gratitude that we no longer live under the sanctions of a theocratic state in which apostasy threatens the constitution and survival of the state itself and is thus criminal and capital. But we then have to face the fact that we owe that social and practical liberation more to the Enlightenment, which broke so-called Christendom's power to enforce legislation like this, than to an understanding of the implications of the NT gospel and its effect on the relationship of God's people to the state in the messianic age. But then we need to recognize also the extent of the penetration of Enlightenment secular presuppositions into the worldview of the church as much as of secular society.

C. S. Lewis once said that if we no longer feel comfortable with the cursing psalms, for example, it is not because of our greater, "Christian" sensitivity, but because of our appalling moral apathy. We no longer feel the passion of the psalmist that God should deal with evil and evildoers and vindicate God's own moral order in the world. We respond to idolatrous, blasphemous evil not with a curse, but a shrug, and then have the gall to claim morally higher ground than ancient Israel. Similarly, if we can no longer identify with the scale of priorities and values that undergird Deuteronomy 13, it is manifestly not because we have acquired a greater appreciation of the value of human life, but because we have lost any sense of the awful majesty of God's reality. The western church, more than it cares to admit, has imbibed that dichotomized, privatized, cultural worldview in which God is no longer the ultimate governing reality and Lord of all human life and community, private and public, domestic and political, local and global. And having for all practical purposes accepted the box into which the surrounding culture has confined God, it is not surprising that we have difficulty with the concept of idolatry. For if the living God is little more than an idol, where do other idols fit? We lack the categories to define them and the tools to discern them. And thus, in reality, their power over us is infinitely enhanced because we don't even recognize them. We can't begin to work on the relevance of a chapter like Deuteronomy 13 when we don't know what it is talking about. We have long since failed the test of verse 3. For only those who know and love the living God "with all their heart (= understanding, mind, intellect) and soul (personal commitment)" know what idols are. One of the most critical missiological tasks facing the church today is to recover, rethink, and reapply a fully biblical understanding of idolatry, with a sober and painful evaluation of the extent of its penetration, not only to the roots of western culture, but into the very bloodstream of the church. We will not find ourselves reviving the legislation of Deuteronomy 13, but we may become more impressed by the sharpness of its delineation between truth and falsehood, between the saving God and lifeless substitutes, and ultimately, between life and death.

Additional Notes §16

13:2 / **Gods you have not known** does not mean gods Israel knew nothing about, as if the Israelites, like Athenians, were to say "We've never heard of that one before, let's try it." It means gods they were not committed to in covenant relationship as a result of saving experience. In that sense, Israel knew no other god (cf. Deut. 4:35; Hos. 13:4) and Yahweh knew no other people (Amos 3:2).

13:3 / Signs of some kind were an expected part of a prophet's credibility. The expectation, however, could produce demands that were little more than an attempt to evade the manifest force of the prophet's **words**, as Jesus discerned (cf. Matt. 12:38ff.; Mark 8:11f.; Luke 11:29–32; John 6:30ff.; 1 Cor. 1:22). It is possible that Jesus himself came under suspicion of being a false prophet and therefore some of the communities he visited may have feared coming under legal or divine judgment for harboring such a one. This type of suspicion would also account for the familial divisions, the predominantly rural ministry, and the severe test of loyalty he engendered (see Neale, "Was Jesus a *Mesîth*?").

13:5 / **Purge the evil from among you:** This expression is used in 17:12; 19:11–13, 19; 21:18–21; 22:22, 23–24; 24:7. These are all cases of serious capital crimes that threatened to bring the wrath and curse of God upon the whole nation. Execution of the criminal was thus a "purgative" or protective action, though deterrence was also a factor (cf. 13:11: "Then all Israel will hear and be afraid, and no one among you will do such an evil thing again"). On the rationale behind Israel's penalties, cf. Wenham, "Legal System."

13:7 / The text makes the exclusiveness of Israel's loyalty to Yahweh as valid worldwide as Yahweh's own uniqueness is valid throughout the heavens (cf. 4:32). The word **land** should really be "earth" (exactly the same as in 28:64). The lordship of Yahweh was not subject to geographical limits or cultural relativities. The one universal God has global loyalty rights.

§17 Israel's Distinctiveness Mirrored in the Home and Farm (Deut. 14:1–29)

It might seem at first sight that the destruction of a whole apostate community and all its property (13:12–16) is worlds away from the question of what you were allowed to cook for lunch, but in fact a common principle governed both—the distinctiveness of Israel as a people wholly and exclusively committed to Yahweh. This principle, which underlies all the preaching of chapters 4–11 and finds its most succinct expression in 7:6, is repeated at the head of this chapter (v. 2) as an introduction to some domestic matters that must also conform to the demands of holiness. Such matters included funeral customs (v. 1), the distinctions between clean and unclean food (vv. 3–21), and the instructions regarding tithes (vv. 22–29). It is important to see this theological continuity of thought, otherwise the laws of this chapter may seem unconnected to the dominant concerns of the book.

14:1 / **You are the children of the LORD your God.** The Hebrew is emphatic, as though intentionally making a contrast with the picture of apostasy and judgment in the preceding chapter: lit. "Sons are you to Yahweh your God." Verse 2 has the same parallel structure, "A holy people are you . . . " The picture of Israel as the child (sg.) of Yahweh has been used twice already (1:31; 8:5). There the stress was on God's action for Israel, in care and discipline. Here, however, the stress is on the other side of the parent-child relationship, namely, the duty of the child to obey the parent's will.

Do not cut (better, "lacerate" or "gash") **yourselves . . . or shave . . . for the dead.** (Cf. also Lev. 19:27f.) Both customs are well-known rites in connection with mourning and were Canaanite cultic practices related to Baal. Special emphasis was given to self-laceration, which was connected with death and fertility ritual (cf. 1 Kgs. 18:28; and Craigie, *Deuteronomy*, pp. 229f.)

The view that it reflects an OT respect for the body may well be, but it is not explicit in the text. Removing some or all of the hair as a response to mourning is found in the OT (Isa. 3:24; 15:2; 22:12; Jer. 16:6; Ezek. 7:18; Amos 8:10; Mic. 1:16), but self-cutting is mentioned only in unusual circumstances (Jer. 16:6; 41:5; cf. 47:5, of the Philistines).

14:2 / This verse is a repetition, word for word, of 7:6 (see commentary there), so our interpretation of the material here needs to be linked to chapter 7's emphasis on Israel's distinctiveness from the nations based on their status as Yahweh's elect people and on Yahweh's own character and action. It is this that ruled out pagan practices associated with death (v. 1), and it is this that also governed the food distinctions that follow—as is further shown by the bracketing reference to holiness in verse 21.

14:3 / This introduction to the food laws provides, by its terse brevity, another link with earlier texts. Israelites were not to eat **any detestable thing.** The word *tô'ēbâ* used here is the same as in 7:25; 12:31; and 13:14. These three earlier uses all depict Canaanite idolatry, whether practiced by Canaanites or by apostate Israelites. Does this mean then that eating an unclean animal was as heinous a crime as worshipping other gods? No, but it means that the *principle* that lay behind the distinction in the animal world in relation to Israel's eating habits was the same as that which required their rejection of Canaanite gods—namely, the holiness (distinctness, difference) of Israel. Incidentally, the uncleanness of certain creatures here is from the perspective of the Israelite as a cook, not as a biologist, nor as an aesthetics critic. The rest of the OT shows that all creatures share in the goodness and wonder of creation and bring glory to God. The selection of some as clean for eating did not denigrate the rest. Cleanness and uncleanness were ritual categories, not moral judgments.

14:4–21 / The list of creatures is divided into the same categories as in Leviticus 11:1–23, according to their primary habitat—land (vv. 4–8), water (vv. 9–10), or air (11–20), probably thereby reflecting the order of the creation narrative. Recent anthropological insights reinforce OT theological concepts in viewing Israel's food laws as *symbolic of their distinctiveness as a nation* (as was so much else in their cult). Clean and unclean animals corresponded symbolically to Israel and other nations (cf. D. P. Wright, "Unclean and Clean (OT)," and G. J. Wenham,

Leviticus, ad loc.). The food laws were thus also a symbolic mirroring of Israel's election. Just as from among all the nations of the earth God had chosen only Israel, so from among all the animals Israel must choose only those deemed clean for eating. The food laws were thus a daily reminder to Israel of their status and role in God's purpose and of the consequent call to holiness in other more morally significant areas of personal and social life. Holiness was woven into everyday life. Every meal should have reminded the Israelite family of God's commitment to them and their commitment to God. A God who governs the kitchen should be not easily forgotten in the rest of life (see additional note).

Covenant commitment and distinctiveness are also important matters for Christians, but Christians, from the earliest NT days, have considered themselves no longer bound by the OT laws on clean and unclean food. Why is this? Mark records Jesus as having explicitly abrogated the distinction between clean and unclean food by declaring that moral distinctions matter more: what counts is not what goes into the mouth but what comes out of the heart (Mark 7:14–23). The OT itself, however, taught the greater priority of moral issues over purely ritual ones (e.g., 1 Sam. 15:22; Hos. 6:6; Ps. 51:16ff.), so it was not this perception alone that led to the abrogation of OT food laws in the NT. In the context of the saying in Mark, Jesus went to Tyre, met a Gentile woman, and healed her daughter. This rare exception to Jesus' normal practice of remaining among Jews pointed forward to the removal of the distinction between Jew and Gentile in the extended and redefined Israel of the Messiah. This end to the distinction is underlined in Acts 10, where Peter's vision taught him (to his great surprise) that the division of the animal kingdom was no longer to be perpetuated and prepared him for his epoch-making visit to the Gentile Cornelius. Thus, the removal of the barrier between Jew and Gentile in Christ meant that, for Christians, the distinctive badge of Jewish separateness had no further theological significance in the new, multi-racial, people of God (cf. Gal. 3:26–29; Eph. 2:11–22). The division of the animal kingdom that had mirrored it was accordingly abolished.

Yet food remains a matter of theological and ethical concern in the NT. What you ate and who you ate with could be controversial and divisive issues (Gal. 2:11–13; Rom. 14; 1 Cor. 8; 10:14–11:1), as could the question of who gets to eat at all (14:28f.; cf. 1 Cor. 11:21!). The Christian *is* required to submit to OT law in matters of food—not, however, to the ritual laws of Leviticus 11 or Deuteronomy 14, but to the more basic law of Leviticus 19:18 and Deuteronomy 10:18f., to *love your neighbor as yourself* (Rom. 13:8–10; 14:15)—expressed in what you do or don't eat in certain company.

14:22–27 / *The annual tithe.* The tithe law begins with the same kind of terse and emphatic summary of the law (v. 22), followed by detailed instructions, as verse 3 provides for the food laws. Another common feature is the verb **eat,** which negatively heads the food laws (**Do not eat,** v. 3) and positively heads the tithe law (**Eat,** v. 23). *Not eating* certain foods would be a sign of Israel's election and holiness (vv. 2–21). *Eating* and enabling others to eat and be satisfied would be a sign of their enjoyment of God's blessing that flowed from obedient response (vv. 22–29). Thus, in structure, theme, and theology, there is more unity within the chapter and between it and the wider theology of Deuteronomy than is first apparent if its contents are treated merely as independent laws. The instruction to **eat your grain, new wine and oil . . . in the presence of the LORD** is a way of acknowledging their source and their status as gifts of blessing (7:13 and 11:14)—they are not mere products of the fertility of nature, still less the gift of any fertility god of Canaan. Deuteronomy's constant educational passion surfaces again at the end of the verse (**so that you may learn . . .**), but with typical Deuteronomic human warmth. Inculcating the fear of God could be achieved during a family party just as much as during family prayers. The allowance made for long-distance commuters (vv. 24–26) only serves to reinforce the intention that the tithe should not be a solemn burden but a joyful celebration (v. 26b).

And do not neglect the Levites (v. 27)—this is a further reminder of the socially inclusive nature of Israel's worship (cf. 12:12, 19; 16:11, 14). This verse may well be an indicator that Deuteronomy's tithe law assumed the use of the tithe to support the Levites and priests serving at the sanctuary and ensures that local Levites should not be excluded from proper provision. The form of the instruction is forceful and possibly deliberately mirrors the command not to forget Yahweh in the context of eating and rejoicing (cf. 8:10–11).

14:28–29 / *The triennial tithe.* This use of the tithe in the third year is a unique provision of Deuteronomy, not found in the other texts. Its importance, however, is underlined by the repetition of its obligation in the solemn religious affirmations of 26:12–15. This triennial tithe was an element of Israel's welfare system for the relief of poverty. Other provisions included the annual gleaning rights (24:19–22), the sabbatical fallow year (cf. Exod. 23:11), and the range of legislation regarding debt, etc. The OT makes a structural, systemic response to economic disparities. Proper storage and controlled distribution of these food stocks would have needed careful supervision, monitoring, and accounting by the civil authorities. Probably the administration of this "social fund" fell among the other responsibilities of community elders. In other words, care for the poor was structured into the regular economic life of the nation. It was not left to *private charity*. Rather, it was a *public duty* that the weakest and poorest should also be enabled to **eat and be satisfied** from the blessing of Yahweh on the whole nation. Only thus, indeed, would that blessing abide (v. 29b). Only by sharing the blessing would the blessing continue—a central spiritual and ethical principle (cf. 15:14, 18).

Thus, the chapter begins with a declaration of Israel's holiness and election (v. 2) and ends with a renewed promise of Yahweh's blessing (v. 29). In between these two fundamentals of Israel's covenant relationship with Yahweh, it picks out, on the one hand, that factor of Israel's life which most illustrated their distinctiveness from the nations at a symbolic level (the food laws), and on the other hand, the dual covenantal response—vertical gratitude to God (the tithes) and horizontal care and support in the community (the triennial tithes). The common theme between the two halves of the chapter is "eating," and the underlying dynamic is the same as the rest of the book preaches constantly: grace experienced in blessing → response → practical obedience in the socioeconomic sphere → continued blessing. This ethical cycle is found with renewed force in Paul's teaching on Christian financial responsibilities: his exhortation in 2 Corinthians 8–9 appeals to the prior grace of God (8:5–9; 9:8), stresses the need for generosity to aim at equality (8:13–15), portrays giving as a matter of responsive obedience (9:13), and breathes an ethos of joy, thanksgiving, and continued blessing (9:6–14).

Additional Notes §17

14:1 / **Children of the LORD your God:** The portrayal of Israel's relationship to Yahweh in child-father terms is very ancient. Possibly the earliest reference to it is in the ancient poetry of Deut. 32:5, 6, 18, 19. In the historical tradition, the assertion that Israel was Yahweh's firstborn precedes the exodus (Exod. 4:22; cf. Hos. 11:1). Analysis of the references elsewhere, primarily in prophetic texts, shows two major usages. (a) When Israel is described in the singular as God's child, or God is spoken of as father, the emphasis is on what God has done, or should do, for the nation as a whole (see e.g., Deut. 1:31; 8:5; 32:6, 18; Exod. 4:22; Hos. 11:1; Jer. 31:9; Isa. 63:16; 64:8). (b) When the Israelites are described in the plural as God's children (as here), then the emphasis tends to be on what is expected of children, namely, obedience and loyalty—which Israel so frequently failed to show (see e.g., Isa. 1:2; 30:1, 9; Jer. 3:22; Mal. 1:6 (sg.); 2:10). Cf. de Boer, *Fatherhood;* C. J. H. Wright, *God's Land,* pp. 15–22; and Wright, *Knowing Jesus,* pp. 118–35.

14:4–19 / Many attempts have been made to explain why certain species were clean and others unclean. Some suggest that animals associated with pagan cults were unclean, but in many cases this does not hold—for example, bulls were sacred in Canaanite Baal worship yet perfectly clean in Israel. A popular view regards hygiene and health as a major factor. It is true that some of the unclean animals (e.g., pigs and carrion birds) are likely to convey contaminations and parasitic infestations. However, while we may recognize the value of such exclusions, this theory does not explain many of the distinctions (e.g., why deer are clean but rabbits unclean) and is not even hinted at in the text itself.

The more recent and more convincing explanation has come from the work of anthropologist Mary Douglas (see esp. *Purity*). She takes note of the three primary classifications (land, water, air) and the references to forms of movement in each element. There is a preference for what is regarded as "normal" in broad terms. The Israelite priestly understanding of holiness and cleanness was strongly based on a concern to preserve the wholeness or integrity of things and to avoid the mixing or confusion of categories, just as the event of creation itself was a matter of careful distinctions between light and darkness, heaven and earth, land and sea, etc. This was carried over into the classification of animals that conformed to a simple picture of what was "standard" for each sphere. Split-hooved ruminants were "standard" domestic land animals, suitable for sacrifice, and so all similar animals could be eaten (vv. 4–8). Fins and scales were the "standard" equipment of sea creatures; anything else was abnormal (vv. 9f.). Birds of prey and carrion eaters obviously ate flesh with its blood and therefore behaved in an "unclean" way (vv. 11–18). Creatures that moved in a mixture of ways and thus disturbed the boundaries or whose movements were wily and unpredictable ("swarming") were also "abnormal" (vv. 19–20). These categories were very general and not biologically precise. All that was at stake was the matter of *edibility*. Uncleanness for *that* purpose was not a rejection of the creature itself or a denial of its place within the wonders of God's praiseworthy creation—as the psalmists and others so often declare. Cf. Patrick, "Unclean and Clean (OT)," and G. J. Wenham, *Leviticus*, pp. 23f., 164–76.

14:21 / The reason for the instruction not to eat the meat of an animal found **already dead** (lit. "a carcass") was almost certainly the likelihood that its blood had not been properly drained out (cf. Lev. 17:15f., and McConville, *Law and Theology*, p. 81).

14:21b / Cf. also Exod. 23:19 and 34:26. In both those texts the prohibition comes after laws about sacrifices and first-fruits, and so it may well apply to some kind of sacrificial ritual, possibly connected with fertility. It is likely that some Canaanite practice was being forbidden. There is some Ugaritic evidence for this, though it is not clearly referring to a sacrifice (cf. Mayes, *Deuteronomy*, p. 243, and Haran, "Seething"). The law is the basis for the Jewish kosher regulations that ensure all milk and meat foods are kept entirely separate.

14:22–29 / Leviticus 27:30–33 and Num. 18:21–29 present a tithe that is for the support of the sanctuary and its personnel—priests and Levites, whereas Deut. describes the tithe as a family meal at the sanctuary (vv. 23–26) and (in the third year) the basis of a food storage scheme for welfare distribution to the needy (vv. 28f.), with apparently only secondary concern for the Levites (v. 27). For a history of the interpretation of these differences, see McConville, *Law and Theology*, pp. 68–78. McConville argues that the difference is wrongly exaggerated by some scholars. It seems likely that Deut. was fully aware of the major purpose of the tithe as a "tax" that served to support the sanctuary and did not intend the "family meal" to replace that. In any case, it is virtually impossible that a family could have consumed the whole of 10% of its annual produce of field and flock in one visit to the sanctuary, or even in several visits after each major harvest. Therefore, it is likely that the ingredients of the symbolic meal were subtracted from the bulk of the tithe that was given to the Levites and dealt with as prescribed in Num. 18. On this understanding, Deut. is not legislating in detail about the tithe, but rather, *assuming* that the regulations and primary purpose of the practice (the support of the sanctuary personnel) as described in Lev. and Num. were well known and still in force. Deuteronomy is adding (or emphasizing) the family feast to reinforce the ethos of the tithe as a matter of rejoicing with gratitude in the presence of a bountiful God.

§18 Release of Debts and Slaves (Deut. 15:1–23)

Those who see the order of the Decalogue reflected in the structure of the laws in Deuteronomy 12–26 relate the whole section from 14:28 to 16:17 to the fourth (sabbath) commandment. The sabbath commandment focused on the needs especially of the dependent sections of the population (5:14) and was motivated by God's redemptive action on behalf of Israel when they were oppressed slaves (5:15). Chapter 15 is saturated with the same social concern and the same motivation. It is the flagship for a flotilla of smaller sections in a similar vein in the following chapters. There is a warmth and compassion to this chapter that we find easier to identify with than the severity of, say, chapter 13. And yet, as was pointed out regarding chapter 14, it is vital that we hold together the theological integrity of the book. The first commandment, amplified by the Shema, is the foundation stone of all else. Total love of the sole God, the God known through historical revelation and experience as Yahweh, is the only adequate basis for the demanding social program outlined in the chapters to follow. The monotheistic passion of chapters 6–13 is the foundation on which the socio-ethical compassion of chapter 15 and related laws can be built.

The Release of Debt Pledges (15:1–11)

15:1–3 / In characteristic fashion, Deuteronomy here recalls an ancient law, adds some modification, and reinforces it with motivational preaching. The original law (Exod. 23:10f.) prescribed a sabbatical fallow year on the land. The similarity of the two laws is not easy to see in the NIV, but the Hebrew phrase translated **you must cancel debts** in Deuteronomy 15:1 uses the same word as that translated "let the land lie unplowed" in Exodus 23:11. It is the root *šmṭ*, meaning "to release." So, in Exodus, the law prescribes, "For six years you are to [work the land], but in the seventh year you shall *release* it." In Deuteronomy, the law says, "**At the end of every seven years,** you shall make *a release (šᵉmiṭṭâ)*." The Deuteronomic law thus expands the scope of the fallow year from release of land from the "burden" of plowing, to the release of human beings from the burden of debt. It thus picks up the humanitarian dimension of the original law, which was for the benefit of the poor (Exod. 23:11b), and consolidates it through a specific measure aimed at alleviating the prime component of poverty—debt.

The probable meaning of verse 2a is that creditors were required to release *the pledges* they had taken for the loans they had made to their debtors (see additional note). In many cases such pledges would have consisted of portions of land, whose produce would be used to repay the loan. As a last resort they would have been human pledges—i.e., dependents of the debtor, working for the creditor to pay off the debt (cf. Neh. 5:1–5), but it is probably primarily material pledges that are in view. It is still debated whether the release of the pledge in the seventh year meant a suspension of repayment in that year or a total cancellation of the debt itself. It may originally have been the former, but later Jewish tradition certainly took it in the latter sense. The law, of course, assumes that repayments of the loan would have been going on, scheduled over whatever period of years remained until the next *šᵉmiṭṭâ*. Even cancellation (as distinct from merely a suspension of payment) in the seventh year, therefore, would not have meant a forfeiture of the *total* debt, but a writing off of whatever remained unpaid by then. The nearer the next *šᵉmiṭṭâ*, therefore, the more likely that a larger part of the debt would remain unpaid, a fact which would naturally discourage lending. Verse 9 addresses this issue with a powerful moral, emotional, and religious appeal.

The distinction in the case of the foreigner (v. 3a) underlines the relational nature of the basic law as a requirement on "neighbors" (NIV **fellow Israelite**s) and kinsfolk. Loans to or by foreigners, who had no stake in the land but were probably traders, were treated differently from loans within the land-kinship network of Israel. Within the latter context, the covenant obligation was paramount, and so the debt-release law is sanctioned by linking it with the Lord of the covenant, Yahweh: (lit.) "Yahweh's release has been proclaimed" (v. 2b). This law is thus a perfect example of the combination of the vertical and horizontal directions of covenantal obligation.

15:4–6 / Coming immediately after the instructions about how to alleviate debt-poverty, the assertion, **However, there should be** (lit. "will be") **no poor among you,** sounds curiously inconsistent. Furthermore, it seems even more contradictory with verse 11, **There will always be poor people in the land.** A tension so obvious to us must also have been obvious to the author or editor of the original text, and thus, must be deliberate. This tension summons the reader/listener to reflect on the interweaving of ideals and realities that pervades the passage. Verses 4–6, on the one hand, portray an ideal situation: an Israel so rejoicing in God's blessing that they **fully obey** God's law, and thereby enjoy further blessing in a mutually reinforcing cycle of gift and response. In such a context, there need be no poverty. It is important, therefore, to set the opening declaration of verse 4a in the context of blessing (v. 4b), which is the consequence of obedience (v. 5), which is itself a response to blessing (v. 6). Verses 7–11, on the other hand, are based on the equally characteristic Deuteronomic awareness that Israel would *not* **fully obey** God in the socioeconomic realm, and therefore those verses build their exhortation on the realistic assumption that there will be those who will need special care and attention in society because of hardship and need. Goldingay coins the phrase "Deuteronomy's pastoral strategy" for this combination of upholding the highest ideal on the one hand and legislating for the realities of a sinful people on the other; for the fruitful ethical tension between what ought to be and what actually is (*Theological Diversity,* pp. 153–66).

The function of verses 4–6, then, is to set the highest possible agenda, to point to the ultimate goal of a perfect confluence of divine blessing and human obedience. Such a vision also functions eschatologically (as all the sabbatical institutions do), pointing to a future hope of a people living in blessing and obedience and without needs. It cannot be accidental that Luke, in his portrayal of the beginnings of the eschatological community of the Holy Spirit, chose to describe them in words taken almost directly from the LXX translation of verse 4, simply changing its future tense to the past ("There were no needy persons among them," Acts 4:34).

It is not an imperialist charter we find in verse 6b, but a matter of economic observation that the links between debt and servitude follow international as well as interpersonal lines. The way to avoid crushing national debts and deficits is not by further exploiting one's own poor, but the reverse. God promises that if the nation will look after its poor, its economy will not suffer. Modern countries would do well to follow this model.

15:7–11 / Having set out, in verses 4–6, the only conditions in which the *š*ᵉ*miṭṭâ* law would *not* be necessary (complete obedience and blessing), these verses proceed to give a portrait of the law in action, on the assumption that it would *always* be necessary (v. 11). It is a remarkable passage, beginning (vv. 7f.) and ending (vv. 10f.) with positive commands to generous lending, sandwiched around a negative warning against self-interested refusal to lend (v. 9). There is thus a double "push-pull" effect on the hearer. Generosity is commanded on the positive basis of God's authority, blessing, and gift, and on the negative basis of God's moral judgment against one who is hostile and grudging to the needy.

Furthermore, the rhetoric of the passage is stylistically emphatic. Hebrew gives weight to an imperative or a promise by a double verb form: infinitive plus imperfect (e.g., "giving you shall give," i.e., "you must surely/freely/generously give."). There is a greater density of this emphatic construction in Deuteronomy 15 than in any other chapter in the book. English translations have to use adverbs—e.g., **richly** (v. 4), **fully** (v. 5), **freely** (v. 8), **generously** (v. 10)—but the Hebrew, with its repetitive verb forms, has a kind of stereophonic double resonance that gives great weight and depth to the central theme of the chapter. This is further doubled by the opening pairs of verbs in verses 7–8. The required response to the needy was, (a) *negatively* (v. 7b), "Do not harden your heart" (the phrase, reminiscent of Sihon, 2:30, has ominous overtones of inevitable judgment), and "Do not shut your hand"; and (b) *positively* (v. 8), "open your hand," and "lend as much as he needs."

These rhetorical effects are reinforced by two other features of the language used here, which is both *physical* and *relational*. There is, first, a concentrated metaphorical use of *body-language* in the chapter as a whole, but especially in this section of it (cf. P. D. Miller, *Deuteronomy*, p. 136). Three terms are used:

The hand. **Cancel** (vv. 2f.) is lit. "release the hand," i.e., renounce one's claim to, or power over, the pledge and thus the debtor. Similarly, in verses 7, 8 and 11, opening or closing the hand (**openhanded, tightfisted**) speaks of the power that the creditor wields over the debtor. The text is thus addressed, significantly, to those who have economic power. The social response to poverty is put squarely in the hands of those who *have* hands— i.e., the power to do something effective about it. It is not left to the self-effort of the unaided poor alone.

The heart. As the seat of the mind and will, the heart governs the intentions and direction of economic action. In each of three uses (vv. 7, 9, and 10) the warning is against a malicious will. The heart can be hard (v. 7), filled with a **wicked thought** (v. 9), or **grudging** (v. 10; lit. "evil"). Deuteronomy is well aware of the self-interest of those who wield economic power and dictate economic policy and realizes that justice for the poor requires a wholly different mindset translated into personal and political will power. It is a perception that has lost nothing of its sharpness and truth with the passing centuries.

The eye. How one looks at another reveals the attitude inside. Wrong attitudes are bound up with wrong actions, just as a wrong mind and will are. Thus, to **show ill will** (v. 9) and to **consider it a hardship** (v. 18) are both translations of Hebrew "eye" metaphors (lit. "give an evil eye" and "it must not be hard in your eyes"). The usage here, and later rabbinic use of the "eye," make it clear that Jesus' reference to the good or bad eye in Matthew 6:22f. also has to do with attitudes of generosity or meanness, as the context indicates (cf. 6:1–4, 19–24).

The vivid body language of the text thus binds together practical, volitional, and attitudinal motivation for the central exhortation. Obedience to "this entire commandment" (v. 5b, NRSV; NIV has again diluted the singular expression into a plural) will require the response of the entire person, in functional effectiveness (hand), decision-making will (heart), and social attitudes (eye).

Secondly, the *relational* language is seen in two ways. On the one hand, the repeated description of the needy person as **neighbor** and **brother** draws on the covenant solidarity that made all Israelites "neighbors" and on the kinship solidarity that made them all likewise "family." And on the other hand, in verse 7 and in verse 11 there is a repetitive, rhyming, piling up of the second person singular possessive suffix, "your." Thus (lit.) "If there is among *you* a needy person, one of *your* brothers, in one of *your* towns, in *your* land . . . " (v. 7). "Therefore I command *you* to open *your* hand to *your* brother, to *your* poor person, to *your* needy person, in *your* land" (v. 11). The effect is missed in English translations when the people concerned are simply categorized as "*the* poor and needy." Deuteronomy insists on relating, not just classifying. Poor and needy people *belong*, they are not just social statistics. They are part of "your" community and are not to be marginalized, excluded, and victimized as an underclass. Alienation is incontrovertibly one of the worst effects of poverty and dependence. Social policies that increase, and even institutionalize, that alienation (even in the name of "welfare" or "charity") are fundamentally contrary to the relational language and community-preserving intention of the biblical vision (cf. the clauses at the end of Lev. 25:35 and 36).

The Release of Hebrew Slaves (15:12–18)

15:12–18 / This law, sometimes called the law of "manumission" (i.e., release from slavery), is also based on the first law in the Book of the Covenant (Exod. 21:2–11). As with the above *šᵉmiṭṭâ* law, which comes straight after the account of the exodus, it preserves the basic intention of the original law (Hebrew slaves should be granted freedom after six years of service) but adds some typically Deuteronomic extras.

If a fellow Hebrew, a man or a woman ... It is very probable that the word "Hebrew" here has a socioeconomic meaning rather than a merely ethnic one. There is wide (though not universal) agreement that the word is linked to *ʿapîru*, a term used throughout the ancient Near East for a class of people who, having been uprooted from their original environment for a variety of reasons, lived by selling their services to host communities as soldiers, agricultural workers, slaves, etc. (see additional note). It is generally agreed that the "Hebrew" slave of Exodus 21 refers to this social class of nonethnic Israelite, landless people who were dependent on Israelite land-owning households for their employment and survival. The Exodus law gave them some rights and protection, effectively allowing them to go free after six years service in one household (which probably meant a change of employer for most of them), unless the "Hebrew" chose to stay permanently. Deuteronomy makes two changes to the Exodus law. Women are now put on an equal footing with men in the law of release (vv. 12 and 17b), and the act of release is to be accompanied by a generous send-off package (vv. 13f.). This generosity is actually a sign of honor—an amazing command for the benefit of one who was, after all, a slave. **Supply him liberally** is literally "you shall *garland* him!" The master was to fashion a rich "necklace" for his departing slave, hanging flocks and grain and wine around his neck in abundance. This would enable the one who now entered the still perilous status of a "freedman" to have some chance of economic viability.

The motivation for this law is drawn from a *theological* matter of principle (vv. 14b–15) and from an *economic* matter of fact (v. 18). The theological reason focuses on present blessing and historical redemption. **Give to him as the LORD your God has blessed you** (v. 14b). This wonderful text, which could have fallen from the lips of Christ himself, perfectly sums up the reciprocal dynamic of obedience and blessing, of doing to others what God has done for you, that Paul also builds into his theology of Christian giving (cf. 2 Cor. 9:6–15). It is based on the historical motivation of the exodus redemption (v. 15). Those who had been "Hebrews" in Egypt and had experienced Yahweh's liberation should not hesitate to grant liberty to "Hebrews" in their midst. Indeed, on such a basis, the response could be unequivocally commanded (v. 15b; cf. v. 11 and 1 Tim. 6:17–19, which is a comparable NT *command*). The words, **remember that you were slaves in Egypt,** recall the Deuteronomic motivation for the fourth commandment (5:15)—another hint of the sabbatical context and flavor of this whole chapter. The words also recall the fact that in the Book of the Covenant, coming straight after the account of the exodus, the law of slave release stands at the very head of the law code—appropriately enough as the first law for a society of escaped slaves! (Exod. 21–23).

The economic reason (v. 18) that the master should not begrudge the "Hebrew" slaves their freedom or their parting gift was that he had benefited by getting their labor at a far lower cost than he could have gotten regular hired workers. When it comes to motivating its socioeconomic vision and program, Deuteronomy is rich in theological and emotional reasoning, but it can do the arithmetic as well. It can preach the message, but it can also present the cost-benefit analysis. The art of persuasion in matters of social reform usually requires skill in both spheres.

The basic law, then, was that "Hebrew" slaves were to "go out" (the very expression is exodus-flavored) in the seventh year of their **service** (v. 18, lit. "work"). Verses 16f. provide for the one and only exception to that rule—namely, if an individual freely chose to stay and explicitly said so. Then the servant status could be made permanent. But the reason is once again relational and moral: **because he loves you and your family and is well off** (lit. "it is good for *him*") **with you.** It is worth noting that the initiative

comes from the *slave's* side and not "because *you* like him and it
is good for *you* to keep him."

The Sacrifice of Firstborn Animals (15:19–23)

15:19–23 / There are several possible reasons why this
law is included in this context. One is that the fuller details of the
original law (in Exod. 13:11–15; cf. also 22:29f.; 34:19f.; Num.
18:15–18) come in close association with the regulations for the
passover, which also follows next in Deuteronomy. Another is
that they both have a link in the catchword "firstborn" (since the
passover celebrated the sparing of Israel's firstborn sons on the
night of the exodus).

However, another more subtle link with the preceding
context lies in the idea of exemption from work. As the slave was
to be released from work ("service," v. 18), so the firstborn ox was
not to be **put to work** (v. 19). The root word is the same in both
cases and was also used for Israel's bondage in Egypt. A further
possible verbal echo or play on words may apply to the firstborn
sheep as well. In Hebrew, **do not shear** *(tāgōz)* sounds very similar
to "Do not **require payment**" *(tiggōś)* in verses 2 and 3. In the
sabbatical year the debtor was not to be "pressed." The firstborn
sheep was not to be "fleeced." Just as the sabbatical principles
regarding land, debt, and slavery required various forms of release, so firstborn animals were to be "released" from the normal
work and produce required of their kind (cf. McConville, *Law and
Theology*, pp. 95–98). They were to be sacrificed like a fellowship
offering (v. 20) unless unfit because of blemish (vv. 21–23). As to
what the animals in question may have thought about the prospect of exchanging a lifetime of hard work and shearing for the
privilege of being eaten instead, our text offers no speculation!
Deuteronomy 15 offers limitless opportunity for ethical
and missiological reflection and action. It is central within the
book of Deuteronomy itself, and its humanitarian warmth sets
the whole ethos for the variety of social and economic legislation
that follows. Now, when we recall that Israel's visibility to the
nations was intended to demonstrate the *righteousness of their
laws* and the *nearness of their God* (4:6–8), we can round out our
understanding of that role from Deuteronomy 15. *This* is what
such righteousness means; *this* is the character and requirement
of that God. A society such as described in this chapter would
undoubtedly be radically distinctive from "the way of the world,"

and would arouse interest and questions. We should not detract from its ethical power and challenge by denigrating the limited extent to which historical Israel ever managed to live by such ideals. Israel's failure no more invalidates Deuteronomy's ethics than the moral failure of the Corinthians invalidates Paul's ethics. The people of God are called to be distinctive, not just in their radical, uncompromising monotheism but also in equally radical commitment to social and economic priorities that reflect God's values and reverse the world's. There can be no doubt that the early church found in Deuteronomy 15 a charter for their attempt to eliminate poverty in their midst, and Luke links the growth of the church as firmly to that social and economic effort as to the evangelistic preaching of the apostles (Acts 2:42–47; 4:32–35). There is missionary power in joyful generosity.

When it comes to working out how such a socioeconomic ethic can be addressed to secular society, we have other hermeneutical steps to take. The first step is the presupposition that Israel was indeed called into existence to be "a light to the nations," so that the social ethic required of Israel has some paradigmatic relevance to all cultures and societies (see introduction). From that base, we can formulate principles that can be used in a modern-day setting. For example, Hamilton suggests the following principles (*Social Justice*, pp. 135–38). First, social justice in Deuteronomy was no mere abstract ideal, but a matter of detailed practical legislation on behalf of the dependent. Secondly, the justness and health of any society is measurable in terms of the quality of its care for the weakest and most vulnerable members of it. Thirdly, the laws aim their rhetorical weaponry at those who have the power to effect change. Fourthly, God is portrayed as the advocate of the powerless, a role that the church can and should take on in God's name. All of these have practical contemporary relevance.

Finally, the sabbatical principle of the chapter is a protest against the allegedly insuperable power of market forces. In modern western society, "the Market" is granted virtually idolatrous status: it is "believed in"; it is personified; it is the alleged source of manifold blessings; its "forces" must be allowed to "reign." But it is also a mechanism for human greed and the relentless forces that drive some people into deeper spirals of debt, dependence, and bondage. To apply sabbatical principles in such a world means to struggle for realistic and effective mechanisms that say "No" to the assumption that this is how it has to be; mechanisms that provide a breathing space ("rest") for recovery; mechanisms that restore the poor and empower them for meaningful belonging and participation in the community; mechanisms, in short, that recognize the reality of v. 11a, but are motivated by the vision of v. 4a, and strive to bridge the gap between them (cf. Miller, *Deuteronomy*, pp. 138ff.).

Additional Notes §18

15:1 / Since the seventh year was a fallow year, there would be no full-scale harvest, so at the end of that year, there was to be a "release" from the repayment of loans.

The *šᵉmiṭṭâ* law of Deut. clearly presupposes the fallow year law of Exod. 23:10f. On the question of the relationship of Deut. 15 to the sabbatical year law of Lev. 25:2–7 and the implications regarding the documentary hypothesis and the relative dating of D and P, see C. J. H. Wright, *God's Land*, pp. 167f.

15:2 / **Every creditor shall cancel the loan he has made . . .** The syntax of the Hb. text here is complicated and open to various exegetical options: *šāmôṭ kol-baʿal maššēh yādô ᵃšer yaššeh bᵉrēʿēhû.* Probably the correct reading is, lit. "Every holder of a pledge in his power/possession (hand) shall release whatever he has received as loan-pledge to his neighbor." In other words, the intention of the law was not simply the cancellation of loans but was also the release of the securities on which the loans had been made—most often probably mortgaged land. The REB is more accurate than the NIV: "everyone who holds a pledge shall return the pledge of the person indebted to him." See North, "*Yâd*," and C. J. H. Wright, *God's Land*, pp. 169–73.

The LORD's time for canceling debts has been proclaimed: Lit. "Yahweh's *šᵉmiṭṭâ* has been proclaimed." There is a formal parallel between this practice and that of some ancient Near Eastern kings, who would proclaim edicts that canceled debts or gave some form of amnesty from taxes. These were occasional: for instance, they were sometimes linked to a king's accession or coronation. The terms used were *mīšarum* (similar to Hb. for act of righteousness) and *andurārum* (probably related to Hb. *dᵉrôr*, meaning release). For a helpful survey of all the relevant material in ancient Near Eastern texts see Hamilton, *Social Justice*, pp. 45–72. The point here is that the proclamation of debt-remission in Israel was not at the whim of a human king, but on the authority of Yahweh, and at regular sabbatical intervals (for which no clear ancient Near Eastern parallel has been found).

15:11 / **There will always be poor people in the land:** It is possible that *hāʾāreṣ* in this first line of the verse means "the earth." In that case, the verse is making a point of the contrast between what is universally true (there are poor people everywhere) and what is to be done about it in Israel (*"your* poor and *your* needy in *your* land"). NRSV translates, "Since there will never cease to be some in need on the earth, I therefore command you, 'Open your hand to the poor and needy neighbor in your land.' "

15:12 / If a fellow Hebrew: Lit. "If your brother (*'āḥîkā*), a Hebrew man or Hebrew woman." Some commentators argue that in Deut., the "Hebrew" has become synonymous with Israelite, since the term "brother" (NIV, **fellow**) is used. However, Hb. *'āḥ* is a broad term that includes resident aliens and was not confined to strictly kinship relatives. It indicates a member of the community. The Hb. word order makes it clear that the "brother" is being defined as a "Hebrew," not in order to indicate his nationality, which would be tautologous, but rather to indicate the precise socioeconomic identity of the persons concerned. The previous law was concerned with "your brother the needy person" (v. 9). This law, which is distinct but with a similar concern, is concerned with "your brother the Hebrew . . . " The literature on the identification of *ʿibrî* and its connection with *ʿapîru* is now enormous. For good representative surveys of the issues, see: Gottwald, *Tribes of Yahweh*, pp. 391–409; Chaney, "Peasant Movements"; Na'aman, "Habiru and Hebrews."

Sells himself to you: The reflexive sense of the Niphal, *yimmākēr*, is correct, rather than the passive ("is sold"). The "Hebrews" were not just ordinary slaves who were bought and sold, but a particular class of people who sold themselves and their services as a way of life because they were landless (not necessarily because of debt). The mortgaged Israelite debtor (vv. 1f.) was quite distinct from the bonded "Hebrew" (vv. 12ff.).

The literary and historical relationship between the manumission laws (laws of slave release) is as problematic as that between the laws regarding the sabbatical year of fallow and debt release. The basic problem is how to reconcile the laws prescribing a seventh year release (Exod. 21:2–11 and Deut. 15:12–18) with the jubilee law prescribing release in the fiftieth year (Lev. 25:10; 39–43; etc.). If all three laws are taken to apply to the same class of people (Israelites) in the same sort of circumstances (debt slavery), then there is a real discrepancy. A possible solution is to argue that the seventh year release applied to those in the category of "Hebrews"—the landless poor who lived by selling their services; whereas the jubilee release applied to Israelite landowners whose land had become temporarily alienated through debt but could still be restored to the family, no later than the second generation after the original crisis. First suggested by Ellison ("The Hebrew Slave"), this view is developed by C. J. H. Wright ("Seven Years" and *God's Land*, pp. 249–59). The most recent full-scale study of the whole matter, which includes a critique of the position suggested above, is Chirichigno, *Debt-Slavery*. For other views, cf. Japhet, "Manumission Laws"; Kaufman, "Social Welfare" and "Deuteronomy 15"; Lemche, "Manumission."

§19 Israel's Rhythm of Celebration: Three Annual Festivals (Deut. 16:1–17)

The sabbatical themes of rest, remembrance, and concern for the poor are all woven into Deuteronomy's summary of the three major annual festivals, which take their place in what Braulik called the "holy rhythm" of Israel's life—sabbath days, seasonal festivals, annual and triennial tithes, sabbatical years ("Die Abfolge," pp. 259ff.)—thus continuing this section's link with the fourth commandment: "remember the Sabbath day by keeping it holy."

The Feasts of Passover and Unleavened Bread

16:1–8 / In these verses Deuteronomy has woven together very closely two of Israel's feasts that elsewhere are described separately. In Exodus 23:15 and 34:18, the Feast of Unleavened Bread is mentioned without reference to the Passover; while in Leviticus 23:5–8, the two feasts are described with Passover immediately preceding. While it is possible that the two festivals had different pre-Israelite roots, it seems that they were combined from an early stage in Israel, through their connection with the exodus, which is the historical basis given for the only Feast of Unleavened Bread in the two Exodus texts cited above. The fact that the two feasts took place within the same week in Spring made it natural to regard them as two parts of a single major festival.

However, the combination of the two in Deuteronomy is more than just a matter of convenience. Rather, it serves Deuteronomy's major purpose of simultaneously looking to the past (the exodus) and facing the future (the land). For the Passover was primarily the celebration of the exodus (vv. 1, 3, and 6), while the Feast of Unleavened Bread, though also rooted in the exodus, could only be celebrated in the context of the land, when Israel could grow their own crops. Exodus 13:3–10 puts the celebration of this festival in the context of the bounty of the promised land, while Joshua 5:10–12 describes the first Passover and Feast of Unleavened Bread after Israel's entry into the land in terms that speak of fulfilled promise and blessing. This backwards and forwards aspect of the law here in Deuteronomy thus reflects the theological perspective of chapters 1–11, with Israel "on the boundary" between blessings past and blessings future. It also anticipates the same dual aspect of the Christian "passover feast": the eucharist or holy communion. For that similarly looks back to the great historical event of our redemption, the cross, but also looks forward to the fulfillment of all God's promises in the messianic banquet of the kingdom of God (Luke 22:14–18; 1 Cor. 11:26).

The Feast of Weeks

16:9–12 / This was the feast that is otherwise known as Pentecost, a word deriving from the LXX translation of Leviticus 23:16, referring to the "fifty day" period from the beginning of the harvest to the celebration of this feast. Full details of the timing and rituals of this feast are given in Leviticus 23:15–21 and Numbers 28:26–31. It included the offering of the firstfruits of the harvest to God and thus was also known as "the feast of harvest" (Exod. 23:16a; cf. 34:22a) or "the day of firstfruits" (Num. 28:26). Deuteronomy does not explicitly mention the offering of firstfruits here (using instead the more general term **a freewill offering**), because they are given a separate section, with heavy theological emphasis, in a position of climax at the end of the legal chapters in Deuteronomy 26.

The main beneficiaries of the offerings associated with this feast were the Levites and priests who served at the sanctuary. The meat of sacrificial animals and the grain of the various vegetable offerings were their main source of food. They were thus in the same position as other classes of dependent people frequently commended to the generosity of Israelite households. So the command of verse 10b that the worshipper's giving should be in proportion to God's blessing was (and remains) a vital principle. It clearly echoes 15:14b and illustrates in the most practical way possible the fundamental Deuteronomic principle that all our "doing" should be grateful and obedient response to the prior blessing of God.

As in chapter 12, we find that the joy of Israel's festivals was to be shared throughout the whole community (cf. 12:12, 18f.). This social inclusiveness of Israel's worship (v. 11) triggers another reminder of the exodus (v. 12). As a harvest festival, the Feast of Weeks had no natural connection with the exodus per se. But although the exodus might not provide the reason for the feast itself, it certainly did provide the reason why everyone, and especially the poor, those without family, and the landless, should benefit from it. Verse 12 is thus a typical Deuteronomic motivation for verse 11, which is itself a typical Deuteronomic expansion of the original liturgical calendar (vv. 9f.).

The Feast of Tabernacles

16:13–15 / Otherwise known as the Feast of Booths, this feast came as the climax of Israel's agricultural year after all the grain and grape harvest was completed (v. 13; cf. also Exod. 23:16; 34:22; Lev. 23:33–43; and Num. 29:12–38). It was a time of great celebration and joy and possibly took its name from the temporary shelters built by the harvesters in the fields at that time of year. Leviticus 23:42–43, however, links the practice to the temporary dwellings that Israel had to make do with after the exodus, thus once again illustrating the characteristic Israelite habit of relating the festivals of the agricultural year to the events of their redemptive history. As with the integration of Passover and Unleavened Bread, the motivation linked with the Feasts of Weeks and Tabernacles combines the past (the exodus, v. 12) and the future (the promised land, v. 15).

16:16–17 / Having drawn from the festival calendars embodied in Exodus 23 and 34, Deuteronomy summarizes the annual feasts using phrases from Exodus 23:15b, 17, and 34:20b, 23. The concluding, emphatic point is to reinforce the necessity of making adequate response to God's blessing. The expression **empty-handed** *(rêqām)* is the same as used in 15:13. There the Israelite householder was urged not to send away his slave in the sabbatical release "empty-handed." The connection is not merely verbal, but typically covenantal. To bring nothing to offer in the sanctuary to God was the vertical equivalent of the horizontal failure to offer anything to a human being in need. Conversely, generous giving to God and generous giving to the released slave were alike appropriate responses to the rich blessing of the covenant Lord (cf. 16:10b and 17 with 15:14b). We shall find the same dual response affirmed even more explicitly and emphatically in chapter 26.

Four notes are sounded several times in this chapter's exposition of Israel's festal calendar. First, there is the *emphasis on history*. The richness of Israel's faith was that it could take the natural and culturally universal celebration of the bounty of nature, as expressed through seasonal feasts and rituals, and tie them to their own redemptive history. Their feasts thus retained their character as cyclical markers of the agricultural year, while avoiding the excesses of the fertility cults. Yahweh was to be worshipped as the saving God of their history and also as the providing God of their land, the giver of all fertility, the Lord of every harvest. It is regrettable that Christian harvest festivals largely ignore this powerful combination of the redemptive-historical with the creation-providential traditions of our biblical faith.

Secondly, there is the *emphasis on joy*. Israelites were *commanded* to rejoice! Just as they were commanded to love, showing that such love was more than a spontaneous emotion, so this fact that joy was commanded indicates that it was more than emotional froth. Praise, thanksgiving, rejoicing—these things were at the core of Israel's faith and religious life, and, as part of a covenant faith, were matters of choice and will and commitment, as the determination to rejoice even in the midst of lament in the Psalms and elsewhere (e.g., Hab. 3:17–19) shows.

Thirdly, there is the *note of social inclusiveness*. Concern for the poor, the weak, the economically and socially vulnerable was not confined to the rhetoric of the prophets but was embodied in the seasonal round. Israel's family festivals reached out to those without family, in an explicit demand that is echoed in the teaching and example of Jesus (e.g., Luke 14:12–14) but has often been stifled or ignored by Christians.

Fourthly, there is the *reciprocal nature of giving and blessing*. The people's giving and feasting was to be an obedient response to God's giving and blessing. But at the same time, God's blessing would be God's continued response to their obedience. It is impossible to separate the two. It is inadequate to speak of obedience being the condition of blessing, or to speak of unconditional blessing unrelated to responsive obedience. There is a dynamic reciprocity between the two. The cycle of nature is mirrored in the cycle of blessing and obedience. Only in this way **your joy**

will be complete (v. 15)—another Deuteronomic jewel that is given a fresh sparkle in a Johannine setting (John 16:24).

Additional Notes §19

For the view that Passover was part of Israel's nomadic heritage, whereas Unleavened Bread was a festival that they took over in Canaan, cf. Mayes, *Deuteronomy,* pp. 255f. For an alternative view, cf. McConville, *Law and Theology,* pp. 100–110.

16:1 / **The month of Abib:** Later known as the month of Nisan, is approximately mid-March to mid-April and is the first month of Israel's OT calendar. Since it was the month of the exodus the twin feasts of Passover and Unleavened Bread were linked to that event (cf. Exod. 12:2, 14–20; 13:3f.; 23:15; 34:18).

16:2 / **An animal from your flock** (i.e., sheep and goats) **or herd** (i.e., cattle): Other Passover texts specify only a lamb (from the flock) as the proper Passover offering. Probably Deut., with its fusion of the Passover (a single meal on one evening) with the Feast of Unleavened Bread (which went on for a week), is referring to the sacrifices of other animals during the week that would be the source of the feasting (cf. 2 Chron. 30:24; 35:6–9).

16:3 / **Bread of affliction:** A term that probably symbolized the harshness of Israel's suffering in Egypt.

16:7 / **Return to your tents:** Obviously, with the feast being centered on the sanctuary, this cannot mean that everyone went *home* after the Passover on the first evening. Rather, it probably refers to temporary shelters that families would have constructed for themselves for the duration of the festival (rather like the modern phenomena of large Christian camping and holiday festivals with worship and teaching!). So although the event was a "national" celebration, its family aspect was preserved.

§20 Leadership in Israel: Judges and Kings (Deut. 16:18–17:20)

Some scholars regard the section 16:18–18:22 as related to the fifth commandment, just as the previous section (usually defined as 14:28–16:17) is based on the sabbatical rhythm of the fourth commandment. The fifth commandment focuses on the honor due to parents, who are the first form of social authority encountered in life. Parental authority, however, is a model for other forms of authority and leadership in society (as is seen in the use of "father" for various kinds of honored or important persons in many societies).

The way Deuteronomy sets four offices of authority and leadership in Israel side by side in this section (judge, king, priest, and prophet) gives us an insight into its "constitutional" intentions. The clear distinction and separation of the different kinds of authority can be seen as a significant precursor of some of the principles of democratic government, especially the separation of powers. No single person could hold all four offices. None of the authorities is given supreme authority over the others. Certainly, the king (who doesn't even come first) does not appoint the others (Jeroboam's appointment of his own priests, thus politicizing a royal religious establishment, is seen as one of the first steps on his road to that great idolatry by which he "made Israel to sin," 1 Kgs. 12:31–33). And the king, though chief executive in the political sphere, has very explicit limitations set on his power. If any priority is evident, it would be in the first and last of the list: the judge (who administers the law of God) and the prophet (who speaks the word of God). The supreme authority is thus Yahweh himself, whose theocratic focus of power and authority in a vertical sense effectively flattens and disperses power at the horizontal level. The constitutional aspects of human authority are thus set firmly in the context of God's transcendent authority and revealed will and word.

Apart from the dimension of covenant theocracy, the principles enshrined here still have political and constitutional relevance. The separation of powers is an important bulwark against tyranny. And there is no doubt that there will be a greater commitment to justice in society when there is some consensual submission to a transcendent norm, however articulated, that stands above all participants in the socio-political process.

Judges and the Courts (16:18–17:13)

16:18–20 / At the basic level, the administration of justice in Israel was largely a matter of local people **in every town** judging themselves through local people elected or appointed for the purpose. Most matters of civil concern were dealt with by the elders, which probably meant the senior males in each "father's house," qualified by their possession of land and family. This text seems to imply that out of this body of elders, some would be elected to function as judges. Job 29:7–25 gives an illuminating account of a day in the life of an elder-judge (with an outstanding record for his defense of the poor), while the following chapter shows how such status was shattered by the loss of family and substance.

These instructions to such **judges and officials** do not typically go into practical detail on the job itself, but rather, emphasize the fundamental moral requirements for the preservation of justice. In this respect they amplify Moses' injunctions in 1:16f. and are also very similar to Exodus 23:6–8 and Leviticus 19:15, in which the integrity of judges is a part of a wider concern for neighborly love in several spheres, all as an outworking of social holiness. The fundamental requirement was that they should **judge the people fairly** (lit. "judge a righteous judgment"). In order to accomplish that, three negative commands (in the same emphatic form as the Ten Commandments) are given in a small series that is echoed in the law and elsewhere and that reflect at a human level the character of Yahweh as the utterly just judge (10:17).

> **Do not pervert justice** (lit. "turn," or "bend" it; cf. Lev. 19:15; Deut. 24:17; 27:19; 1 Sam. 8:3; Amos 5:12; Isa. 10:2).

> **Do not show partiality** (lit. "regard faces"; cf. Ps. 82:2; Prov. 18:5; 24:23; 28:21; Mal. 2:9).

Do not accept a bribe (cf. Ps. 15:5; Prov. 17:23; Isa. 1:23; 5:23; 33:15; Ezek. 22:12).

As against such practices, commonly decried elsewhere, Deuteronomy hoists its own banner in verse 20, (lit.) "Justice, justice, you shall pursue!" and motivates it with the familiar concern for prosperous life in the land. This last phrase of the verse should not be taken lightly as a stock phrase. Deuteronomy uses it repeatedly in chapters 5–11 as a major motivation for covenant loyalty and fulfillment of the demands of the first commandment. Prosperous life in the land could not continue if they abandoned Yahweh. But likewise, it could not continue if judicial corruption set in like a cancer at the social level. The integrity of the judicial system was (and still is) basic to the preservation of society. Any society will have some levels of crime and some levels of injustice, but if the means of restitution and redress themselves become corrupt, then there is only despair. Justice itself turns to wormwood (Amos 5:7, 10).

16:21–17:1 / These few laws may have been included here because they describe the kind of religious syncretism that would lead to covenant transgression (17:2), and thence to the sort of court case that judges would have to deal with.

The **wooden Asherah pole** (v. 21, either a wooden pole or a living tree, as a female symbol) and the **sacred stone** (v. 22, as a phallic symbol) were the typical props of the Canaanite fertility cult (cf. 7:5; 12:3). Given that they were to be destroyed at Canaanite shrines, the very idea that they could be planted or erected beside **the altar you build to the LORD your God** was abhorrent. It would be unacceptable syncretism and incompatible with covenant loyalty (**hates** is covenant vocabulary, as is its opposite, "loves"; it means that Yahweh could enter into no relationship with, make no accommodation to, such symbols of other gods). Precisely such syncretism, however, later became endemic in Israel and was the target of more prophetic anger than probably any other offense. Defective sacrifices (17:1) were a mark of a careless and ungrateful people—again, signposts on the slippery slope to outright covenant violation (cf. 15:21; Lev. 22:17–25; and Mal. 1:6–14).

17:2–7 / This case illustrates the operation of the judicial procedure. An accusation of breaking the first commandment would be the most serious case likely to come before any court in

Israel (cf. ch. 13). This would be **evil in the eyes of the** LORD . . .
in violation of his covenant, and contrary to my command. It
would thus provide the supreme model of how all cases should
be dealt with.

Several points are significant in assessing Israel's judicial
practice. First, the law applies to both men and women without
distinction (vv. 2, 5). Neither chauvinism nor chivalry is to distort
the proper response to crime (cf. the collusion of the sexes in Jer.
44:15–25). Secondly, the charges are to be public knowledge; this
is not to be a means of settling a private vendetta justified on the
grounds of the victim's alleged idolatry (v. 4a, reads lit. "and it
has been declared to you and you have heard"). Thirdly, there is
to be full investigation and clear proof that the charge is true. In
other words, innocence is assumed until guilt is conclusively
established (v. 4b; cf. 13:14; 19:18). The law is as concerned to
protect the innocent from false charges as to make sure the
genuinely guilty are punished—a concern that is equally relevant in modern times. Fourthly, the trial and execution are to be
conducted in public (v. 5; the **city gate** is the open space where all
public business is carried on), not in some secret court where
"witch-hunt" mentalities could fester. Fifthly, there must be more
than one witness for the prosecution (v. 6). This obvious precaution, which is expanded in 19:15–21 and was known to Jezebel
(1 Kgs. 21:10), is wisely applied to matters of church discipline in
the NT (cf. Matt. 18:16; 2 Cor. 13:1; 1 Tim. 5:19). Sixthly, those who
brought such serious charges must be prepared to take the lead
in carrying out the execution itself (v. 7). Along with the other
law concerning false witness (19:16–19), this ruling must have
had a strong psychological deterrent effect against frivolous or
false accusation in local communities where accuser and accused
would be acquaintances. Perjury, if successful in a capital case,
would turn the false witness into a murderer.

Whatever our views on capital punishment in the modern
secular state, there is no doubt that the *procedural* concerns of
Deuteronomy's judicial instructions are impressive and point to
objectives still well worth striving for.

17:8–13 / These verses describe the higher level of judicial administration in Israel. Verse 16:18 speaks of local tribal
judges in the settlements. But here we find the establishment of
a court of referral for those cases that prove beyond the compe-
tence of the local judiciary. This law thus puts on a permanent

footing the arrangements originally suggested by Jethro for Moses himself (cf. Exod. 18:22 and Deut. 1:17b). The kinds of cases that might prove too difficult for local judges are listed carefully: **bloodshed, lawsuits or assaults** (lit. "one kind of blood and another, one kind of case and another, one kind of striking and another"). The REB paraphrases, "whether it be a case of accidental or premeditated homicide, civil rights, or personal injury." These are complicated areas in any society, and OT law is well aware of some necessary distinctions (cf. Exod. 21:12–14, 18f.; Num. 35:16–25).

The higher court is to be established in the same place as the central sanctuary, thus endowing it with the sacredness and authority of the presence and name of Yahweh. Those in charge will be **the priests, who are Levites, and the judge who is in office at that time** (v. 9). Jehoshaphat's reform strengthens this central court in Jerusalem (2 Chron. 19:8–10), including in the panel of judges both Levites (presumably for their detailed knowledge of the law that they are supposed to preserve and teach) and "heads of Israelite families" (possibly selected local elders, chosen for their experience and wisdom in practical application of the law in court). It is probably this high court that Jeremiah faces directly when accused of false prophecy about the destruction of Jerusalem and the temple (Jer. 26). The authority of this court is final, and its decisions are to be meticulously carried out (vv. 10f.) under threat of death for **contempt** of court, which is really contempt for Yahweh himself (v. 12). The high duty of judges (16:18–20) is to be matched by a high respect by the people for their words. Anything less will bring evil and wrath on Israel. Hence the strong deterrent policy of verse 12. Sadly, the history of the nation tells us that many prophetic words of condemnation were brought against the judges themselves, for their contempt of the Torah of God and their corruption of justice.

The King (17:14–20)

It may seem strange that in this section on leadership in Israel the king comes second rather than at the head of the series. The reason is that whereas sound judicial administration by impartial judges is at the very heart of Israel's covenant theocracy, monarchy as a particular form of political authority is not. The nation can and does survive without kings both before and after

the centuries of actual monarchic government. Although in other
OT traditions the king can be seen as the human embodiment of
Yahweh's kingship, this is not in view here. In Deuteronomy the
judge stands closer to divine functions and is a more true successor to Moses than a king. "The way of the righteous judge reflects
the way of the Lord (cf. 16:18–19 with 10:17). The way of the king
in Deuteronomy is not a reflection of the deity but a model of the
true Israelite" (P. D. Miller, *Deuteronomy,* p. 147). This section,
therefore, is permissive rather than prescriptive legislation. It
does not command monarchy but allows for it.

    17:14–17 / Kingship in Israel is immediately set in an
ambivalent light. On the one hand, if it comes it will be by the
people's own request (v. 14), but on the other hand, the individual king is to be Yahweh's choice (v. 15). The people's anticipated
request, **"Let us set a king over us like all the nations around
us,"** need not be negatively colored by the historical account of
1 Samuel 8. That account clearly portrays the request when it
comes as stemming from motives that compromise the distinctiveness of Israel and reject the covenant sovereignty of Yahweh
in the military sphere (vv. 5, 20). Though the literary account
of the request in 1 Samuel obviously echoes the Deuteronomic
phraseology, the Deuteronomic law is not itself negative or hostile to the people's request. There is no harm in asking. The
people ask other things of God that meet with approval (e.g.,
12:20; 18:16f.). If the request for a king had been *intrinsically*
incompatible with theocracy, it would doubtless have received a
resounding rejection in the language of chapter 7. Yahweh is
Israel's supreme judge, but that does not rule out human judges
as his agents. Likewise, Yahweh is the true king in Israel (cf. Exod.
15:18; Num. 23:21; Deut. 33:5; Judg. 8:23), but that does not
totally exclude human kings (even though it certainly induced a
strong resistance to kingship in Israel for several centuries and
never allowed monarchy to feel totally naturalized within the
theocratic-covenant tradition).
    However, even if the request for a king is not antitheocratic
in principle, Israel's most recent experience of kingship was the
imperial tyranny of Egypt, from which it had been liberated.
Against that negative background, therefore, these verses make
two requirements and three restrictions on the exercise of kingship in Israel. The king must be **the king the LORD your God
chooses** (v. 15). The human request must accept the divine choice

(cf. 1 Sam. 10:24; 16:1–13; etc.). And he must be **a brother Israelite.**
The ban on having a foreigner as king is doubtless for the same
reasons as the ban on marriage or any kind of alliance with the
Canaanites, namely, the threat of apostasy and idolatry (cf. 7:2–4).
The three restrictions (vv. 16f.) are remarkable because
they quite explicitly cut across the accepted pattern of kingship
throughout the ancient Near East. *Military power,* through the
building up of a large chariot force (the point of having **great
numbers of horses**), the prestige of *a large harem* of **many wives**
(frequently related to international marriage alliances), and
the enjoyment of *great wealth* (**large amounts of silver and
gold**)—these were the defining marks of kings worthy of the title.
Weapons, women, and wealth: why else be a king? But Deuteronomy starkly declares, "Not so in Israel." If any negative light is
shed on the people's request of verse 14, it lies here. Israel might
admire the kings of the nations. But the king they are to have is
to be as unlike the kings of other nations as one can imagine.
Clearly the issue is not merely if Israel should have a king or not,
but what kind of king that should be. What matters fundamentally for Deuteronomy is whether or not the whole covenant
people of Israel will remain wholly loyal to Yahweh their God.
The value of a king is assessed solely by the extent to which he
will help or hinder that loyalty. A king who will trust not in God
but in his own defenses (cf. 3:21f.); a king whose heart turns away
because of many wives (cf. 7:3f.); a king whose great wealth leads
to the snares of pride (cf. 8:13f.)— such a king will quickly lead
the people in the same disastrous directions. History proves the
point with depressing regularity, as the Deuteronomistic historians show.

17:18–20 / These verses lay one overriding duty on the
king: pay careful attention to the law. It is facetious to mock these
verses as piously idealistic, since kings had so many other duties
to see to in the course of a day. As is so often the case, Deuteronomy mentions only what matters. In this case, it avoids the
small print of an exhaustive job description for royalty and con-
centrates on the fundamental priority. The law is to permeate the
king's behavior in every sphere, whether political, administra-
tive, judicial, or military. He should be a model of what was
required of *every* Israelite (v. 19b). These verses no more suggest
that the king would do nothing else all day but *read* the Book of

the Law than 6:6–9 imagine that the Israelite family would do nothing else all day but *talk* about it.

In his submission to the law, the king must **not consider himself better than his brothers** (v. 20), even though he has been **set over** them in political terms (v. 14). Functional authority must be exercised in a context of covenant equality, a principle that the NT applies to leaders in the church (e.g., 1 Pet. 5:1–4). Even the dynastic succession (**he and his descendants will reign**) will be conditional on such obedience to the law. Jeremiah expressed most forcefully the subordination of the dynastic principle to the demands of the Sinai law at the very gate of the palace (Jer. 22:1–5).

One could say, first, that the Deuteronomic law of the king should be included in any attempt to derive ethical principles for political life from the OT. A radically different, consciously distinct, and counter-cultural model of political leadership is offered here. It is a model that limits military power, prestige, and private gain and puts all political executive authority firmly under the authority of the law itself. The failure of so many of Israel's kings to abide by its standards does not invalidate its moral force. We know how much they failed only and precisely because of the presence of a law like this. The concept of servant-kingship has penetrating political relevance in addition to its NT christological dimension.

Second, just as the NT picks up aspects of Israel's judicial rules to apply to the internal discipline of the church (see commentary on vv. 2–7), so the model of leadership before us here is a challenge to those in Christian leadership in churches or parachurch organizations. Christians are as vulnerable to the temptations of power, prestige, and wealth as Israelite kings, and the warning of Jesus (Luke 22:24–27) never loses its relevance. Both by example and by teaching Jesus modeled the more down-to-earth requirements of this law, for "he was one who sought and received none of the perquisites of kingship, who gave his full and undivided allegiance to God, and who lived his whole life by the instruction, the torah, of the Lord" (Miller, *Deuteronomy*, p. 149). The disciple, even in leadership, is not above his master (John 13:12–17).

Additional Notes §20

On the constitutional and political relevance of this section, cf. Lohfink, *Great Themes*, pp. 55–75. On the way in which Yahweh, as supreme judge and king, "flattened" the differentials of human functional authority in Israel, cf. Gottwald, *Tribes of Yahweh*, pp. 608–21.

16:18 / On the role of elders in Israel, and especially their judicial functions and the administration of justice, see J. L. McKenzie, "Elders," D. A. McKenzie, "Judicial Procedure," and C. J. H. Wright, *God's Land*, pp. 78–81. The **officials** (*šōṭᵉrîm*) were probably a rank of assistants to the judges. They may have had clerical duties, supervision of the parties to the case, or supervision over any punishment to be exacted (cf. 1:15).

16:19 / Bribery is singled out as the worst form of judicial corruption, because it **blinds the eyes of the wise;** that is, it makes those who should have the wisdom to act with insight and understanding behave as if they were foolish and uninformed. And it **twists the words of the righteous.** This might mean that bribery can persuade those who would otherwise give honest testimony to falsify it, or that the testimony of honest witnesses gets twisted by bribed judges, or that bribery "subverts the cause of those who are in the right" (NRSV)—in any case, it causes a serious miscarriage of justice. Cf. Goldberg, "Gifts or Bribes."

17:3 / Cf. Deut. 4:19; 5:9; 8:19; 11:16; 29:26; 30:17.

17:14 / Although it is difficult to read these verses without thinking of Solomon and the later kings, and although the literary account of Solomon has clearly been written with these verses as a background, it is not necessary to assume that this law of kingship must be a post factum reflection of Solomon. The nature of ancient Near Eastern monarchies was common knowledge, and Israel, from its earliest origins, had plenty of dealings with nations headed by kings (e.g., already, Sihon of the hard heart and Og of the hard bed, Deut. 2:30; 3:11). Any leader or legislator in Israel had enough knowledge of what kings *could* be like to know what a king in Israel *should not* be like (Deut. 17:16f.) or, indeed, to warn Israel about what a king *would* eventually be like if they chose that road (1 Sam. 8:10–18). For a positive view of the Deuteronomic attitude to monarchy, cf. Gerbrandt, *Kingship*, and the review article, Howard, "The Case for Kingship."

17:16 / **Horses** were the "engines" of chariots, the "tanks" of ancient armies. To **make the people return to Egypt to get more of them** might simply describe merchants sent to trade, but it could refer to the actual trading of men for horses—i.e., selling Israelites as mercenary soldiers in exchange for horses. Solomon exchanged Israelite towns for timber (1 Kgs. 9:11–14), and there is some hint that he may have traded in this manner so as to acquire horses (1 Kgs. 10:26–29). The antipathy to any **return to Egypt** is echoed in the prophets who condemned reliance on Egypt and/or horses and chariots (cf. Isa. 2:7; 30:1–7; 31:1–3; Jer. 2:18, 36; Hos. 14:3; Mic. 5:10). There is no direct record of the saying attributed to God, **"You are not to go back that way again,"** but cf. Deut. 28:68 (a threat) and Exod. 14:13 (a promise). A return to Egypt would obviously speak of a virtual reversal of salvation-history. Cf. Reimer, "Return to Egypt."

17:20 / Cf. 1 Kgs. 12:7, and Weinfeld, "King as Servant."

§21 Leadership in Israel: Priests and Prophets (Deut. 18:1–22)

After the two sections on "secular" leadership (the judge and the king), we now have two sections on the "spiritual" leadership provided by the priest and the prophet.

Priests and Levites (18:1–8)

The responsibilities of the tribe of Levi were broadly two-fold: the service of the sanctuary, especially the role of the priests at the altar; and the preservation and teaching of the law (cf. Lev. 10:11; Deut. 10:8; 33:10; 2 Chron. 15:3; 17:8f.; 35:3; Neh. 8:7–9). They also had judicial (17:9; 21:5) and military (20:2–4) duties. This law, however, is concerned with their rights in relation to the rest of the nation.

18:1–2 / These verses restate the basic fact about the tribe of Levi as a whole, namely, that they did not have a territorial inheritance like the other tribes. There was to be no slice of the land that would be called "Levi," as there would be for Judah, Ephraim, and the other tribes. However, they were provided with forty-eight cities scattered throughout all the tribes, with some surrounding pasture land (cf. Num. 35:1–8; Josh. 21). And they were to be supported by the gifts and offerings of the people, along with the portions of the sacrifices that were given to the priests (for details, cf. Num. 18, which is probably what the text refers back to in the expression, **as he promised them**). Because they were supported by what was actually given to the Lord, the expression is frequently used that **the LORD is their inheritance.** This was not a pious spiritualization of a life of ascetic poverty but a statement of the principle that they would receive the full material blessing of their inheritance to the extent that the people of Yahweh were faithful in their worship of him and in covenant commitment to one another.

What these verses stress, then, is that although the tribe of Levi had no *landed* inheritance, they most definitely did have an inheritance. They would live in the land, and they must benefit from it along with **their brothers.** Deuteronomy's characteristic concern is for the unity of the nation, the sense of kinship solidarity, and the equality of sharing the blessings of the gift of the land. This concern, as applied to the Levites, has already been expressed and was clearly of considerable importance to Deuteronomy (cf. 12:12, 18f.; 14:27, 29; 16:11, 14). After these two verses of general introduction to the principle requirement, verses 3–5 apply it to the benefits to be enjoyed by the Levites who were priests, while verses 6–8 apply it to those Levites who lived in the scattered towns, but wished at some time to come and serve at the central sanctuary.

18:3–5 / These verses summarize the shares that the priests received from the sacrifices and offerings of the people. Much fuller detail is given elsewhere (Lev. 7:28–36; Num. 18:8–32). As so often, Deuteronomy is concerned not to repeat detailed legislation but to underline the theological and social point of it. Verse 5, therefore, motivates the command to treat the Levites with generosity by referring to their status and task. **The LORD your God has chosen them . . . out of all your tribes.** Interestingly, this describes the Levites in terms that verbally echo God's choice of *Israel* as a whole out of all the *nations* (cf. 7:6). The implication is that the Israelites should treat the Levites as God had treated Israel. The Levites function as "model" Israelites, both in their *dependence* (on the rest of the Israelites, as the Israelites in turn depended on God) and in their *benefits* (from the rest of the Israelites, as the Israelites in turn were blessed by God).

18:6–8 / Levites were scattered throughout the territories of the tribes of Israel. Some would have been able to work as priests or in assisting roles at the central sanctuary, wherever it was situated (from the time of David on, it was in Jerusalem; cf. additional notes on 12:5 for a discussion of the place of Israel's worship). Their teaching role could have been exercised anywhere. These verses continue to be concerned for the preservation of the Levites' benefits and for the same equality within the tribe as between tribes. If a Levite chose to leave his country town and move to the central sanctuary and serve there, then he was to receive the same share in the same benefits as the Levites already there. The main point of the law is thus verse 8, not verse

7, which should be included among the conditions that begin in verse 6 (see additional note). The translation, **He is to share equally,** conceals the point that the Hebrew verb is "to eat" (lit. "portion like portion [i.e., equal portions] they shall eat"). As we have seen elsewhere, Deuteronomy rejoices that the good land will enable God's people to "eat and be satisfied" (e.g., 8:10ff.) and urges that proper provision be made to enable even the poorest to do so (14:28f.). Here is another law concerned with eating—this time with the equal rights of all Levites to the food benefits of the sanctuary.

The NT never calls those who serve the church in its leadership "priests." Priesthood is applied only to either Christ (Heb. 7, etc.), or the whole community of believers (1 Pet. 2:9, echoing the same collective use in Exod. 19:4–6). Nevertheless, some reflections on the position of the Levites are relevant to Christian ministry. First of all, it was a bold stroke that consigned Israel's priestly tribe to landlessness. This meant that Israel was not meant to be a nation in which a clerical hierarchy could wield economic power (and all its derivative forms of social influence) as an exploitative, land-owning elite. In this way Israel was remarkably different from surrounding societies. In Egypt, for example, the temples and priests were major landholders. But in Israel, the priesthood of Yahweh the liberator was not to be a tool of religiously sanctioned oppression. In the history of the Christian church, somehow the "clergy" sadly forgot this aspect of its biblical roots and pursued economic wealth and power, while reintroducing sacerdotal aspects of OT priesthood that it was meant to have shed in the light of the sacrifice of Christ.

But secondly, the landlessness of Israel's priestly tribe was not intended to impoverish them. They would be *dependent,* indeed. But dependence on an *obedient* people should have meant perfectly adequate provision for their material needs, just as Israel's dependence on their faithful God would include full provision. The principle that those who serve God and teach God's people should be fully provided for by God's people is emphatically reapplied in the NT. Galatians 6:6 applies it to Christian teachers (cf. 1 Tim. 5:17f.). Paul actually makes reference to OT priestly dues, along with many other supporting arguments (including another Deuteronomic law, 25:4, and a command of Christ), in establishing the responsibility of Christian churches to provide for the material needs of those who work for the cause of the Gospel (1 Cor. 9:13). Paul had freely chosen to waive this right in his own personal case, but he explicitly makes himself an *exception* to the principle he insists on for others. Unfortunately, some Christian organizations have turned Paul's exception, rather than his rule, into a policy imposed on their workers. But in view of the teaching of both OT and NT, churches or other Christian groups that fail to pay their workers adequate living wages are not "living by faith," but are simply living in disobedience.

The Prophet (18:9–22)

The prophet comes last in the listing of Israel's different leadership roles. Almost certainly this is deliberate and significant, like the putting of the judge before the king. Maintaining justice was a higher priority than having a dynastic monarchy. Judge and king must both submit to the law of God, just as the priest must faithfully teach it. But what if those entrusted with such forms of leadership were themselves to go astray? Then the last word was God's. And God would put that word in the mouth of God's prophet.

18:9–13 / To prepare the way for the section on the role of the prophet, Deuteronomy first outlines some of the pagan practices by which the Canaanites looked for answers to the riddles of life and the future. They are lumped together as **the detestable ways of the nations** and headed by the horrific rite of child-sacrifice (cf. 12:31), which was not a divinatory rite, but sets the tone for the way the following practices were to be viewed. It is a universal human desire to know the unknown, to have some preview of the future, to get guidance for decisions, to exercise control over others, to harm others and ward off the harm others may aim at oneself. Alienated from the living God, humans devise the dark arts of verses 10b–11 for such purposes. Their effect is usually to compound the fear that led to their being practiced in the first place. The list of practices here is comprehensive and not at all out-of-date, since all these forms of occult, magic, and spiritism are still widespread today. And we must assume that, given the consistency of God, they are just as **detestable to the LORD** now as they were then. That they should be put in the same "**detestable**" category as child-sacrifice is an interesting window on biblical values. God knows there are more things that destroy human life and dignity than physical fire. The same severe moral assessment of the occult is implied in the statement that **because**

of these practices the LORD your God will drive out those nations (v. 12), which is a reminder of the moral context in which
the OT sets the conquest (cf. Lev. 18:24–28, 20:22f.). By contrast,
Israel was called to be different, distinctive, **blameless** (cf. Lev.
18:3–5).

18:14–19 / **But as for you . . .** : the contrast is immense
and stark. From the foul fog and darkness of occultism to the
clarity and authority of the prophetic word; from the futility of
human attempts to penetrate the confusions of alienation from
God's will and purpose to the direct communication of God, on
God's own initiative—**God will raise up for you a prophet.** At the
same time, by recalling the request of the people at Mt. Sinai
(vv. 16f., **This is what you asked of the LORD**), Moses makes the
people responsible on one level for the gift of prophets. The verse
obviously recalls 5:22–29, when the people had been afraid to
hear the voice of God so directly. They had accepted, however,
the mediatorial role of Moses. Here, God promises to extend that
role by raising up a prophet like Moses, to continue bringing
God's word.

These verses are of great importance in understanding the
nature of true prophecy. Four points are significant. First, true
prophecy would be a matter of *God's initiative* (vv. 15, 18). Prophecy was neither for self-appointed egoists nor for a self-perpetuating
mantic guild. It was God who wanted to do the speaking, God
who had guidance and laws to give, God who would address
God's own people with words of warning and encouragement.
Prophecy, unlike all the divinatory arts aforementioned, would
not be what humans could discover, but what God would reveal.

Secondly, true prophecy would follow *God's model,* namely
Moses himself (**a prophet like me** [v. 15], **a prophet like you**
[v. 18]). The immediate context speaks of Moses' role as the mediator of God's word and will, and that would certainly be the
hallmark of all true prophets to come. But further reflection
suggests other ways in which Moses was the model and criterion
for true prophecy. He had a distinct experience of God's call, for
which he felt great inadequacy. He was sent into a specific situation of need and crisis, within which he had to address the
challenging word of God both to God's own people and to the
political authorities. He predicted events beforehand and interpreted them afterwards. He gave to Israel the foundational theological and ethical constitution that undergirded the message of

centuries of later prophets. He was faithful in intercession and passionate concern for the good of his people, as well as in declaring God's specific judgments. He suffered with and for his people and finally died without seeing the full fruition of his life's mission. In these respects he not only set a model for subsequent true prophets, but, given that *no* OT prophet was really "like" him (cf. 34:10–12), he also prefigured the one prophet who was not only like him (cf. Acts 3:22ff.) but indeed surpassed him as a son surpasses a servant (cf. Heb. 3:2–6).

Thirdly, the true prophet would speak *God's message*. **I will put my words in his mouth;** this is as direct a statement of the link between God's word and the prophets' words as could be made (cf. 2 Pet. 1:20f.). Only by divine initiative could God's words be expressed through a human mouth, even reluctantly, as in the case of Balaam (Num. 22:28; 23:5, 12, 16). But the fact that they could is the presupposition that lies behind every "Thus says the LORD" (cf. Isa. 6:5–7; Ezek. 2:9–3:4; Jer. 1:9; 5:14).

Fourthly, the true prophet carried *God's authority*, for he or she would speak **my words . . . in my name** (v. 19). Therefore, those who heard the prophet heard God; whatever response they made to the prophet they made to God, and they would take the consequences.

18:20–22 / All the marks of true prophets have been stated; now the danger of false prophets have to be faced. Two kinds of falsehood are defined. First, anyone who spoke **in the name of other gods** (v. 20b) would be easily recognizable as a serious violator of the covenant and would be severely punished (cf. 13:1–5). But second, and this threat is much more insidious, the person who claimed to speak in the name of Yahweh but whose words were his own, not the Lord's (v. 20a), was a false prophet. Verse 22 sets up a single criterion: *fulfillment*. A prophet whose words did not come true had not spoken God's message. This shows that prediction, although not the only or main aspect of the prophetic message, was an expected means of establishing a prophet's credentials. But it is very significant that the test is framed *negatively*. It cannot be reversed to imply that if a prophet's prediction came true he was therefore necessarily a true prophet *for that reason alone*. Chapter 13:1f. shows very clearly that false prophets could produce remarkable predictions, signs, and wonders—and still lead the people astray. Thus, non-fulfillment would prove falsehood, but fulfillment could not *by* *itself* prove authenticity—an important caution when assessing remarkable apparent feats of clairvoyance and prediction in any age, including our own.

How else, then, could people distinguish true from false? They could hardly "wait and see" every time a prophet opened his mouth. And how long were they to wait? If, as in the case of Jeremiah, the prediction was the ultimate destruction of Jerusalem, were they to respond to his message only after his prediction came true—by which time it would be too late? This was in fact part of the terrible dilemma that Jeremiah faced. The one thing that would have established beyond all doubt his credentials before a people who rejected and disbelieved him was the one thing he least wanted to happen. Clearly people *should have* been able to recognize his truth and reject the falsehood of other prophets on grounds other than fulfillment alone.

Our text provides another clue to the distinction, even though it is not included in the "test" verses at the end. The prophet whom God would raise up would be *like Moses*. This was a qualitative criterion. There was some standard by which to measure the moral and spiritual credentials of prophets. Those who pandered to the nation's wickedness were not "like Moses." Those who posed no challenge to oppressive government were not "like Moses." Those who were immoral in their own lives, or self-seeking in their ambitions, were not "like Moses." It was on these grounds that Jeremiah actually attacked the false prophets of his own generation (cf. Jer. 23). In the NT, prophets were subject to testing (cf. 1 Cor. 14:29–32). In our age, when we are faced with the multiplication of prophetic cults and sects, the adulation of people with "prophetic ministries," and the proliferation of all kinds of "miracle" attested claims on our attention by the purveyors of consumer religion, ordinary Christians could be excused for being as confused as the contemporaries of Jeremiah, were it not for the fact that we possess far richer resources for exercising discrimination: the whole canon of Scripture and the teaching and example of one "greater than Moses."

Additional Notes §21

18:1 / **The priests, who are Levites—indeed the whole tribe of Levi:** There has been much critical debate as to the history of the priesthood in Israel and its precise relation to the tribe of Levi. One view claims that people struggled over membership in the priesthood, as membership prerequisites changed. At first, members of any tribe could become priests, then a potential priest needed to be a Levite, and finally, priests needed to come from the family of Aaron. On this view, the present law in Deut. represents a stage in that struggle, when all Levites could be priests, and Levites were granted equal rights to the benefits of the central sanctuary. Deuteronomy, on this view, held no distinction between priests and common Levites; this distinction was only clearly articulated by P (cf. Driver, *Deuteronomy,* pp. 213–21). This view is clearly at variance with the Pentateuchal presentation of the origins of the Levitical priesthood and the special role of Aaron and his descendants. For surveys of the reconstruction, see Rehm, "Levites and Priests," and Hubbard, "Priests and Levites."

Much of the debate has centered on the precise syntax of the opening words of 18:1, "the priests, the Levites, the whole tribe of Levi." Those who follow the view that for Deut. all Levites were (or potentially could be) priests, argue that all three phrases are synonymous and that Deut. was unaware of any distinction within the tribe of Levi between those who were priests at the altar and those who had other duties in the care of the sanctuary (e.g., Emerton, "Priests"). In my view, it is preferable to regard the last phrase as inclusive of, but wider than, the combined first two. That is, "the priests (the limited family of Aaronids within the tribe), the Levites (a wider group of sanctuary servants), indeed the whole tribe of Levi (including its scattered members who had no direct connection with the sanctuary)." (For this view see G. E. Wright, "Levites.") More recently, the view seems to be prevailing that Deut. *was* aware of a distinction within the tribe of Levi and did not simply use "priest" and "Levite" synonymously. See, Abba, "Priests," and McConville, "Priests and Levites."

McConville makes a strong case for rejecting the idea that Deut. 18:1–8 can be seen as a precise piece of legislation whose intention was to effect a change in the position of the Levites and thus as evidence for a specific historical development in Israel's priesthood, dated to the seventh-century reform of Josiah. Deuteronomy was fully aware of distinctions between altar priests and other Levites, but its purpose was to present the claims of *the whole tribe* in relation to the kinship and equality of *all the tribes* of Israel as regards their inheritance (*Law and Theology,* pp. 124–53).

18:6–8 / **In all earnestness, v. 6:** This is a possible interpretation of the phrase, lit. "with all the desire of his soul." The identical phrase is found in 12:15, where it means "as much [meat] as you want."

So it could mean "whenever he likes"; cf. NRSV, "and he may come whenever he wishes." In other words, the option for Levites to come and serve at the central sanctuary was always open, and probably only temporary service was envisaged.

Money from the sale of family possessions, v. 8: This, like most of the other translations, is a guess at a very problematic phrase, lit. "besides his sellings according to the fathers." It has usually been taken to mean some income the Levite has gained from the sale of his patrimony. However, this has never seemed very satisfactory, given the antipathy in Israel to the selling of family land, and the fact that Levites did not have tribal territory, but towns and some pasturage around them. There is some merit, therefore, in the suggestion of L. S. Wright that it has nothing to do with patrimonial land but should be translated "sellings according to ancient custom." He suggests that the "sellings" refers to the sale of the carcasses of animals sacrificed as sin and guilt offerings, for which some money values were set (cf. Lev. 5:15, 18; 6:6), and that it was this priestly income from sacrifices that the priests refused to donate for the temple repairs (2 Kgs. 12:16; L. S. Wright, "*MKR*").

It is no longer thought probable that vv. 6–8 are connected with Josiah's program of destroying the rural sanctuaries and centralizing worship. It used to be thought that this law permits the redundant priests of those sanctuaries to come to Jerusalem, but they did not do so (2 Kgs. 23:9). However, the Deuteronomic text speaks of Levites in their towns, not of priests in sanctuaries. In any case, priests of rural high-places were deemed apostate by Josiah and would not have been brought to the temple. There is probably no link at all between 2 Kgs. 23:9 and Deut. 18:6–8. Cf. McConville, *Law and Theology,* pp. 132–35, and Mayes, *Deuteronomy,* p. 278f.

Furthermore, it is almost certainly a misreading of the syntax of vv. 6–8 to take v. 7 as the main clause, and thus to make the Levite's coming to the central sanctuary the main thing legislated. Most probably, v. 8 should be taken as the main point of the whole sentence, taking v. 7 as the continuation of the "If . . . " clauses from v. 6. The NIV, by translating **he may minister,** takes the law as a *permission* for Levites to minister at the central sanctuary. The more natural reading of the Hb. takes the law as *assuming* the right of ministry, but stipulating equal share in the material benefit—primarily food. Thus, the sense is, "If a Levite moves . . . and comes . . . and ministers . . . then he shall eat equal portions" (cf. NEB and REB). Cf. Duke, "The Portion of the Levite."

18:15 / On NT comparison of Jesus with Moses, cf. Moessner, "Luke 9:1–50."

§22 Manslaughter, Murder, and Malice (Deut. 19:1–21)

The whole section 19:1–21:9 may be thematically linked to the sixth commandment, "you shall not murder." This is clearest in 19:1–13 and 21:1–9, but there are some links in the intervening laws as well, particularly 19:15–21. The organization is not overly tidy, however, and other commandments can be detected; the eighth and tenth, for example (19:14), and the ninth (19:16–19).

Israel needed structures of authority and leadership that would preserve their societal commitment to justice and obedience to God's Torah. However, even in a nation living with the ideal standards and patterns of life of 14:28–16:17 and with the ideal leaders of 16:18–18:22, things could go wrong. Premature deaths could happen, by accident (19:5–7), by design (19:11–13), in war (ch. 20), or through causes unknown (21:1–9). It was all very well to have the fundamental rule, "You shall not kill," but not all killing was the same. Certain crucial distinctions were needed for the purpose of protecting the innocent and vulnerable—a pervading concern in the preached law of Deuteronomy.

19:1–13 / This ancient law of asylum for the accidental manslayer is based upon Exodus 21:12–14, which, while prescribing the death penalty for murder, carefully distinguishes between intentional premeditated murder and unintentional killing that "God lets happen." In the latter case, the accidental killer can "flee to a place I will designate," by which was meant the altar of Yahweh (Exod. 21:14).

Moses had set aside three named cities east of Jordan as places of sanctuary for accidental killers (4:41–43). Three (as yet unnamed) cities (with the possibility of three more, vv. 8f.) were to be designated as places of refuge in the land itself, west of Jordan. Joshua 20 records the selection of these cities (Kedesh in the North, Shechem in the center, and Hebron in the South of the country) and further explains their purpose and the procedures to be followed by all the parties, especially the elders of the cities, who were the primary judicial adjudicators. As to how the system worked, Deuteronomy avoids the intricate details of Numbers 35:6–34. Instead it states the basic rule (vv. 1–3), explains and illustrates it (vv. 4–7), expands it where necessary (vv. 8–10), qualifies it with an obvious exception (vv. 11–13), and bases it on a fundamental theological and legal principle (vv. 10 and 13).

It is this final principle that attracts interest. What was at stake was **the guilt of shedding innocent blood** (v. 13). But the law shows a careful concern for two kinds of innocence. On the one hand there was the innocent victim of a deliberate murder. But on the other hand there was the innocent person who had accidentally caused someone else's death, with no **malice aforethought**. This unfortunate person needed protection from the injustice of a wrongful revenge killing, just as the premeditated murder victim needed the vindication of having the murderer brought to justice. Verse 10 emphatically states that to allow an accidental killer to be slain would be as much a matter of shedding innocent blood as the deliberate murder of verse 13. The law thus enshrines a legal principle of fundamental magnitude: *the innocent should not be punished, and the guilty should not go unpunished.* Significantly, it notes that anger and haste are likely causes of injustice being done (**pursue him in a rage,** v. 6). The most notorious cases in recent British legal history of wrongful arrest and imprisonment of persons later shown to be innocent were the result of public anger at IRA terrorist outrages and the pressure on British police to produce immediate results.

We may have moved a long way from cities of refuge, but unless current criminal justice systems can improve on their own recent record of wrongful imprisonment of innocent people and failure to punish the manifestly guilty, we would do well not to imagine ourselves superior to the much caricatured OT legal system. On the contrary, we may find ourselves deserving of the prophetic scorn of Hosea (6:8–9), who, with heavy sarcasm for the violence of Israel's society and the double failures of its judicial guardians, portrayed one city of refuge ([Ramoth] Gilead) as full of deliberate murderers who should not have been allowed sanctuary there, and another (Shechem) as the hiding place of priests who murdered those who were genuinely fleeing for refuge.

19:14 / Although an attack on a neighbor's property might not seem as serious as an attack on his life, it was nevertheless a matter of great weight. The land was God's gift to the whole nation. It was to be divided up between tribes and clans, and even the extended families. Possession of a share in the **inheritance** was thus the means of economic survival for each family and also the family's tangible proof of membership in the covenant people. Loss of land was a terrible thing, with spiritual as well as socioeconomic consequences. Encroachment, therefore, by stealthy moving of the boundary stone, was virtually an attack on the neighbor's livelihood. It was a violation of the eighth commandment, and Micah 2:1–2 shows how it was rooted in ignoring the tenth commandment as well (cf. Isa. 5:8). In fact, as an attack on a covenant neighbor, striking at his share of the covenant land given by God, theft was indirectly a crime against God. This explains why the offense appears again in the list of curses in chapter 27. Indeed, it comes high on that list, after idolatry and dishonoring parents (27:17). Elsewhere in the OT, the crime of boundary encroachment is listed among the worst offenses (cf. Hos. 5:10; Prov. 23:10f.; Job 24:2–4). Cf. C. J. H. Wright, *God's Land,* pp. 128–31.

19:15–21 / The purpose of the plurality of witnesses (cf. 17:6) is clearly the protection of the accused, especially the protection of the weaker individual from the vindictiveness of a more powerful opponent. Obviously this precaution could be flouted, as Naboth discovered (1 Kgs. 21), but it provided at least some safeguard.

Verses 16–19 expand the basic rules for witnesses given in Exodus 23:1–3. This text is notable, first, for its insistence on great care and diligence in establishing the truth of each case, on the assumption that all matters of justice are decided **in the presence of the LORD,** the supreme judge. Second, this text has a simple but effective deterrent to perjury. Anyone proved to have lied in court is to suffer whatever penalty would have been inflicted on the accused if the false accusation had been successful. If the case is capital, then the risk to a malicious witness was very great indeed. And even in less serious matters, such a law would decidedly dampen any frivolous "taking the neighbor to court," with all the undesirable social side effects of uncontrolled litigation. The severity of this law reflects the way justice in Israel was a matter of the utmost seriousness. Yahweh, by his character as well as his action, demanded commitment to social and judicial justice among the people who claimed his name. The most essential components of that justice were the impartiality of judges and the integrity of witnesses; hence the presence of the ninth commandment in the Decalogue and hence this direct and uncompromising attack upon perjury. Its deterrent effect is openly acknowledged as quite intentional (v. 20), and one wonders if the adoption of a remotely comparable law in relation to perjury would not have a salutary effect on the truthfulness of witness in modern courts.

Additional Notes §22

19:2–3 / On the concept and practice of asylum, cf. Greenberg, "Asylum."

19:4 / On the distinctions involved in various kinds of homicide, cf. Daube, "Direct and Indirect Causation," and McKeating, "Homicide."

19:6 / **The avenger of blood** (Hb. *gōʾēl haddām*): The word *gōʾēl* is used of the kinsman who has the duty of protecting or redeeming a member of the family or clan who is in difficulty or debt (cf. Johnson, "Primary Meaning"). The addition of "blood" (i.e., murder), is usually taken to mean that it was the responsibility of a member of the family of any slain person to seek out the killer and avenge the death. This ancient and common custom could obviously lead to blood feuds between families, and legal developments in many societies indicate how this kinship duty is brought within the control of public law. In the OT, while the **avenger of blood** has the right to seek the killer (accidental or deliberate), his scope for action is clearly limited by the intervention of the elders, both in the city of refuge and in the killer's own city (v. 12). This civil involvement effectively lifts homicide out of the sphere of private or kinship vengeance and puts it in the sphere of properly constituted courts.

19:14 / For possible reasons why this law appears in this context, cf. Carmichael, "Deuteronomic Laws," and Mayes, *Deuteronomy*, p. 288. Carmichael suggests that it may be due to the historical associations of the preceding law on asylum cities. The earlier reference to those cities (4:41–43) came in the context of the division of the land east of Jordan (3:12–17). So here, the law of asylum "triggers" a reminder of the sanctity of that allocation as part of the requirement **in the inheritance** received from God (v. 14, cf. v. 10).

19:21 / **Eye for eye, tooth for tooth:** Possibly no other OT text has been the victim of more misunderstanding and exaggeration than this one, the lex talionis, or law of retribution. This verse, understood in its most literal and vengeful sense, has entered popular imagination as the summation of all OT ethics. (This can be the only reason why my own book on OT ethics was unilaterally given the title *An Eye for An Eye* by its American publishers, instead of its original British title, *Living as the People of God!*). Yet it is abundantly clear to any reader of Deut. alone that such a view is a misunderstanding that totally ignores the ethos of compassion, generosity, concern for the weak, and restraint of the powerful that pervades the book. The sequence, with minor variations, occurs in just three places: Exod. 21:23–25; Lev. 24:17–20; and here. In the first two it is clearly a matter of punishment and compensation for injury. Here it is more loosely linked to the idea of equivalence in punishment.

Contrary to the popular view, the law does not condone rampant physical vengeance but has precisely the opposite intention. It is designed to ensure that penalties in law are strictly proportionate to offenses committed—a perfectly proper and still valid legal and ethical principle. It is very likely that the phraseology was standard and stereotypical, expressing the principle of proportionality, not necessarily intended to be followed literally in all cases (except that of deliberate taking of human life). Other forms of proportionate compensation for injury (e.g., monetary) may well have been acceptable. In Exodus, this seems certain, since any injury to an unborn child would not include its teeth! Historians of ancient law suggest that the lex talionis, which is found elsewhere in Semitic cultures, represents a legal development that was actually *an improvement* on an earlier practice of uncontrolled vengeance. Cf. Diamond, "Eye for an Eye."

The antithesis set up by Jesus in the Sermon on the Mount (Matt. 5:38–42) was not, then, an attack upon "OT ethics" as a whole. He was saying that the principle governing legal decisions in court cases (which was the legitimate goal of strict equivalence) should not be taken as the model for all behavior in personal relationships and attitudes. It was possible to suffer wrong without seeking personal or legal retaliation and to extend generosity even to one's enemy. Such transformed behavior within the kingdom of God had roots in the OT (e.g., Lev. 19:17–18).

§23 Policies and Limits in the Conduct of War (Deut. 20:1–20)

This chapter does not pretend to be a manual for military operations and it is hermeneutically futile to read it or criticize it as if it were. Rather, as in the law of the king (which is no manual for government administration either), it is concerned with fundamental principles, principles that must govern Israelites at war as in any sphere of life. The two most basic covenantal principles of Israel's life under God were: love for Yahweh (6:5) and love for one's neighbor. This vertical and horizontal duality was fundamental to the covenant dynamic. Love (as covenant loyalty and trust) for God can be seen operative in the opening challenge of 20:1–4, but is there any way that love for neighbor can be operative in the context of war? Two responses may be made to this question.

First, love of neighbor clearly does not mean a facile niceness to everybody in all circumstances. Love of neighbor is not incompatible with discipline and punishment. One's duty to one's neighbor may include, for example, the duty to expose the apostate or idolater or to execute the criminal. Love of neighbor did not exclude the need to "purge the evil from among you." On a wider canvas, likewise, the historical execution of divine justice upon the wickedness of the Canaanites is not incompatible with the overall belief in God's ultimate intention to bless the nations through Israel (cf. commentary on ch. 7). Nor does it prevent the remarkable degree of social compassion and legal protection afforded to the foreigner within Israel, even in Deuteronomy. The mere fact, then, that Deuteronomy makes provision for war does not invalidate all it has to say concerning human ethical duties of compassion, neighborliness, and generosity.

Secondly, it is precisely within the imperfections and fallenness of human life that love for neighbor has to operate. And Deuteronomy is well aware that sometimes the priority is to work for the humane within the inhumane, to mitigate the worst effects of human sin, to control the worst human instincts, to protect the interests of those most vulnerable in contexts of brokenness (cf. its laws on polygamy, slavery, and divorce). Seen from this perspective on the one hand, and in the light of the horrors and extremes of cruelty in ancient warfare on the other, the provisions of 20:5ff. and 21:10–14 are an exercise of neighbor love within the constraints of the grim reality of warfare.

20:1–4 / Horses and chariots were the pride of the great ancient Near Eastern imperial armies, and Israel did indeed face them in the Canaanite wars. To a mere human calculation of odds they would induce a crippling inferiority complex. But the odds were not merely human, for Israel already celebrated their history in a song that is not noted for its awe of chariots (Exodus 15:1):

> I will sing to the LORD, for he is highly exalted.
> The horse and its rider he has hurled into the sea.

This same God who **brought** them **up out of Egypt** would be **with** them in any future engagement (always assuming it was in obedience to him; cf. the sharp lesson of 1:41–44). **God . . . with you** (vv. 1, 4): the language of Immanuel is already being spoken, significantly in the context of salvation (**to give you victory,** is lit. "to save you"). These verses thus express the Deuteronomic perspective that the wars Israel would fight in obedience to Yahweh would effectively be Yahweh's own wars against his enemies. It is this theological assumption that undergirds the chapter and determines its selection of contents.

20:5–9 / Certainly, this faith assumption is required to justify what is prescribed here. There is no attempt to match force with force. There is no competitive arms race. The whole spirit of this chapter is actually *antimilitaristic.* Faced with superior technology and superior numbers (**an army,** [lit. a people] **greater than yours,** v. 1), Israel's response was to announce coolly several exemptions that would actually *reduce* the size of their own army, and would do so by sending home some of what were probably the youngest and fittest men! Dependence on Yahweh's superiority liberated Israel from dependence on human superiority and thereby freed some Israelites from military service. The exemptions reflect a very distinctive set of national priorities.

The first three exemptions (**a new house, a new vineyard,** a new wife) seem to form an integral series, to which the fourth

(v. 8) has been added as a final pruning of the forces. To build a house but not live in it, or to plant a vineyard but not enjoy its fruit, or to betroth a wife but not marry her were all elements in "futility curses," widely known throughout the ancient Near East (cf. the stylized language of Ps. 109 and Deut. 28:30). Thus, part of the reason for military exemption for these categories would be that a man should not be slain in battle in circumstances that made him seem under a curse, with all that would entail for his surviving dependents. Another possible reason, however, was that the wars envisaged here were wars connected with possession or defense of the land. Enjoyment of the blessing of the land was thus their end purpose. It would be tragic if Israelites should be killed without experiencing the very gifts and blessings for which the war was being fought. "Thus, in these exemptions from military service, it is clear that the important aspects of normal life in the land take precedence over the requirements of the army, but this somewhat idealistic approach (in modern terms) was possible only because of the profound conviction that military strength and victory lay, in the last resort, not in the army, but in God" (Craigie, *Deuteronomy,* p. 274). Once again, then, we observe how Deuteronomy's distinct theology produces an equally distinct humanitarian rationale for its laws. Family and community life stood *above* the war effort and were not to be sacrificed to it—a remarkable limitation and a reversal of the assumptions of modern concepts of war.

It has been suggested that the offer of verse 8 would have had the psychological effect of boosting courage since nobody would have admitted to being afraid (cf. Mayes, *Deuteronomy,* p. 293). No such embarrassment, however, seems to have afflicted a sizable proportion of Gideon's initial group of soldiers (Judg. 7:2f.)!

20:10–18 / The distinction drawn in verses 15–16 between cities at a distance and cities of the Canaanite nations rests on the same theological rationale as was expressed most starkly in chapter 7. The Canaanites were to be destroyed, not merely as judgment upon their wickedness, but because of the long-term threat of idolatry and syncretism that they presented to Israel (v. 18). The nature of the text as preaching, not military briefing, is very apparent here.

In the case of other cities, the element of restraint is again present, though modern ears may easily miss it. First, there was a preference for peace through negotiation if possible, thus

avoiding war and slaughter. **An offer of peace** probably implies
a vassal treaty in which the city would become subject to Israel.
The terms of surrender strictly include only such subject labor.
No other humiliation, violation of human rights, excessive bru-
tality, or plunder were to be allowed. Subjection itself may seem
bad enough, but when one sees carved in stone what the Assyrians, for example, did to their conquered or surrendered victims
(e.g., some were impaled on stakes; captives were chained to one
another by hooks through the nose), or merely reads of the
known excesses reported by Amos (1:3, 6, 9, 13), "restraint" is the
correct word for what is permitted here. Secondly, if the city
chose war, then in the event of victory, only the male combatants
were to be military targets (v. 13). Defeat in war always meant
capture and plunder, and this is assumed here, but in 21:10–14 a
most remarkable restraint is placed upon the Israelite soldiers as
regards female captives.

20:19–20 / Centuries before environmentalist and "green"
pressure groups, Israel's law called for ecological restraint in the
conduct of war. If this was set up in contrast with practices of
Israel's contemporaries, (destruction of enemy agriculture, especially vineyards, olive groves, and date palms), how much more
it is a poignant protest against atrocities like the defoliation of
Vietnam or the pollution of the Gulf, to mention only two of the
most recent ecological war crimes of our day.

When we allow ourselves, then, to see past the slaughter
of the Canaanites as a moral stumbling block to the other features of Deuteronomy's rules of war, we can hardly remain
unimpressed. Without a Geneva Convention, Deuteronomy
advocates humane exemptions from combat; requires prior negotiation; prefers nonviolence; limits the treatment of subject
populations; allows for execution of male combatants only;
demands humane and dignified treatment of female captives;
and insists on ecological restraint. We may even, as in the case
of slavery, detect something that seems to undermine war itself,
even if only in whispers (cf. Miller, *Deuteronomy*, pp. 159f.).

Additional Notes §23

The term "holy war" has been increasingly criticized as inadequate and misleading (especially in view of modern applications of the phrase). "Yahweh war" has been preferred for expressing the fact that some of the wars of Israel were described and celebrated as the wars of Yahweh against his enemies. It should be remembered, however, that not all the wars fought by Israel in the OT fall into this category, and sometimes kings were prophetically challenged over wars that were not sanctioned by Yahweh. See Jones, " 'Holy War,' " and Craigie, *War*. As regards the humaneness of the laws of war in Deut., cf. Rofé, "The Laws of Warfare." Rofé, however, regards these laws as late idealizations, quite unrelated to the actual practice of warfare during the conquest or monarchy eras. While it is true that Israel's practice did not follow what is prescribed here, it seems to be as likely that the idealization *preceded* Israel's wars in the land (i.e., as a prior statement of what should have happened, but did not), as that it was a seventh-century *post*idealization of what should have happened, but everybody knew had not. It is hard to see what possible point the distinctions of vv. 10–18 would have had centuries after the actual settlement of Israel in the land, or indeed what purpose this ch. would have served at all in relation to a seventh-century reformation.

As regards the moral and theological question of how Christian readers of the OT should view the wars of the OT, or the kind of instructions given in this ch., we should note first the degree of humaneness and restraint in Deuteronomy's laws of war, which is often overlooked in generalized criticisms of "OT violence." Secondly, one must be careful to set the whole issue of war in the OT in the theological context in which it is clearly set in Deut. It is seen not merely as a matter of Israel's supremacy over the nations (on the contrary, the reverse was usually the case in military terms, cf. 20:1), but of Yahweh's supremacy over all other gods and as the exercise of Yahweh's legitimate moral judgment on human wickedness in the context of God's overall sovereignty in history. McConville stresses this need to evaluate the place of war in Deuteronomic theology in terms of its own categories, especially: Yahweh as the only true God; Yahweh as the God of history; and Israel's election in relation to Yahweh's purpose of salvation. Seen in this light, "the victory over Canaan, therefore, is not merely a demonstration of power, but also a vindication of truth" (McConville, *Grace in the End*, p. 141). On the moral and theological questions, see also J. Wenham, *The Goodness of God*, pp. 119–47.

20:11 / **Forced labor** (Hb. *mas*): As it turned out, Israel disobediently imposed forced labor on Canaanite cities, not just those at a distance (v. 15); cf. Josh. 16:10; Judg. 1:27–36; 1 Kgs. 9:21. The early monarchy even established an arm of government to administer this imposition (2 Sam. 20:24). Cf. Mettinger, *Solomonic State Officials*, pp. 128–39.

§24 Rectifying Public and Private Wrongs (Deut. 21:1–23)

Each of the five sections of this chapter deals with a situation of human distress or misconduct and seeks either to rectify the wrong or to mitigate its worst effects. We have seen already that this is a characteristic feature of Deuteronomy—part of its "pastoral strategy." Another feature is that the first and fifth of the laws both require actions that involve removing pollution from the sight of God and from the land.

21:1–9 / *Atonement for an unsolved murder.* Chapter 19 deals with procedures where a killer (intentional or accidental) is known to the community. But if the killer is not known, it is not enough just to "leave the case open." Bloodshed defiles the land (the land whose special character is emphasized in verse 1 and repeated in verse 23), and brings guilt on the whole people (cf. v. 8), thus exposing them to Yahweh's anger. So this law provides a ritual to deal with that guilt and pollution and to exonerate the community.

The details of the ritual are clear enough (vv. 3–8a), and the involvement of elders, judges, and priests shows how seriously the matter is to be taken. The town nearest to the murder site is held responsible through its elders for proper action that would protect the rest of the nation. The ultimate purpose of the ritual is also clear: namely, that **the bloodshed will be atoned for** (v. 8), and **the guilt of shedding innocent blood** will be purged away. What is less apparent is the exact significance of the killing of the cow and reason for the place in which it was to be done. For a survey of the various explanations that have been offered, see D. P. Wright, "Rite of Elimination." Since the text itself gives no explanation of the ritual, we cannot be dogmatic, but the two most likely explanations are as follows.

(a) It represents a vicarious execution of the unknown criminal. The cow is a symbolic substitute for the murderer. Kill-

ing it, therefore, is not a sacrifice (there is no altar and probably
no shedding of blood since the neck was broken instead), but an
"execution." Nevertheless, it has some of the *effect* of a sacrifice by
achieving **atonement** (a "covering" or "wiping away") for the
guilt. This view, however, does not readily explain the unusual
location of the ritual (in an uncultivated **valley** with a **flowing**
stream). One might have expected such a symbolic execution to
have taken place in the public place where a real execution would
have happened.

(b) Alternatively, the ritual has been explained as a symbolic reenactment of the murder in an uninhabited place, which,
by first transferring the guilt away from the human settlement
and then "flushing it away" in the running water, removes all its
threat from the community. This seems better in explaining the
location of the rite and the action of handwashing over the
carcass. Such "elimination rites" have parallels in the OT itself
(e.g., the released bird in Lev. 14:1–7 and the scapegoat in Lev.
16:20–22) and are widely known in Hittite and Mesopotamian
texts. Even in modern times, the practice of symbolic removal of
sin and its guilt is found when, for example, Christians are invited to write down their sins or besetting failures of the past, and
then burn the paper or nail it to a symbolic cross. Any benefit of
such action lies, of course, not in the ritual itself or any kind of
sympathetic magic, but in the objective basis of God's atoning
grace. In the same way, the elders pray for God's forgiveness of
the people, not merely because of the ritual they have carried out,
but on the basis of God's historical redemption and the covenant
relationship (**your people Israel, whom you have redeemed, O**
LORD; v. 8). The same covenant faithfulness of God's character
provides the hope of forgiveness when Israel's sins will be
metaphorically hurled into "the depths of the sea" (Mic. 7:18–20),
just as the guilt of an unknown crime is flushed down the **flow-**
ing stream.

It is often when the OT seems most culturally remote from
us that we need to pay closest attention to its challenge. What
ought to strike us from this law is not the oddity of a cow with a
broken neck in an uninhabited wadi, but the expected response of
a whole community through its civic, judicial, and religious leaders to *a single human death*. In our society, a violent death has to be
particularly gruesome or shocking (e.g., of a child or of the defenseless aged) to become even newsworthy, let alone a matter for
public penitence. We have lost not only any concept of corporate

responsibility for blood guilt (having rejected a sovereign moral God to whom we might be corporately responsible), but we have increasingly lost any sense of the sanctity of life itself. We (or at least our emergency services) can cope with hundreds of thousands of road deaths. We can tolerate millions of abortions. What need have we for rituals of cleansing that would acknowledge responsibility even where personal guilt cannot be assigned? **Shedding innocent blood** (v. 9) has become a fact of life, silently sanitized by statistics. Symbolic reenactment is left to the commercialized catharsis of cinema and television.

21:10–14 / *The female prisoner of war.* Here we have another law that on first reading seems not only remote from our normal experience but superficially harsh. But on closer inspection, it furnishes a good example of the value of asking the kind of questions suggested in the introduction of this book for getting at the underlying objectives and priorities of OT laws. We might like to live in a world without wars and thus without prisoners of war. However, OT law recognizes such realities and seeks to mitigate their worst effects by protecting the victims as far as possible. If we ask whose interests this law serves, the answer is clearly the female captive. If we ask whose power is being restricted, the answer, equally clearly, is the victorious soldier. The law is thus a paradigm case of the OT's concern to defend the weak against the strong, war being one of the most tragic human expressions of that situation.

There are four ways in which this law benefits the captured woman. (a) She is not to be raped or to be enslaved as a concubine, but is to be accorded the full status of a wife (vv. 11, 13). The instruction in Hebrew is quite clear that only marriage is intended. (b) She is to be given time to adjust to the traumatic new situation and to ritually mourn for the parents who are now dead as far as she is concerned. This is to take place within the security of her new home, not in some prisoner or refugee camp. (c) The law compassionately restricts even the soldier's "bridegroom's rights," by postponing any sexual intercourse with the woman until this month of mourning and adjustment is over. (d) If the man finally changes his mind and will not undertake marital responsibility toward her, she is to leave as a free woman. He can take no further advantage over her by selling her as a slave. Thus, the physical and emotional needs of the woman in her utter vulnerability are given moral and legal priority over the desires and claims of the man in his victorious strength. The case could be written up as a matter of human rights. Deuteronomy characteristically prefers to express it as a matter of responsibilities. As such, its relevance is clearly applicable beyond the realm of war to all kinds of analogous situations of weakness and power.

21:15–17 / *The right of the firstborn son.* The next two laws balance each other. The first protects a son from an unfair father; the second protects parents from an unruly son. Together they illustrate the balance of rights and responsibilities that exist in a family, and even more so, in wider society.

Polygamy was permitted in Israelite society but was probably not very common. It was a sign of wealth and prestige and so was something of a perk of royalty (in spite of Deut. 17:17). Bigamy (as defined in this law) may have been more common. The law accepted it, but by pointing out its emotional and economic dangers, possibly offered tacit criticism of the practice. The law reckoned with inevitable favoritism, but acted to prevent it from denying the firstborn son his proper rights. There are, of course, stories in the OT where the order of inheritance was reversed or overturned (e.g., Jacob and Esau, Isaac and Ishmael, Ephraim and Manasseh), but the basic legal principle was to stand. A son was not to suffer because his mother was no longer his father's favorite.

21:18–21 / *The fate of the rebellious son.* If a son should not suffer because of his father's whims, then neither should parents (indeed the whole family) suffer because of one son's incorrigible behavior. This is another law that at first seems harsh. In our modern society, which frowns upon even the simplest forms of corporal punishment, the idea of *executing* a child for disobedience seems to typify all the alleged barbarity of the OT. Once again, however, a closer look uncovers important features that put the law in its proper context and indicate a contemporary relevance.

(a) The law is not talking about naughty young children but about seriously delinquent young adults. If the law intentionally balances the preceding one, then it may envisage a firstborn son who is proving totally unworthy of his inheritance. There is a conflict of interests between the individual and the whole family, which could affect the family's economic viability for posterity. If this is how the son behaves while still a minor, then what will he do with the family's substance when he inherits it?

His behavior is both an offense in the present and a threat to the future of his family. (b) The law recognizes both the importance and the limits of internal family discipline. The case is brought to the elders only after prolonged parental discipline has manifestly been disregarded. The son **does not obey his father and mother and will not listen to them when they discipline him** (v. 18); a point that they make explicitly to the elders in their testimony. The law thus admits that the wisdom of Proverbs 22:6 ("Train a child in the way he should go, and when he is old he will not turn from it") and Proverbs 15 was a general rule to which there could be exceptions. Possibly an awareness of this law lies behind Proverbs 19:18. (c) The exercise of family law does not extend to the right of life and death over children (as is sometimes falsely alleged about ancient Israel). If serious action is required, the matter has to be brought into the arena of civil law, before the elders. The law thus recognizes a valid role for civil authorities, representing the interests of the whole community, when domestic issues become a threat to the well-being of a family and thereby the welfare of the whole community. The family is not loaded with the total burden of delinquent behavior on its own. The whole community becomes involved in exercising a serious social responsibility. Since the offense also involves a blatant and persistent breach of the fifth commandment, the elders are also acting to protect the community from the covenantal anger of Yahweh. (d) The role of father and mother together reflects the way the fifth commandment demands honor for *both* parents. The presence of the mother in the legal proceedings may also be an element of protection for the son. As in the preceding law, a son is not to suffer for the unfairness or harshness of a father.

There is no account of this law ever being invoked in OT Israel. It is in its own terms a very last resort. Yet its mere existence indicates the serious nature of the fifth commandment. And its balancing of familial with civil responsibilities in the matter of young adult delinquency is not without relevance to the same issue today.

21:22–23 / *The body of an executed criminal.* The purpose of this law is to prevent the land from being polluted by improper treatment of a human corpse (cf. 21:1–9). The difference here, of course, is that the corpse is of an executed criminal, not a murder victim. Hanging is not the means of execution (which is stoning), but a kind of intensification, perhaps for its deterrent effect. The law does not *prescribe* that the body of a person put to death under the law should be hung up in open view. But it is a known custom, occasionally recorded in exceptional circumstances in the OT itself (e.g., Num. 25:4; Josh. 8:29; 10:26f.; 2 Sam. 21:5–9). This law *limits* the exposure to the remaining daylight hours of the day of execution. The explicit reason for the ruling is sacral—the offense to God and the desecration of the land. But it is not unlikely that part of its intent (and certainly its practical effect) is to spare the victim from further degradation beyond death itself, and to spare the criminal's family further emotional suffering (cf. Brown, *Deuteronomy*, p. 211).

Additional Notes §24

A possible link between the five laws of this ch. as matters involving life and death, or the intrusion or expectation of death, is suggested by Carmichael, "Common Element."

21:1–9 / Some scholars have claimed, by source critical analysis of the text, that there are several layers of material that indicate a historical development of the ritual from a pre-Israelite propitiatory sacrifice to the gods of the earth, to early Israelite expiation of blood-guilt before Yahweh, to the later nonsacrificial ritual of Deut. Cf. Zevit, "Deuteronomy 21:1–9." Tracing such a complex history from a single text, however, remains highly speculative.

21:3 / **The elders of the town nearest the body,** as representatives of that community, have to assume responsibility for the crime, even though they are not guilty of it. The ritual that follows combines acknowledgment of the crime, its guilt, the need for atonement, and the need for forgiveness with declaration of innocence on the part of those involved in, or represented at, the ritual.

21:4 / **Break the heifer's neck:** This unusual method of slaughter indicates the action is not a sacrifice. This method is used to kill a first-born donkey (an unclean animal) that has been not redeemed (Exod. 13:13; 34:20).

21:5 / **The priests** play no major part in the ritual, but their presence is evidence of the serious and sacral nature of the proceedings. Possibly they respond on God's behalf with words of atonement in response to the elders' prayer (vv. 7–8a).

21:6 / **Wash their hands:** This common rite for declaring innocence (cf. Pss. 26:6; 73:13), was used most famously (and proverbially) by Pontius Pilate (Matt. 27:24).

21:7 / **This blood** refers primarily, of course, to the blood of the human murder victim. Most commentators believe that breaking the neck of the cow meant that none of its blood was shed. D. P. Wright, however, considers that the slaughter would have involved some bloodshed from the cow, into the running stream. In his view the killing of the cow was a symbolic reenactment of the murder; thus, when the elders deny that they had shed "this blood," they are referring to the cow's blood as symbolic of the blood of the human victim.

21:8 / **Accept this atonement:** A better translation would be, "Clear, or forgive, your people." The Hb. verb *kippēr* means either "to cover over" or "to wipe clean" and is most widely used in the sacrificial texts in Lev. 1–7. Thus the last phrase of the verse means, "the bloodshed will be wiped clean, or blotted out"; i.e., the pollution is gone.

21:10–14 / This law does not contradict the prohibition on intermarriage in 7:3 that deals with the Canaanite inhabitants of the land. This law presumably refers to captives taken from enemies outside the land (cf. 20:14f.). Also, the prohibition in ch. 7 is explicitly to prevent idolatry as a result of intermarriage. The permission granted in 21:10–14 indicates that the concern over foreign marriages is not a matter of racial prejudice per se.

21:15–17 / On the special status of the firstborn son, cf. Mendelsohn, "Preferential Status." There is evidence in the ancient Near East and in the OT (e.g., Gen. 48:13–20; 49:3f.) that a father could sometimes choose which of his sons would have firstborn rights. This law aims to prevent such arbitrary choice from becoming common practice.

21:18 / The words **stubborn and rebellious** (*sôrēr* and *môreh*) are terms for serious and persistent rejection of authority, in this case tantamount to a renunciation of the parental bond. They are used frequently of Israel's disobedient response to Yahweh (e.g., Pss. 78:8; 106:7; Neh. 9:29; Isa. 1:23; Jer. 5:23; Hos. 9:15). On their theological appeal to Deut., cf. Bellefontaine, "Rebellious Son." She suggests that Deut. included this law because it mirrored the book's theological concern over Israel's stubborn and rebellious nature, which would lead in similar fashion to a disciplinary "death."

On the failure of parental discipline, vv. 18–21, so praised in Prov., cf. Callaway, "Proverbial Wisdom and Law."

21:20 / **He is a profligate and a drunkard:** These are not so much the accusation as part of the evidence. They are publicly visible illustrations of the real crime, namely, persistent rebellion against parents. The young man is not to be executed for gluttony and drunkenness in themselves, but for incorrigible flouting of the fifth commandment in ways that were squandering and endangering the family's substance.

21:23 / **Anyone who is hung on a tree is under God's curse:**
There is disagreement in both Jewish and Christian exegesis as to
whether the Hb. ("a curse of God is the hanged one") is a subjective
genitive ("accursed by God") or an objective genitive ("a curse [i.e., an
offense] to God"). Both are possible. The majority verdict favors the
former (as NIV). Cf. Bernstein, "Early Jewish Exegesis." It is important to
note that the hanging was an expression of the cursed status of the
criminal, not the reason for it. "The body was not *accursed of God* . . .
because it was hanging on a tree; it was hanging on a tree because it was
accursed of God" (Craigie, *Deuteronomy*, p. 285).

Deuteronomy 21:23 entered early into Christian interpretation of
the death of Christ on a "tree" (cf. Acts 5:30; 10:39f.; 1 Pet. 2:24), though
only Paul explicitly quotes the verse and relates it to the curse of the law
(Gal. 3:13). Cf. Tuckett, "Paul's Conversion," and Caneday, " 'Curse of
the Law.' "

§25 Respect for Life in All Its Forms (Deut. 22:1–12)

The heading above echoes Mayes' suggestion (*Deuteronomy*, pp. 305–9) that, apart from verse 5, the laws in 22:1–12 are loosely concerned with respect for life, animal and human. As such, they would fittingly end the section mainly related to the sixth commandment, "you shall not murder."

22:1–4 / This warmhearted law builds on Exodus 23:4–5, where it occurs in a list of rules for those taking part in court cases. That is why the animals are said to belong to "your enemy" or "one who hates you," i.e., contestants in a court case. The point is that animals should not have to suffer because of human disputes. Deuteronomy lifts the law from the judicial context of Exodus and changes "your enemy's ox" to **your brother's ox**, thus widening its relevance to all Israelites at any time. Animals should not have to suffer because of human neglect either. Deuteronomy adds some other details to the original law: the animal should be cared for until a distant or unknown owner claims it (v. 2); the same principle should be applied to any form of lost property (v. 3); help should be given to a neighbor in difficulty (v. 4).

The significant phrase in these verses is **do not ignore it** (vv. 1, 3, 4), lit. "Do not hide yourself from it," which counteracts the instinctive human reaction "not to get involved," as supremely illustrated by the priest and the Levite who pass the injured man on the Jericho road (Luke 10:30–35). Care for others means care for what they own and giving practical help in time of need. It is a fundamental principle of biblical ethics. Indeed, the first steps of broader application (**do the same if . . .**) found in verse 3 could be infinitely extended, as the sage exemplifies (Prov. 12:10; 29:7).

22:5 / This law is not about styles or fashions in clothing, though it has been quoted in earnest pamphlets urging Christian women not to wear jeans (though not, as far as I am aware, in relation to Scotsmen's kilts!). Almost certainly it is about the perverted crossing of genders either in orgiastic rites involving transvestitism, or in some form of pagan worship, or both. The final phrase of the law shows that some form of serious immorality or idolatry was involved.

22:6–7 / Some see this law as another example of Deuteronomy's humanitarian spirit (cf. 25:4), though the mother bird, of course, may not have been so impressed on this score. Others have invoked a sacral reasoning (cf. Lev. 22:27f.). Perhaps the most likely rationale, through comparison with the fruit trees of 20:19–20, is the conservationist principle of preserving a source of food supply for the future by not consuming it all in the present. Long term prudence should set limits to short term greed. This is certainly a principle applicable well beyond birds' nests. Sadly, this is so ignored today that environmentalists warn us that our current ecological destruction (most of it for short-term greed, or because of need, poverty, and injustice) is putting the possibility of any "long term" in question. This gives point to the final phrase of the verse: our own **long life** is bound up with how we treat the rest of creation.

22:8 / The flat roof of Israelite homes is used for a variety of purposes: sleeping, relaxation, entertainment of guests. The possibility of someone falling off to injury or death is very real. "Building regulations and planning permission begin with God" (Brown, *Deuteronomy*, p. 214). This law is thus a very basic safety precaution, which not only protects the householder's family and guests but also protects the householder from **the guilt of bloodshed.** This phrase means that if a houseowner fails to provide a parapet and someone has a fatal fall, the houseowner can be guilty of indirect homicide. Like Exodus 21:33f., this was probably a paradigm law, setting a precedent for similar cases where injury or death was caused by avoidable accidents.

The number of human deaths around the world that are caused, not by malice, but by negligence and carelessness, industrial dangers, inadequate maintenance, unhealthy work environments, etc. must be simply incalculable. Christians (like the Clapham Sect in Britain) were in the forefront of the struggle for basic safety, hygiene, and worker protection laws. Yet still, the **guilt of bloodshed** lingers through far too many deaths and injuries caused by negligence and apathy.

22:9–11 / The reason for these rules (cf. Lev. 19:19) may lie in their symbolic value as "badges" of Israel's distinctiveness from the nations. This is certainly the rationale behind the clean/unclean distinction, and we know from the criteria listed in Leviticus 11:1–8 that the ox was clean and the donkey unclean, though it was eaten in dire emergency (2 Kgs. 6:25). In other words, even at everyday levels, Israel was to be reminded of the importance of not "mixing" with paganism.

22:12 / Numbers 15:37–41 explains the purpose of these tassels as being a reminder to Israelites (by day and night, since the cloak was clothing by day and a blanket by night) of the law and their obligation to covenant loyalty.

Additional Notes §25

22:5 / The first line includes not only clothing but also any articles typically associated with men (e.g., weapons).

22:6–7 / Jewish rabbis explicitly called this "law of the nest," "the least of the commandments." They deduced from it the importance of the *whole* law (since this "least" law has the same major theological justification as the fifth commandment) and also the importance of human beings. Such reflection probably underlies what Jesus has to say about birds and people in the sermon on the mount, as well as his use of the expression in Matt. 5:19. Cf. Johnston, " 'The Least of the Commandments.' "

22:8 / It is disputed whether **the guilt of bloodshed** meant that the houseowner would have faced a legal charge of homicide. Phillips argues (correctly, in my view) that he would (*Criminal Law*, p. 94). Daube, however, believes it would have been very unlikely ("Direct and Indirect Causation").

§26 The Integrity of Marriage and Sexual Relationships (Deut. 22:13–30)

The progression through the Ten Commandments as a framework for other laws continues with this short section fairly obviously related to the seventh commandment forbidding adultery (see the commentary and additional notes on 5:18). These laws relating to marriage, adultery, fornication, rape, and incest were not merely matters of sexual morality alone but have at heart the vital integrity of the family as the fundamental unit of the covenant community—a concern that explains the severity of the penalties attached to these laws.

22:13–21 / *A wife accused of premarital unchastity.* In this case, a man makes a charge against his new wife that constitutes a legal accusation against her parents (see additional notes). It is a serious charge because, since betrothal is virtually tantamount to marriage, the girl is accused of adultery and the parents are accused of giving a daughter as bride under false pretenses. If the charge cannot be disproved (vv. 17, 20), then the wife faces the same judgment as a convicted adulteress (vv. 20f.). Because of this, the law provides a strong deterrent to a false charge. A man who viciously tries to get rid of an unloved wife by this means (and presumably reclaim the bridal gift he had paid to the father) faces a whipping (implied by **take the man and punish him,** v. 18), a fine that is double the average bridal gift (cf. v. 29), and the loss of any right of subsequent divorce.

The law is thus a strongly protective measure for a young wife at her most vulnerable. It not only defends her good name (vv. 14, 19) but also provides for her future security against his likely desire to divorce her. The law takes the view that the security and provision of a household—even in the home of such a man—is preferable to the insecurity of a divorced woman that nobody else is likely to marry. Such a law protects women, who in many cultures are vulnerable to cruel husbands. An example of this cruelty is seen in the scandalous incidence of "dowry deaths" (often by burning) of young brides in India. When husbands and in-laws want more in material goods or favors than the bride's family can afford, the bride is abused and even killed, freeing the man to remarry and gain another dowry. Thousands of such deaths happen every year, but they are rarely investigated or prosecuted with any success.

22:22 / For further discussion, see commentary and additional notes on 5:18. See also Leviticus 20:10. The inclusion of the guilty *man* in the sentence shows that the law did not support a double standard of sexual morality, as did those who brought only the woman caught in adultery to Jesus (John 8:2–11).

22:23–29 / This series of three laws relating to unlawful extramarital sexual intercourse shows a similar concern to make important distinctions and qualifications as for the laws on homicide (ch. 19), and indeed makes that comparison (v. 26). Since betrothal is tantamount to marriage, intercourse with a woman **pledged to be married** (vv. 23, 25) is tantamount to adultery. But the circumstances in which it occurs affect the assumptions the court might make regarding *intention* and thus also affect its allocation of guilt and punishment. The contrast between a busy town and the deserted countryside makes an obvious difference to what could be assumed regarding the woman's consent. The difference is also expressed in the vocabulary. In verse 23, **and he sleeps with her**, need not imply force or violence (and thus allows for the possibility of the woman's agreement to the unfaithful act), whereas in verse 25, **and rapes her**, is in Hebrew (lit.): "he seizes her and sleeps with her." In the latter case, the court should accept what could only be the woman's own testimony in the matter and assume her innocence. Probably we are again dealing with "paradigmatic" law, that is, the detailing of specific circumstances with a view to giving judges basic principles and precedents on which to evaluate the great variety of individual cases that might come before them. It was of equal importance that the guilty should be fully punished (and others deterred) and that the innocent should be protected.

Intercourse with a girl as yet **not pledged to be married** is of a different category; it is not adultery (vv. 28f.). The verb in verse 28 is different from that in verse 25 and means simply "handle" or "take hold of," rather than the NIV's stronger translation, **rape**. Legally, and with carefully defined limits, children in

Israel were the "property" of the father (in a way that the wife was *not* the property of the husband), and so to violate a girl (even with her consent) was also an offense against her father. Since the matter had been **discovered**, the girl would no longer attract another potential bridegroom and the exchange of gifts and dowry that went along with the marriage. It is for this loss that the man must compensate the father (v. 29a). When this law is compared with Exodus 22:16f., it can once again be seen how Deuteronomy modifies earlier law in the interests of the weaker party. It gives the offender no option but to marry the girl (and the father no right to refuse), with no easy way out through a quick subsequent divorce. The girl is thus assured of security and provision, in place of virtual widowhood if she had been abandoned after the loss of her virginity.

22:30 / (Cf. Lev. 18:8; 20:11; and Deut. 27:20.) The **father's wife** would not have been the man's own birth mother, but either another of his father's wives in a bigamous or polygamous situation or (more probably) his stepmother, i.e., a woman married by his father after the death of the son's mother and quite possibly of the same age or younger than the son. In either case the purpose of the law was to maintain the sexual integrity of the nuclear marital units within the extended family even when the relationship would not be strictly incestuous in a biological sense. The moral wrongness of the act was still insisted on by Paul (1 Cor. 5:1ff.).

Additional Notes §26

On the unity of 22:13–29, cf. Wenham, "Drafting."

22:13–21 / Wenham, "Marriageable Age," argues that the husband's accusation is that his new wife is not menstruating, which he suspects is because she is already pregnant from some act of premarital unfaithfulness. The parents' "evidence" would be an article of clothing with menstrual bloodstains to prove that she had not been pregnant before the wedding. It has also been suggested that the cloth might have been the bloodstained sheet from the wedding night, preserved by the parents; this custom is known in many cultures, but there is no evidence of it in the OT. The difficulty with this explanation is that if the husband knew that such a piece of cloth had been witnessed and handed over to the bride's parents, he would have been pretty foolish to bring this charge. Cf. also C. J. H. Wright, *God's Land,* pp. 214–16.

A disgraceful thing in Israel, v. 21: This expression, sometimes rendered "folly in Israel," is used for something utterly contrary to expected standards of behavior among the covenant people (cf. Gen. 34:7; Josh. 7:15; Judg. 20:6, 10; Jer. 29:23). Cf. Phillips, "*NEBALAH.*"

22:22 / The fact that the legal penalty for the wife who commits adultery is execution weighs strongly against the idea that wives in OT Israel are legally no more than the property of their husbands. If adultery is merely an offense against another man's "property," why destroy the "property" as well as punishing the guilty man? Furthermore, it would be quite exceptional, inasmuch as no other property offense in OT law is punishable by death. For a full discussion of the issue, see C. J. H. Wright, *God's Land,* ch. 6, esp. pp. 200–208.

22:29 / **Fifty shekels of silver** is probably the average amount given to the parents of brides by bridegrooms or their families. The term elsewhere used for this marriage gift is *mōhar* (Exod. 22:17 [MT v. 16]), but it is wrong to translate it "bride-price" (as NIV). The custom of exchanges of money and other gifts between families in the context of marital arrangements is widespread in many cultures and is usually a part of the cementing of relationships and investing in the stability and permanence of the new union. The idea that it reduced marriage to a matter of mere purchase or the wife to mere property has long been shown to be a misunderstanding of the whole phenomenon (in India, dowry is paid by the woman's family to the man's—the reverse of the biblical direction—but it certainly does not mean that the husband is thereby the purchased property of the wife!). For a survey of the debate and recent understanding, cf. C. J. H. Wright, *God's Land,* pp. 191–94. On the property value of children and its limitations, see pp. 222–24.

22:30 / The interpretation in the commentary assumes that the unlawful act takes place while the father is still alive and thus invades his marital privacy. Some think, however, that it assumes the father's death, in which case the law was intended to prevent a son "inheriting" his deceased father's wife or wives as though they were merely property to be passed on. Cf. C. J. H. Wright, *God's Land,* pp. 208f., and also Phillips, "Uncovering."

§27 Community Laws: Defining and Protecting the Community (Deut. 23:1–25)

These last chapters of the central law code have a "flavor" of concern for a compassionate and caring community that takes seriously the claims of kinship and the needs of the weak and vulnerable. That community itself, however, needs clear definition and measures to protect its religious distinctiveness and purity. This need explains the presence, alongside laws that immediately appeal to us by their charitable nature, of other laws that appear much harsher and exclusive.

23:1–8 / **The assembly of the LORD** means the assembly of those who belong fully to the covenant community and gather for worship, for the reading of the law, or for festivals. This body is not quite coextensive with the whole nation, which includes various people who are not full members of the worshipping community. Three groups are here excluded from membership of the assembly.

Eunuchs (v. 1). The practice of castration was sometimes done for religious reasons in ancient Near Eastern culture and sometimes for entry into particular forms of government service. The prohibition on eunuchs belonging to the worshipping assembly is not explained here, but it may have had the same motivation as the rules that barred from the priesthood men suffering from genital damage (Lev. 21:17–20; cf. Lev. 22:24), namely, a concern for wholeness and a rejection of that which appeared to mutilate nature and God's design for creation (as cf. 14:1). Or it may have been because self-inflicted castration was a feature of certain religious rites that Israel so utterly rejected.

*Those **born of a forbidden marriage** (v. 2).* The rare Hebrew word *mamzēr* [MT v. 3] refers not merely to children born out of wedlock ("bastard" in older versions) but also to those born as a result of incest or marriages that broke the prohibited degrees of relationship (Lev. 18:6–20; 20:10–21).

Certain foreigners (vv. 3–6). It should be noted that this is not an exclusion of *all* foreigners per se, but of specific groups. The tradition of Genesis 19:30–38 may have influenced the permanent exclusion of Moabites and Ammonites from the sacred assembly, but this reason is not explicitly stated. Instead, Deuteronomy draws on the more recent historical experience of the Israelites and pinpoints the Ammonites' failure to help the needy (Deut. 2:26–30) and the Moabites' hostility in the attempt to curse Israel (Num. 22–24).

Another reason for the exclusion of eunuchs and some foreigners from the sacred assembly may be found in the fact that in preexilic Israel, kinship and land were vital factors in membership in the covenant community (cf. C. J. H. Wright, *God's Land*). A eunuch's inability to produce or continue a family and the foreigner's lack of any share in the land may have been a factors in their exclusion from the assembly. Certainly, awareness of the former disability is the point of the eunuch's despair in Isaiah 56:3b, and it is answered by the promise that God would grant blessings "better than sons and daughters" to eunuchs who would choose to bind themselves to God. A corresponding promise is made to foreigners. These promises in Isaiah 56:3–8 apparently repeal the exclusion laws of Deuteronomy 23 (though some scholars question whether the prophetic text does refer to Deut. 23) and look forward to an Israel redefined and extended by the ingathering of hitherto excluded people. This was an important factor in the missionary theology and practice of the early church (cf. Eph. 2:11–19). There is, perhaps, a touch of divine humor in the fact that among the earliest notable converts was one who was both a eunuch and a foreigner—and was reading Isaiah! (Acts 8:26–40).

The claims of kinship (Edomites) and hospitality (Egypt) allowed the grandchildren of resident aliens from these nationalities to be included in the covenant community (vv. 7f.). It is notable that Israel's historical memory extends back behind the oppression of the later years of their experience in Egypt and rewards the original hospitality offered to their ancestors in time of famine and need. Likewise, it may be that a reason for the acceptance of Ruth within the community of Israel (and eventually her inclusion within the genealogy of David), is that her people showed hospitality to the family of Elimelech and Naomi in their need and distress.

23:9–14 / These two laws show that the old saying "cleanliness is next to godliness" is more biblical than some may have imagined! The requirement that soldiers on campaign maintain ritual purity and **keep away from everything impure** is part of the rules of "Yahweh warfare" (cf. 1 Sam. 21:1–6). The text refers to ritual impurity, not immoral behavior, since the remedy is merely a day's quarantine and washing.

The instructions of vv. 12f. have obvious hygienic benefits, even though the explicit reason given is religious (v. 14). There are many countries where the routine burial of excrement would have a marked effect on the health of millions of the world's population where, without adequate latrines, people defecate in the open and insect borne diseases spread easily. Since God was aware of the effects of germs long before humans knew of their existence, we may be impressed yet again with the correlation between holiness and health. Physical cleanliness, ritual cleanness, and moral holiness were interrelated.

23:15–16 / This is an astonishing law. It is diametrically opposite to the whole thrust of slave legislation in other ancient Near Eastern law codes, and indeed in the legislation governing slavery in more modern times. The normal, common rule in such legislation is that (a) any slave who runs away is subject to extreme penalties (sometimes death), and (b) anyone who harbors a runaway slave is also subject to heavy penalty (see, for example, the death penalty in the Code of Hammurabi, 15–20, Pritchard, ed., *Ancient Near Eastern Texts*, pp. 166f.). The simple **do not hand him over** in the middle of verse 15 makes this OT law the direct negation of standard slave law, which would have insisted on returning the slave to his master.

If this law applies to slaves in general and not just to *foreign* slaves, as suggested by some (though without any textual support), then it implies two things. First, the law seems to assume that the experience of slavery in Israel would not be so intolerably harsh that there would be a glut of runaways. Indeed, the slave release law allows for the possibility that a slave might be so content in his relationship with his master that he (or she) would prefer permanent slavery to freedom (15:16f.). When reading the OT, we need to put out of our minds pictures of slavery derived from Roman galley slaves or more recent black slavery because these are quite inappropriate analogies for what a slave was in Israel. The word *ᶜebed* meant a servant-worker, who could hold a wide range of social positions. The law allows for the fact that *some* slaves *might* run away from unfair or brutal masters, but does not envisage an institution of such widespread savagery that *most* slaves *would want to* if they could.

Secondly, the radical nature of the law must be given full weight. To legislate so *contrary* to the universally accepted norms for the treatment of slaves indicates an intentional critique of the very nature of the institution itself. That is, the legal rights and expectations intrinsic to slavery as a social institution are subordinated to the rights of the slave as a human being with needs. Old Testament law characteristically values needs above claims. In this case, the needs of the weaker party (the slave seeking refuge) are given explicit legal preference over the claims of the stronger (the master seeking his return). Thus, the legal right to hold property in the form of persons (slaves) is not abolished, but it is certainly relativized and subordinated to higher moral obligation. This Deuteronomic law on slavery is pointing in a direction that ultimately undermines slavery itself. In Job 31:13–15 the same awareness of the rights of the slave as a human being is founded explicitly on the created equality of slave and master. There is no higher statement of that equality after Job 31:15 until Paul declares the redeemed equality of slave and free in Christ (Gal. 3:28).

One final remarkable feature of the law, somewhat obscured by the NIV rendering, **Let him live among you wherever he likes,** is that the slave is given a freedom to choose his own place of residence in words that echo precisely God's own choice of a place: "With you let him live, in the midst of you, *in the place which he will choose in one of your towns* as is good for him" (v. 16). This is a significant example of the way Deuteronomy reinforces its social legislation on behalf of the poor and the weak, by using phrases that echo its primary theological foundations (cf. the use of the exodus in ch. 15). When the phraseology of the "chosen place," which is used so extensively in Deuteronomy to denote the *sanctuary* where Yahweh would place his name, is used in connection with the free choice of a *slave*, it gives that law a deep theological resonance (cf. Hamilton, *Social Justice*, pp. 117–21).

23:17–18 / Cult prostitutes were a common part of temple personnel and functioned in fertility cults in the religious cultures surrounding Israel. Israel's law outlawed prostitution in general (Lev. 19:29), and this law (in v. 17) prohibits it in the context of worship. The normal practice with cult prostitution in the surrounding cultures was for the money given to a shrine prostitute to be paid to the sanctuary (cf. Mic. 1:7), but since the practice itself was illegal, any money made from it could not be used for the sanctuary (v. 18).

23:19–20 / The prohibition on charging interest is found three times in OT law (cf. Exod. 22:25; Lev. 25:35–37). Once again we find that Israel's law stands in marked contrast to surrounding ancient Near Eastern countries, where the charging of interest, often at very high rates, was common. In Israel, it was among the defining marks of righteousness that a person did *not* lend at interest; conversely, the charging of interest was morally and socially condemned (cf. Ps. 15:5; Prov. 28:8; Ezek. 18:8, 13, 17). The strength of feeling in these texts indicates a high level of ethical priority. Three comments may be made.

First, the texts clearly ban all interest-charging between Israelites. The word "usury," found in some translations, suggests an exorbitant and greedy level of interest in modern English, but its original sense in English (i.e., *any* interest charged on a loan) matches the Hebrew. For this reason, the NIV's insertion of "excessive" in several places is an unwarranted interpretation, suggesting that only the *amount* of interest was challenged, not the charging of interest itself, whereas the OT texts cited above simply ban interest per se, without defining any level at which it becomes excessive.

Secondly, the primary focus of this law is consistent with surrounding legislation in Deuteronomy on behalf of the needy. The versions in Exodus and Leviticus specify that the prohibition applies to loans given to those in acute need. This would primarily apply to Israelite farmers in need of food or seed grain in a difficult season or (in Leviticus) those who had fallen into severe poverty over a longer term. Such is the evil of human nature, that desperate human need is commonly an opportunity for unscrupulous exploitation. True to OT ideals of justice and compassion, the ban on interest in Deuteronomy, Exodus, and Leviticus is primarily concerned to stop the hardhearted from making a profit out of hard times. This may, as some think, be the reason why the ban did not apply to foreigners. The foreigners in mind (though not, it must be said, stated in the law) may have been commercial traders, with whom interest bearing transactions were allowed.

Thirdly, the impact and influence of the OT ban on interest has been remarkably extensive in Jewish, Christian, and Islamic history. Only with the dawn of the modern era did the Christian church shift from its position that interest was unlawful and a moral evil. Both Jews and Christians found ways of getting around the law and concealing interest in transactions, but the official position was disapproval of interest up to the medieval period. It was Calvin's carefully qualified approval of the legitimacy of interest in commercial transactions that paved the way for the economic developments of the following centuries (see additional note). Although it would be difficult to see how the modern economic system, so fueled by interest and inflation, could be changed (though Islamic banking poses a notable challenge to the norm), it is still worth asking what the OT ban on interest has to contribute to Christian economic ethics even if it would never be literally reestablished.

To answer that question, we need to set the specific law on interest in the context of the overall ancient Israelite economic system and see its purpose in the light of that. The law is a typical OT response to poverty in the way that it restrains the power of the lender to exploit the need of the borrower (a restriction that has not lost its importance in modern life). It also strengthens the economic aspect of kinship bonds. Since it is a legal and moral duty to lend to the kinsperson in need, and since loans from a kinsperson can be obtained without interest, the extended family gains an advantage by keeping such transactions within the kin group rather than going outside. The centrality of the family in Israel's life and faith is thus given practical economic muscle as well. Economic life is linked to primary relationships, not treated as a detached, autonomous sphere of market forces. It is ironic that some of our modern giant financial institutions grew out of smaller, local networks of self-help and mutual assurance, built upon relationships of family or neighborhood trust. The loss of that element is a factor in the rise of gigantic fraud and it is interesting that there has been a resurgence in the forming of local credit unions and neighborhood banking schemes, designed specifically to keep interest low (basically to cover costs) and provide genuine help to the needy in a more human, relational, and personal way.

23:21–23 / Though entirely voluntary (v. 22, cf. Num. 30), once a vow to the Lord is made it is a serious matter and must be fulfilled (cf. Pss. 56:12f.; 61:5, 8; 66:13–15; 116:12–14). Wisdom warns against hasty promises (Prov. 20:25; Eccl. 5:4–6). The abiding relevance of the law is that commitments have great value and significance. **Whatever your lips utter you must be sure to do** (v. 23), is a principle that applies to many areas of life, not just promises made to God in moments of great stress or relief. Casual carelessness regarding commitments, especially among Christians, flouts both the third and the ninth commandments.

23:24–25 / This law is another example of the OT's characteristic priority of needs over rights. Neighborly hospitality should allow a hungry traveler to have something to eat from one's crops without charge or grudge. On the other hand, this ancient (and still common) privilege should not be abused by actions tantamount to theft (the use of a **basket** or **sickle**). Laws like this, deliberately imprecise, require considerable maturity and social trust and presuppose a people prepared to put very practical flesh on to the basic principle of loving God through loving the neighbor.

Additional Notes §27

23:7 / **Do not abhor,** means not to treat as ritually unclean and therefore to be excluded from the worshipping community.

23:10 / **A nocturnal emission** (lit., "what happens at night") could mean an emission of semen (cf. Lev. 15:16) but could also mean urinating in the camp instead of going outside (vv. 12ff.).

23:14 / The verb translated **moves about** is the rare hithpael form of *hālak* ("to walk" [MT v. 15]), used also of God strolling companionably with Adam and Eve in the garden (Gen. 3:8) and of God's promised presence among an obedient people (Lev. 26:12).

23:17 / The Hb. for **shrine prostitute** is *qᵉdēšâ* [MT v. 18], lit. "a holy one." The person was "holy," not in the moral sense but in being "set apart," i.e., dedicated to the god of the shrine for the purposes of ritual sex, often as part of fertility cults. The practice is still found in some parts of the world. In India, though it is officially outlawed, many young girls are made into "devadasis," i.e., to serve as religious prostitutes.

23:19–20 / Calvin discusses the texts on interest in his "exposition" of the eighth commandment, *Harmony* IV, pp. 125–33. He carefully observes the law's prime objective of protecting the poor from exploitation and argues that this is a universal principle: "the common society of the human race demands that we should not seek to grow rich by the loss of others." He shows that God was against any hidden additions to the original loan and then goes on, cautiously: "I have, then, admonished men that . . . all unjust gains are ever displeasing to God, whatever color we endeavor to give to it. But if we would form an equitable judgment, reason does not suffer us to admit that all usury is to be condemned without exception." He cites prolonged failure to repay a debt, or a loan taken by an already monied person in order to purchase land. He insists that the biblical prohibition is specifically in regard to the poor and does not apply to interest agreements between the rich. His caution proceeds: "I should, indeed, be unwilling to take usury under my patronage, and I wish the name itself were banished from the world [later he refers to 'this plague of usury']; but I do not dare to pronounce upon so important a point more than God's words convey." However, he will admit that "usury is not now unlawful, except in so far as it contravenes equity and brotherly union. Let each one, then, place himself before God's judgment-seat, and not do to his neighbor what he would not have done to himself." This is hardly the capitalist's charter that Calvin is often accused of providing.

§28 Community Laws: A Portrait of a Caring Society (Deut. 24:1–22)

The majority of laws in this chapter have to do with restraining exploitation and greed for the sake of protecting the needy. The eighth and tenth commandments (prohibiting theft and coveting) seem most closely linked to this section, but as before, the order of laws is not sharply defined.

24:1–4 / As Jesus himself points out (Matt. 19:7–8), this law is not a *command* to divorce wives but a provision that regulates those instances when a divorce takes place, and therefore presupposes that divorce is *permitted*. Since the law is concerned with what happens *after* a divorce, it does not provide details as to the grounds of divorce itself. The expression **something indecent** (v. 1) is nonspecific. In any case, it seems that divorce is basically a matter of internal family law that does not require the involvement of the civil authorities (the elders) to examine the causes or grounds of the divorce.

The main requirement of the law comes in its final clauses in verse 4: a man may not remarry a wife he has divorced if she has subsequently been married by **another man** and then divorced or widowed. The practical effect of this rule is to protect the unfortunate woman from becoming a kind of marital football, passed back and forth between irresponsible men. It is likewise for the woman's protection that a **certificate of divorce** is to be given to the woman (lit. "into her hand"), since it proves her status as free to marry the second man. Otherwise she (and he) could be accused of adultery. Although the second marriage is perfectly legitimate and not legally adulterous, from the point of view of the first marriage it may have been considered morally so. This might explain the description of the woman as **defiled** (i.e., ritually unclean, or out of bounds) in relation to the first husband. Jesus draws out the full implication in his explicit teaching (Matt. 5:31f.). For other views, see additional note.

Three prophets use the divorce law in their message. Jeremiah asks whether Israel, having deserted Yahweh for other lovers, could simply be taken back by Yahweh. The answer is that what may have been impossible under the law was possible by God's grace, given genuine repentance (Jer. 3:1–5; 4:1f.). Isaiah looks for the certificate of divorce between Yahweh and Israel, and finding none leaves open the possibility that though Israel has been sent away for its unfaithfulness, a formal divorce has not taken place and there could be restoration (Isa. 50:1f.). For Hosea divorce is a painful personal experience. It seems God suspends the prohibition on remarriage of a divorced wife in Hosea's case, in commanding him to recover Gomer after her unfaithfulness, though it may be significant that she had returned to prostitution and had not, perhaps, been *married* to another man (Hos. 3:1–3).

24:5 / This generous law extends the compassionate leave from active military service in war granted to the newly married (20:7) into a one-year exemption from all other civil duties. The underlying purpose of the exemption is doubtless so that the new couple could have time to become parents and thus ensure the continuity of the family, a joy that Deuteronomy expresses with characteristic warmth: it would allow the man to **bring happiness to the wife he has married,** or in the delightful phraseology of the KJV, he "shall cheer up his wife which he hath taken!"

24:6 / This law goes along with verses 10–13, 14f., 17f., and 19–22, as legislation for the benefit of the poor. The regulation of credit and debt in any society is one of the touchstones of humaneness or oppression. Lending (as distinct from simply giving) to those in need is commended in the OT (e.g., Ps. 15:5), but such is human greed and callousness that the power of lenders to squeeze and exploit their debtors calls for control. To take, as a security for a debt, something indispensable to its owner, is a form of pressure that this law prohibits. The **pair of millstones** is the small family mill for producing daily bread. To take it would threaten the poor family's very lives (lit. "that would be taking a life in pledge"). The law thus protects the poor who borrow from lending conditions that actually worsen their plight rather than alleviate it. The moral force of the law is still powerfully relevant to the need for legislative controls on unscrupulous forms of lending.

24:7 / This law is the only exception to the OT's rule that theft is not punishable by death. Theft of property cannot be measured against a human life. But in this case the theft *is* of a human life; **kidnapping** is lit. in Hb. "stealing the life" *(nepeš)* of a fellow Israelite. Even though there is no killing, the act was a kind of "social murder" (Craigie), since the victim is cut off from the covenant people by being sold, presumably into foreign slavery (cf. Exod. 21:16). The value system that places human life and freedom above property is still inadequately represented in modern law and penal policy.

24:8–9 / Deuteronomy's concern for the religious and moral health of society here extends to the physical health also (cf. 23:11–14). **Leprous diseases** translates a word *(ṣāraʿat)* that probably did not indicate leprosy proper as known today (Hansen's disease). It seems to be a general term for any kind of infectious skin problem, characterized by scaly or flaky flesh, roughness, redness, or itch. It is one of the tasks of the priests, like public health inspectors, to diagnose and deal with such outbreaks (Lev. 13–14). Deuteronomy characteristically reinforces its advice with historical warning (Num. 12).

24:10–13 / The concern for the poor continues here, picking up similar themes found in 23:19f. and 24:6. Deuteronomy is determined to protect the poor not only from commercial exploitation (hence the ban on interest), not only from life-threatening pressures from lenders (hence the ban on taking essentials in pledge), but even from invasion of their privacy. Human dignity matters. Poverty robs a person of so much, but the poor should be allowed to control what they still own and should be given respect in their own homes. Verses 10f. are typical of Deuteronomy's blend of realism and challenge. They accept the reality of poverty and debt and the necessity of loans. But they seek to mitigate the harshness of that reality by inculcating an ethos of compassion and respect, which, while not a matter of enforceable legislation, insists on preserving the humanity and dignity of every member of the community. Those who work among the world's poor realize that the answer to exploitation is not "charity" alone. More important than material help is the recognition and affirmation of the dignity of poorer people, often through enabling and empowering them to exercise some measure of discretion and control over what they do own.

Verses 12f. expand the original law of Exod. 22:26f. Just as
the millstones are essential for daily bread, so the **cloak** (a garment
by day and a blanket by night) is essential for nightly sleep. If it is
taken as security for a loan, it is to be returned before nightfall,
thus again preventing the poor from being subjected to intolerable pressures (cf. Amos 2:8a). If the pledge was to be returned so
quickly, was there any point in taking it at all? Possibly not, from
the lender's point of view. But it has been suggested that the very
basic and physical nature of the pledge would prevent the borrower from entering into several separate loan arrangements (he
could not give his cloak to more than one lender), and thus getting
entangled in multiple indebtedness, to the detriment of borrower
and lenders alike. Whether or not this was a subsidiary economic
purpose of the law, both Exodus and Deuteronomy focus on the
primary moral obligation, which is not merely a horizontal matter
of compassion for a fellow human being, but a fundamental vertical duty to God, that God takes very seriously (negatively in
Exod. 22:27b, positively in Deut. 24:13b). This is not, therefore,
mere charity, but this is righteousness before God. In a similar way
Paul regards the money he is collecting from Gentile churches for
the Jerusalem Jewish Christians not merely as producing human
gratitude (cf. Deut. 24:13b) but also as a proof of obedience to the
gospel of Christ (2 Cor. 9:12ff.).

24:14–15 / The interest in economics continues with this
law regarding proper treatment of workers. The law is concerned
that the *conditions* of work should be fair and not exploitative (the
translation, **do not take advantage of,** is far too weak; the Hb.
word ʿāšaq, means to oppress by robbery or fraud, as it is properly
translated in the parallel law in Leviticus 19:13) and that the
payment for work should be prompt. The OT shows remarkable
interest in the welfare of working human beings and even working animals (cf. the sabbath commandment and 25:4). This law
refers to a particular category of workers who were likely to be
poor and needy, namely, **hired** laborers. These were people who
had no permanent (i.e., basically residential) employment, but
were hired for short-term jobs, and were often paid a daily wage.
They were therefore more vulnerable and easily exploited than
slaves, for whom owners had a legal and economic duty of care.
Since daily pay was essential for daily food, any delay in payment
meant immediate hunger for the worker and his family. Hence
the urgency of verse 15, and hence also the point of the generosity

of the vineyard owner, whose decision to pay a day's wage for an hour's work recognized the need of the man who had to feed his family regardless of how long he worked (Matt. 20:1–15).

The concluding challenge of the law (v. 15b) is the negative counterpart to the positive conclusion of the preceding law (v. 13b). When a creditor deals humanely with a debtor, "it will be righteousness in the eyes of the Lord" for him. When an employer fails to pay his worker, "it will be sin" in him. The deliberate parallel pattern of words is unmistakable and illustrates Deuteronomy's covenant ethic. Employment legislation is also divine *torah*. Workers' rights are responsibilities before God. Unjust pay and conditions are not just social problems, they are sin against God. For this reason, OT prophets can direct the judgment of God against those who fail to pay workers properly (Jer. 22:13f.; Isa. 58:3b), and a NT apostle can do the same with equal vehemence (Jas. 5:4).

The moral force and necessity of the OT's laws on workers' rights is undiminished today. It is not only in Two-Thirds World countries that there is horrific exploitation of day laborers. Western countries, where movements that won rights and protections for workers had Christian origins, often exhibit callous and exploitative practices in this sphere. Wage councils, which regulated minimum wages for lowest paid workers in Britain, have recently been abolished. Employers keep workers only up to the point at which they would have statutory rights and quickly lay them off with impunity. Small firms with a few local workers are forced out of business by large firms who deliberately delay payment of bills for work done. Part-time workers are denied many benefits. To be actively concerned about rectifying such abuses is a question not merely of party politics, but of fundamental biblical ethical categories of righteousness and sin.

24:16 / This law must be seen in its proper context— namely, the administration of criminal law in human courts. Deuteronomy elsewhere expresses a deep understanding of corporate solidarity of the people of God, through the covenant that spans the generations. However, while it is true theologically that each generation's commitments and failures affect those that follow, the basic legal principle of individual responsibility is to be strictly applied. This is a principle that does not "emerge" in Israel at a later period (as is mistakenly alleged on the basis of Jeremiah 31:34 and Ezekiel 18) but is fundamental to their earliest recorded laws, such as the Book of the Covenant (Exod. 21–23). This law contrasts, probably intentionally, with the laws of Hammurabi, which prescribe that if a builder builds a house that collapses and causes the death of the houseowner's son, the builder's son was to be put to death (§ 230). This law in Deuteronomy 24:16, like that in Exodus 21:31, certainly excludes "vicarious" punishment of that kind. It also excludes "collective" punishment, i.e., the execution of a criminal's children along with him in normal judicial procedures. This is how the law was interpreted in 2 Kings 14:5f. in a case of regicide. The law fits in the present context because, like the surrounding laws, it is concerned to protect the vulnerable—in this case the relatives of one found guilty of a capital offense, who, though personally innocent, might be exposed to community anger or vengeance.

24:17–22 / Although the paragraphs of the NIV divide these verses into two separate laws, it is likely that the whole section should be taken together. Unifying these verses is the repetition of the phrase **the alien, the fatherless and the widow** and of the motivation for just behavior (in vv. 18 and 22). When the section is read as a whole, it seems also likely that the opening injunction, **do not deprive the alien or the fatherless of justice**, extends to the entire section. The phrase is literally "do not turn aside (or away) the case (cause, rights; Hb. *mišpāṭ*) of the alien, etc." It obviously applies to legal justice, and therefore includes the importance of treating the cases of the poor with equal care and justice as those of the rich or important (something Job recalls doing energetically in the days of his health, Job 29:12–17). But *mišpāṭ* is broader than courtroom justice and includes a person's rights in general. The GNB is thus close to the breadth of the phrase in translating, "Do not deprive foreigners and orphans of their rights." The rules that follow are thus a matter of rights, not charity. In God's sight, a widow has a right not to be robbed of essential clothing to get a loan. And the gleaning provisions of verses 19–21 are also rights, not hand-outs. Thus, by putting together the gleaning law (cf. Lev. 19:9f.) with the general law against oppressing the alien, orphan, and widow (cf. Exod. 22:21–24), Deuteronomy makes the former a practical illustration of the latter. To harvest in such a way as to leave no gleanings would be to **deprive the alien or the fatherless of justice**. This message is strengthened by the repeated phrase **for the alien**, etc. The NIV's **Leave it for** . . . is not quite what the Hebrew says

here (though it is in Lev. 19:10). Deuteronomy says, "To the alien
. . . it shall be"—an expression normally used to indicate ownership. The sense is therefore, "Do not pick the forgotten sheaf, the
remaining olives and grapes, *they belong to* the alien, orphan, and
widow." The remainder of the harvest *is theirs;* they have every
right to do the final harvesting themselves. This means that the
landless are not to be totally dependent on handouts from the
landowners after every scrap of the crop has been harvested by
them. Rather, they are to have the opportunity to work for their
own benefit in the fields of God's land. Those who do not, for
various reasons, have a share in the *ownership* of the land are still
to be given the chance to share in the *blessing* of the land as the
bounty of the true landowner.

When the principle of the law is expressed thus, it can be
seen to be relevant beyond its immediate context of harvest
gleaning—a practice that modern harvesting methods render
somewhat unprofitable (though gleaning schemes have been
tried with some success in North America by one Christian
group). The law asks us, however, not to ban combine harvesters,
but to find means of ensuring that the weakest and poorest in the
community are enabled to have access to the opportunities they
need in order to be able to provide for themselves. "Opportunities" may include financial resources, but could also include
access to education, legal assistance, investment in job opportunities, etc. Such things should not be leftovers or handouts, but a
matter of rights and responsibilities in a caring society.

Such community care is itself dependent on corporate
awareness of the grace of God. Twice Israel is reminded here of
the exodus and its proof of God's generosity to Israel in its time
of utter need (vv. 18, 22). *When Israel forgot its history, it forgot its
poor.* The prophets have to remind them of both. It is not surprising either that in modern Western culture, which has systematically been squeezing the biblical God out of its definition of
reality and truth, there is a corresponding resurgence of callousness toward the vulnerable. If the alien, the orphan, and the
widow of Deuteronomy have anything in common with the
immigrant, the refugee, the homeless, the single parents, the
aged, etc. of today, then it is clear that our society is massively
guilty of "turning aside justice and rights" from many people in
those categories. The portrait of a caring society in these chapters
is of a society with a memory at the center of its whole system of
moral and social values and norms—the memory of God and

God's power. The phrase "moral vacuum" is being used of the increasingly anarchic callousness of the West. It is a vacuum manufactured by the sucking out of that memory and the denial of any transcendent reality that would undergird our values or challenge our behavior. The gods we worship, though unrecognized as gods, are not the God of exodus. The social gleanings for the poor are accordingly very lean indeed.

Additional Notes §28

24:1 / The expression, **something indecent** (*ʿerwat dābār;* lit. "nakedness of a thing"), cannot mean full sexual unfaithfulness, since the penalty for that would have been death, not divorce. Most commentators believe that either some kind of serious immodesty or indecent behavior is meant.

24:4 / **Detestable in the eyes of the LORD:** Yaron, "Restoration," argues that far from giving any suggestion that the second marriage was adulterous, the law was seeking to protect precisely the second marriage by preventing any further interest in the woman from the former husband. As far as he was concerned, she was now "defiled"—i.e., not immoral, but "out of bounds," not to be touched again. Wenham, "Restoration," suggests further, in comparison with Lev. 18 and 20, that marriage was deemed to produce a bond equivalent to kinship. Therefore, remarrying a former wife would be tantamount (under such a perception) to marrying one's sister—one of the "detestable practices" forbidden there.

24:14 / The **hired man** (Hb. *śākîr*) was part of a group of dependent laborers, closely linked to the "strangers" (*gērîm*) and "resident aliens" (*tôšābîm*), who are frequently singled out in the law as being in need of fair and compassionate treatment. Whereas the latter two groups probably tended to be fairly permanent residential employees (similar in practice, though not in status, to slaves), the hired workers had no such security and survived only by finding short-term employment for their labor or skills. For surveys of the economic and social details of Israel's working population, cf. Sulzberger, "Status of Labor," Lang, "Social Organization," and C. J. H. Wright, *God's Land,* pp. 99–103, 159f.

24:16 / This law may seem at variance with two other features of OT history and law. First, there are three (though only three) cases where whole families were executed for the crimes of the heads of the household (Num. 16; Josh. 7; and 2 Sam. 21:1–9). However, these were clearly exceptional cases. The first two involve serious rebellion and apostasy, and the breaking of the solemn *ḥērem* at a crucial stage of Israel's entry to Canaan. And the response is clearly a matter of divinely specified judgment, not simple penalties in a human court. The third involves concepts of bloodguilt "clinging" to generations, and in any case is an act of Canaanite revenge, not of Israelite judicial practice. In fact, none of the three cases illustrate Israelite law in normal or typical operation.

Secondly, this law is often wrongly thought to contradict the words of the second commandment regarding God visiting the sins of the fathers upon the children (Deut. 5:9). The commandment, however, is stating the reality that sin in one generation will afflict following generations in its consequences. Children cannot escape the effects of parental sin—especially if it involves fundamental covenant disloyalty. But this law is saying that it is not for human courts to inflict specific punishment on those who are legally innocent.

> The two cases are thus altogether different: it is one thing that, in virtue of the physical and social conditions in which they live, children should suffer for their fathers' sins; it is another that, by the deliberate intervention of human authority they should be punished for criminal acts which they have not committed (Driver, *Deuteronomy*, pp. 277f.; cf. C. J. H. Wright, *God's Land*, pp. 224–30, 235–37).

25:1–3 / The concern for human dignity and the protection of the vulnerable continues in this law regarding corporal punishment. Beating, probably with a rod not a whip (cf. Exod. 21:20), was one of Israel's forms of legal punishment. (Apart from the death penalty and the rare case of Deut. 25:12, the only other forms were restitution, compensation, or slavery. Imprisonment is not prescribed for any offense in pentateuchal law.) Physical punishment could easily degenerate into physical abuse if, for example, a local community were particularly angered by some offense. This law therefore sets down four requirements:

(a) There must be a *proper trial* (v. 1). Although the administration of justice in Israel is a relatively local affair, that does not mean "taking the law into your own hands." Conflicts are to be brought to recognized **judges** for their decision. (b) There is to be *proper supervision* (v. 2). If the court sentences the offender to corporal punishment, the court must ensure it is properly administered and not left to the mercy or cruelty (or venality) of the person in charge of the beating, who would face competing pressures and pleas from the family of the offender on the one hand and of the victim on the other. The judge must supervise the beating **in his presence.** (c) There must be *proper proportion* (v. 2b). **The number of lashes** must be precisely fixed as the number **his crime deserves** and carefully counted; there would be a beating only **if the guilty man deserves to be beaten.** (d) There must be a *proper limit* (v. 3). There is to be no prolonged or indefinite beating. If **forty lashes** is the maximum penalty, it can be assumed that judges would normally sentence offenders to less.

The final explanatory clause of the law bases the above requirements on (a) covenant bonds: the criminal is still **your brother** and that status must be borne in mind even when he is being punished; and (b) human dignity: viciously prolonged beating is "degrading" and humiliating for any human being (the Hb. is lit. "your brother will be *made light of*"; the verb *qll* is the same word used for dishonoring parents in 27:16). It is sad that in the popular perception the OT is so often vilified for the severity of its punishments, whereas this law with its careful limitations and its explicit protection of the rights and dignity of criminals is overlooked.

25:4 / The compassionate spirit of 22:1f., 4, and 6f. is here applied to working animals. In a procedure still practiced in nonmechanized communities, harvested sheaves are spread out on the ground and a tethered animal walks round and round dragging a heavy wooden sledge embedded with stone or metal pieces that sever the grains from the stalks. Muzzling the beast prevents it from eating any of the grain. So this law bans the muzzle to enable the animal to have a share in the food that its labor is making available for human beings. It is as though the gleaning rights of the poor (24:19–22) have been extended to include working animals as well. Such practical concern even for animals is commended by the sage as a mark of righteousness (Prov. 12:10) and indeed reflects God's own heart (Jonah 4:11).

Paul's use of this law (twice, in 1 Cor. 9:8–12 and 1 Tim. 5:17f.) is hermeneutically instructive. It is not really a case of "allegorizing" (Mayes) or of "spiritualizing" (Thompson, Brown). For Paul does *not* merely draw a spiritual meaning out of the law. On the contrary, he uses it to mandate a different, *but equally practical* and material duty, namely, proper payment for Christian workers. His argument is that if God requires such fair treatment of a working animal, how much more does he require fair treatment of working human beings, and in particular those who work for the sake of the gospel or in teaching the church. Paul has identified the principle at the heart of the law and *redirected* its authority in support of Christian responsibilities. His rhetorical question, "Is it about oxen that God is concerned?" is not a denial of the original intention of the law (which obviously *is* a sign of God's concern for oxen), but a leading question designed to show that a God who cares about the daily food of an ox would not care any less about the material needs of those humans who serve God. Thus Paul can legitimately say, "This is written for us," as a very practical example of the overall conviction expressed in 2 Timothy 3:16f.

25:5–10 / The practice of *levirate marriage* (from the Latin word *levir,* "brother-in-law") was widespread both in ancient Israel (cf. Gen. 38) and throughout the ancient Near East. Some forms of it are still found in some cultures. If a man died without a male heir, it was the duty of his brother to marry his widow and seek to produce a son, who would then inherit the deceased brother's name and property. The institution thus (a) provided for the security of the widow in her bereavement and offered the hope of removing the stigma of not having borne a son; (b) prevented any loss of property or land to the wider family, which would happen if she married **outside the family;** and (c) ensured that the dead man's name would be carried forward for posterity in his family. The law is set in the context of the centrality of the family in Israel's life and faith. Each family had a share in the land, through the original tribal division and distribution; that family inheritance was to be held inalienably; and when it was threatened by natural misfortunes such as premature or childless death, steps had to be taken to protect it. The second part of the law (vv. 7–10) recognized the fact that although levirate marriage was a strong moral duty, it could not be enforced against the determined will of the brother-in-law. The law therefore makes such a refusal a matter of social disgrace instead. The removal of the sandal was possibly a symbol of renunciation of property rights (cf. Ruth 4:7f., but see additional note for an alternative explanation), but this was to be accompanied by words and gestures that showed maximum disapproval for the man's selfishness. The act also freed the woman from remaining a widow indefinitely pending levirate "rescue." She could remarry without stigma.

Clearly the means by which any society cares for the bereaved and the childless, and the mechanisms by which it preserves the economic integrity and future of family units, will vary from culture to culture. The strength of feeling expressed here about the levirate practice shows that the moral responsibility it embodies is meant to be taken seriously. The NT brings the same intense feelings to bear on Christian duties by describing those who will not care for their own families in need as having denied the faith and as being worse than unbelievers (1 Tim. 5:3–8).

25:11–12 / Like the previous law, this law is concerned with actions that threaten family continuity. There, the unwilling brother-in-law threatens the survival of his deceased brother's name, since he will remain childless. This woman's action threatens the assailant's ability to have children, if serious damage is inflicted on his genitals. This seems a more likely reason for the severity of the law than simply that it is regarded as gross immodesty on the woman's part. The law is unique in that, although it strikes us as shockingly severe (though see additional note), it is in fact the *only* case in OT law in which any form of physical mutilation is prescribed for a specific offense (apart from the *lex talionis*—"an eye for an eye," which may have been more a principle of equivalence than a literal description of penalties in some cases). And the offense would seem to be a relatively remote and unlikely occurrence in any case. In this, OT law is in marked contrast with other ancient Near Eastern law, especially Assyrian law, where all kinds of very nasty physical mutilations were prescribed for many offenses.

25:13–16 / **Two differing** sets of measures are of course for the dishonest purpose of obtaining more than standard measure when purchasing and giving less when selling. Fair trade is one of the essential hallmarks of any human society seeking to protect everybody's interests in a civilized way. In this OT form of a law that is commonly found in the ancient Near East, the covenant sanctions of Israel's own specific constitution are significantly brought to bear. There is, on the one hand, the positive promise that commitment to honesty in trade will bring the covenant blessing of long life **in the land** (v. 15); and, on the other hand, there is the negative warning that dishonesty stands under the covenant curse as something "detestable" (an abomination) to Yahweh (v. 16). In the parallel law in Leviticus 19:35f., the law is based on the fundamental identification of Yahweh as the God of the exodus. These theological sanctions remind us of the OT's scale of values, in which the same strong word ("abomination to Yahweh"—insulting to his character) could be used as much about commercial malpractice as about idolatry, sexual perversions, and pagan cults. The reason is that it is precisely such cheating and sharp dealing in the world of trade and commerce that lies behind so much of the exploitation and poverty of those whom Deuteronomy cares so passionately about elsewhere. The same zeal to expose dishonesty because of its social destructiveness inflamed Amos (Amos 8:4–6).

25:17–19 / The reason for the particular curse upon the Amalekites (which here probably does not refer to Exod. 17:8–16 but to other unspecified attacks) ties in with Deuteronomy's wider concern in these chapters. They were *merciless to the weak.* They showed total lack of compassion in attacking Israel in their extreme vulnerability immediately after the exodus. Those

lagging behind would have been the elderly and the very young, the sick, pregnant women, etc. To attack such defenseless people is a sign of extreme human callousness, which in turn is evidence of **no fear of God.** It is interesting, here as in Amos 1–2, that noncovenant nations are still assumed to be morally accountable to God for fundamental norms of human behavior. The Amalekites are to be judged, then, not just because they had been *anti-Israel,* but because they had been *anti-human* by disregarding basic human obligations instilled by the creator God. The prophets proclaimed God's punitive judgment on Israel too, when lack of the fear of God led to similarly barbaric behavior toward the weak and defenseless in Israel's own society (e.g., Mic. 2:1–2, 8f.). In our day of mind-numbing violence, from muggings, rape, and robbery in "civilized" cities, to horrendous war crimes around the world, it is difficult to know how to cope with such reality alongside our faith in the God who cares for the weak and claims to defend the defenseless. We know that the command to exterminate the Amalekites is no longer the way for the disciples of Christ. Yet we affirm the reality of God's sovereign historical justice and the reality of judgment to come on those who persist, with no fear of God, in trampling on other human beings made in God's image. If the crimes of Amalek were "written in a book," then we know that there will come a day when "the books will be opened" (Rev. 20:11–15) and the judge of all the earth will do right.

Additional Notes §29

25:3 / **Not . . . more than forty:** Later Jewish tradition, in order to avoid the risk of transgressing this limit, set the maximum penalty at thirty-nine strokes. The Apostle Paul tells us he received it five times (2 Cor. 11:24).

25:4 / For a discussion of the exegetical and hermeneutical significance of Paul's use of this verse as regards the ethical authority of the OT, cf. Kaiser, "Current Crisis."

25:5 / **If brothers are living together:** This conditional clause probably limited the applicability of the levirate obligation to the situation where the father of the brothers was dead and their living together means that the family estate had not been divided up into separate independent shares. This may have been ideal but not very common in practice (perhaps why it is commended in Ps. 133). Cf. C. J. H. Wright, *God's Land*, pp. 54f. The law also specifies that the brother had died **without a son.** Inheritance was normally through the male line, but female inheritance was possible (cf. Num. 27:1–11; 36:1–12).

25:7 / **If a man does not want to marry his brother's wife:** The reasons for such a refusal were most probably economic, not personal. Since the brothers were still **living together,** it is probable that if one died childless, his share of the family inheritance would eventually pass to the next brother on the death of the widow or be divided among the surviving brothers. Greed might make the surviving brother(s) prefer that prospect to incurring the cost of maintaining the widow and raising a son who would inherit that share. This is probably what made the nearer kinsman than Boaz waive his right of redeeming Naomi's land when he heard that he must take Ruth as well, since ultimately any son born to Ruth would inherit the land the kinsman had invested in (Ruth 4:5f.). On the levirate institution, see Leggett, *The Levirate;* Carmichael, "Ceremonial Crux"; E. W. Davies, "Inheritance Rights"; Gow, *The Book of Ruth*, pp. 143–82.

25:9 / Since "the feet" was sometimes a euphemistic way of referring to the male genitals, it has been suggested that the removal of the sandal was a symbolic exposure of the unwilling brother's genitals—an act of gross contempt. If this were the meaning, it would shed light on the immediately following law. The legal permission for a *symbolic* attack of this sort on the genitals of one who threatened a wife's (deceased) husband's progeny must never be construed as condoning a *literal, physical* attack on the genitals of an assailant who likewise threatened a wife's (living) husband. See Eslinger, "Drafting."

25:12 / The phrase, **you shall cut off her hand,** may not be meant literally, but may be a euphemism for the female genital region (as, cf. "feet" for male genitals, above). If the lex talionis were being strictly applied and she had damaged the man's genitals, then some form of punishment was to be inflicted on hers (possibly female circumcision, practiced in some cultures though otherwise unknown in Israel, but unlikely; or possibly a denial of sexual relations, and thereby a denial of further children). The word for hand here is *kap* (not *yād*), usually referring to the palm of the hand. In Gen. 32:25, 32 (Hb. 26, 33) and in the erotic imagery of Song Sol. 5:5, *kap* (along with *yād* in the latter), is possibly a euphemism for the genitals, male and female. See Eslinger, "Immodest Lady Wrestler."

25:15 / **Accurate and honest:** The words in Hb. are *šᵉlēmâ*, lit. "whole," (cf. "shalom"), and *ṣedeq*, lit. "of righteousness."

25:17 / The Amalekites remained an inveterate enemy of Israel for many years after the settlement (cf. Judg. 3:13; 6:3–5, 33; 7:12; 10:12). Saul failed to eliminate the threat (1 Sam. 15; 28:18), and they were still pillaging in David's day (1 Sam. 30). They seem to have finally disappeared in Hezekiah's time (1 Chron. 4:43).

§30 Celebration and Commitment
(Deut. 26:1–19)

The legislative section of the book (chs. 12–25), which flowed *out of* a worshipping, grateful response to the acts and gifts of God (1–11), now flows *into* renewed worship that sanctifies the claim to have obeyed God's requirements (26:14b). The three sections of this chapter provide a very beautifully balanced expression of the logic and dynamic of the covenant. First (vv. 1–11), there is celebration of the vertical blessing of God that each Israelite has experienced. Second (vv. 12–15), there is commitment to the horizontal obligations through which Israelites are to express their covenant loyalty to God and each other, and which will lead to fresh blessing in a dynamic cycle of blessing → obedience → blessing. Third (vv. 16–19), there is a summary statement of the heart of the covenant relationship and its wider purpose for Israel as the people of God among the nations. The chapter is thus a wonderful presentation of covenant *grace*, covenant *obedience*, and covenant *blessing*. As such, it is virtually a condensing of the total message and burden of the whole book of Deuteronomy—into two actions and three liturgical declarations.

26:1–11 / The most prominent feature of these verses is the emphasis on the land as Yahweh's *gift*. The verb *nātan* occurs six times (vv. 1, 2, 3, 9, 10, 11). It is not meant to deny or discount that the land would have to be taken by armed struggle, any more than it overlooks the fact that the fruit of the harvest would have to be gained by hard labor. But the prior reality is God's grace. The land itself and the fruit of the land are gifts of grace and that must be acknowledged. Thus, the Israelite is called on to make two liturgical declarations. The first (v. 3) is a simple acknowledgment of fact—**I have come to the land that the LORD swore to our forefathers to give us.** This historical fact is attributed to divine promise and divine gift. The words are thus the response of faith to grace. It is not a *claim*—"I own this land because I conquered it"—but an *acknowledgment*—"I have come because God gave it." The second (vv. 5–10) is a confessional narrative that "colors in" the historical fact by recalling the fundamental redemptive events, thus anchoring grace not just in the blessings of nature but in the facts of history. The Israelite farmer, in this remarkable declaration, connects together several centuries of *history* (from the ancestors of Israel to his own generation), a *theology* of election, redemption and land-gift, and personal *experience* of God's blessing.

There is also in this section an attractive blending of corporate blessing (*we* **cried out. . . . the** LORD **brought** *us* **out. . . . he brought** *us* **to this place and gave** *us* **this land**), individual blessing (**the firstfruits of the soil that you, O** LORD, **have given** *me*), and shared blessing (**you** *and* **the Levites** *and* **the aliens among you shall rejoice**). In this way, the vertical dynamic of the covenant relationship is channeled to the nation as a whole and to the individual also, and at the same time the individual is reminded of the horizontal dynamic, which comes into focus in the next section.

26:12–15 / These verses repeat a law already given—the triennial tithe for the benefit of the poor (cf. 14:28f.). But by setting it here alongside the harvest thanksgiving in the context of worship, Deuteronomy emphasizes it as the representative of all the rest of the book's legislation on behalf of the needy. The two explicit references to **the Levites and the aliens** (v. 11) and **the Levite, the alien, the fatherless and the widow** (v. 12) show that the socially and economically deprived were not to be excluded either from the spiritual blessings of covenant worship or from the material blessings of covenant obedience. This Deuteronomic ethos breathes again in the challenging teaching of James regarding the social and economic demands of Christian worship and fellowship (Jas. 2, note esp. vv. 2–4, 15–17).

In the liturgical declaration, the Israelite claims to have fully obeyed the law; this is expressed both negatively (v. 13b) and positively (v. 14b). This declaration is linked specifically to the distribution of **the sacred portion** (i.e., that which specially belongs to God) among the needy. Thus, giving to the needy is not only a sacred duty to God, but it also is the defining point for any claim to have kept the law. *The law is kept only if the poor are cared for.* Only when Israel responds to the needy by enabling *everyone* in the community to **eat and be satisfied** can they affirm **I have done** *everything* **that you commanded me.** This shows once again the essential thrust of OT ethics—that love for the neighbor is the practical proof of any claimed love for God. It also shows how the enacted love for the poor and needy is the practical proof of genuine, God-honoring love for the neighbor. The Torah itself thus agrees with the way the prophets later pinpoint and prioritize care for the poor as somehow definitive or paradigmatic of Israel's response to God as a whole. They argue passionately that callous neglect of the weak in society utterly invalidates all the claims of their enthusiastic religious observance. Sacred rites are no atonement for social wrongs.

The prayer for continued blessing (v. 15) thus rests on continued obedience. But it should not be seen as *deserved* by obedience. The blessing of God on the people is already written into the title deeds of the land as **given,** and prior even to that, was bound into the promise at the heart of the covenant of grace made with the fathers. The thrust of the verse is therefore *not,* "we have obeyed so you must bless us," *but,* "you have already blessed us in history and in the present, and we have responded in obedience, so graciously continue to bless." There is thus a dynamic cycle in the whole chapter that binds together "gospel" facts (vv. 1–11) with "law" response (vv. 12–14) and looks for God's blessing in both arenas.

26:16–19 / Verse 16, with its reminder to **follow** and **carefully observe** the **decrees and laws,** deliberately echoes 12:1 and thus functions editorially to indicate the completion of the whole section of law that began there. Verses 17 and 18 follow with reciprocal commitments by Israel and by God. The essence of the covenant is that Yahweh is Israel's God (v. 17) and that Israel is Yahweh's people (v. 18). This central covenantal reality is then reinforced by Yahweh's promise that Israel will be his **treasured possession** and by Israel's commitment to **walk in his ways,** to **keep his decrees,** and to **obey him.**

Verse 19 then expands this essence of the covenant relationship with a declaration of its goal, in terms that echo Exodus 19:4–6—a text that has already been brought to mind by the term **treasured possession.** At first sight it might seem that there is nothing more than national chauvinism in the expectation that Israel will be set **in praise, fame and honor high above all the nations.** But first of all, Israel's place among the nations is never to be a matter of national pride, since it is due neither to numerical nor to moral superiority (7:7; 9:4–6). Furthermore, the reputation of Israel among the nations is ultimately to be for the sake of Yahweh's own name. Their obedience will be visible to the nations and arouse questions (4:5–8). Thus, it is possible that the text actually means that the **praise, fame and honor** are *for Yahweh*. The Hebrew reads "He will set you high above all the nations he has made *for praise and for a name and for honor.*" The NEB/REB translates this, quite legitimately, "to bring *him* praise and fame and glory." This understanding of the very purpose of Israel's existence, which will be fulfilled only by its obedience to the covenant, is expressed with the same phraseology by Jeremiah in his acted prophecy (Jer. 13:1–11; cf. 33:9). If these close parallels are allusions to the Deuteronomic text, then they support the understanding that it is primarily the honor of Yahweh that is the goal of the exaltation of Israel. And this impression is further strengthened by the final phrase of the chapter, that Israel would be **a people holy to the LORD,** for this is another clear echo of Exodus 19:6, where holiness is linked to Israel's role as God's priesthood in the midst of the nations and both are linked to covenant obedience.

The chapter thus brings the whole legal section to a close with the reminder that obedience to the law was not an end in itself. Nor was it merely the means of keeping Israel secure in the land. Ultimately there was a missionary purpose to the law. Just as it had been founded upon the basis of God's redeeming grace in the past, so it was motivated by the vision of God's name being known and honored among the nations in the future. Seeing the law of the OT as thus *framed between grace and glory* is of immense importance, theologically, hermeneutically, and missiologically. We can handle the law rightly only when we understand its role in relation to the identity and mission of Israel, historically (in their own experience of God's saving action) and eschatologically (as the vehicle of God's saving purpose for all nations). Distortion of the law, whether toward legalism or toward antinomianism, usually creeps in when God's people forget either the grace of God on which alone they stand or the glory of God for which alone they exist. The Apostle Paul's efforts to establish an authentically scriptural understanding of the law in relation to God's grace did not take place alone. Rather, it happened alongside his efforts to establish an equally scriptural understanding of the mission of Israel to the nations, which he saw as being eschatologically fulfilled in his own Gentile mission to bring about "the obedience of faith among the nations" for the glory of God: "so that all nations might believe and obey him—to the only wise God be glory forever through Jesus Christ! Amen" (Rom. 16:26f.).

Additional Notes §30

26:4, 10 / First the priest sets the basket of firstfruits down before the altar (v. 4), then the worshipper is told to **place the basket before the LORD** (v. 10). Some see a contradiction or evidence of different layers of redactional activity. However, given the liturgical nature of the material, it is not at all unlikely that two placings may have been intended, accompanied by the two verbal responses (cf. Craigie, *Deuteronomy*, p. 320).

26:5–10 / These words were first described as an ancient Israelite "credo" by von Rad, who also proposed that the whole Sinai tradition (which is not explicitly mentioned here) was originally separate from this historical land-gift tradition (cf. "Problem"). His views have received considerable criticism and must be regarded as broadly rejected with regard to the separation of Sinai from the historical tradition. But, it is still plausible to see in Deut. 26:5–10 (and 6:21–23) a succinct statement of Israel's redemptive history which, by sheer repetition in the context described, must have functioned in a liturgically credal way in the faith of Israel. For thorough surveys of the matter, cf. Nicholson, *Exodus and Sinai;* Wright, *God's Land,* pp. 13–15, 24–43; and Daniels, "Creed."

26:5 / **A wandering Aramean:** Almost certainly Jacob. The Hb. ʾōbēd, can mean "perishing," "ailing," or "lost" and may allude to the tenuous state of Jacob and his family as a result of the famine that drove them to seek refuge in Egypt or may refer to Jacob's earlier life, especially his flight from Laban. Jacob is called an "Aramean" probably because of his links with that region (Gen. 24:10, 24) and the years he spent with Laban there. There is also some evidence that may link ʾōbēd to the ʿapîru, that class of rootless, stateless persons who are found in various contexts of the ancient Near East, sometimes as refugees. "To the Israelite settled in his Promised Land, who came with his firstfruits to God, the contrast of his 'confession' would be all the greater. His ancestor was a political refugee and social misfit; he, the descendant, was cultivating his own land as a citizen of an established nation" (Millard, "A Wandering Aramean").

§31 Covenant Renewal and Covenant Curse (Deut. 27:1–26)

Structurally, we are moving into the second half of the "inner frame." Chapter 27 balances chapter 11, thus functioning as a framework for the detailed legislation in chapters 12–25. This is clear not only from the reference in both chapters to the ceremony at Mt. Ebal but also from the emphasis in both on covenant choice and commitment.

27:1–8 / The first point in these verses is the *permanence* of the law. If the covenant is to endure through the generations, then the covenant law must be properly preserved in a permanent way that can function as a regular reminder of the obligations the people had undertaken. This may also be the reason for the otherwise unusual addition of **the elders of Israel** (v. 1) and of **the priests, who are Levites** (v. 9) to Moses. Moses is soon to pass from the scene. But the preservation and administration of the law he has given will become the responsibility of precisely these groups of people—priests and elders. Setting up **large stones** with writing was a common ancient Near Eastern practice for preserving significant public documents. To **coat them with plaster** (a kind of whitewash) and then **write on them** was an Egyptian practice, as distinct from the Mesopotamian preference for carved lettering.

A second point is the *clarity* of the law. The instruction is to **write very clearly** the whole law (v. 8). The unusual verb expressing this *(bāʾēr)* is the same as is used in 1:5 to describe how Moses undertook to "explain," "expound," "make clear" the whole law. It is coupled here with *hêṭēb*, "to do [something] well," cf. REB, "clearly and carefully." An important feature of the OT law is that it is assumed to be available to all, intelligible to all, and observable by all. It is not to be the esoteric preserve of a special privileged caste. It is entrusted to the priests, but precisely for them to teach it to the people. This is a theme that will be expanded more forcefully in chapter 30.

Thirdly, the ceremonies described here draw their significance from *when* and *where* they will happen. It will be **when you have crossed the Jordan** (vv. 2, 3, 4); i.e., when the promise will be finally fulfilled, when all that the book of Deuteronomy looks forward to and is predicated upon will have finally become a reality. The monumental expression of the law and Israel's commitment to it will come after their experience of God's grace in the fulfillment of God's promise. This is underlined by the reminder (as if it were needed) of the place as **the land the LORD your God is giving you, a land flowing with milk and honey** (cf. 11:9), **just as the LORD, the God of your fathers, promised you** (v. 3). The land itself will be an even greater monument to God's grace than the stones erected upon it. The stones will bear witness to God's covenant law. The land they stand on will bear witness to God's covenant faithfulness. Even in physical symbolism, the law is grounded in grace.

Fourthly, the whole event is to be bathed in worship (vv. 5–7). The instructions to **build an altar** follow closely the altar law of Exodus 20:24ff. The two types of sacrifice specified are often found together; **burnt offerings** are wholly offered to God as the most "vertically-oriented" sacrifices, whereas the **fellowship offerings** involve the greatest sharing of the meat of the sacrificed animal among the worshippers and are thus the most "horizontally-oriented" sacrifices. Love for God and love for neighbor permeate even the worship that celebrates the renewal of the covenant in the land.

27:9–10 / These verses reaffirm the basic covenant relationship and its basic obligation and do so in the now familiar order: Israel's identity by God's redemptive grace (God's people) and what Israel must do (be obedient). Obedience is well motivated. Between the opening command to keep "this entire law" (v. 1) and the renewed call to obedience in verse 10 comes the gift of the land, the promise to the patriarchs, the rejoicing in sacrificial worship, and the status of Israel as Yahweh's people.

27:11–13 / Mt. Ebal and Mt. Gerizim stand, respectively, to the north and south of the valley close to the site of Shechem, which had very early associations with Israel's religious history (Gen. 33:18–20; Josh. 24:1–26; 1 Kgs. 12:1). The ceremony described here is reported as having taken place during the conquest period under Joshua (cf. Josh. 8:30–35). Whether it was intended to be periodically reenacted is unclear. Certainly, the mere identification of the two mountains with curse and blessing would remind Israelites, every time they passed through that valley, of the straightforward choice that faced them day by day—loyalty and obedience or disloyalty and disobedience—and of the serious consequences of the choice (cf. 11:26–32; 30:15–18). It may be, however, that while the text envisaged a single nonrecurring event, nevertheless that single historical event contributed to the ongoing liturgy of Israel's worship. The litany of curses and their responsive "Amens" may have functioned as part of the entrance liturgy, rather like Psalms 15 and 24, to remind worshippers of the moral seriousness of any approach to God in worship.

27:14–26 / This list of curses differs from that found in chapter 28 in that here there is a selection of specific actions that are placed under a curse without the nature of the curse being spelled out, whereas in chapter 28 the content of the curse is described in graphic detail. Two points may be made about the twelve curses of this chapter.

First, there is an interesting combination of the very public nature of the declaration of the curses with the generally private nature of the actions described (cf. Alt, "Israelite Law," pp. 114f.). The list speaks primarily of offenses that have an air of secrecy, either explicitly (vv. 15, 24) or in the obvious nature of the offense. By their nature, therefore, they are not likely to come into open court for trial and judgment. The purpose of the curses, therefore, is to remind Israel that Yahweh sees and knows what happens in secret. The criminal who escapes the wrath of the civil community will not escape the wrath of God. The repeated demand that **all the people shall say, "Amen!"** had the effect that all wrongdoers are obliged to pronounce their own curse. If these curses did form part of public worship in Israel's later life, then they were an enormously challenging piece of liturgy.

Secondly, like some other lists in the OT (most notably, of course, the Decalogue itself, but also texts such as Job 31; Ps. 15; and Ezek. 18), this list provides a window of insight into Israel's scale of religious and ethical values and thus witnesses to an order of priorities that clearly reflects some of the key commandments of the Decalogue, coupled with some of the major concerns of Deuteronomy itself. The first and greatest covenant obligation, loyalty to Yahweh alone, comes first. The opening curse (v. 15) probably includes both first and second commandments in its scope. Significantly, this is followed by the family, as the sequence jumps straight to the fifth commandment (v. 16), reinforcing the centrality of the family within the national covenant relationship. Since the economic viability of the family on its own inherited share of the land is paramount, the next curse is directed at those whose greed attacks the original land division and who change boundaries to their own advantage (v. 17). This is followed by two curses against those who exploit the weak and vulnerable—perhaps the second most prominent concern of Deuteronomy after its covenantal monotheism (vv. 18f.). Sexual integrity is also central to healthy family structures in society, and so four curses condemn incest and perversion (vv. 20–23).

Finally, the curses return to the Decalogue with two based on the sixth commandment and the sanctity of human life (vv. 24f.). The list of curses clearly focuses most on the social life of Israel. But the whole list is suspended from the fundamental question of loyalty to Yahweh or going after idols. Again and again the message of the OT is that if you choose the wrong gods you will end in social decay. Biblical monotheism, far from an abstract creed, affirms that only when God is properly honored will society be just and compassionate. Modern western society, reaping the fruit of two centuries of systematically excluding the living God from all practical public relevance, is now plagued by the loss of family stability, respect for property, social compassion, sexual integrity, and the sanctity of life. Those who will not love God soon find it irksome (or uneconomical) to love their neighbors.

Additional Notes §31

27:1 / **All these commands:** Again, the NIV has turned a Hb. singular into the plural. The Hb. phrase "this whole commandment" emphasizes the unity and completeness of the law considered as a whole. Occurring here after all the detail of the intervening legislative chapters (12–26), it echoes its double use in 11:8 and 22 (cf. 6:1, 25).

27:2 / **When you have crossed . . . :** The Hb. here is lit. "On the day you cross . . . " Taken literally, this suggests that it was intended that inscribed stones be set up close to the river Jordan as soon as Israel had crossed it. This would conflict with v. 4, where the Hb. is not so specific and the stones were to be set up at Mt. Ebal—a considerable distance "inland" from the Jordan. One can take v. 2 in a general sense (as the Hb. idiom allows) and thus solve at least the geographical problem, but this still leaves the awkward repetitions of vv. 2, 4, and 8. Various scholarly attempts exist to trace the sources and redactional history of the ch., on the assumption of its composite nature (cf. Mayes, *Deuteronomy*, pp. 340ff.), but they do not inspire much confidence. On the basis of comparison with ancient Near Eastern land-grant treaties and the Babylonian *kudurru* stones that give details of local land ownership, Hill offers a more unified interpretation of the chapter as a Hebrew variant of the ancient Near Eastern land-grant form, and as a distinct subcategory within the wider covenant framework of the book. The Ebal ceremony related specifically to the grant of the land and its legitimate possession—"a ceremony within a ceremony." See Hill, "The Ebal Ceremony."

27:5 / The instruction here to set up an altar at Mt. Ebal clearly conflicts with the assumption that ch. 12 prescribes the exclusive centralization of worship in one place—"the place the LORD your God will choose"—if that place is asumed to be Jerusalem. Since the so-called "centralization formula" is not used here, the chapter obviously does not intend that Mt. Ebal was that place. But then, if it was not, we have an exception to the alleged "rule" that no other sanctuaries were to be allowed—an exception that, in view of its significant position in the book, raises questions about the assumption that Deut. in its origins was so fundamentally intended to achieve centralization.

27:15–26 / On the relation of these curses to Israel's earliest law, and especially the "prohibitives," cf. Bellefontaine, "The Curses of Deuteronomy 27."

§32 Blessings and Curses (Deut. 28:1–68)

It is not hard to understand why this is perhaps the most difficult chapter in Deuteronomy for a modern reader to cope with. And yet the fact is that in its ancient context this list of blessings and the even longer list of curses would have been *expected* at this point. Deuteronomy is structurally modeled on the secular treaty format, and a consistent feature of those treaties is the section of blessings and curses that follows the detailed stipulations of the treaty in order to give them a solemn and binding force. Since the vassal state had to be made unmistakably aware of the inevitable consequences that would follow if the treaty was broken, the curses tend to dominate. Indeed, many of the curses recorded in Deuteronomy 28 were identical to those in secular treaties. The litany of calamity was familiar enough, and even the rhetoric with which it was delivered was fairly standardized.

Theologically, we should not treat the blessings and curses as though they were comparable opposites. The headings of the NIV unfortunately give that impression: "Blessings for Obedience" and "Curses for Disobedience." Likewise, some popular versions of the "Prosperity Gospel" give the impression that all the material blessings of verses 2–14 will come pouring out of the heavenly slot machine if you press the right behavior buttons. However, although it is clear that if the curses happen, they will come as deserved punishment, there is no corresponding sense in which the blessings can be earned as some kind of reward. The whole thrust of Deuteronomy would protest at such an idea. Israel is bluntly warned to make no equations between military or material success and its own merits (8:17f.; 9:4–6). Rather, God's blessing on God's people is already *there* in the very fact that they are God's people at all. It is intrinsic to the promise to Abraham and to the covenant relationship. Blessing is the prior reality of God's grace. It is there to be enjoyed, but can be enjoyed only by living in God's way in the land God is giving them.

Obedience, therefore, like faith, is the means of *appropriating* God's grace and blessing, not the means of *deserving* it.

28:1–14 / The opening promise (v. 1), should be read in the light of the commentary on 26:19. The heart of the chapter is really the liturgical-style blessings of verses 3–6, which find their counterpart in the curses of verses 16–19. Both are then expanded in the verses following them. The focus of the blessings is very obviously the enjoyment of the land, which would depend on being protected from invading enemies (v. 7), on fertility (v. 11), and on the rain (v. 12). So all these things are promised as part of God's blessing on an obedient people. The whole section, rather like 7:12–15, is a kind of coloring in of the fundamental outline of the Abrahamic covenant. God promised to bless Abraham's descendants in the land. What else could that mean than the basic realities described here?

Echoes of the Abraham covenant are also heard in the universal missionary thrust of verse 10. Obedience will not only ensure the enjoyment of God's promised **blessing** but also spread the knowledge of God's **name**. The very reason for Israel's existence is for the sake of the nations, and so here Israel's obedience is linked to that national mission. The scope is universal: **all the peoples on earth,** which in its immediate context may be a rhetorical flourish but in the overall context of biblical eschatology is a sober and solid expectation. Elsewhere in the OT, coming to know the name of the God of Israel is the first step in the ingathering and salvation of the nations (e.g., Isa. 19:19–22; Jer. 12:14–17; Amos 9:12). Ultimately all humanity will know the name of the God of Israel through the multinational community who bear the name of Israel. As ever, we find the close integration of *ethics and mission* for the envisaged spread of the knowledge of Yahweh's name through the Israelites (v. 10) is bound up with their being **his holy people** by keeping **his commands** and walking **in his ways** (v. 9; cf. Gen. 18:19 and the discussion in the introduction). And likewise we find the link between *blessing and mission*. The purpose of God blessing *this* people is ultimately so that God can bless **all the peoples on earth.**

28:15–68 / Four things may be said about this lengthy tale of suffering. First, it does not spring from morbid imagination. Such things were a matter of grim reality, experienced by many a nation in the ancient world (and not unfamiliar in parts of the modern world as well). The list of catastrophes includes:

disease and blight (vv. 21f., 27, 35, 59–61); drought, famine and other calamities in the food chain (vv. 23f., 38–42); all the dire results of defeat in war, especially the horrors of prolonged siege (vv. 25f. 30–34, 49–57); and the distress, fear, and frustration of land loss, deportation, and exile (vv. 36–37, 63–68). In the course of its history, Israel experienced all of these things, culminating in the final exile of Judah in the sixth century. The prophets explained such disasters in terms of God's judgment, thereby either directly or implicitly accusing Israel of breaking the covenant (cf. Amos 4:6–13; Jer. 11:1–8).

Secondly, the curses include specific negative echoes of the blessing of Abraham and of the exodus. Disobedient Israel will find history inverted. Instead of the Abrahamic blessing of national growth and greatness in the land of promise, it will wither away to insignificance and through expulsion from the land (vv. 43f., 62f.). Instead of exodus deliverance from their enemies, the Israelites themselves will suffer all the plagues once laid on the Egyptians and finally go back into the very kind of captivity from which they had been rescued (vv. 27–29, 60f., 68).

Thirdly, there is a polemical implication here also. Israel went after other gods because they thought they could provide the desired blessings of rain, fertility, success, victory, etc. The tragic irony is that the pursuit of such idolatries ultimately brought the dire opposite of what those false gods promised. There is a persistent tendency in human society toward idolatry—seeking answers and solutions in everything but the living God. Modern western idolatries include the ideologies of materialism ("the Market"), consumerism, individualism, militarism, etc. But these do not give us the salvation they appear to promise. On the contrary they only lead us deeper into the realms of judgment and curse, in which the frustrations, anger, and despair that run through these verses of Deuteronomy 28 become increasingly real and demoralizing. "All our gods have failed," was the climax of a secular journal's assessment of the moral failure of late twentieth-century British society. It was the task of the prophets of Israel to bring them to the same realization, not just as a figure of speech but as a sober assessment of reality (cf. Jer. 2:27f.; 3:23f.; 14:22).

Fourthly, the conditional nature of this whole section should be given its full weight. There is nothing *inevitable* about the chain of events described here. The whole point of the chapter is to *warn* the Israelites of the consequences of certain behavior so that they can avoid them. The curses are not "fated." Only if they engage in persistent rebellion against God's grace and blessing will such consequences become unavoidable. They will then bring the curses on themselves. The thrust of this horror preview, then, is not to portray a horrific God (v. 63 must be taken as rhetorical, not literal) but to make a powerful appeal to a legitimate consequentialism: "Think what will happen if you deliberately choose the path of rebellion and disobedience." Choices matter.

§33 Summary and Renewal of the Covenant (Deut. 29:1–30:20)

In terms of the *rhetorical* nature of the book, Moses' third speech to Israel begins here at 29:2 (which is 29:1 in the Hebrew text). In terms of the *concentric* structure of the book, we are still within what Christensen calls "the inner frame" (chs. 27–30), which is in a position corresponding to chapters 4–11 (cf. introduction, p. 4). And in terms of the *message* of the book, this section picks up and summarizes much of the earlier material, setting it once again within a recognizable treaty/covenant pattern. The following elements of the treaty pattern can be discerned: historical prologue (29:1–9); parties to the agreement (29:10–15); basic stipulation (29:18); curses for disobedience (29:19–28); possibility of restoration and blessing (30:1–10); witnesses (30:19). Clearly, however, these elements have not been simply stuck together mechanically, but have been woven into a speech that, precisely because it condenses the message of the whole book into such a short space, generates great rhetorical power and spiritual challenge. It concludes with almost evangelistic fervor, and it is not surprising that the second half of chapter 30 finds echoes in the teaching of Jesus and Paul.

29:1–9 / *The fundamental covenant history.* The speech begins characteristically with a historical review, condensing the longer recollections found in chapters 1–3, which are themselves a summary of the full narratives in Exodus and Numbers. The climactic miracle of the exodus (vv. 2f.), the prolonged miracle of Israel's survival in the wilderness (vv. 5f.), and the early victories over Transjordan kingdoms that enable a preliminary sharing of the land (vv. 7f.) are highlighted. These are the historical givens of Israel's faith. There is no denying them. Whatever wandering paths Israel's religion might take, there is an unchangeable objective core to it in the historical fact of these events. This historical grounding is as important for OT faith as the events of the life, death, and resurrection of Jesus are for the Christian gospel. The biblical faith is not something speculatively invented in religious fervency but is in response to events in which God has acted. In both testaments, the gospel is not a good *idea;* it is good *news.*

The gospel nature of what is summarized here is further embossed by the emphasis on God's initiative of grace. **Your eyes have seen** *all that the* LORD *did* (v. 2): these words are an unmistakable echo of Exodus 19:4, the first words Israel heard from Mt. Sinai even before the commandments and the law were given. Those whom God calls into covenant relationship, those from whom God demands covenant obedience, are those whom God has already acted to save. God's love already is demonstrated. Ours is awaited.

If God's historically proven grace can, in a sense, be taken for granted, the human response certainly cannot. Verse 4 injects a surprisingly paradoxical note, yet one that is consistent with Moses' unvarnished realism elsewhere. He knows that the eyes that had witnessed the exodus have not become eyes of faith (cf. 1:30–32). The ears that heard the thunder of Mt. Sinai have not become ears of obedience, in spite of good intentions (cf. 5:26f.). The hearts that learned the message from these events, namely, that Yahweh alone is God (cf. 4:35, 39; 7:9; 29:6b), are still capable of turning away and worshipping other gods (cf. vv. 18f.). It is this perennial fickleness of human nature, even among the redeemed people of God, that generates the apparent contradiction between verses 2f. (**your eyes have seen . . . with your own eyes you saw**) and verse 4 (**the** LORD **has not given you . . . eyes that see**). People can see the very works of God, hear the very voice of God, and yet still neither trust nor obey God. This awful fact dogs the footsteps of Jesus himself, breaks his heart, and leads him to respond in Isaianic echoes of this very verse (Matt. 13:14f. [note the earlier context of the Beelzebub controversy, 12:22–32]; Isa. 6:9f.). Paul also reflects on this verse in his interpretation of the rejection of Jesus by some of his contemporary Jews (Rom. 11:8), in a broader context (Rom. 9–11) heavily influenced by this whole section of Deuteronomy.

Returning to our text, we must face the question of what is meant by the words **the** LORD **has not given you** . . . On the surface, it may appear to suggest that Israel's failure to understand, trust, and obey was somehow God's fault. Such a suggestion, however, runs right against the whole thrust of the book, which rebukes the Israelites for their own failure and challenges them instead to respond properly to God. There is furthermore the clear word of 5:28f. in which God welcomes Israel's declaration of intent and fervently wishes it could always be true. Nor can the verse mean that somehow Israel was *incapable* of trust and obedience. Such a thought is faced and decisively rejected in this very speech (30:11–14). The urgent appeal of 30:15–20 would be a cynical charade if God had somehow decreed in advance that Israel *could not* respond to it. It seems, therefore, that this phrase reflects a feature of Hebrew language and thought in which events and processes that today would be expressed as consequences of human choice are attributed to God's active will. The sovereignty of Yahweh encompasses even those things that oppose him.

The words also express a deeper truth, namely, that hearts understand, eyes see, and ears hear only through the gift of God. Knowledge of God, trust, and obedience are themselves gifts of grace, at the same time as they are matters of human choice and response. In some sense, therefore, however mysterious, the persistent and wholly culpable failure of Israel to make the right response to God and to live accordingly was indeed because the gift was not yet fully given. Thus, the words of Moses on the boundary of the promised land gather eschatological force as they echo through later generations, until they are eventually taken up into more explicit prophetic visions of the day when God would indeed "give" the people hearts to know and obey, in the context of not merely a renewed covenant, but a new covenant altogether (cf. Jer. 24:6f.; 31:33; Ezek. 11:19f.; 36:26–28). Indeed, such a possibility is already envisaged through the grace of God beyond the fires of judgment (30:6): *God will give what the covenant demands*—circumcision of the heart for love and obedience.

29:10–15 / *The fundamental covenant relationship.* The core of this section is the core of the covenant itself, the mutual commitment of people to God and God to people (vv. 12f.). Though the commitment is reciprocal, the initiative is God's. It is God who is **making** and **sealing** the covenant, in order **to confirm** (or establish) Israel as the people of God. And in doing so, God keeps not only the promise to them but also the original promise to their ancestors, Abraham, Isaac, and Jacob. To God's grace is added God's faithfulness through the centuries and generations.

On either side of this central covenantal fulcrum two other key truths are balanced. (a) The *social inclusiveness* of the covenant is spelled out in remarkable detail by listing a whole variety of people in the community, **all** of whom are included in the covenant relationship, from national leaders to the most menial laborers, women, children, and men, aliens and native born (vv. 10f.; cf. 31:12). No caste system in Israel excludes the lowest social groups from participation and blessing. The woodchopper is no less a member of the covenant community than the king. No matter who stands before whom in daily life, all find themselves **standing in the presence of the LORD,** a radically leveling posture. Such an understanding of the unity and social equality of God's people underlies the strong words of James 2. (b) The *perennial continuity* of the covenant is recalled (cf. 5:2f.; 11:2–7) and doubly underlined by including **those who are not here today** (i.e., not those accidentally absent but those as yet unborn), and by the chiming repetition of **today . . . today,** which echoes down the ages every time these words are read. For every new generation, the challenge of the covenant would always be "today" (cf. Ps. 95:7b–11), just as for every generation of Christians the Lord's coming is always "soon." The Christian church, especially at the local level, has much to learn from this social and trans-generational inclusiveness of OT Israel.

29:16–21 / *The fundamental covenant demand.* The third section of the speech moves on, logically, to the most foundational stipulation of the covenant—namely, the total renunciation of all other gods and idols out of exclusive loyalty to Yahweh (the first and second commandments). Again Moses appeals to experience as a counterbalance to any attractiveness that Canaanite idolatry might hold. Just as eyes that had seen the works of the living God ought to be eyes of faith, so eyes that had seen the hideousness of idolatry ought to recognize it as something to be avoided at all costs. The two words used for **detestable images and idols** are unusual (*šiqqûṣîm,* cf. Hos. 9:10; and *gillûlîm,* cf. Ezek. 37:23) and express disgust and contempt (v. 17 [MT v. 16]). The trouble is, of course, that idolatry only tempts people because its enticements initially outweigh its wretchedness and cost, a lesson always learned too late.

The insidious nature of idolatry and the hypocrisy it engenders (vv. 18f.), as well as the severity of the penalties that follow, indicate the serious nature of such behavior. God's refusal

to forgive (v. 20) probably indicates this person's refusal to repent. Such sin in Israel would be sin against the light, in this
context against what one has seen with one's own eyes, and
hence ties in with the similar verdict of Jesus on such sin (cf. Matt.
12:22–32). The blotting out of **his name** and the threat that God
will **single him out** (lit. "separate him") are clear evidence that
the OT has as sharp an understanding of individual accountability before God as any NT text. To be sure, God deals with the
nation as a whole, in blessing and in judgment. But no individual
is lost to God's view in either event.

29:22–28 / *An open stage.* "A city set on a hill cannot be
hidden." The behavior of God's people and God's own actions
toward them are performed in full view of the rest of world and
in the full glare of history. This public position could be positive
or negative. Israel could become the means of the nations coming
to know God because of the blessing that would accompany their
obedience (28:10), or they could become "an object of scorn and
ridicule to all the nations" because of the judgments that would
befall them in their disobedience (28:37). This missiological understanding of the role of Israel in relation to God and the nations
is also expressed in the powerful challenge of 4:5–8. An obedient
Israel will raise questions among the nations, questions about
Israel's God and the quality of Israel's society. In chapter 29 there
is a kind of photographic negative of that picture in 4:5–8. **All the
nations** will still be asking questions, but the questions will now
be triggered by disaster (v. 24). Far from being a model of righteousness, Israel will join Sodom and Gomorrah as a model of
deserved wrath and destruction (v. 23).

The presence of both texts (4:5–8 and 29:22–28) so prominent in the "inner framework" structure of the book underlines
the awesome responsibility that lies upon the Israelites in their
mission as the people of God, as God's priesthood in the midst of
the nations. The very name of God is invested in their fulfillment
of that mission. Success will make Yahweh's name known as a
matter of admiration; failure will drag his name to the depths of
profanity. The solemn warning of this section is that the disaster
of destruction and exile will be as much an expression of the logic
of the covenant (**Why? . . . Because . . .**) as anything else in
Israel's history. Ezekiel sees and feels this most keenly, standing
as he does amidst the smoldering wreckage after the judgment
has indeed fallen. But in that perception Ezekiel sees the seeds of

hope, for Yahweh will always finally act for the vindication of his own name (Ezek. 36:16–36). Only in that fact can there be a future for the people who bear that name and a future for the nations who will witness the restoration of God's people.

30:1–10 / *An open future.* After the dire curses of chapter 28 and the compressed warning of 29:22–28, this section comes like an oxygen mask to revive hope. History is ultimately open-ended. God will not be defeated by Israel's response or bound and imprisoned by the past. For beyond past, present, and even future failure, stands the covenant faithfulness and purpose of Yahweh. There is great faith inherent in the *assumption* of verse 2, that the people *will* **return to the LORD . . . and obey him.** The sentence is not conditional, but simply a continuation of the temporal clauses with which the chapter begins (i.e., not if, but when). Similarly there is tremendous hope expressed in the **even if** of verse 4. No matter how severe the judgment or how **distant** the exile, God *will* **restore** the people. All hope is placed in God, who is the subject of most of the verbs in these verses.

But that hope in the grace and power of God is integrally linked to the need for Israel to **turn** and **obey.** In fact, the whole section has a concentric arrangement that interweaves the divine and the human very powerfully.

A When you and your children return (v. 2a)
B and obey . . . with all your heart and soul (v. 2b)
C then you will have restoration to the land and more prosperity than the fathers (vv. 3–5)
D *God will circumcise your hearts so that you will love him with all your heart and soul* (v. 6)
C' you will have prosperity in the land, like the fathers (vv. 8–9)
B' if you obey the LORD your God (v. 10a)
A' and turn to the LORD . . . with all your heart and soul (v. 10b)

The condition that frames the promise of restoration is Israel's wholehearted turning back to God in obedience (vv. 2 and 10). But the central verse (v. 6), by its repetition of the key phrase **with all your heart and with all your soul,** makes it clear that even such turning cannot happen apart from the gracious decision of God to **circumcise** the Israelites' **hearts** *so that* they could love him in that way. Thus the fundamental demand of the law (to love God with all one's heart and soul) is presented as the ultimate fruit of God's grace in the human heart. As with much of the content of these two chapters, the echoes of chapter 4 are very clear. The hope of Israel lies not in its unaided capacity to respond but in God's unending commitment to remember mercy (4:28–31). This simultaneous proclamation of the transforming grace of God and the urgent call to repentance finds its clear echo in the prophets (e.g., Jer. 31:23ff.; 32:37–41; Ezek. 36:24–38).

30:11–14 / *An open word.* This short interlude before the final appeal reassures Israel that God's law *can* be kept. The text refers to the law in the singular, literally, "this commandment which I am commanding you today" (rather weakly rendered **what** in NIV). It is referring to God's covenantal demand on God's people, considered as a whole. Two negative things are said about it (v. 11), reinforced by two suggestive metaphors (vv. 12f.), followed by a powerful positive affirmation (v. 14).

God's commandment is **not too difficult,** nor is it **beyond your reach.** The law is not among those things that the humble person does not bother with (Ps. 131:1) or that even the wise find beyond their understanding (Prov. 30:18). It is not, therefore, impossibly idealistic, impracticable, unachievable. We have noticed earlier the balance achieved between ideal standards and earthly realities. The idea that God deliberately made the law so exacting that nobody would ever be able to live by it belongs to a distorted theology that tries unnecessarily to gild the gospel by denigrating the law. The frequent claims by various psalmists to have lived according to God's law are neither exaggerated nor exceptional. They arise from the natural assumption that ordinary people can indeed live in a way that is broadly pleasing to God and faithful to God's law, and that they can do so as a matter of joy and delight. This is neither self-righteousness nor a claim to sinless perfection, for the same psalmists are equally quick to confess their sin and failings, fully realizing that only the grace that could forgive and cleanse them would likewise enable them to live again in covenant obedience. Obedience to the law in the OT, as has been stressed repeatedly, was not the means of achieving salvation but the response to a salvation that was already experienced.

The two spatial metaphors (**up in heaven . . . beyond the sea**), significantly rule out the idea that the law is somehow only for those capable of rising to the heights of understanding it or that it is attainable only after great struggles and journeys. Once again we note how Israel's faith eschewed elitism or asceticism. The law is intelligible to all and accessible to all. Thus, to say that the law **is not too difficult** does not mean that obedience is *easy* but rather that it is *simple*. It is not complicated and distracted by obscure philosophies, complex rules, or esoteric religious rituals, accessible only to the privileged few. All those who are included in the covenant relationship (cf. 29:10–15; 31:12–13) are deemed capable of understanding and obeying the covenant law.

The positive truth is expressed with powerful brevity in verse 14 (lit.): "But near to you is the word, exceedingly, in your mouth and in your heart to do it." The nearness of God's word here echoes the nearness of God's self in 4:7. In chapter 4, the nearness of God is the basis of Israel's distinctiveness among the nations. In chapter 30, the nearness of God's word is the basis of their moral response to God, which enables their distinctiveness to be visible. There could be no clearer indication that the OT knows and understands the importance of internalizing the law in the mind and heart (cf. the impact of Pss. 1; 19; and 119). The idea that for Israel the law was merely an external code likewise belongs to the mythology of distorted theologies that, misled and misleading, try to prove the superiority of Christianity by denigrating Judaism.

Paul's use of this verse in Romans 10:5–13 is entirely Christocentric. His argument should not be seen as a mutually exclusive contrast between the law and faith, since he quotes from Leviticus and Deuteronomy (both part of the law) on both sides of his argument. Rather, his point is that in Christ the true response to the law (i.e., faith and obedience), expressed in the law itself, is possible.

> For Paul, the word of God, the way of the Lord, the means to life are all so completely given in Jesus Christ, the end or goal of the law (Rom. 10:4), that what Deuteronomy means is crystal clear. Nowhere is the availability of God's gift of life more readily transparent and demonstrated than in the word made flesh and the word preached. . . . Paul reminds us that the way to life and the way to live are fully set before us in Jesus Christ, in who he was and what he said and did. (P. D. Miller, *Deuteronomy*, p. 216)

30:15–20 / *An open choice.* And so this powerful summary of the whole book reaches its climax charged with evangelistic energy, emotion, and urgency (cf. Ezek. 18:30–32). All the

points expressed have been made before, but combining them in
this fashion increases their intensity. The issue is a matter of **life**
and **death**. The context shows that the whole nation and its
continuing prosperity on the land are in view. Yet the passage, so
typically of Deuteronomy, is expressed in the second person
singular, thus presenting the whole matter as an intensely personal choice—a choice that matters more than any other in life.

The opening words of the appeal, **See, I set before you
life . . .** , echo the opening words of Moses in the speech that
sets the context for the whole book, as Israel stands on the
boundary of the land: "See, I have given you this land . . . " (1:8;
the verb is the same in Hb. as 30:15). The link between land and
life is explicit all the way through the book. The previous generation of the exodus had the land set before them, refused it,
and "chose" death and destruction as a consequence. This generation, even when they enter the land, must still go on choosing life through obedience, love, and loyalty to their covenant
Lord God (cf. Josh. 24:15). This is the framework for understanding the whole of the inner contents of Deuteronomy with
its detailed outworking of the choice.

What then is life? The reply Jesus gives to the rich man who
asks such a question is authentically scriptural (cf. Matt. 19:17;
Lev. 18:5). In the words of verse 16, life is loving God, walking **in
his ways** and keeping **his commands.** In the words of verses 19f.,
life is *loving* God, *listening* to God, and having *loyalty* to God. Life,
in the end, is not found in the law itself, but in the God who gave
it; for ultimately, **the LORD is your life.**

Additional Notes §33

29:19 / **Disaster on the watered land as well as the dry:** The
NIV inserts "land" as a way of making some sense of what was probably an abbreviated proverbial expression. The Hb. is simply "on the
moist and on the dry." Perhaps it was an idiomatic phrase that implied totality: "on everybody." The sense would then be that although
the sin might appear to be hidden and individual, its punishment
would affect everybody. Others have taken it to mean, "on the innocent and on the guilty."

29:29 / It is difficult to know whether this concluding verse should be linked to what precedes or what follows. If linked to the preceding context, then **the secret things** could be a way of referring to the as yet unknown future. God alone knows what will happen in the future history of God's people. The future is not a matter of blind fate, nor of inevitability. The threats of the previous verses still function as a warning that may yet be avoided. So leave the unknown future to God and concentrate on **the things revealed**, namely, God's known law that can be obeyed. If, on the other hand, the verse is linked to what follows, and especially to 30:11–14, then it is part of the affirmation that God's law is clear and accessible. There may be much that remains hidden from our understanding (a characteristic Wisdom viewpoint), but God has revealed all that is needed for us to know and obey God. The verse then takes its place among many that bear on a biblical doctrine of revelation in relation to ethics.

30:11–14 / It is important to recognize that Paul's use of these verses in Rom. 10 is intended not to negate the law as such, but to affirm that the law, as something good, was always intended to be lived out by faith in the God who gave it. On the paradoxical understanding of the law in Paul, see N. T. Wright, *Climax*, and especially his discussion of Rom. 9–11.

30:15 / Derrett, "Power of Choice," finds in the question of Jesus to the synagogue in Mark 3:4 a midrash on this verse ("good or evil; life or death") and goes on to find other echoes of the whole Deuteronomic context of curse and choice in these chapters in the incident and its sequel.

§34 A Song for the Future (Deut. 31:1–32:47)

At this point we move finally to the "outer frame" of the book, composed of chapters 1–3 and 31–34. The links between the two sections are very clear, and they could be read together continuously. The common theme, especially at the "join" (cf. 3:21–28), is the commissioning of Joshua to lead the Israelites into the land, in view of the fact that Moses would not do so but would die outside it. However, whereas chapters 1–3 focus primarily on the past, chapters 31–34 shift to the future. Not just the immediate future is in mind, with the transfer of leadership and prospect of conquest, but the long-distance history of Israel is surveyed in the prophetic Song of Moses. This encapsulates a realistic and historically vindicated view of Israel's unfaithfulness as well as a profound theology of God's purposes through Israel in relation to the nations; this seals the missiological significance of the book and deeply influences Paul's missionary theology and vision.

31:1–8 / Transfer of leadership is a critical time for any community, sacred or secular. The Bible actually focuses on the issue quite frequently, and with characteristically consistent features (e.g., Samuel to Saul, David to Solomon, Elijah to Elisha, Jesus to his disciples, and even Paul to Timothy). Even when Moses is at the helm, however, the true leader of the people is God. That reality does not change when Moses passes from the scene. Accordingly, the first point Moses makes in his transfer speech is to reassure the people that **the LORD your God himself will cross over ahead of** Israel into the land (v. 3a). Their survival and success depend on God's leadership; their victories will be God's (v. 4). They can face the future with boldness and courage founded on the perennial promise of God's own presence (v. 6).

Divine leadership, however, is "incarnational"—it is earthed in human leaders. And thus verse 3 abruptly repeats exactly the words used about God to describe Joshua also: "he is the one about to cross over ahead of you." The people can be free from anxiety. God will neither desert them after the death of Moses nor leave them without a human leader.

Joshua, no doubt awed by the prospect of taking over from Moses, need have no anxiety, for the same original promises made to Moses himself—the presence of God with him to empower him to carry out his task—will rest on Joshua. This commissioning and encouragement of Joshua is given great emphasis by sheer repetition (cf. Num. 27:18–23; Deut. 1:38; 3:21, 28; 32:3, 7f., 14, 23; 34:9). It actually becomes the single event that most binds the Pentateuch to the historical books that follow, since the book of Joshua opens with yet another and still fuller account in direct divine speech to Joshua himself (Josh. 1:1–9). The key words in the commissioning are **Be strong and courageous** (v. 7)—words that countless numbers of those called to leadership in God's people have needed and heeded. These words are not merely for a psychological boost. They are based on two great truths. First, the people one is called to lead are those whose very existence proves the faithfulness of God (v. 7b). God has invested God's word and name in the future of this people and so ultimate responsibility for them is God's own—a fact Moses uses so effectively in his intercession (cf. 9:26–29). Secondly, the leader can count on the unfailing presence of God. What was covenantally true for the people (v. 6b) will be no less personally true for their leader (v. 8).

31:9–13 / What use would there be in the law being accessible and intelligible (30:11–14) if it were lost, forgotten, or otherwise became unknown? In the secular treaty texts, arrangements were normally specified for the storage and periodic reading of the treaty; here this task is entrusted to the religious leaders (**the priests;** v. 9) and the civil leaders (**the elders;** v. 9). Both are important because the law embraces the whole of life, just as the covenant embraces the whole community (notice again the social inclusiveness of the covenant relationship in verse 12: **men, women and children, and the aliens**). The occasion of the public reading of the law is also pregnant with significance. In the sabbatical year, **the year for canceling debts,** the law will be heard in the context of widespread liberation from debt and release of slaves, based upon the historical recollection of God's own liberation of the Israelite slaves from Egypt (Deut. 15). And at **the Feast of Tabernacles,** the reading of the law will be engulfed in the mood of harvest-time gratitude to God (Deut. 16:13ff.). Thus, the law would forever be heard alongside *the memories of historical redemption* and in the midst of rejoicing at *the generosity of God's grace*. If only the law had gone on being heard (and read) in such a context, the Christian church might have avoided some of its more distorted handlings of the OT law in relation to the NT gospel.

31:14–29 / The chapter begins to appear repetitive and disjointed. References to Joshua are split up into several contexts (vv. 7–8, 14f., 23). The writing, reading, and preservation of the Book of the Law is likewise split between verses 9–13 and 24–29. The central section of the chapter (vv. 16–22) is a prose introduction to the theme of the Song of Moses and seems to go naturally with 31:30ff. Those who reckon on several editions of the book and supplementary work of later Deuteronomists attribute the unevenness to that redactional process (e.g., Mayes, *Deuteronomy,* pp. 371–80), though even so it is hard to see why a later redactor would not have put verses 16–22 immediately prior to the Song. It may be, however, that Deuteronomy's remarkable penchant for concentric arrangements of material has affected the chapter and produced the apparent linear disjointedness. The following pattern emerges from verse 9 to the end.

> A Writing of the law; entrusting to Levites; "Assemble" people for
>   reading of law (vv. 9–13)
>   B Commissioning of Joshua (vv. 14f.)
>   C Reason for the Song of Moses (vv. 16–22)
>   B' Commissioning of Joshua (v. 23)
> A' Writing of the law; entrusting to Levites; "Assemble" elders to
>   hear the testimony (vv. 24–29)

If this concentricity is intentional, then even though the gloomy prediction of the people's future unfaithfulness haunts the center of the chapter, there is still a frame of words of promise that God will guarantee the gift of the land through Joshua. Then this unconditional gift of land itself is framed by the demands of obedience to the law as the condition for life in the land. There is a theological interweaving that makes sense of the literary pattern. Yahweh's faithfulness to his long-term covenant purposes for Israel is maintained in spite of his knowledge of Israel's future covenant unfaithfulness (v. 21). Even the promise of God's presence (v. 23) is set alongside the expectation that sin will entail God's absence (vv. 17f.).

It is in the theological depth of these interwoven paradoxes that the prophets find the sources of their message as, on the one hand, they explain the disasters that indeed befall Israel from generation to generation in terms of their persistent unfaithfulness (even the vocabulary is echoed: "prostitution," "forsaking," "breaking"), and, on the other hand, they hold on to a hope for the future in the promises of this oath-taking God whose patience with Israel was already a matter of historical record before they even entered the land. If there is to be a future at all, it must lie with God, not in the capacity of Israel. That much has already been demonstrated by the previous generation, and there is no reason to expect future generations to be markedly superior. God has no illusions (v. 21). Neither has Moses (v. 27). But then, neither God nor Moses nor the Bible as a whole deals in illusions. The future prophetically described in the Song of Moses, whether predictive or retrospective, was no illusion, but a matter of historical fact as the centuries of Israel's OT history unfolded and ultimately became the basis for an equally non-illusory eschatological theology of history and mission in the hands of Paul.

31:30 / Moses may well have **recited the words of the song from beginning to end,** but from our point of view, it is helpful to first observe its structure, sections, and changes of direction. The first part of the song (vv. 1–25) has the form of a *rîb,* that is, a structured lawsuit. This formal pattern is known from the secular treaty texts as a means of accusing a vassal of disloyalty before acting in punishment through military attack. The prophets made use of this form in what has come to be called the "covenant lawsuit." This is a way of both announcing and justifying God's imminent judgment on Israel. However, since the formal structure of the *rîb* is followed only up to verse 25 or 26, it is clear that the song as a whole goes beyond a simple declaration of judgment. Some scholars have labeled the rest of the chapter as mere "expansions" to the basic lawsuit. But this does not do justice to the overall unity and message of the song. Wiebe, "Song of Moses," observing that the song includes a vital element of divine reflection and reconsideration, calls it a "deliberative *rîb.*" He further argues that the same fundamental features are to be found in some prophetic texts in which there is the same pause for consideration and questions before the sentence is either carried out, postponed, or transformed in some way. The secular form has thus been given a fresh interpretation in the context of

Israel's covenantal theology. Wiebe suggests the following analysis of the song, which is broadly convincing.

A. 1–6   Introduction, summoning of witnesses,
              case stated
B. 7–14   The prosecutor's speech; historical review
C. 15–18   The specific indictment
D. 19–26   The sentence
E. 27–33   An act of lamentation
F. 34   The judge's deliberation
G. 35–42   The decision following deliberation
H. 43   Concluding doxology

32:1–6 / The song opens with a summons to the **heavens** and the **earth** to listen. Secular treaty texts had lists of witnesses, usually gods and goddesses, who could be appealed to if either side breached the treaty. This role is metaphorically entrusted to the heavens and the earth in Deuteronomy 4:26, 30:19, and 31:28, and so here they are summoned to fulfill their duty in the impeachment of Israel (cf. Ps. 50:1–4; Isa. 1:2; Mic. 6:1f.).

Though in form this is a lawsuit, the purpose of the song is didactic. It is described as **teaching** (v. 2) and its teaching nature has already been made clear in the prose introduction in chapter 30. History itself may be a poor teacher, but history interpreted by the word of God is a fertile source of real learning. Sadly, even with the prophets as additional teachers, Israel did not learn the lessons of this song. Furthermore, although the central content of the song is the indictment of Israel, the ultimate purpose of the singer is doxological (v. 3). The song is bracketed (vv. 3f. and 43) with praise to Yahweh, the God whose glory will outshine all the failures of historical Israel and ultimately be acknowledged by all nations. The mysterious ways of God with the nations ultimately find their only true response in doxology (cf. Rom. 11:33–36).

But it is that very doxology that sets the context for the basic charge against Israel. There can be no greater contrast than that between verses 4 and 5. Verse 4, lustily sung as a chorus, affirms the character of God in repetitive, overlapping parallelism. As **the Rock,** God is utterly dependable, empty of any wrongdoing, the very foundation of all integrity and justice. Verse 5, not so often sung at all, affirms the lamentable opposite in Israel's case. These people are corrupt, slippery, unstable, **warped and crooked.** That would be bad enough, but the charge is aggravated by the reminder of what Israel owes to this God (verse 6). The metaphor changes from "Rock" to "Parent" and "Maker." Israel's sin was not merely a failure to be like God in character but a refusal to recognize the obligations of their relationship with God and of all God had done for them (**is this the way you repay . . . ?**).

The fundamental clashing questions of the song are thus starkly set out: How can such a people escape judgment? But how can such a Rock God abandon this purpose; how can such a Parent God sever this relationship? The answers go deep into the divine cosmology and eschatology, and ultimately lead Paul in Romans 9–11, via this song, through Christocentric missiology back to doxology.

32:7–14 / Meanwhile, back in the courtroom, the case proceeds with a speech by the "prosecutor," speaking on behalf of God and recounting all God has done for the accused. It opens with a characteristic word of Deuteronomy: **Remember** . . . The prosecution is appealing to no secret files of information, but simply laying out what is common knowledge to every generation of Israelites. The accused cannot plead ignorance. It is characteristic of all the covenant-lawsuit passages in the OT that they make some reference to the history of God's redemptive actions on Israel's behalf as a backdrop to the charge of infidelity. Here the full story is told, starting even before human history with the divine election of Israel as the special portion of Yahweh (vv. 8f.), moving on to the historical events of exodus and God's tender care in the wilderness (10–12), and climaxing in God's abundant generosity in the land (13f.). Election, redemption, and land-gift embodied the essential acts of God on which the covenant with Israel is founded, and therefore the grounds on which the prosecution's case is established (cf. chs. 1–11). If no other God than Yahweh had guided their history, then no other gods had any claim on their worship.

Whereas most other prophetic-lawsuit passages focus on a selection of particular *historical* events (most commonly the exodus and/or the wilderness themes), this song provides "an entire cosmology of the nation of Israel" (Wiebe, p. 133), and indeed of the other nations. Verses 8–9 take the origins of Israel right back to the divine allocation of nations and locate the election of Israel in the creative sovereignty of God over **all mankind.** Prior even to the choice of Abraham (the usual Deuteronomic starting-block for election theology), these verses see Israel's uniqueness in terms of the divine ordering of all human geography and history. Verse 8 echoes the theological affirmations of God's multinational sovereignty in history (2:10–12, 20–23; 4:19), while verse 9 echoes the unique relationship between Yahweh and Israel alone among the nations (cf. 7:6; 10:14–15). Verse 8 thus embodies a universal, providential understanding of God in relation to the nations of humanity at large, while verse 9 expresses the particular elective-redemptive relationship of God to Israel. This is reflected in the two names used: **the Most High** ("Elyon," otherwise not used in Deuteronomy, but elsewhere associated with non-Israelite nations, e.g., Gen. 14:18–22; Num. 24:16) and **the LORD** (Yahweh, the redemptive, covenant name of God as known in Israel). Yahweh, of course, is synonymous with Elyon here. There is no possibility that Yahweh is simply one of the "sons of the gods" to whom nations are allocated. The point is that the one and only God, known to Israel as Yahweh, is the same Most High God who is sovereign among the nations of humanity. While it is true, then, that verses 8–9 function in their *immediate* context to reinforce the special relationship between Yahweh and Israel, they also function to keep the wider context in mind in a way that will be important later in the song. Yahweh, Most High, is God of the whole earth and all nations and *as such* is uniquely the God of Israel. This universal framework becomes the primary grounds for the *judgment* of the nations later in the song, but the concluding call to the nations to "rejoice" (v. 43) hints at more hopeful possibilities for the nations that are developed by psalmists, prophets, and apostles.

32:15–18 / Just as verses 7–14 expand the benevolence of God in verse 4, so verses 15–18 now expand the basic charge made against Israel in verse 5, with verse 18 also echoing verse 6. This section, then, is the specific indictment of Israel. It casts in pithy poetic form the fundamental sins that earlier chapters of Deuteronomy warned against in familiar rhetorical prose. As a result of their prosperity in the land (paradoxically, therefore, as the result of God's very blessing), Israel has become **fat** (v. 15a, i.e., proud and complacent; cf. 8:12–14; Hos. 13:6; Jer. 8:7–28). They have **abandoned, rejected,** and **deserted** their creator and savior God (vv. 15b, 18a) and gone after other gods—demonic, unknown, upstart, non-God gods (vv. 16f.). The offensiveness of such behavior is underlined again by reference to the parenthood of God. In verses 4 and 6 the pictures of God as Rock and as Father are distinct. In verse 18 they are dramatically combined into a single metaphor. But the parent metaphor itself is extended to include both genders. God is both the one who **fathered** Israel and the one who **gave you birth**; both father and mother of the people (cf. Num. 11:12). The combination of roles makes the point even more strongly. To dishonor or disobey one's *human* father and mother was a covenant offense that carried the death penalty. What then did Israel deserve for this treatment of the father-mother *God*? The answer follows directly.

32:19–25 / God, the rejected parent, declares the rejection of such perverse offspring. There is anger in verses 19f., but also pain. The God who sees (v. 19) cannot bear to see and so hides God's face (v. 20). The pain turns to bitter irony in the sarcastic wordplay of verse 21: "They have made me **jealous** by a *no-god (lōʾ-ʾēl)*; I will make them jealous by a *no-people (lōʾ-ʿām)*." Israel would suffer at the hands of a nation as worthless in their eyes as their gods were worthless in God's eyes. In this context, the verse simply reinforces the tragedy of Israel's pathetic idolatry and the historical sovereignty of God over the nations as agents of judgment. The idea, however, of God making Israel *jealous* by the nations kindles a flame of hope beyond the fire of judgment in the thinking of the Apostle Paul. For God is in the business of turning "no-peoples" into God's people (cf. Rom. 9:24f., quoting Hosea 2:23 and 1:10). And if that should succeed in fanning Israel to jealousy, and thereby to repentance, faith, and salvation, then Paul's personal mission strategy would be vindicated (Rom. 10:19; 11:11–14). For Paul, the amazing mystery of God's purpose is that the very judgment of Israel for their unbelief will lead to the extension of salvation to the nations, which in turn will lead to the repentance and restoration of Israel. It is a missiology with broad roots throughout the OT, and at least one of its roots lies here in Deuteronomy 32.

Returning, however, to the immediate purview of our text: the fire of God's judgment will burn. That is the sentence, and it is spelled out in graphic detail derived from the stereotypical language of the covenant curses (vv. 20, 22–25)—an absent God, fire, arrows, famine, plague, wild beasts, snakes, slaughter (cf. 28:15–68). "The anger of God is an awesome and terrible thing because it follows from a rejection of the equally pervasive love of God" (Craigie, *Deuteronomy*, p. 384).

32:26–34 / Suddenly, there is a turning point in the song:
but . . . (v. 27). The judgment in verse 26 seems total and irrevocable: **blot out their memory from mankind.** Its implication is
clear: if the sentence is to be fully executed, then Israel would
be no more. But then what? Yahweh would have destroyed his
own "allotted inheritance!" The Israelites would become a "no-
people" like those God used to execute judgment upon Israel
(v. 21). All that God had done and had yet to do among the
nations would be destroyed. And worse, what would then become of Yahweh's own reputation? The triumphant enemies of
Israel, claiming credit for their victory, would not be likely to
accept that it was actually accomplished by Yahweh, the God of
their victims (v. 27b)! On the contrary, Yahweh would be a laugh-
ingstock, himself the victim of **the taunt of the enemy** (v. 27a).
This intolerable thought, here found in the mouth of Yahweh
himself (and cf. Isa. 48:9–11; Ezek. 20:9ff.; 36:19–23), had been
used to great effect in the mouth of Moses in his intercessions
on previous occasions when God had threatened the destruction of Israel (e.g., 9:26–28; cf. Exod. 32:11f.; Num. 14:13–16).
Does the song suggest that the merging of identity between
God and Moses is such that not only does Moses think God's
thoughts, but God thinks Moses'? At any rate, the effect is to
inject a pause in the proceedings. Judgment is suspended while
the judge deliberates. (See additional note on whether Israel
repents at this point.)

Verses 28–33 can be confusing unless one recognizes who
they, their, and **them** refer to in this section. It seems probable,
in view of the immediately preceding reference to enemies in
verse 27, that the **they** and **them** of verse 28 means *the enemies*
of God and Israel (not the Israelites themselves). God (the
speaker in v. 27) observes that they (the enemies) cannot per-
ceive what is really happening or its end result (v. 29). They
could never have defeated Israel in their own strength (v. 30a)
but did so only because Israel's rock of defense had **given them
up.** The enemies' victory is Yahweh's doing, and even they will
eventually recognize that their own gods (**their rock**) are no
match for Israel's (v. 31). Of themselves, the enemies are as
corrupt as **Sodom** and **Gomorrah,** so their victory is not a
matter of moral superiority (vv. 32f.). On the contrary, are they
not the ones who should be punished?

Such deliberations were going on in the depths of God's
own mind, in the realms of God's secret plans and purpose (v. 34;

cf. 29:29). The question form of verse 34 is typical of the divine deliberation and is more clearly seen in the prophetic examples of the form (e.g., Mic. 6:10f.; Hos. 6:4; 11:8; Jer. 5:29; 31:20). Behind the anthropomorphism of a questioning, deliberating, wrestling God lies the profound truth of the problem the world poses to its maker, and even more so the problem God's people pose to their divine Parent. While it may be true that "nothing is too hard for the Lord," it is equally true that nothing is too easy for the Lord either, as the sweat and blood of Gethsemane and Calvary finally demonstrate.

32:35–42 / The result of the deliberation is now made known in a revised decision. God will act in judgment, but those boastful enemies will themselves **slip** and be overtaken by **disaster** and **doom** (v. 35). Their judgment is decreed in the standard poetic language for such oracles of doom (vv. 40–42). This is the consistent message of the later prophets, that the nations who are agents of God's judgment against Israel will themselves one day face their own judgment at God's hands (cf. Isa. 10:5–19, 24–27; 47; Jer. 25:12–14; 50–51). And in that act of judgment on their enemies, Israel will experience the vindicating grace of God. Verse 36 is another of Deuteronomy's gems of grace. We might have expected a verse beginning **the LORD will judge his people** to conclude with words of wrath and destruction. But that is precisely the ending that the divine deliberation has gone beyond. **Judge** (Hb. *dîn*) would here be better translated, "vindicate," for it involves the final putting things right for God's people. And that will be the triumph of God's gracious **compassion** toward those God deigns to transform from unfaithful children into **servants**. Grace is suffused with pity when God sees the utter destitution of the people (v. 36b), but it is not without rebuke, as God reminds them of the futility of their useless idols (37f.). The divine irony is in play again: the very gods the Israelites looked to for rocklike strength and shelter have left them weak and defenseless. Such is always the way of idolatry in human society, ancient and modern. False gods never fail to fail. Sadly, we never fail to forget.

And so in the climax of the song, before its final summons to praise, Yahweh alone is left on the field, supreme, unique, all-powerful (v. 39). The poetry of the song reechoes the rhetoric of the preacher in 4:35, 39 and echoes again with even richer harmonies in the lyrics of Israel's greatest prophet after Moses (Isa. 42:8; 43:10–13, 25; 45:18, 20–22).

32:43–47 / The final doxology of the song is a call to praise (v. 43), but unfortunately the MT is almost certainly corrupt (lit. "Rejoice, nations, his people" or, grammatically less likely, "Praise, O nations, his people"). Longer texts are found in the LXX and Dead Sea Scrolls (cf. footnotes of NIV and NRSV and additional note below), which suggest that *the heavens* are being summoned to praise (cf. v. 1), along with the angelic beings ("sons of God"; cf. the quotation of the LXX of this verse in Heb. 1:6). Alongside this cosmic rejoicing, the **nations** are summoned to rejoice along with **his people,** in view of the vindicating work of God as judge and as the one who will cleanse the land and people. Wiebe suggests that the call to "heavens and earth" in verse 1 is also a call to those who dwell there—respectively, the heavenly beings in the cosmic council of God and the nations on earth ("Song of Moses," pp. 140f.). This would be a fitting parallel to verse 43, if the reconstruction is correct.

The call to the nations to rejoice over what God has done in and for Israel is paradoxical since, at the human historical level, they were on the receiving end of Israel's victories. Psalm 47 presents a similar paradox, where the nations are summoned to applaud Yahweh because he had subdued them under Israel's feet. Such a call makes sense only if, in the mystery and imagination of faith, the nations are deemed to have benefited in some way from the history of Israel. If they are to praise God for it, it must be ultimately for their good. Psalm 47 ends even more surprisingly by referring to the nations *"as the people of the God of Abraham"* (an identification that may make theological, if not grammatical, sense out of the MT of Deut. 32:43a, "nations his people"). This faith vision, in the context of worship, of the nations praising Yahweh is particularly found in the Psalms where Yahweh's kingly rule is celebrated, with special reference to his righteous judgment over all the earth (cf. Pss. 22:27f.; 96; 98). It is not surprising, then, that in the final biblical vision of all the nations of redeemed humanity acclaiming the rule of God and Christ, the song on their lips will be "the song of Moses the servant of the Lord and the song of the Lamb," celebrating precisely the ingathering of all nations through the saving work of God (Rev. 15:3f.).

The song thus ends where it began, in the cosmic realms, but with a vision that encompasses the intersection of God's cosmic rule with history, first through the election and redemption of Israel, but ultimately in the praise of all nations for God's righteous acts of salvation. Such is the profound power of this song in the light of the rest of biblical history that it offers us an integration of creation with redemption, of God's cosmic purposes with God's historical action, of the historical particular with the eschatological universal, of judgment with salvation, of past event with future vision, of wrath with grace. The song encompasses the whole of Israel's OT history in its scope, but only the cross and resurrection of Israel's messiah ultimately plumbed its depths and resolved its questions and paradoxes. And having recognized that, it is no wonder Paul found in it a powerful engine of mission as he strove to make Israel's messiah known as the savior of the nations, so that they too might praise the Lord God of Israel (cf. the quotation of Deut. 32:43 in Rom. 15:10 and the surrounding context, Rom. 15:8–12; cf. also the introduction).

Additional Notes §34

31:9–13 / On the verbal parallels between these verses (along with vv. 24–29) and 10:1–5, 8f., see Begg, "The Tables." Evidence for the reading of the law every seven years is detected in the book of Jeremiah by Holladay, "Seven-Year Recitation."

31:17 / **Our God is not with us:** The Hb. is in the singular (lit.) "because my God is not in the midst of me all these evils have come upon me." This intense personalizing of the matter corresponds to the common use of the singular second person in addressing the nation.

31:19, 26 / Both the **song** and the **Book of the Law** are described as **a witness** against Israel, i.e., in the presumed "court case" between Yahweh and his people. This has led some to regard the **words of this law** in v. 24 as actually referring back to the immediately preceding description of the writing of the song (v. 22). Lundbom has argued ("Lawbook") that the Book of the Law found in the temple during Josiah's reign was actually the Song of Moses (i.e., Deut. 32), not the whole book of Deuteronomy (or whatever part of it is usually assumed to have been the "Josianic" Deuteronomy—12–26 or 5–26). On the whole, however, it seems preferable to regard the song and the Book of the Law as separate entities, even if they came to be included in the same document, each intended to function as a **witness** against the

Israelites if and when they broke the covenant. Hence the importance attached to the Israelites actually learning and singing the song (v. 19, 22). Its witness must be on their own lips.

31:26 / **Place it beside the ark of the covenant:** Only the tablets of the Ten Commandments were actually *in* the ark. The distinction is thus preserved between the special character of the ten words and all the rest of the law that applied and developed them (cf. 5:22).

31:30 / The Song of Moses (actually the second one; the first was sung on the shores of the Red Sea, Exodus 15) has generated a large quantity of scholarly study. There is general, though not unanimous (see, e.g., Mayes, *Deuteronomy*, pp. 381f.), agreement that the song is a poem of considerable antiquity, some regarding it as premonarchic. Its Hb. has various archaic features, and it seems preferable to regard these as natural evidence of an early date rather than deliberate archaisms in a later composition. Cf. Cassuto, "Song of Moses;" Albright, "Remarks"; and Robertson, *Linguistic Evidence.* On the poetic structure, with emphasis on the unity and integrity of the poem, cf. Skehan, "Structure." On the similarities in form with the treaty lawsuit, cf. G. E. Wright, "Lawsuit," and for a contrary view, attributing the Song to Samuel, see Mendenhall, "Samuel's 'Broken *Rîb.*' "

32:4 / **He is the Rock:** This is a very ancient title for God in the OT (cf. Gen. 49:24) used six times in this song (vv. 4, 15, 18, 30, 31). With its obvious metaphorical force (stable, dependable, unmoveable, safe), it remained a favorite title, particularly in times of historical danger and change (cf. 2 Sam. 22:2f.; Pss. 18:2, 31; 19:14; 95:1; Isa. 26:4; 44:8). It is a title for deity also found in Canaanite and wider ancient Near Eastern religion, so there is quite probably a polemical dimension to the use of it here. That is, Yahweh, not Baal, is the rock who gave birth to and protects his people (vv. 15–18; procreative imagery in relation to mountains was also a feature of Canaanite religion); but Yahweh is greater than any or all other deities who claim to be "rocks" (cf. v. 31). And what makes God distinctive is not merely God's power as the refuge and deliverer of God's people, but God's moral character and absolute justice—precisely the Sinai attributes affirmed in this verse. Cf. Knowles, "The Rock."

32:6 / **Is he not your Father?:** The fatherhood of God is not a NT invention, but has deep roots in the relationship between God and Israel (cf. Exod. 4:22). The imagery of protective care and parental discipline has already been used in Deut. 1:31 and 8:5 (cf. 32:10f.). Here the emphasis is on father as creator (cf. v. 18). Later God's fatherhood was appealed to as the basis for mercy under judgment (Isa. 63:16; 64:8). Cf. also Geller, "Dynamics."

32:8–9 / **According to the number of the sons of Israel:** Almost certainly the reading given in the NIV footnote is to be preferred in this case. The Dead Sea Scrolls and LXX have "the sons of God." This expression usually means angelic, heavenly beings, not simply "gods" (as NRSV). Whereas other nations were allotted to angelic powers for "supervision," Yahweh reserved Israel for himself. Thus, although all nations live under the sovereignty of the Most High God, mediated through angelic deputies, Israel lives in a uniquely direct relationship with God through their covenantal knowledge of God as Yahweh. The concept of angelic powers associated with nations is found elsewhere in the OT (e.g., Isa. 24:21; Ps. 82 [esp. v. 6, "sons of Elyon"]; and Dan. 10:20f.). The link seems to be particularly with the political and judicial authorities in the nations and their territorial jurisdiction, and it is misleading in my view to use this verse as a biblical legitimation of the *religions* of other nations (as Miller, *Deuteronomy*, p. 229).

32:15 / **Jeshurun** was an alternative poetic title for Israel, probably derived from the word *yāšār*, "upright one." Its use here is therefore deliberately ironic (cf. 33:5, 26; Isa. 44:2).

32:17 / The description of foreign gods as **demons** is significant, though rare. In Ps. 106:36–39 the same word links the demonic nature of idolatry to destructive cruelty and degradation. Paul warns that, although alleged gods and idols may be "nothing" in the sense that they have no *divine* reality, they may be agents or vehicles of the demonic in some contexts, and thereby arouse very Deuteronomic sounding divine jealousy (cf. 1 Cor. 10:18–22).

32:27–33 / Wiebe, "Song of Moses," claims to detect in these verses an "act of lamentation/repentance," in which the people lament the fact that their rock sold them to the enemy, which they find intolerable in view of the evil and corruption of that enemy (vv. 30–33). He assumes (though there is no hint of it in the text) that this would have included some act of repentance as well (perhaps reflected in v. 36b?). But though he rightly points to examples of this motif in some prophetic deliberative lawsuits (e.g., Hos. 6:1–3; Jer. 3:1–3; 4:1–4), it is not at all clear in these verses. Rather it seems that vv. 26–34 are all part of the deliberation that leads up to the fresh decision in vv. 35ff.

32:43 / Various attempts have been made to restore the MT here on the assumption that the Dead Sea Scrolls (4QDt) and LXX have preserved a reading closer to the original. All textual reconstruction remains tentative, of course, but that suggested by Albright ("Remarks") is reasonably probable.

> Shout for joy, O heavens, before him,
> Worship him all you sons of God.
> Shout for joy, O nations with his people,
> give might to him all you messengers of God.
> (Wiebe's translation of Albright's reconstruction)

Apart from the textual support for this reconstruction, it also has the contextual plausibility of combining the "heavens," the "sons of God," and "the nations" in exactly the way the content of the song has combined the heavenly/cosmic and the earthly/historical dimensions of God's activity.

§35 The Last Mountain: The Blessing and Death of Moses (Deut. 32:48–34:12)

The speeches have been made, the sermon has been preached, the song has been sung. All that remains is for Moses to bid farewell and leave the stage, which he does in typical fashion (typical of him, and typical in another sense of his great successor), by climbing a mountain. Just before the final ascent, however, comes his parting blessing on the tribes of Israel. There is something beautiful in the fact that after all the dark chapters of curses, challenge, warning, and melancholic prediction, these last words are so rich in warmth, hope, and comfort. More than beautiful, it is the abiding theological truth of Deuteronomy, this monumental exposition of covenantal realities, that its final words acclaim the God who eternally loves God's people and a people eternally saved by their God (33:27–29).

32:48–52 / (Cf. Num. 27:12–14.) The **Abarim Range** of mountains lie at the northeastern end of the Dead Sea, **across from Jericho,** and thus had a view of much of the land of Canaan, with the southern hills of what would be Judah to the left, the central region of later Ephraim in front, and the northern hills of future Galilee to the right. In the first part of the "outer frame" of the book, the fact that Moses will die outside the land and not enter it is connected loosely to the rebellions of the people (1:37; 3:26). Here the sad fact is explained in terms of an action of Moses himself (cf. Num. 20:1–13 and commentary on 3:23–27).

33:1 / The introduction virtually sets Moses among the *patriarchs,* by portraying him as the father of his people, pronouncing over them a deathbed blessing (except that Moses, setting out for Mt. Nebo, was far from bedridden). There are similarities with the blessings of Jacob especially (Gen. 49). The title, **Moses the man of God** (cf. Josh. 14:6; Ps. 90, heading), however, sets Moses among the *prophets,* since this is a phrase later used of seers and prophets (e.g., 1 Sam. 9:6, 10, etc.). The title "servant of the Lord" (34:5) is also used of prophets, but the final assertion of the book will be that Moses held a unique place, unrivaled by any successor (34:10–12). Moses is a patriarch, a prophet, and more.

33:2–5 / These opening verses are balanced by the closing verses of the chapter (vv. 26–29) in celebrating the power of Yahweh as guide, king, and protector of Israel. They have been regarded as two stanzas of what was originally one single hymn, into which the tribal blessings have been inserted after the reference to the tribes in verse 5. This may well be so, though there is no reason why the poem could not have been constructed intentionally as it now stands.

The flow of thought in these verses describes the Sinai theophany as a cosmic event involving Yahweh and his heavenly hosts (v. 2) and also as the historical occasion when Israel submits to Yahweh as guide and instructor (v. 3), through the law given by Moses (v. 4). As a result, Yahweh is established as king in Israel (v. 5). The clipped poetry thus binds together, in the same way as did chapter 32, the *heavenly* realm (God and God's hosts) with *historical* events (the gathering of the tribes at Sinai) and also links *divine* authority (Yahweh as king) with *human* agency (Moses as lawgiver). Three main emphases thus occupy this first stanza.

(a) The transcendent power of Yahweh is acclaimed by reference to the Sinai theophany. Sinai is remembered not merely as the place of the giving of the law, but as the occasion when the awesome cosmic power of Yahweh was demonstrated and as the place from which Yahweh marched forth victoriously at the head of his heavenly hosts and his mobilized earthly people. That is why Deborah and Habakkuk and the author of Psalm 68 all refer to Yahweh as "God of Sinai" (or as coming from that region—Paran, Seir, etc.) in the context of military victory or acute military need, in poems that have much in common with this opening stanza of Deuteronomy 33 (see Judg. 5:4f.; Hab. 3:3–6; Ps. 68:7f.). Yahweh was "the One of Sinai" (Ps. 68:8) and "if *this* God be for us, who can be against us?" (b) The covenantal relationship is defined again as one of committed love from Yahweh's side (v. 3a), and reciprocal obedience from Israel's (v. 3b), through the *tôrâ* mediated by Moses (v. 4). (c) The kingship of Yahweh is affirmed on this double basis of his "military" power in defense of Israel and his role as lawgiver. This is the third of three references in the Pentateuch to the kingly reign of Yahweh, each of which reflects a significant aspect of the functions and expectations of kingship in the ancient world (and indeed of governments in the modern world too). In the earlier Song of Moses Yahweh's kingship is the crowning deduction from *the defeat of Israel's enemies*—Pharaoh and his army (Exod. 15:18). It is next found in the mouth of Balaam as *the grounds of Israel's security*—nothing can harm them while they are defended by the power of such a king (Num. 23:21–23). Finally, in Deuteronomy 33:2–5 it is linked with Yahweh's role as *the giver of Israel's laws* (cf. Isa. 33:22 for the same combination of roles). Defeat of enemies, protection and security, good laws—these are the things expected of kings and these are the things Yahweh as the true king provides for Israel.

33:6–25 / The opening stanza has thus set the context in which the blessings on the tribes appropriately follow. The theme of divine protection and defeat of enemies is continued in the blessings (vv. 7, 11, 12, 17, 20, 25), but it is supplemented with the promise of abundance in the fruitfulness of the land ahead. This is the main emphasis of the longest of the blessings on Joseph (vv. 13–16) and the briefer sayings for Zebulun (v. 19), Gad (v. 21), Naphtali (v. 23), and Asher (v. 24c). The prime foci of the list are the two longer blessings on Levi and Joseph.

The blessing on Levi is unusually long because, uniquely among the blessings, it gives historical reasons for the blessing and describes the two main functions of the priestly tribe (33:8–11). On at least two occasions of great apostasy among the people, the Levites had proved faithful to the demands of covenant loyalty by being willing to be agents of God's judgment even at personal cost (cf. Exod. 32:25–29; Num. 25:6–13). Verse 9 is not a warrant for disowning one's family; its point is that the Levites are prepared to put loyalty to Yahweh and the covenant above even family bonds in circumstances where they stand in conflict. Jesus calls for no less from all who submit to the reign of God (Matt. 10:34–39; Luke 14:26). The covenant faithfulness of the tribe is thus seen as a factor in their being entrusted with the double priestly work of teaching and sacrificing.

While the work of the priests in the sanctuary and at the altar is familiar (v. 10b), we should not overlook the fact that, after parents, the priests were meant to be the main teachers in Israel (v. 10a; cf. Lev. 10:10f.). Through the priests the knowledge of

God and the law was to be communicated to the rest of the people. Understandably, therefore, when the moral and social state of the people betrayed an utter lack of knowledge of God, it was the priests who were blamed by the prophets for the situation (cf. Hos. 4:1–9; Jer. 2:8; Mal. 2:1–9). On other more positive occasions, the Levites were used as agents of teaching in the great reforms of Hezekiah (2 Chron. 31:4) and the program of "theological education by extension" of Ezra (Neh. 8:7f., 13). Alongside this teaching work, the priestly work of the tribe included, of course, the service of the sanctuary. *Through the priests, God came to the people in the teaching of the torah. Through the priests, the people would come to God in the offering of the sacrifices.* Such a role speaks volumes when God elsewhere gave to the people as a whole the identity and mission of being God's priesthood in the midst of the nations (Exod. 19:4–6).

The blessing on Joseph is the most lyrical of all, with its exquisite listing of all the sources of God's material bounty (33:13–17). It invokes all the beneficence of the great magnitudes of creation—the **heaven above**, the **deep waters below**, the **sun and moon**, the **ancient mountains**, the **earth** itself. But its broadbrushed beauty conceals a polemical edge, for its point is that all the blessings God's people may desire from these primordial natural sources are from the hand of the one God, Yahweh, their creator and controller, and no other. Paganism and polytheism are excluded. If ever Israel should look to the sun and the moon themselves in astral cults, or to the earth itself in fertility cults, or to the mountains in the many forms of Canaanite hill worship, then they would find no blessing in them. But let them stay loyal to the living God of creation and redemption, and all the bounty of creation could be legitimately appreciated and enjoyed.

The description of Yahweh as **him who dwelt in the burning bush** (v. 16) is the only reference to that event outside the story itself in Exodus 3. Poetically, the phrase produces a brilliant bathos: after the list of nature's enormities, the blessing seeks the favor of the God who was found in a *bush*. But theologically, it is the climax of the blessing, for all the power of the God of such creation had been concentrated into that bush for the purpose of launching Israel's liberation from slavery into covenant relationship with God.

33:26–29 / The blessings are now rounded off with the second stanza of the encasing poem. Like the first stanza

(vv. 2–5), it begins with God and ends with Israel. Whereas the first stanza celebrates God as cosmic leader and king and speaks of Israel's commitment to obedience, this stanza portrays God as the great protector and therefore rejoices in Israel's security. So much of the book of Deuteronomy has expressed the uniqueness of Yahweh and the derived uniqueness of Israel as the people of Yahweh that it is highly apt that the book virtually closes on that double note by the resounding affirmation, **There is no one like the God of Jeshurun** (v. 26; cf. Exod. 15:11) and the rhetorical question, **Who is like you, O Israel?** (v. 29).

The affirmation of God's eternal, enveloping care for those who find refuge in **the everlasting arms** (v. 27a) is a reality claimed and proved by untold numbers of believers. It is not, however, a picture of *repose* in the arms of God. There are battles ahead, literal and spiritual, and we are reminded that Deuteronomy is a book "on the boundary" as the people prepare to cross over into the land. There they will face enemies, as the people of God always have and always will when they move forward with God. The reassurance, therefore, is not one of a peaceful paradise, but of divine protection and deliverance in the midst of conflict. Israel, then and now, can move forward in the confidence, "We rest on thee, our Shield and our Defender; We go not forth alone against the foe."

34:1–4 / No deathbed requiem for Moses! He is last seen climbing. The purpose of this final ascent is not just to admire the view. Although he is not permitted to set foot in the land, he is granted a formal viewing that may have been perceived as declaring possession in advance for his people. This ties in with the words of God to Moses in verse 4. Moses will not *enter* the land of promise, but in his viewing of it the promise is as good as fulfilled. The Pentateuch thus ends with a final reference to what has been its fundamental theme and purpose all the way through—God's promise to Abraham, a promise already two parts fulfilled in the growth of the nation and the blessing of covenant relationship and with the third part now shimmering from horizon to horizon beneath Moses' gaze.

34:5–8 / The reader has been well prepared for this final description of the death of Moses by some seven advance references to it (1:37; 3:23–29; 31:2, 14, 16, 27–29; 32:48–52). This gives an additional testamentary seriousness to the whole book. We have already noted the dual explanation of the apparently tragic

event as related to the sin of the people and as owing to Moses'
own sin (see commentary on 3:23–29). Centuries of Jewish reflection on Moses' death outside the land have produced various
explanations. One interesting view is that the scriptures had to
emphasize the human mortality of Moses in order to balance the
emphasis through the Pentateuch (and especially in Deut.) on his
closeness to God. There was a danger that one who had spent so
much time face to face with God (v. 10), one who spoke for God
almost interchangeably at times, one who had mediated the
blessings and the judgments of God, might come to be unduly
venerated. Hence the stress on his mortality, supplemented by
the note that since nobody knew where his grave was it could
not become a distracting and potentially idolatrous shrine. For
all his greatness, Moses is no more and no less than **the servant
of the LORD.**

34:9 / This editorial note paves the way for the opening
of the next book in the canon, Joshua, though sadly the people
listened to him and did what the LORD had commanded Moses
only for a short time after the generation of Joshua himself (cf.
Josh. 24:31; Judg. 2:7–13).

34:10–12 / Deuteronomy, which has so stressed the incomparability of Yahweh, finally closes with an acknowledgment
of the incomparability of Moses himself. Indeed, one Jewish tradition links the two rather beautifully by envisaging God declaring as a profoundly affectionate compliment, "Moses said of me,
'There is none like Yahweh,' and so I in turn bear witness that
'There is none like Moses' " (see additional note). The posthu-
mous decoration in these verses helps to soften the denial of a
physical presence in the land. And so this mountain of a man
reached the summit of his last mountain, with the final act of his
remarkable vigor (v. 7). The prospect from Pisgah was not merely
geographical. Moses had already envisaged with the eyes of faith
the people he had led out of Egypt living in that land for generations to come, with ultimate consequences for all the nations
included in the scope of God's great purpose. He would never set
foot in the land, but his prophetic vision was doubtless as clear as
his physical eyesight. And as Moses' undimmed eyes scanned the
northern mountains, perhaps one may be allowed to imagine a
twinkle in the eyes of the LORD God, looking forward to that day
when Moses, the servant of God, would stand at last on another
mountain *in* the land, conversing with the Son of God about the

even greater "exodus" that he would accomplish in Jerusalem for Israel and for the world (Luke 9:28–31).

Additional Notes §35

33:2–5 / The Hb. text of these vv. is not easy, and its somewhat cryptic and archaic poetic form has led some to indulge in major emendation. However, apart from minor changes, it is probable that the text we have now should not be reconstructed in any major way; there is a remarkable degree of metrical equivalence with the balancing stanza of vv. 26–29. The similarities extend to sub-syllabic level and can hardly be accidental. For a detailed prosodic analysis of vv. 2–5 and 26–29 that concludes that the equivalence meant that they could have been composed to be sung to the same melody, see Christensen, "Two Stanzas," and cf. Freedman, "Poetic Structure."

We are still left with the task of translation, however, and a glance at a few major English versions will show that there is considerable variety, particularly in vv. 2b and 3a. The NIV gives an acceptable sense, though the last line of v. 2 is more probably "at his right hand, heavenly warriors," or "a host of his own" (NRSV). See Cross and Freedman, "Blessing"; Miller, "Two Critical Notes"; and Komlos, "Deut. 33:3."

Verse 4 has often been suspected as an addition. However, when taken as a subordinate relative clause in apposition to the **instruction** of v. 3b (as the NIV does), it makes good sense. Cf. C. J. H. Wright, *God's Land*, pp. 40–43, to whose syntactical and contextual arguments must now be added the metrical argument of Christensen above.

He was king (v. 5) must refer to Yahweh. Although grammatically it could refer to Moses, the subject of the subordinate clause in v. 4, there is no hint anywhere else in the Hb. Bible that Moses was ever regarded as a king in Israel. It is also unlikely that the opening phrase, *wayyᵉhî melek*, means "and there arose a king," since the establishment of the monarchy lies outside the scope of the poem, which is reckoned by many scholars to be premonarchic in any case. Cf. Seeligmann, "Psalm from Pre-regal Times"; Cassuto, "Deuteronomy"; and Herman, "Kingship of Yahweh."

33:6–25 / On the similarities and differences between this list of tribal blessings and the blessings of Jacob in Gen. 49, see Mayes, *Israel*, and Steck, "History."

33:6 / The NIV footnote is the more correct translation—"but let his men be few." Reuben survived as a tribe, but became small and insignificant, a fact that conflicts with his position as the eldest brother but is given an explanation in Gen. 49:4.

33:7 / The blessing on Judah probably relates to protection in battle and may reflect the tribe's position in the call-up as the first contingent to march out (cf. Num. 2:9).

33:8 / The **Thummim and Urim** were the sacred stones used as lots for getting a "yes" or "no" decision in questions addressed to God and were carried in a pouch of the High Priest's breastpiece (cf. Exod. 28:30; Lev. 8:8).

33:18f. / **The abundance of the seas:** The northern tribes of Zebulun and Issachar would benefit from the opportunities and resources of the Mediterranean Sea and the Sea of Galilee.

33:20f. / Gad had been allocated the table land in the northern Transjordan, but was committed to supporting the other tribes in their conquest of the land to the west of the river (cf. 3:12–20; Num. 32; Josh. 22:1–9).

33:24 / The blessing on Asher is a "pun" on the name, which means "happy" or "blessed." Asher's territory on the northwestern coast was fertile and rich in olive trees, hence the abundance of **oil.**

33:26 / **There is no one like the God of Jeshurun:** The NIV has adopted (probably correctly) a very minor change in the pointing of the Hb., which in the MT reads, "There is no one like God, O Jeshurun." As we saw in the earlier chapters (especially chs. 4 and 6), the challenge of Deut. is not simply monotheism (the singularity of deity), but the uniqueness specifically of God as Yahweh, revealed and known in Israel.

34:1–4 / On viewing as an act of anticipated possession, see Daube, *Studies*, pp. 25–39, who cites Gen. 13:14f. and Matt. 4:8f. as other examples, along with extrabiblical material. His views, however, are contested, e.g., by Mayes.

34:5–8, 10–12 / On Jewish traditions regarding the death of Moses, see Goldin, "The Death of Moses."

For Further Reading

Commentaries

Brown, R. *The Message of Deuteronomy: Not By Bread Alone*. Leicester: InterVarsity, 1993.

Cairns, I. *Word and Presence: A Commentary on the Book of Deuteronomy*. Grand Rapids: Eerdmans; Edinburgh: Handsel, 1992.

Christensen, D. *Deuteronomy 1–11*. Word Biblical Commentary. Dallas: Word, 1991.

Clifford, R. *Deuteronomy with an Excursus on Covenant and Law*. Wilmington, Del.: Michael Glazier, 1982.

Craigie, P. C. *The Book of Deuteronomy*. Grand Rapids: Eerdmans; London: Hodder & Stoughton, 1976.

Driver, S. R. *A Critical and Exegetical Commentary on Deuteronomy*. Edinburgh: T. & T. Clark, 1895.

Mayes, A. D. H. *Deuteronomy*. Grand Rapids: Eerdmans; London: Marshall, Morgan & Scott, 1979.

Miller, P. D. *Deuteronomy: Interpretation, A Bible Commentary for Teaching and Preaching*. Louisville: John Knox, 1990.

Rad, G. von. *Deuteronomy: A Commentary*. London: SCM, 1966.

Thompson, J. A. *Deuteronomy: An Introduction and Commentary*. London: InterVarsity, 1974.

Weinfeld, M. *Deuteronomy 1–11: A New Translation with Introduction and Commentary*. New York: Doubleday, 1991.

Other Works

Abba, R. "Priests and Levites in Deuteronomy." *VT* 27 (1977), pp. 257–67.

Albright, W. F. "Some Remarks on the Song of Moses in Deuteronomy XXXII." *VT* 9 (1959), pp. 339–46.

Alt, A. "Das Verbot des Diebstahls im Dekalog." In *Kleine Schriften zur Geschichte des Volkes Israel*. Volume 1, pp. 333–40. Munich: C. H. Beck, 1953.

_____. "The Origins of Israelite Law." In *Essays on Old Testament History and Religion*. Pages 101–71. Oxford: Blackwell, 1966.

Anderson, G. W. "Israel: Amphictyony: AM; QAHAL; EDAH." In *Translating and Understanding the Old Testament*. Edited by H. T. Frank and W. L. Reed. Pages 135–51. Nashville: Abingdon, 1970.

Andreason, N.-E. A. *The Old Testament Sabbath*. SBLDS 7. Missoula: Scholars, 1972.

Baker, J. A. "Deuteronomy and World Problems." *JSOT* 29 (1984), pp. 3–17.

Balentine, S. E. *Prayer in the Hebrew Bible: The Drama of Divine-Human Dialogue*. Minneapolis: Fortress, 1993.

Beckwith, R., and W. Stott. *This is the Day*. London: Marshall, Morgan & Scott, 1978.

Begg, C. T. "The Tables (Deut. 10) and the Lawbook (Deut. 31)." *VT* 33 (1983), pp. 96–97.

Bellefontaine, E. "The Curses of Deuteronomy 27: Their Relationship to the Prohibitives." In *No Famine in the Land: Studies in Honor of John L. McKenzie*. Edited by J. W. Flanagan and A. W. Robinson. Pages 49–61. Missoula: Scholars, 1975.

_____. "Deuteronomy 21:18–21: Reviewing the Case of the Rebellious Son." *JSOT* 13 (1979), pp. 13–31.

Bernstein, M. J. "כי קללת אלהם תלוי" (Deut. 21:23): A Study in Early Jewish Exegesis." *JQR* 74 (1983), pp. 21–45.

Boecker, H.-J. *Law and the Administration of Justice in the Old Testament and Ancient East*. Minneapolis: Augsburg, 1980.

Boer, P. A. H. de. *Fatherhood and Motherhood in Israelite and Judean Piety*. Leiden: Brill, 1974.

Bosch, D. *Transforming Mission*. Maryknoll: Orbis, 1992.

Braulik, G. "The Sequence of the Laws in Deuteronomy 12–26 and in the Decalogue." In *A Song of Power and the Power of Song*. Edited by D. L. Christensen. Pages 313–35. Winona Lake, Ind.: Eisenbrauns, 1993.

_____. *Die deuteronomischen Gesetze und der Dekalog*. Stuttgarter Bibelstudien 145. Stuttgart: Katholisches Bibelwerk, 1991.

_____. *Die Mittel Deuteronomischer Rhetorik*. Analecta Biblica 68. Rome: Pontifical Institute, 1978.

Brichto, H. C. "Kin, Cult, Land and Afterlife—a Biblical Complex." *HUCA* 44 (1973), pp. 1–54.

Brueggemann, W. *The Land*. Philadelphia: Fortress, 1977.

_____. *The Prophetic Imagination*. Philadelphia: Fortress, 1978.

Callaway, P. R. "Deut. 21:18–21: Proverbial Wisdom and Law." *JBL* 103 (1984), pp. 341–52.

Calvin, J. *Commentaries on the Four Last Books of Moses Arranged in the Form of a Harmony Vols. I–IV.* Translated by C. W. Bingham. Edinburgh: Calvin Translation Society, 1852–55.

Caneday, A. " 'Redeemed from the Curse of the Law': The Use of Deut. 21:22–23 in Gal. 3:13." *Trinity Journal* 10 (1989), pp. 185–209.

Carmichael, C. A. "A Common Element in Five Supposedly Disparate Laws." *VT* 29 (1979), pp. 129–42.

_____. "Ceremonial Crux: Removing a Man's Sandal as a Female Gesture of Contempt." *JBL* 96 (1977), pp. 321–36.

_____. "Deuteronomic Laws, Wisdom, and Historical Traditions." *Journal of Semitic Studies* 12 (1967), pp. 198–206.

Carson, D. A. ed. *From Sabbath to Lord's Day*. Grand Rapids: Eerdmans, 1982.

Cassuto, U. "Deuteronomy Chapter xxxiii and the New Year in Ancient Israel." In *Biblical and Oriental Studies I*. Pages 47–70. Jerusalem: Magnes, 1973.

_____. "The Song of Moses (Deuteronomy Chapter xxxii 1–43)" [1938]. In *Biblical and Oriental Studies I*. Pages 41–46. Jerusalem: Magnes, 1973.

Chaney, M. L. "Ancient Palestinian Peasant Movements and the Formation of Pre-monarchic Israel." In *Palestine in Transition: The Emergence of Ancient Israel*. Edited by D. N. Freedman and D. F. Graf. Pages 52–57, 72–83. Sheffield: Almond, 1983.

Childs, B. S. *Exodus*. London: SCM, 1974.

Chirichigno, G. C. *Debt-Slavery in Israel and the Ancient Near East*. Sheffield: JSOT Press, 1993.

Christensen, D., ed. *A Song of Power and the Power of Song: Essays on the Book of Deuteronomy*. Winona Lake, Ind.: Eisenbrauns, 1993.

_____. "Two Stanzas of a Hymn in Deuteronomy 33." *Biblica* 65 (1984), pp. 382–89.

Clements, R. E. *Deuteronomy*. Old Testament Guides. Sheffield: JSOT Press, 1989.

_____. "Deuteronomy and the Jerusalem Cult Tradition." *VT* 15 (1965), pp. 300–312.

_____. *God's Chosen People: A Theological Interpretation of the Book of Deuteronomy*. London: SCM, 1968.

_____, ed. *The World of Ancient Israel: Sociological, Anthropological, and Political Perspectives*. Cambridge: Cambridge University Press, 1989.

Clines, D. J. A. *The Theme of the Pentateuch*. Sheffield: JSOT Press, 1978.

Craigie, P. *The Problem of War in the Old Testament*. Grand Rapids: Eerdmans, 1978.

Cross, F. M., and D. N. Freedman. "The Blessing of Moses." *JBL* 67 (1948), pp. 191–210.

Daniels, D. R. "The Creed of Deuteronomy xxvi Revisited." In *Studies in the Pentateuch*. Edited by J. A. Emerton. Pages 231–42. Leiden: Brill, 1990.

Daube, D. "Direct and Indirect Causation in Biblical Law." *VT* 11 (1961), pp. 249–69.

_____. *Studies in Biblical Law*. Cambridge: Cambridge University Press, 1947.

Davies, E. W. "Inheritance Rights and the Hebrew Levirate Marriage." *VT* 31 (1981), pp. 257–68.

_____. "The Meaning of *pî š^enayim* in Deuteronomy 21:17." *VT* 36 (1986), pp. 341–47.

Davies, G. I. , *The Way of the Wilderness: A Geographical Study of the Wilderness Itineraries in the Old Testament*. Cambridge: Cambridge University Press, 1979.

_____. "The Significance of Deuteronomy 1:2 for the Location of Mount Horeb." *Palestine Exploration Quarterly* 111 (1979), pp. 87–101.

Davies, W. D. *The Gospel and the Land: Early Christianity and Jewish Territorial Doctrine*. Berkeley: University of California, 1974.

Dearman, J. A. *Property Rights in the Eighth-Century Prophets*. Atlanta: Scholars, 1988.

Derrett, J. D. M. "Christ and the Power of Choice (Mark 3:1–6)." *Biblica* 65 (1984), pp. 168–88.

Diamond, A. S. "An Eye for an Eye." *Iraq* 19 (1957), pp. 151–55.

Douglas, M. *Purity and Danger*. London: Routledge & Kegan Paul, 1966.

Drews, R. "The 'Chariots of Iron' of Joshua and Judges." *JSOT* 45 (1989), pp. 15–23.

Duke, R. K. "The Portion of the Levite: Another Reading of Deuteronomy 18:6–8." *JBL* 106 (1987), pp. 193–201.

Ellison, H. L. "The Hebrew Slave: A Study in Early Israelite Society." *EvQ* 45 (1973), pp. 30–35.

Emerton, J. A. "Priests and Levites in Deuteronomy." *VT* 12 (1962), pp. 129–38

Eslinger, L. M. "The Case of an Immodest Lady Wrestler in Deuteronomy 25:11–12." *VT* 31 (1981), pp. 269–81.

_____. "More Drafting Techniques in Deuteronomic Laws." *VT* 34 (1984), pp. 221–26.

_____. "Watering Egypt (Deuteronomy xi 10–11)." *VT* 37 (1987), pp. 85–90.

Flusser, D. "The Ten Commandments and the New Testament." In *The Ten Commandments in History and Tradition.* Edited by B.-Z. Segal and G. Levi. Pages 219–46. Jerusalem: Magnes, 1990.

Freedman, D. N. , ed. *ABD.* 6 volumes. New York: Doubleday, 1992.

_____. "The Poetic Structure of the Framework of Deuteronomy 33." In *The Bible World: Essays in Honor of C. H. Gordon.* Edited by G. Rendsburg et al. Pages 25–46. New York: Ktav, 1981.

Fretheim, T. E. *The Suffering of God: An Old Testament Perspective.* Overtures to Biblical Theology. Philadelphia: Fortress, 1984.

Freund, R. A. "Murder, Adultery and Theft?" *Scandinavian Journal of the Old Testament* 2 (1989), pp. 72–80.

Geller, S. A. "The Dynamics of Parallel Verse: A Poetic Analysis of Deut 32:6–12." *HTR* 75 (1982), pp. 35–56.

Gerbrandt, G. E. *Kingship According to the Deuteronomistic History.* Atlanta: Scholars, 1986.

Gnuse, R. *You Shall Not Steal: Community and Property in the Biblical Tradition.* Maryknoll: Orbis, 1985.

Goldberg, M. L. "The Story of the Moral: Gifts or Bribes in Deuteronomy." *Interp* 38 (1984), pp. 15–25.

Goldin, J. "The Death of Moses: An Exercise in Midrashic Transposition." In *Love and Death in the Ancient Near East: Essays in Honor of Marvin H. Pope.* Edited by R. M. Good and J. H Marks. Pages 219–25. Guilford, Conn.: Four Quarters, 1987.

Goldingay, J. E. *Theological Diversity and the Authority of the Old Testament.* Grand Rapids: Eerdmans, 1987.

Goldingay, J. E., and C. J. H. Wright. " 'Yahweh Our God Yahweh One': The Oneness of God in the Old Testament." In *One God, One Lord: Christianity in a World of Religious Pluralism.* Edited by A. D. Clarke and B. W. Winter. Pages 43–62. Grand Rapids: Baker; Exeter: Paternoster, 1992.

Gottwald, N. K. *The Tribes of Yahweh: The Sociology of Liberated Israel, 1250–1050 BCE.* Maryknoll: Orbis; London: SCM, 1979.

Gow, M. D. *The Book of Ruth: Its Structure, Theme and Purpose.* Leicester: Apollos, 1992.

Grassi, J. "Matthew as a Second Testament Deuteronomy." *Biblical Theology Bulletin* 19 (1989), pp. 23–29.

Greenberg, M. "The Biblical Concept of Asylum." *JBL* 78 (1959), pp. 125–32.

_____. "Some Postulates of Biblical Criminal Law." In *Yehezkel Kaufmann Jubilee Volume.* Edited by M. Haran. Pages 5–28. Jerusalem: Magnes, 1960.

Halpern, B. "The Centralization Formula in Deuteronomy." *VT* 31 (1981), pp. 20–38.

Hamilton, J. M. *Social Justice and Deuteronomy: The Case of Deuteronomy 15.* Atlanta: Scholars, 1992.

Haran, M. "Seething a Kid in Its Mother's Milk." *JJS* 30 (1979), pp. 23–35.

Harrelson, W. *The Ten Commandments and Human Rights.* Philadelphia: Fortress, 1980.

Hasel, G. F. "Sabbath." *ABD.* Volume 5, pages 849–56. New York: Doubleday, 1992.

Herman, W. R. "The Kingship of Yahweh in the Hymnic Theophanies of the Old Testament." *HTR* 16 (1988), pp. 169–211.

Hess, R. H. "Yahweh and His Asherah? Religious Pluralism in the Old Testament World." In *One God, One Lord: Christianity in a World of Religious Pluralism.* Edited by A. D. Clarke and B. W. Winter. Pages 13–42. Grand Rapids: Baker; Exeter: Paternoster, 1993.

Hill, A. E. "The Ebal Ceremony as Hebrew Land Grant." *JETS* 31 (1988), pp. 399–406.

Hirsch, E. G. "Phylacteries." *The Jewish Encyclopaedia.* Edited by I. Singer. Volume 10, pages 21–28. New York: Funk & Wagnalls, 1905.

Holladay, W. L. " 'On Every High Hill and Under Every Green Tree.' " *VT* 11 (1964), pp. 170–76.

_____. "A Proposal for Reflections in the Book of Jeremiah of the Seven-Year Recitation of the Law in Deuteronomy (Deut. 31, 10–13)." In *Das Deuteronomium: Enstehung, Gestalt und Botschaft.* Edited by N. Lohfink. Pages 326–28. Leuven: Leuven University Press, 1985.

Hoppe, L. J. "The Meaning of Deuteronomy." *Biblical Theology Bulletin* 10 (1980), pp. 111–17.

Houten, C. van. *The Alien in Israelite Law.* Sheffield: JSOT Press, 1991.

Howard, D. M. Jr. "The Case for Kingship in Deuteronomy and the Former Prophets." *Westminster Theological Journal* 52 (1990), pp. 101–15.

Hubbard, D. A. "Priests and Levites." In *New Bible Dictionary.* Edited by J. D. Douglas et al. Pages 967–72. Downers Grove: InterVarsity, 1982.

Hyatt, J. P. "Were There an Ancient Historical Credo in Israel and an Independent Sinai Tradition?" In *Translating and Understanding the Old Testament.* Edited by H. T. Frank and W. L. Reed. Pages 152–70. Nashville: Abingdon, 1970.

Ishida, T. "The Structure and Historical Implications of the Lists of Pre-Israelite Nations." *Biblica* 60 (1979), pp. 461–90.

Jackson, B. *Essays on Jewish and Comparative Legal History.* Leiden: Brill, 1975.

_____. "Liability for Mere Intention in Early Jewish Law." In *Essays on Jewish and Comparative Legal History.* Pages 202–34. Leiden: Brill, 1975.

_____. *Theft in Early Jewish Law.* Oxford: Oxford University Press, 1972.

Janzen, J. G. "On the Most Important Word in the Shema (Deuteronomy vi 4–5)." *VT* 37 (1987), pp. 280–300.

Japhet, S. "The Relationship between the Legal Corpora in the Pentateuch in Light of Manumission Laws." In *Studies in Bible, Scripta Hierosolymitana* 31. Pages 63–89. Jerusalem: Magnes, 1986.

Johnson, A. R. "The Primary Meaning of *gʾl.*" *Congress Volume.* Edited by G. W. Anderson. Pages 67–77. VTSup 1. Leiden: Brill, 1953.

Johnston, R. M. " 'The Least of the Commandments': Deuteronomy 22:6–7 in Rabbinic Judaism and Early Christianity." *Andrews University Seminary Studies* 20 (1982), pp. 202–15.

Jones, G. " 'Holy War' or 'Yahweh War'?" *VT* 25 (1975), pp. 642–58.

Kaiser, W. C. Jr. "Current Crisis in Exegesis and the Apostolic Use of Deuteronomy 25:4 in 1 Corintians 9:8–10." *JETS* 21 (1978), pp. 3–18.

Kaufman, S. A. "Deuteronomy 15 and Recent Research on the Dating of P." In *Das Deuteronomium: Enstehung, Gestalt und Botschaft.* Edited by N. Lohfink. Pages 273–76. Leuven: Leuven University Press, 1985.

_____. "A Reconstruction of the Social Welfare Systems of Ancient Israel." In *In the Shelter of Elyon.* Edited by W. B.

Barrick and J. R. Spencer. Pages 277–84. JSOTSup 31. Sheffield: JSOT Press, 1984.

Kline, M. G. *Treaty of the Great King: The Covenant Structure of Deuteronomy.* Grand Rapids: Eerdmans, 1963.

Knight, G. A. F. *Isaiah 56–66: The New Israel.* International Theological Commentary. Edinburgh: Handsel; Grand Rapids: Eerdmans, 1985.

Knowles, M. P. " 'The Rock, His Work is Perfect': Unusual Imagery for God in Deuteronomy xxxii." *VT* 39 (1989), pp. 307–22.

Komlos, O. "תָּכּוּ לְרַגְלֶךְ (Deut. 33:3)." *VT* 6 (1956), p. 436.

Lang, B. "The Social Organization of Peasant Poverty in Biblical Israel." *JSOT* 24 (1982), pp. 47–63.

Leggett, D. A. *The Levirate and Goel Institutions in the Old Testament.* Cherry Hill, N. J.: Mack, 1974.

Lemche, N. P. "The Manumission of Slaves—The Fallow Year— The Sabbatical Year—The Jobel Year." *VT* 26 (1976), pp. 38–59.

Lenchak, T. A. *"Choose Life!" A Rhetorical-Critical Investigation of Deuteronomy 28,69–30,20.* AnBib 129. Rome: Pontifical Institute, 1993.

Lilley, J. P. U. "Understanding the Ḥērem." *TynBull* 44.1 (1993), pp. 169–77.

Lohfink, N., ed. *Das Deuteronomium: Enstehung, Gestalt und Botschaft.* Leuven: Leuven University Press, 1985.

_____. *Das Hauptgebot: Eine Untersuchung literarischer Einleitungsfragen zu Dtn 5–11.* AnBib 20. Rome: Pontifical Institute, 1963.

_____. *Great Themes from the Old Testament.* Edinburgh: T. & T. Clark, 1982.

_____. "חָרַם *ḥāram;* חֵרֶם *ḥērem,*" *Theological Dictionary of the Old Testament.* Edited by G. J. Botterweck and H. Ringgren. Translated by D. E. Green. Volume 5, pages 180–99. Grand Rapids: Eerdmans, 1986.

Lundbom, J. R. "Lawbook of the Josianic Reform." *CBQ* 38 (1976), pp. 293–302.

Luyten, J. "Primeval and Eschatological Overtones in the Song of Moses (Dt 32,1–43)." In *Das Deuteronomium: Enstehung, Gestalt und Botschaft.* Edited by N. Lohfink. Pages 341–47. Leuven: Leuven University Press, 1985.

Manley, G. T. *The Book of the Law.* London: Tyndale, 1957.

Mann, T. W. "Theological Reflections on the Denial of Moses." *JBL* 98 (1979), pp. 481–94.

Mayes, A. D. H. "Deuteronomy 4 and the Literary Criticism of Deuteronomy." *JBL* 100 (1981), pp. 23–51.

_____. *Israel in the Period of the Judges.* London: SCM, 1974

McBride, S. D. "Polity of the Covenant People: The Book of Deuteronomy." *Interp* 41 (1987), pp. 229–44.

_____. "The Yoke of the Kingdom: An Exposition of Deuteronomy 6:4–5." *Interp* 27 (1973), pp. 273–306.

McCann Jr. , J. C. "Sabbath." *ISBE.* Edited by G. W. Bromiley. Volume 4, pages 247–52. Grand Rapids: Eerdmans, 1988.

McCarthy, D. J. "Notes on the Love of God in Deuteronomy and the Father-Son Relationship between Yahweh and Israel." *CBQ* 27 (1965), pp. 144–47.

_____. *Old Testament Covenant: A Survey of Current Opinions.* Oxford: Blackwell, 1972.

McConville, J. G. "God's 'Name' and God's 'Glory'." *TynBull* 30 (1979), pp. 146–63.

_____. *Grace in the End: A Study in Deuteronomic Theology.* Grand Rapids: Zondervan; Carlisle: Paternoster, 1993.

_____. *Law and Theology in Deuteronomy.* Sheffield, JSOT Press, 1984.

_____. "Jerusalem in the Old Testament." In *Jerusalem Past and Present in the Purposes of God.* Edited by P. W. L. Walker. Pages 21–51. Grand Rapids: Baker; Carlisle: Paternoster, 1994.

_____. "Priests and Levites in Ezekiel: A Crux in the Interpretation of Israel's History." *TynBull* 34 (1983), pp. 4–9.

McKay, J. W. "Man's Love for God in Deuteronomy." *VT* 22 (1972), pp. 426–35.

McKeating, H. "The Development of the Law on Homicide in Ancient Israel." *VT* 25 (1975), pp. 46–68.

_____. "Sanctions against Adultery in Ancient Israelite Society, with Some Reflections on Methodology in the Study of Old Testament Ethics." *JSOT* 11 (1979), pp. 57–72.

McKenzie, D. A. "Judicial Procedure at the Town Gate." *VT* 14 (1964), pp. 100–104.

McKenzie, J. L. "The Elders in the Old Testament." *Bib* 40 (1959), pp. 522–40.

Mendelsohn, I. "On the Preferential Status of the Eldest Son." *Bulletin of the American Schools of Oriental Research* 156 (1959), pp. 38–40.

Mendenhall, G. E. "Ancient Oriental and Biblical Law." *Biblical Archaelogist* 172 (1954), pp. 24–46.

_____. "Samuel's 'Broken *Rîb.*' " In *A Song of Power.* Edited by D. Christensen. Pages 169–80. Winona Lake, Ind.: Eisenbrauns, 1993.

Mettinger, T. N. D. *Solomonic State Officials: A Study of the Civil Government Officials of the Israelite Monarchy.* Coniectanea Biblica, Old Testament Series 5. Lund: Gleerup, 1971.

Millard, A. R. "King Og's Iron Bed: Fact or Fancy?" *Bible Review* 6 (April 1990), pp. 16–21, 44.

_____. "A Wandering Aramean." *Journal of Near Eastern Studies* 39 (1980) pp. 153–55.

Miller, P. D. "Fire in the Mythology of Canaan and Israel." *CBQ* 27 (1965), pp. 256–61.

_____. "Moses, My Servant: A Deuteronomic Portrait of Moses." *Interp* 41 (1987), pp. 245–55.

_____. "Two Critical Notes on Psalm 68 and Deuteronomy 33." *HTR* 57 (1964), pp. 240–43.

Moberly, R. W. L. "Abraham's Righteousness (Genesis xv 6)." In *Studies in the Pentateuch.* Edited by J. A. Emerton. Pages 103–30. VTSup 41. Leiden: Brill, 1990.

_____. *At the Mountain of God: Story and Theology in Exodus 32–34.* JSOTSup 22. Sheffield: JSOT Press, 1983

_____. *The Old Testament of the Old Testament.* Overtures to Biblical Theology. Philadelphia: Fortress, 1992.

_____. "Yahweh is One: The Translation of the Shema." In *Studies in the Pentateuch.* Edited by J. A. Emerton. Pages 209–15. VTSup 41. Leiden: Brill, 1990.

Moessner, D. P. "Luke 9:1–50: Luke's Preview of the Journey of the Prophet like Moses of Deuteronomy." *JBL* 102 (1983), pp. 575–605.

Moor, J. C. de. *The Rise of Yahwism: The Roots of Israelite Monotheism.* Leuven: Peeters, 1990.

Moore, R. D. "Canon and Charisma in the Book of Deuteronomy." *Journal of Pentecostal Theology* 1 (1992), pp. 75–92.

Moran, W. L. "The Ancient Near Eastern Background of the Love of God in Deuteronomy." *CBQ* 25 (1963), pp. 77–87.

_____. "The Conclusion of the Decalogue (Ex 20,17 = Dt 5,21)." *CBQ* 29 (1967), pp. 543–54.

Na'aman, N. "Habiru and Hebrews: The Transfer of a Social Term to the Literary Sphere." *Journal of Near Eastern Studies* 45 (1986), pp. 271–88.

Neale, D. "Was Jesus a *Mesith*? Public Response to Jesus and his Ministry." *TynBull* 44.1 (May 1993), pp. 89–101.

Nicholson, E. W. *Deuteronomy and Tradition.* Oxford: Blackwell, 1967.

_____. "The Decalogue as the Direct Address of God." *VT* 27 (1977), pp. 422–33.

_____. *Exodus and Sinai in History and Tradition.* Oxford: Blackwell; Richmond: Knox, 1973.

Nicol, G. G. "Watering Egypt (Deuteronomy xi 10–11) Again." *VT* 38 (1988), pp. 347–48.

Nielsen, E. "Some Reflections on the History of the Ark." Edited by G. W. Anderson. Pages 61–74. VTSup 7. Leiden: Brill, 1959.

_____. *The Ten Commandments in New Perspective.* London: SCM; Naperville: Allenson, 1968.

North, R. G. "*Yâd* in the Shemitta-Law." *VT* 4 (1954), pp. 196–99.

Noth, M. *The Deuteronomistic History.* Sheffield: JSOT Press, 1981.

O'Connell, R. H. "Deuteronomy viii 1–20: Asymmetrical Concentricity and the Rhetoric of Providence." *VT* 40 (1990), pp. 437–52.

Patrick, D. P. "Unclean and Clean (OT)." *ABD.* Volume 6, pages 739–41. New York: Doubleday, 1992.

Perlitt, L. *Bundestheologie im Alten Testament.* Neukirchen: Neukirchener Verlag, 1969.

Phillips, A. *Ancient Israel's Criminal Law.* Oxford: Blackwell, 1970.

_____. "Another Look at Adultery." *JSOT* 20 (1981), pp. 3–25.

_____. "*NEBALAH*—A Term for Serious Disorderly and Unruly Conduct." *VT* 25 (1975), pp. 237–42.

_____. "Prophecy and Law." In *Israel's Prophetic Tradition: Essays in Honour of Peter R. Ackroyd.* Edited by R. Coggins, A. Phillips, and M. Knibb. Pages 217–32. New York: Cambridge University Press, 1982.

_____. "Uncovering the Father's Skirt." *VT* 30 (1980), pp. 38–43.

Polzin, R. *Moses and the Deuteronomist.* New York: Seabury, 1980.

_____. "Deuteronomy." In *The Literary Guide to the Bible.* Edited by R. Alter and F. Kermode. Pages 92–101. London: Collins, 1987.

Porter, J. R. *The Extended Family in the Old Testament.* London: Edutext, 1967.

Pritchard, J. B., ed. *Ancient Near Eastern Texts Relating to the Old Testament,* 3d ed. Princeton: Princeton University Press, 1969.

Rad, G. von. "The Problem of the Hexateuch." In *The Problem of the Hexateuch and Other Essays.* Pages 1–78. Philadelphia: Fortress, 1984.

_____. "The Promised Land and Yahweh's Land in the Hexateuch." In *The Problem of the Hexateuch and Other Essays*. Pages 79–93. Philadelphia: Fortress, 1984.

_____. *Studies in Deuteronomy*. London: SCM, 1953.

_____. "There Remains Still a Rest for the People of God." In *The Problem of the Hexateuch and Other Essays*. Pages 94–102. Philadelphia: Fortress, 1984.

Rehm, M. D. "Levites and Priests." *ABD*. Volume 4, pages 297–310. New York: Doubleday, 1992.

Reimer, D. "Concerning Return to Egypt: Deuteronomy xvii 16 and xxviii 68 Reconsidered." In *Studies in the Pentateuch*. Edited by J. A. Emerton. Pages 217–29. VTSup 41. Leiden: Brill, 1990.

Robertson, D. A. *Linguistic Evidence in Dating Early Hebrew Poetry*. SBLDS 3. Missoula: Scholars, 1972.

Rofé, A. "The Laws of Warfare in the Book of Deuteronomy: Their Origins, Intent and Positivity." *JSOT* 32 (1985), pp. 23–44.

_____. "The Tenth Commandment in the Light of Four Deuteronomic Laws." In *The Ten Commandments in History and Tradition*. Edited by B.-Z. Segal and G. Levi. Pages 45–65. Jerusalem: Magnes, 1990.

Rosner, B. " 'No Other God': The Jealousy of God and Religious Pluralism." In *One God, One Lord: Christianity in a World of Religious Pluralism*. Edited by A. D. Clarke and B. W. Winter. Pages 149–59. Grand Rapids: Baker; Exeter: Paternoster, 1992.

Scobie, C. H. H. "Israel and the Nations: An Essay in Biblical Theology." *TynBull* 43 (1992), pp. 283–305.

Scott, J. M. "Restoration of Israel." In *Dictionary of Paul and His Letters*. Edited by G. F. Hawthorne and R. P. Martin. Pages 796–805. Downers Grove and Leicester: InterVarsity, 1993.

Seeligmann, I. L. "A Psalm from Pre-regal Times." *VT* 14 (1964), pp. 191–210.

Segal, B.-Z., and G. Levi, ed. *The Ten Commandments in History and Tradition*. Jerusalem: Magnes, 1990.

Senior, S., and C. Stuhlmueller. *The Biblical Foundations for Mission*. Maryknoll: Orbis; London: SCM, 1983.

Skehan, P. W. "The Structure of the Song of Moses in Deuteronomy (Deut. 32:1–43)." *CBQ* 13 (1951), pp. 153–63.

Smith, M. *The Early History of God: Yahweh and the Other Deities in Ancient Israel*. San Francisco: Harper & Row, 1990.

Soggin, J. A. "Cultic-Aetiological Legends and Catechesis in the Hexateuch." In *Old Testament and Oriental Studies*. Edited by

J. Swetnam. Pages 72–77. Biblica et Orientalia 29. Rome: Biblical Institute, 1975.

Stamm, J. J., and M. E. Andrew. *The Ten Commandments in Recent Research.* London: SCM; Naperville: Allenson, 1967.

Steck, J. D. "A History of the Interpretation of Genesis 49 and Deuteronomy 33." *Bibliotheca Sacra* 147 (1990), pp. 16–31.

Sulzberger, M. "The Status of Labor in Ancient Israel." *JQR* New Series 13 (1922/23), pp. 245–302, 397–459.

Tigay, J. H. *You Shall Have No Other Gods: Israelite Religion in the Light of Hebrew Inscriptions.* Atlanta: Scholars, 1986.

Tuckett, C. M. "Deuteronomy 21,23 and Paul's Conversion." In *L'Apotre Paul.* Edited by A. Vanhoye. Pages 345–50. Leuven: Leuven University Press, 1986.

Van Leeuwen, R. C. "What Comes out of God's Mouth: Theological Wordplay in Deuteronomy 8." *CBQ* 47 (1985), pp. 55–57.

Vasholz, R. I. "A Legal 'Brief' on Deuteronomy 13:16–17." *Presbyterion* 16 (1990), pp. 128–29.

Vaughan, P. H. *The Meaning of 'Bāmā' in the Old Testament.* Cambridge: Cambridge University Press, 1974.

Vaux, R. de. *Ancient Israel.* New York: McGraw Hill, 1961.

_____. *Studies in Old Testament Sacrifice.* Cardiff: University of Wales, 1964; Mystic, Conn.: Verry, 1966.

Wall, R. W. " 'The Finger of God': Deuteronomy 9.10 and Luke 11.20." *New Testament Studies* 33 (1987), pp. 144–50.

Walton, J. H. "Deuteronomy: an Exposition of the Spirit of the Law." *Grace Theological Journal* 8 (1987), pp. 213–25.

Weinfeld, M. *Deuteronomy and the Deuteronomic School.* Oxford: Clarendon, 1972.

_____. "The King as Servant of the People: The Source of the Idea." *JJS* 33 (1982), pp. 189–94.

Wenham, G. J. "Betulah—A Girl of Marriageable Age." *VT* 22 (1972) pp. 326–48.

_____. *The Book of Leviticus.* New International Commentary on the Old Testament. Grand Rapids: Eerdmans, 1979.

_____. "Deuteronomy and the Central Sanctuary." *TynBull* 22 (1971), pp. 103–18.

_____. "Drafting Techniques in Some Deuteronomic Laws." *VT* 30 (1980), pp. 248–52.

_____. "Law and the Legal System in the Old Testament." In *Law, Morality and the Bible.* Edited by B. N. Kaye and G. J. Wenham. Pages 24–52. Leicester: InterVarsity, 1978.

_____. "The Restoration of Marriage Reconsidered." *JJS* 30 (1979), pp. 36–40.

Wenham, J. *The Goodness of God.* London: InterVarsity, 1974.

Whitney, J. T. " 'Bamoth' in the Old Testament." *TynBull* 30 (1979), pp. 125–47.

Wiebe, J. M. "The Form, Setting and Meaning of the Song of Moses." *Studia Biblica et Theologica* 17 (1989), pp. 119–63.

Wilson, I. *Out of the Midst of the Fire: Divine Presence in Deuteronomy.* Missoula: Scholars, 1996.

Wright, C. J. H. "The Authority of Scripture in an Age of Relativism: Old Testament Perspectives." In *The Gospel in the Modern World: A Tribute to John Stott.* Edited by M. Eden and D. F Wells. Pages 31–48. Leicester and Downers Grove: InterVarsity, 1991.

_____. "The Ethical Authority of the Old Testament: A Survey of Approaches." *TynBull* 43.1 (1992), pp. 101–20 and 43.2 (1992), pp. 203–31

_____. *God's People in God's Land: Family, Land, and Property in the Old Testament.* Grand Rapids: Eerdmans; Exeter: Paternoster, 1990.

_____. *Knowing Jesus through the Old Testament.* London: Marshall Pickering, 1992.

_____. *An Eye for an Eye* (in the UK, *Living as the People of God*). Downers Grove and Leicester: InterVarsity, 1983.

_____. "The People of God and the State." *Themelios* 16 (Oct.–Nov. 1990), pp. 4–10.

_____. "Ten Commandments." *ISBE.* Edited by G. W. Bromiley. Volume 4, pages 786–90. Grand Rapids: Eerdmans, 1988.

_____. *Walking in the Ways of the Lord: The Ethical Authority of the Old Testament.* Leicester: Apollos, 1995; Downers Grove: InterVarsity, 1996.

_____. "What Happened Every Seven Years in Israel? Old Testament Sabbatical Institutions for Land, Debt and Slaves." *EvQ* 56 (1984), pp. 129–38, 193–201.

_____. *What's So Unique About Jesus?* Tunbridge Wells: Monarch, 1990.

Wright, D. P. "Deuteronomy 21:1–9 as a Rite of Elimination." *CBQ* 49 (1987), pp. 387–403.

_____. "Unclean and Clean (OT)." *ABD.* Volume 6, pages 739–41. New York: Doubleday, 1992.

Wright, G. E. "The Lawsuit of God: A Form-Critical Study of Deuteronomy 32." In *Israel's Prophetic Heritage: Essays in Honor of*

James Muilenburg. Edited by B. W. Anderson and W. Harrelson. Pages 26–67. New York: Harper & Row, 1962.

_____. "The Levites in Deuteronomy." *VT* 4 (1954), pp. 325–30.

Wright, L. S. "*MKR* in 2 Kings 12:5–17 and Deuteronomy 18:8." *VT* 39 (1989), pp. 438–48.

Wright, N. T. *The Climax of the Covenant: Christ and the Law in Pauline Thought.* Edinburgh: T. & T. Clark, 1991.

_____. *The New Testament and the People of God.* London: SPCK, 1992.

Yaron, R. "The Restoration of Marriage." *JJS* 17 (1966), pp. 1–11.

Zevit, Z. " *Egla* Ritual of Deuteronomy 21:1–9." *JBL* 95 (1976), pp. 377–90.

Zimmerli, W. *I Am Yahweh.* Atlanta: John Knox, 1982.

Subject Index

Scripture Index